John Eliot's Puritan Ministry to New England "Indians"

John Eliot's Puritan Ministry to New England "Indians"

DO HOON KIM

☙PICKWICK *Publications* • Eugene, Oregon

JOHN ELIOT'S PURITAN MINISTRY TO NEW ENGLAND "INDIANS"

Copyright © 2021 Do Hoon Kim. All rights reserved. Except for brief quotations in critical publications or reviews, no part of this book may be reproduced in any manner without prior written permission from the publisher. Write: Permissions, Wipf and Stock Publishers, 199 W. 8th Ave., Suite 3, Eugene, OR 97401.

Pickwick Publications
An Imprint of Wipf and Stock Publishers
199 W. 8th Ave., Suite 3
Eugene, OR 97401

www.wipfandstock.com

PAPERBACK ISBN: 978-1-6667-0979-7
HARDCOVER ISBN: 978-1-6667-0980-3
EBOOK ISBN: 978-1-6667-0981-0

Cataloguing-in-Publication data:

Names: Kim, Do Hoon [author].

Title: John Eliot's puritan ministry to New England "Indians" / Do Hoon Kim.

Description: Eugene, OR: Pickwick Publications, 2021 | Includes bibliographical references and index.

Identifiers: ISBN 978-1-6667-0979-7 (paperback) | ISBN 978-1-6667 0980-3 (hardcover) | ISBN 978-1-6667-0981-0 (ebook)

Subjects: LCSH: Eliot, John, 1604–1690 | Indians of North America—Missions—History | Missions—North America—History | Indians of North America—Missions—Massachusetts | Puritans—Massachusetts

Classification: E78.M4 K56 2021 (paperback) |E78.M4 (ebook)

11/11/21

I would like to dedicate this book
to my grandparents Byung Shik Kim and Jung Suk Yoo,
my parents Young Sup Kim and Soon Yee Park, and
my parents-in-law Young Taik Jeong and Hee Im Hwang.

I also desire to dedicate this book to my beloved wife Sae Rom Jeong,
my daughter Christine Ye-Kyung Kim, and
my son David Min-Jun Kim.
Without them, I could not have finished this book.

Contents

Acknowledgments | ix

Abbreviations | xi

Part 1 | Relocating John Eliot

1. Historiographical Introduction and a Proposition for a New Perspective | 3
2. Puritan Migration, Millenarianism, and Indian Conversion: Re-envisioning the Motives for John Eliot's Indian Ministry | 29
3. The Historical and Theological Background of Seventeenth-Century Puritan Ministry in Old and New England in Relation to the Motives for Indian Ministry | 65

Part 2 | John Eliot and the Indians

4. Praying Towns and Indian Churches | 123
5. John Eliot's Practice of Indian Ministry | 157
6. Conversion Narratives and Indian Expression of Christianity | 190
7. Conclusion | 224

Bibliography | 233

Index | 263

Acknowledgments

I WOULD LIKE TO confess that this book, as a revised version of my PhD thesis submitted to the University of Edinburgh, is absolutely from the abundant grace of God, and to acknowledge my deep thanks for the varieties of unforgettable help from many individuals, schools, and churches. First of all, I would like to express my sincere thanks to Rev. Professor Susan Hardman Moore, my supervisor, with the deepest respect. I appreciate her splendid academic knowledge, insight, guidance, and care, not only as an excellent puritan scholar, but also as a mentor and teacher with a warm caring heart for her students. Also, I would like to thank my external and internal examiners for my thesis, Professor Crawford Gribben and Professor Jane Dawson. It was a great honor for me to meet these excellent scholars as my examiners. My thanks should also go to the scholars and teachers that I have met during my nine years of study abroad in the US and UK. I would like to thank the late Rev. Dr. Syngman Rhee, a distinguished visiting professor at Union Presbyterian Seminary and the first Korean moderator of the PCUSA, and his wife Dr. Haesun Rhee. I can never forget their help, support, and enormous love for me. I would like to thank Professors Harry Stout and Kenneth Minkema as my advisors at Yale, and Professors Joseph Chinnichi, Christopher Ocker, Eugene Ludwig, and Randi Walker as my advisors and teachers in history department at the GTU. The teachings, advice, and insights which these scholars offered to me have been and will be a great asset for my academic journey.

I would like to express my thanks to the staffs of: New College Library and Main Library of the University of Edinburgh, National Library of Scotland, Cambridge University Library, British Library, St. Andrews University Library, and King's College London Library, which have provided me essential resources. I would like to give my special thanks for financial support from the schools where I have studied, as well as several Korean churches. The excellent scholarships from UPS, Yale, GTU, and Edinburgh have been essential supports for my studies. Also, the scholarships and fellowships from Myung-Sung Presbyterian Church, So-Mang Presbyterian Church, God's Will Church, and Youngnak Presbyterian Church of LA have been tremendously important help for my studies and life in foreign countries.

A brief and revised portion of chapter 2 was published as "A Reinterpretation of the Relationship between the Great Migration and Indian Evangelization: A Reconsideration of 'City upon a Hill' Theory," in *Mission and Theology* 37 (Oct. 2015). I am grateful for permission to use the material in the journal here. I also thank the editorial staff of Wipf and Stock Publishers, for their professionalism, help, and care.

I will never forget the spiritual fellowship and help from the pastors and church members in my mother church in Korea. I would like to thank Rev. Kyu Ho Lee, a former moderator of PCK (Tonghap), and his wife, deaconess Heung Ae Park, as well as Rev. In Dae Jang, the senior pastor of Kyung-Ju Gujung Presbyterian Church. Along with them, the prayer and warm concern from the church members have been a great consolation to me. Also, I would like to express my deep thanks and love to the members and co-pastors of Ross Chapel in Edinburgh and all my current beloved members of New Haven Korean Church in Connecticut. The ministry and fellowship in the churches have been a great joy and significant spiritual nourishment for my life in Edinburgh and Connecticut.

My thanks to my own family is the last. However, it does not mean that their help has been the smallest, but rather the most important and the biggest. I could never reward enough the support and love of my parents, elder Young Sup Kim and deaconess Dr. Soon Yee Park, and my parents-in-law, Rev. Dr. Young Taik Jeong and Hee Im Hwang. I am also grateful to my only brother Chae-Hoon and his wife Soong-Yoon. My biggest thanks and love should go to Sae Rom Jeong, my lovely wife, and Christine Ye-Kyung Kim and David Min-Jun Kim, my beloved daughter and son. Without the faithful and sincere love, support, and sacrifice of my wife for her humble husband and her family, and the bright and untainted smiles and love of my children towards their "studying" daddy, I could never have finished this work. Their being with me has itself been the best help and the biggest consolation to me.

Soli Deo Gloria.

Abbreviations

WORKS BY JOHN ELIOT
THE ELIOT TRACTS

New Englands First Fruits (1643)	[Thomas Weld, Hugh Peter, and Henry Dunster], eds. *New Englands First Fruits; in Respect, First of the Conversion of Some, Conviction of Divers, Preparation of Sundry of the Indians*. London, 1643.
Day-Breaking (1647)	[Thomas Shepard], ed. *The Day-Breaking, If Not the Sun-Rising of the Gospell with the Indians in New England*. London, 1647.
Clear Sun-shine (1648)	[Thomas Shepard], ed., *The Clear Sun-Shine of the Gospel Breaking forth upon the Indians in New-England*. London, 1648.
Glorious Progress (1649)	Edward Winslow, ed. *The Glorious Progress of the Gospel amongst the Indians of New England*. London, 1649.
Light Appearing (1651)	Henry Whitfield, ed. *The Light Appearing More and More towards the Perfect Day or a Farther Discovery of the Present State of the Indians in New England*. London, 1651.
Strength out of Weaknesse (1652)	Henry Whitfield, ed. *Strength out of Weaknesse, or a Glorious Manifestation of the Further Progresse of the Gospel among the Indians in New England*. London, 1652.
Tears of Repentance (1653)	John Eliot, and Thomas Mayhew Jr., eds. *Tears of Repentance: Or, A further Narrative of the Progress of the Gospel amongst the Indians in New-England: Setting forth, Not Only Their Present State and Condition, but Sundry Confessions of Sin by Diverse of the Said Indian*. London, 1653.

Late and Further Manifestation (1655) — John Eliot ed. *A Late and Further Manifestation of the Progress of the Gospel amongst the Indians in New England ... Being a Narrative of the Examinations of the Indians, about Their Knowledge in Religion, by the Elders of the Churches.* London, 1655.

Further Accompt (1659) — John Eliot, ed. *A Further Accompt of the Progresse of the Gospel amongst the Indians in New England and of the Means Used Effectually to Advance the Same.* London, 1659.

Further Account (1660) — John Eliot, ed. *A Further Account of the Progress of the Gospel amongst the Indians in New England: Being a Relation of the Confessions Made by Several Indians (in the Presence of the Elders and Members of Several Churches) in Order to Their Admission into Church-Fellowship.* London, 1660.

Brief Narrative (1671) — John Eliot, ed. *A Brief Narrative of the Progress of the Gospel amongst the Indians in New England, in the Year 1670.* London, 1671.

ET — Michael P. Clark, ed. *The Eliot Tracts: With Letters from John Eliot to Thomas Thorowgood and Richard Baxter.* Westport, CT: Praeger, 2003.[1]

OTHER WORKS BY JOHN ELIOT

Indian Dialogues (1671) — John Eliot. *Indian Dialogues for Their Instruction in That Great Service of Christ, in Calling Home Their Country-Men to the Knowledge of God, and of Themselves, and of Iesus Christ.* Cambridge, 1671.

ID — Henry Bowden, and James P. Ronda, eds. *John Eliot's Indian Dialogues: A Study in Cultural Interaction.* Westport, CT: Greenwood Press, 1980.[2]

CORRESPONDENCE

CGTNEC — John W. Ford, ed. *Some Correspondence between the Governors and Treasurers of the New England Company in London and the Commissioners of the United Colonies in America The Missionaries of the Company and Others between the Years 1657 and 1712 to Which Are Added the Journals of the Rev. Experience Mayhew in 1713 and 1714.* London: Spottiswoode, 1896.

---

1. This edition contains the whole texts of eleven Eliot Tracts. This book refers to the texts in this edition.

2. This edition contains the whole texts of Eliot's *Indian Dialogues* (1671). This book refers to the texts in this edition.

CJC   John Cotton. *The Correspondence of John Cotton*, edited by Sargent Bush Jr. Chapel Hill, NC: University of North Carolina Press, 2001.

CRBJE   F. J. Powicke, ed. *Some Unpublished Correspondence of the Reverend Richard Baxter and the Reverend John Elliot, the Apostle of the American Indians, 1656–1662*. Manchester: Manchester University Press, 1931.

JEI   Wilberforce Eames, ed. *John Eliot and the Indians, Being Letters Addressed to Jonathan Hammer of Barnstaple, England, Reproduced from the Original Manuscripts in the Possession of Theodore N. Vail*. New York: Adams & Grace, 1915.

Other Primary Sources

CPC   Williston Walker, ed. *The Creeds and Platforms of Congregationalism*. New York: Scribner's Sons, 1893.

HCINE   Daniel Gookin. *The Historical Collections of the Indians in New England*. 1674.

HADSINE   Daniel Gookin. *An Historical Account of the Doings and Sufferings of the Christian Indians in New England*. 1677.

JJW   John Winthrop. *The Journal of John Winthrop*, edited by Richard S. Dunn et al. Cambridge: Belknap, 1996.

LJE   Cotton Mather. *The Triumphs of the Reformed Religion in America: The Life of the Renowned John Eliot*. Boston, 1691. Reprinted in Cotton Mather, *Magnalia Christi Americana*. London, 1702.

MHSC   Massachusetts Historical Society Collections.

RMB   Nathaniel B. Shurtleff, ed. *Records of the Governor and Company of the Massachusetts Bay in New England (1626–86)*. Boston, 1853–54. Reprint, New York: AMS, 1968.

TSC   Thomas Shepard. *Thomas Shepard's Confessions*, edited by George Selement and Bruce C. Woolley. Publications of the Colonial Society of Massachusetts Collections 58. Boston: Society, 1981.

Monographs and Reference Works

ANB   *American National Biography*. 24 vols. Oxford: Oxford University Press, 1999. https://www.anb.org.

JEMI   Richard W. Cogley. *John Eliot's Mission to the Indians before King Philip's War*. Cambridge: Harvard University Press, 1999.

ODNB   *Oxford Dictionary of National Biography.* 61 vols. Oxford: Oxford University Press, 2004. https://www.oxforddnb.com.

PPEA   Francis J. Bremer, and Tom Webster, eds. *Puritans and Puritanism in Europe and America: A Comprehensive Encyclopedia.* 2 vols. Santa Barbara, CA: ABC-CLIO, 2006.

Part 1

Relocating John Eliot

1

Historiographical Introduction
and a Proposition for a New Perspective

"By prophesying to the wind, the wind came and the dry bones lived." This is a paraphrased biblical passage from Ezek 37:9–10, the text of John Eliot's first preaching to the Indians in 1646.[1] Ezekiel's vision of the revival of "the dry bones" through prophesying in the wind was the very dream of Eliot, who devoted more than a half century of his life to indefatigable labors in Indian ministry.

John Eliot was a puritan minister, born and educated in England, who emigrated to New England in 1631 for a pastoral ministry with the English settlers.[2] Eliot was initially a teacher of the Boston church, and from 1632 a teacher and pastor of the Roxbury church, until he died in 1690.[3] As a religious leader of New England, he participated in the examination and excommunication of Anne Hutchinson, who argued for Antinomianism.[4] Also, he was one of the writers and publishers of *The Bay Psalm Book* (1640), which was the first book printed in North America. John Eliot as "The Apostle of the Indians"[5] devoted himself as a preacher and minister for New England Indians from 1646 until his death in 1690, while he was

1. *Clear Sun-Shine* (1648), 135.

2. *JJW*, 59. Fausz, "Eliot, John."

3. *JJW*, 83. See also Thwing, *History of The First Church in Roxbury*. For more resources on Eliot's English ministry, see the section on historiography below.

4. Winship, "Hutchinson, Anne."

5. Baxter, *Reliquiae Baxterianae* (1696), 131; Sewall, *The Diary of Samuel Sewall*, 63.

actively involved with pastoral ministry in New England settlements. Eliot established fourteen Praying Towns as Indian Christian communities in Massachusetts.[6] Also, he established the first native Indian church at Natick Praying Town in 1660. After that church, five more Indian churches were established by Eliot. John Eliot was the author of *The Christian Commonwealth* (1659), *The Communion of Churches* (1665), and *Indian Dialogues* (1671). Eliot was the first Indian Bible translator. He translated and published the New Testament and the whole Bible in the Algonquian Indian language, in 1661 and 1663, respectively. Eliot also translated and published many pastoral and educational resources for the Indians, including *The Indian Primer* (1654), *The Psalter* (1658), and *The Logick Primer* (1672). In addition, Eliot translated Richard Baxter's *A Call to the Unconverted* (1658), Lewis Bayly's *The Practice of Piety* (2nd ed., 1612), and Thomas Shepard's *The Sincere Convert* (London, 1640), in 1664, 1665, and 1689 respectively.[7]

My book will examine John Eliot's puritan ministry to New England Indians, which in modern missiological perspectives has been normally interpreted as "mission." John Eliot has been explored from a "mission" perspective adopted by missiologists and ethnohistorians, who applied the term "mission" to Eliot, a seventeenth-century puritan, and interpreted his work with New England Indians as "missionary" work, without providing an explanation of the terminological and hermeneutical applications of the terms. The basic research questions we are driven to engage with are whether we can apply the term "mission," as defined by modern missiologists, to John Eliot and his Indian ministry; as well as asking what kind of understanding of "mission" he had, in his seventeenth-century context. In order to answer

---

6. New England Indians who became Christians were known as "Praying Indians" and John Eliot established fourteen Christian Indian towns called "Praying Towns." John Eliot explained the use and meaning of the term "Praying Indians" in *Tears of Repentance* (1653): "Their frequent phrase of Praying to God, is not to be understood of that Ordinance and Duty of Prayer only, but of all Religion, and comprehendeth the same meaning, with them, as the word [Religion] doth with us: And it is observable, because it seemeth to me, That the Lord will make a Praying people: and indeed, there is a great Spirit of Prayer pow[e]red out upon them." *Tears of Repentance* (1653), 261. See also Winslow, *John Eliot*, chs. 10, 13; *JEMI*, chs. 5–6. "New England Indians" in this book signifies Algonquian Indians. "Algonquian" is "ethnological term denoting the original people who inhabited much of the eastern continent, as well as their culture and language. Algonquian culture encompassed the Massachusett, Wampanoag, Pennacook, and other New England tribes. The beliefs, practices, and language of this people differed somewhat from those of the Iroquois, who principally populated New York and who included the Mohawk." Morrison, *A Praying People*, 237.

7. For Baxter, Bayly, and Shepard, see Keeble, "Baxter, Richard"; Jones and Larminie, "Bayly, Lewis"; Jinkins, "Shepard, Thomas." According to Jones and Larminie, the year of the first edition of *The Practice of Piety* is unknown.

these basic research questions, this book seeks to refocus understandings of Eliot to set him in the context of seventeenth-century puritanism. Eliot has often been described as a "puritan missionary," and in this book not only the seventeenth-century sense of word "missionary," but also the word "puritan," will come under scrutiny. The definition of puritanism has been seriously debated among scholars. Scholars have interpreted the term "puritan" and "puritanism" in their own complicated political, social, cultural, and religious contexts. Among many definitions, this book understands puritanism as a pietistic Protestant reforming movement based on Reformed theology.[8] In addition, recent scholarship on puritanism is also related to the understanding of Eliot and his work with the Indians. The general understanding of John Eliot's work with New England Indians as "mission" has been based on missiologists' own interpretations of the Great Migration of puritans to New England as a missionary enterprise to make a model society through Indian evangelization, based on Perry Miller's "errand into the wilderness" thesis. However, this book will argue that the purpose of the Great Migration to New England was not a missionary enterprise, but was for the pursuit of religious purity that puritans could not actualize under Laudian policy in England.[9] In this sense, understanding Eliot and his work with the Indians only from a modern missionary perspective without careful theological and historical consideration of puritanism can cause serious conceptual and historical misunderstandings.

My book starts from these initial questions, which require reinterpretation of Eliot and his work with the Indians through serious consideration of puritan historical contexts. Based on this argument, the study suggests a seventeenth-century puritan theological and historical perspective from which to view John Eliot. The necessity of a new approach to Eliot can be supported by reflection on previous research. A historiographical survey in the next section will reveal previous dominant perspectives and methodologies.

Previous Research on John Eliot

Before presenting an argument for a new perspective for understanding Eliot, we need to pay attention to previous Eliot research. Although John Eliot has been called "The Apostle of the Indians" and one of "the Grandparents of modern Protestant missions,"[10] and has been the subject of at least some

8. For historiographical approaches and definitions of puritanism, see chapter 3.
9. For detailed argument, see pp. 20, 31–41 below.
10. Carpenter, "The New England Puritans," 519–32.

scholarly treatment since the seventeenth century, he did not receive intense academic attention until the 1960s.

The first two biographical descriptions of Eliot and his ministry were written by his contemporaries Daniel Gookin[11] and Cotton Mather.[12] Through those books, one can see the earliest biographies of Eliot and his ministry within his own religious and historical circumstances. Mather provided a hagiographical description of Eliot. Gookin, colonial administrator and superintendent of the Praying Indians, provided what has been called "the most comprehensive first-hand account of the missionary project."[13]

John Eliot was also considered by some scholars in the 1800s and early and mid-1900s.[14] However, conspicuous research on Eliot did not appear until the 1960s. From this time Eliot and his "mission"[15] have again been of interest to scholars, such as Frederick F. Harling, Sidney H. Rooy, Ola Elizabeth Winslow, and Alden T. Vaughan.[16] Harling and Winslow's biographies offered detailed historical descriptions of Eliot, together with an understanding of the circumstances in seventeenth-century New England, through a rediscovery and examination of extant historical resources that had not been sufficiently explored previously. For Harling, Eliot was not only "a saint of New England way," but also a sustained and energetic missionary for Indians. For Winslow, Eliot was "the gentlest and beloved" mission pioneer for New England Indians. For both scholars, Eliot was not a "cultural imperialist" (particularly for Harling), but a sincere missionary pursuing the religious conversion of Indians more than cultural change.

11. Thompson, "Gookin, Daniel." See *HCINE* and *HADSINE*. The former was published in 1792 and first appeared in the *Massachusetts Historical Society Collections*, and the latter was published in 1836 and appeared in the *American Antiquarian Society's Transactions and Collections*. See *JEMI*, 264; *ET*, 48. For Gookin, see *JEMI*, 224–30.

12. Hall, "Mather, Cotton." See *LJE*.

13. *ET*, 7.

14. Clark, *Historical Account of John Eliot*, 5–35; Moore, *Memoirs of the Life and Character of Rev. John Eliot*; Biglow, *History of the Town of Natick*; Francis, *Life of John Eliot*; Adams, *The Life of John Eliot*; Caverly, *Lessons of Law and Life from John Eliot*; Winters, "Notices of the Pilgrim Fathers, John Eliot and His Friends," 267–311; Normandie, *An Historical Sketch of the First Church in Roxbury* (1896); Normandie, *Address on the Apostle Eliot*; Normandie, "John Eliot, the Apostle to the Indians," 249–370; Byington, "John Eliot," 109–45; *JEI*; Polack, *John Eliot*; Chamberlain, *Eliot of Massachusetts*; Morison, "John Eliot," *Builders of the Bay Colony*; Cornish, "John Eliot"; Winship, *The New England Company of 1649 and John Eliot*.

15. The terms "mission" and "missionary," which are generally applied to John Eliot by scholars, require careful and further discussion of their usage, at least definition in seventeenth-century puritan studies. I will discuss this more below.

16. Harling, "A Biography of John Eliot"; Rooy, *The Theology of Missions*; Winslow, *John Eliot*; Vaughan, *New England Frontier*.

Despite their unprecedented historical account of Eliot's life based on various primary sources, these scholars described Eliot's work for Indians as missionary work, and focused on a description of the mission process, rather than on a theological and ministerial analysis of Eliot's work from the perspective of puritan theology and ministry.

Rooy, in his *The Theology of Missions in the Puritan Tradition* (1965), gave a fine theological analysis of the relationship between puritan theology and mission. Rooy aimed to relate puritan theology to mission, to discover the theological foundations of Protestant missions. Rooy identified the following themes as foundations for modern Protestant mission: puritans' undivided attention to human conversion through the propagation of the gospel, their emphasis on human responsibility (particularly as stressed by Richard Sibbes and Richard Baxter), their ecclesiology for church establishment, and their eschatology for the redemption of the world. For Rooy, Eliot's theological ideas on mission were in line with the theology of Sibbes and Baxter, and Eliot's missionary work was an actualization of puritan missionary ideas.

Alden T. Vaughan, in *New England Frontier: Puritans and Indians, 1620-1675*, opened up a new approach by analyzing the relationship between the Indians and English puritans, focusing on the social and political relations between the two groups. Vaughan emphasized the puritans' genuine purpose for mission and their labor and passion for this, but also argued that the puritans had treated the Indians with respect and had not forced them from their land or driven them to despair through unjust or cruel treatment. The puritans' efforts towards Indian conversion were not vigorous. Additionally, he argued that the rise of the English in New England was not the crucial reason for the decline of the Indians.[17]

There are four common aspects in research on Eliot in the 1960s, as undertaken by scholars like Rooy and Vaughan. The first is an acknowledgement of the authenticity of Eliot's missionary purpose. Second, the major focus in the literature is a description of Eliot as a missionary. Third, the work commonly emphasizes the positive impact of puritan missions on the Indians. Lastly, the scholarship is based on a highly English-centered viewpoint rather than an Indian perspective.

English-centered descriptions of John Eliot and the understanding of the Indian-English relationship presented by Harling, Winslow, and Vaughan met severe criticism in the early 1970s, especially from Francis Jennings. Jennings argued "the mission was conceived as a means to an

---

17. Vaughan, *New England Frontier*, 326-35.

end rather than as an end in itself."[18] For Jennings, puritan mission in New England was not implemented for the sincere purpose of Indian conversion (as Vaughan and Winslow had argued), but was instead used as a means for the expansion of English imperialism. Jennings stated that the enforcement of Indian conversion by the puritans, and the impact of the puritans on the Indians, had led the Indians to severe degeneration and despair. Jennings strongly argued for the victimization of the Indians by the puritans in his work.[19] Jennings's work, based on an Indian-centered ethnohistorical viewpoint,[20] drew scholarly attention to the socio-economic relationship between the Indians and puritan missionaries.[21] In the wake of Jennings's work, new research issues about puritan missions, such as socio-economic analysis of Indian-puritan relations, cultural encounter and conflict, the relationship between puritan mission and English imperialism, and the reasons for the Indian conversion, have been treated as major topics by ethnohistorians. After Jennings's ground-breaking revisionist interpretation of puritan mission, John Eliot, the most notable puritan missionary in New England, came under intense scrutiny. In fact, Eliot became an object of serious critique by ethnohistorians.

In the 1970s–1980s, many scholars followed Jennings by contributing to Indian-centered and socio-economic interpretations of puritan missions

18. Jennings, "Goals and Functions of Puritan Missions to the Indians," 207.

19. Jennings, "Goals and Functions of Puritan Missions to the Indians"; Jennings, *Invasion of America*.

20. A generally agreed definition of ethnohistory is "the use of historical methods and materials to gain knowledge of the nature and causes of change in a culture defined by ethnological concepts and categories." Methodologically, ethnohistory which is not a separate discipline (or even sub-discipline) pursues "a hybrid method, process, or approach applicable to a variety of historical problems." Therefore, it is an "exacting but flexible approach to the problems of cultural process and change, problems that are shared by the complementary disciplines of history and anthropology." Axtell, "The Ethnohistory of Early America," 113–14. For the resources of definition and methodology of ethnohistory, see Axtell, "The Ethnohistory of Early America," nn12–14. Ethnohistory rose out of the critique and reflections on the dominant white-centered perspective in American scholarship. Some scholars such as Joseph Kinsey Howard, Bernard De Voto, and William N. Fenton criticized white-centrism in American history and culture research in their work in the 1950s and the American Indian Ethnohistoric Conference was established at Indiana University in 1954 after which, ethnohistory was developed as a definite scholarly discipline. For early ethnohistorical research on the native American Indians in 1950s, see Howard, *Strange Empire*; Bernard De Voto's "Introduction," in Howard, *Strange Empire*; Fenton, *American Indian and White Relations to 1830*; Axtell, "The Ethnohistory of Early America," 112–44; Hedges, "Strangers, Foreigners, and Fellow Citizens," 1–7.

21. For Jennings' further argument about victimization of the Indians by the English, see Jennings, *The Ambiguous Iroquois Empire*; Jennings, *The Founders of America*.

and Indian-puritan relations.²² The scholars who followed Jennings in the 1970s–1980s include, for example, Neal Salisbury, Kenneth M. Morrison, Wilcome E. Washburn, Elise Brenner, and Henry Warner Bowden.²³

There were also revisionists who critiqued Jennings's arguments, one of whom is James Axtell.²⁴ Although Axtell followed Jennings's main argument criticising English imperialism in the puritan mission in New England, he revised the one-sided victimization of the Indians demonstrated by Jennings and his followers. Axtell tried to emphasize the ability and activity of the Indians by treating the puritan mission in the context of a mutual cultural encounter between the Indians and English, yet still criticising the puritan mission as a means of expanding English imperialism.²⁵ For Axtell, Indian conversion and Christianization was not achieved via unilateral enforcement by the puritans with the Indians in a passive role, but by the Indians' active participation in the puritan mission project of their own accord, in order to avoid cultural and racial extinction.²⁶ Axtell's revision of Jennings was adopted by scholars such as James P. Ronda, Robert James Naeher, and Harold W. Van Lonkhuyzen.²⁷

Another new approach to "puritan mission" in New England appeared partially in the 1970s, but mainly in the 1980s. Unlike previous scholars like Jennings and his followers, who had analyzed the puritan mission and Indian-puritan relations based on ethnohistorical and socio-economic interpretations, a fresh band of scholars interpreted the puritan mission through puritan millenarianism. In the 1970s, puritan millenarianism in New England was examined by scholars such as James A. De Jong and James F. Maclear. Maclear argued that Vaughan, Winslow, and Jennings did not

---

22. Richard W. Cogley calls the interpretation used by Jennings's group "material interpretation." Cogley, "Idealism vs. Materialism," 165–82.

23. Salisbury, "Conquest of the 'Savage'"; Salisbury, "Red Puritans," 27–54; Salisbury, "Prospero in New England," 253–73; Salisbury, "Squanto," 228–46; Salisbury, *Manitou and Providence*; Morrison, "'That Art of Coyning Christians,'" 77–92; Washburn, *The Indian in America*; Brenner, "To Pray or be Prey," 135–52; Bowden, *American Indians and Christian Missions*. See also *ID*.

24. Axtell, *America Perceived*; Axtell, *White Indians of Colonial America*; Axtell, *The European and the Indian*; Axtell, *The Indian Peoples of Eastern America*; Axtell, *The Invasion Within*; Axtell, *After Columbus*; Axtell, *Beyond 1492*. For Axtell's main arguments, see Hedges, "Strangers, Foreigners, and Fellow Citizens," 1–48.

25. Axtell, *The European and the Indian*, 85–86.

26. Axtell, *After Columbus*, 120; Axtell, *The European and the Indian*, 85–86.

27. Ronda, "'We Are Well as We Are,'" 66–82; Ronda, "Generation of Faith," 369–94; Naeher, "Dialogue in the Wilderness," 346–68; Lonkhuyzen, "A Reappraisal of the Praying Indians," 396–428.

discover millenarianism in John Eliot.[28] In the 1980s, further information appeared on puritan millenarianism related to Eliot and the puritan mission, for example in the work of James Holstun, Theodore Dwight Bozeman, Timothy J. Sehr, and Richard W. Cogley, who contributed significantly to the topic. For them, Eliot's ministry for Indians' conversion clearly reflected his millenarian ideology.[29]

In the 1990s and 2000s, readers have seen ongoing debates between Vaughan and Jennings. Vaughan, in his reprinted *New England Frontier*, has continued to dispute Jennings's arguments about the one-sided victimization of the Indians, the sincerity of the puritans' mission purpose, and their positive impact on the Indians.[30] Also, new angles for examining Eliot and puritan mission have come to light. For example, Andrew H. Hedges, in his dissertation, revised one of the major arguments of ethnohistorians.[31] Hedges argued that puritan missionaries had not been racialists or cultural and political imperialists who had brought about the extinction of Indian culture and identity. For Hedges, the Indians preserved their culture and identity although they received puritan Christianity. Emphasizing the reasons for Indian conversions, Hedges took issue with Axtell's argument that conversion was primarily to preserve their traditional cultures and identity. Yet, he also demonstrated Indians' sincere conversion and the importance of "personal-self-interest" as a reason for conversion.[32]

Richard W. Cogley's work in the 1990s was a significant contribution to research on Eliot. In his earlier work in the 1980s, Cogley had already convincingly demonstrated the importance of millenarianism in Eliot's puritan ministry in Praying Towns.[33] He continued to state that Eliot's millenarianism was essential for understanding Eliot's efforts toward Indian conversion and his Indian ministry. For Cogley, the importance of millenarianism for Eliot's mission was not discovered by ethnohistorians

---

28. Jong, *As the Waters Cover the Seas*; Maclear, "New England and the Fifth Monarchy," 223–60.

29. Holstun, *A Rational Millennium*; Bozeman, *To Live Ancient Lives*, 263–86; Sehr, "John Eliot, Millennialist and Missionary," 187–203; Cogley, "The Millenarianism of John Eliot"; Cogley, "John Eliot and the Origins of the American Indians," 210–25. For seventeenth-century puritan millenarianism, see Gribben, *The Puritan Millennium*. See also Gribben, *Evangelical Millennialism*, 37–50.

30. Vaughan, *New England Frontier*.

31. Hedges, "Strangers, Foreigners, and Fellow Citizens."

32. Hedges, "Strangers, Foreigners, and Fellow Citizens," 90–149. See Axtell, *After Columbus*, 120; Axtell, *The European and the Indian*, 85–86.

33. Cogley, "The Millenarianism of John Eliot"; Cogley, "John Eliot and the Origins of the American Indians," 210–25; Cogley, "Seventeenth-Century English Millenarianism," 379–96.

pursuing a socio-economical interpretation of the puritan mission in New England. Cogley criticized the inadequacy of Jennings's "materialistic" evaluation, and indicated that his misunderstanding of Eliot came from "his misunderstanding of religion."[34] Cogley's book, *John Eliot's Mission to the Indians before King Philip's War* (1999)[35] offers the most detailed description of Eliot's missionary work in New England in the last twenty years. Cogley, who did not work from an ethnohistorical perspective, described a mission process of Eliot focusing on the genuineness of the work, rather than a socio-economic analysis of puritan mission and the Indian-puritan relations as argued by ethnohistorians. Cogley, who had already explored the relationship between millenarianism and Eliot's work with the Indians in his doctoral dissertation in 1983, stressed that millenarianism is essential to understand Eliot's Indian mission. For Cogley, the mission became important for Eliot, who had not initially been interested in Indian mission, because Eliot came to appreciate their humanity and to sympathize with their problems.[36] In addition, Cogley offered a more concrete description of Praying Towns as the field and product of Eliot's puritan mission, which was not sufficiently explored in previous research. Through his work, Cogley consequently disputed the misunderstanding of ethnohistorians which characterized Eliot as an imperialistic cultural destroyer and coercer of a Christian faith. For Cogley, Eliot as a sincere missionary tried to Christianize Indians without introducing fundamental and destructive cultural changes, while acting with compassion and deep respect toward the people and their cultures.

Another piece of work produced by Cogley in 1999 is an article examining John Eliot's puritan ministry in New England towns.[37] A significant fact in this article is that Cogley clearly distinguished "puritan ministry" from "puritan mission." Cogley did not consider Eliot's work with the Indians to be a puritan ministry, and therefore excluded Eliot's work with the Indians from this article. Although this article just focused on a brief historical description of the pastoral activities of Eliot as a pastor, writer and publisher, millennialist, educator, and religious and civil leader in New England towns (without a theological analysis or reflection on his thoughts and practices from the perspective of puritanism), the article is one of only

---

34. Cogley, "Idealism vs. Materialism," 165–82. See also Cogley, "John Eliot and the Millennium," 227–50; Cogley, "Pagans and Christians on the New England Frontier," 95–109. Cogley also offers a helpful historiographical essay for Eliot research. See Cogley, "John Eliot in Recent Scholarship," 72–92.

35. *JEMI*.

36. *JEMI*, 249.

37. Cogley, "John Eliot's Puritan Ministry," 1–18.

a few works investigating Eliot's puritan ministerial activities in puritan towns which stresses Eliot as a puritan pastor.[38]

Another interesting scholarly tendency of the 1990s–2000s was that more intensive attention has been paid to primary sources on Eliot and the puritan mission, through linguistic and literary analysis. The literary and linguistic approach to Eliot and the puritan mission can be seen in several recent doctoral dissertations by Kristina Kae Bross, Cynthia Marie Moore, Zubeda Jalalzai, Joseph Patrick Cesarini, and Kathryn Napier Gray.[39] Bross examined the identity of Praying Indians in relation to puritan missionary work through primary sources, especially those written by Eliot. For Bross, the identity of Praying Indians was crucially related to the puritans' self-definition and redefinition, which in turn relates to and reflects their changing transatlantic context. Bross argued that Christianized Praying Towns were the realization of the puritan ideals. For Bross, the identity of Praying Indians was constructed by the puritans, and it ultimately reflected the identity of the puritans themselves in the New World.

Cynthia Marie Moore has argued through literary textual analysis that the Indians' conversion narratives, and the puritan missionaries' narratives, were used for the management of the puritans' congregations in Old and New England. For Moore, the Indians' conversion narratives (printed for an English audience) revealed the ideas of the puritans' New England experiment to show a model of puritan society to congregations in England. Also, according to Moore, missionaries' narratives about the Indians' conversion were ultimately used to encourage New Englanders who ignored Indian mission to participate in the work.

Zubeda Jalalzai has argued that the puritan mission was "a primary site of puritan imperial power because the missions were the initial justification for the settlement." Missions affected relations between Old and New England, as well as between New England as a colony and "the wilderness."[40] For Jalalzai, the Indian conversion narratives in the Eliot Tracts reveal the puritans' self-understanding, and puritan utopias and puritan missions in New England, and ultimately reflect English imperialism.

Joseph Patrick Cesarini, in his dissertation "Reading New England's Mission: Indian Conversion and the Ends of Puritan Rhetoric in the

---

38. For Eliot's puritan ministerial activities in puritan towns, see Harling, "A Biography of John Eliot," chs. 3–5; Winslow, *John Eliot*, chs. 3–5.

39. Bross, "'That Epithet of Praying.'" See also Bross, "Dying Saints, Vanishing Savages," 325–52; Moore, "'Rent and Ragged Relation(s)'"; Jalalzai, "Puritan Imperialisms"; Cesarini, "Reading New England's Mission"; Gray, "Speech, Text and Performance in John Eliot's Writing."

40. Jalalzai, "Puritan Imperialisms," 18.

Seventeenth Century" (2003), argues that the published records of puritan mission in the seventeenth century were not propaganda for the imperialistic expansion of England as many ethnohistorians argue, but rather the expression and explanation of genuineness of puritan mission, the progress of it, and the relationship between the Indians and the puritans. These can be discovered through the rhetoric of the mission records.

The last among these recent dissertations is a study by Kathryn Napier Gray. Gray, observing that there is no comprehensive literary analysis of Eliot's work, despite scholarly attention from historians of the colonial period, has examined written records of direct speech, conversations, speeches, dialogues, and deathbed confessions of Algonquian Praying Indians, in order to investigate the use and manipulation of written and spoken communicative strategies. Despite the general recognition of a scarcity of resources for Eliot research, recent literary-analysis-centered research (such as Gray's) reminds us of the significance of using various approaches to reinterpret primary sources.

From this chronological survey of scholarship over the last forty years, one can see four major streams in Eliot research. The first stream is a biographical and puritan-centered approach towards Eliot and his Indian ministry, mainly written before the 1970s. Together with Eliot's contemporaries, Daniel Gookin and Cotton Mather, and other biographers in the 1800s and the early 1990s, the work of the 1960s argues for the sincerity of the mission and positive impact of the puritans on the Indians, from an English-centered perspective.

The second stream is the ethnohistorical and socio-economic analytical approaches used by Jennings and his followers that emerged in the early 1970s, arguing the one-sided victimization of the Indians, and the puritan mission as a significant means of English imperialism.

The third type of approach to Eliot focuses on millenarianism as a critical angle for analyzing Eliot and his puritan mission. In particular, Cogley argues the inadequacy of a non-religious "material" ethnohistorical perspective, then offers a religious perspective focusing on puritan millenarianism as a new angle to investigate Eliot and to correct previous views on Eliot and his work in New England.

Finally, a conspicuous amount of research focuses on literary and linguistic approaches, as mainly seen in several dissertations in the 1990s–2000s. They pursue an exploration of the identities of the Indians and puritans in New England contexts, Indian-puritan relationships and their minds, ideologies, and attitudes, mainly through a careful literary and linguistic analysis of primary texts related to Eliot's Indian mission.

Although scholars in the four general streams of scholarship have pursued their own directions, they have shared a common perspective for seeing John Eliot. Despite different research foci and interpretations of Eliot, they have commonly seen Eliot as a puritan "missionary." From the modern perspective of "mission," they have analyzed Eliot and his works in the specific context of seventeenth-century New England and have considered whether he was a "sincere missionary" or a wicked conspirator with English imperialism. These perspectives draw on out-dated interpretations of puritanism and migration to New England. Also, the modern "mission" perspectives lack sufficient understanding of Eliot's historical and ideological context. In the next section, I will suggest a new angle to set John Eliot in the context of seventeenth-century puritanism.

John Eliot and Puritan "Mission": An Argument for a New Perspective

Reflecting on earlier research, I would like to point out some problematic elements in previous work on John Eliot, while acknowledging their significant scholarly contributions. First of all, it is important to grasp the perspective which has been taken in previous research to analyze Eliot and his ministry in New England. Previous researchers, whether consciously or unconsciously, adopted the modern perspective of "mission" in their interpretations of Eliot as a seventeenth-century puritan figure. The modern "mission" perspective adopted by many scholars has two aspects: terminological and hermeneutical. In this section, I will briefly discuss these two aspects through an examination of the definition and theological meaning of "mission" and the terminological and hermeneutical application of the conception of the term. Also, I will delineate some problematic issues of the perspective based on the two aspects of the mission perspective.

Traditional Understanding of "Mission" in Relation to Seventeenth-Century Puritans

When considering previous research, almost all scholars have called Eliot a "missionary," and his Indian ministry "mission," without a satisfactory explanation of the terms. Use of the terms, especially in seventeenth-century puritan studies, without careful consideration of the definition, origin and various applications of the terms, can cause a terminological and conceptual misunderstanding.

The term "mission" originated from the Latin *mitto* (I send), which is the equivalent of *apostello* (to send) in Greek. A "missionary" is a "sent one," a synonym for "Apostle," from the Greek *apostello* (I send). The basic meaning of the term "mission," which does not come from the Bible, is "sending someone forth with a specific purpose."[41] However, although the term "mission" does not come from biblical languages, one can see that the concept of "being sent out for a certain purpose" in the Christian faith is a biblical idea. Based on this meaning, M. R. Spindler describes "mission" as "being sent out," "to make disciples of all nations, deliverance, emancipatory action," and "witness" for the Christian faith.[42]

In Christian history, "mission" has been specifically applied to the propagation of the Christian faith, especially among non-Christians. "Mission" has been one of the key tasks of the Christian Church from the beginning.[43] However, until the sixteenth century, the term "mission" was used exclusively in relation to the doctrine of the Trinity: the sending of the Son by the Father and of the Holy Spirit by the Father and the Son. In the sixteenth century, the Jesuits were the first to use it to mean the spreading of the Christian faith among people who were not members of the Catholic Church.[44] Since then the term has normally been related to foreign missionary activities.[45]

David J. Bosch, acknowledging that traditionally "mission" has been conceived as only related to the non-Western world,[46] offers a comprehensive understanding of the traditional meaning of "mission" in church history.[47] Bosch offers three categories of circumstance to which "mission" was applied until the 1950s. First of all, "mission" referred to: "the sending of missionaries to a designated territory, the activities undertaken by such missionaries, the geographical area where the missionaries were active, the agency which dispatched the missionaries, the non-Christian world or mission field." The term also referred to a slightly different situation: "a local congregation without a resident minister and still dependent on the support

---

41. Moreau, *Evangelical Dictionary of World Missions*, 636; Glover, *The Progress of World-Wide Missions*, 3; Walls, *The Missionary Movement in Christian History*, 255.

42. Spindler, "The Biblical Grounding and Orientation of Mission," 127–30.

43. Cross, *The Oxford Dictionary of the Christian Church*, 1100.

44. Bosch, *Transforming Mission*, 1. See also Bowden, *Christianity*, 762.

45. Douglas, *The New International Dictionary of the Christian Church*, 664.

46. Bosch, *Witness to the World*, 15.

47. For Andrew F. Walls, "David Bosch was the most complete missiologist of our generation, perhaps of the whole century." Walls, *The Cross-Cultural Process in Christian History*, 273. For the life and work of David Bosch, see Walls, *The Cross-Cultural Process in Christian History*, 273–77.

of an older, established church, or a series of special services intended to deepen or spread the Christian faith, usually in a nominally Christian environment." In sum, the traditional understanding of the Christian "mission" is the propagation of the Christian faith and gospel by missionaries, dispatched by the Christian world to the non-Christian world. Here, one can notice three natures of the traditional understanding of "mission." First, "mission" is basically a proclamation of the gospel and propagation of the Christian faith. Second, "mission" has a geographical dimension: "mission" is the churches' or Christians' task abroad in non-Christian or pagan countries. Third, the objects of "mission" are non-Christians who have never heard of the Christian faith. This is the "theological nature" of "mission."[48]

With its three natures, "mission" can be distinguished from "evangelism" in traditional understanding.[49] The word "evangel" is *euangelion* in Greek, translated as "gospel" meaning "good tidings," or "good news." Therefore, simply speaking, "evangelism" is the proclamation of the gospel, and an "evangelist" is "one who proclaims the gospel."[50] The Church of England's Commission on Evangelism adopted the following definition of the term "evangelize" in 1918 (and reaffirmed it in 1945): "To evangelize is so to present Christ Jesus in the power of the Holy Spirit that [people] shall come to put their trust in God through him, to accept him as their Saviour, and serve him as their King in the fellowship of his Church."[51] In terms of the propagation of the gospel, "mission" has the same meaning as "evangelism." However, in their geographical and theological natures, "mission" is distinguished from "evangelism." If "mission" is acting in non-Christian territories abroad, the context of "evangelism" is the evangelist's own place. Also, if the main objects of "mission" are "not-yet-Christians," "evangelism" is for "no-more-Christians."[52]

Bosch, in offering a traditional concept of "mission," argues that in changing modern times, especially after the 1950s, the traditional concept of "mission" is being modified and is in a so-called "paradigm shift."[53] According to Bosch, until the 1950s, the term "mission" was not frequently used. Since the 1950s, the term has circulated and become popular among

---

48. Bosch, *Witness to the World*, 12.

49. For the conceptual differences between "mission" and "evangelism," see Bosch, *Witness to the World*, ch. 1; Bosch, "Mission and Evangelism," 161–91; Kirk, *What is Mission?*, 56–57, 60–74.

50. Richardson and Bowden, *A New Dictionary of Christian Theology*, 192; Douglas, *The New International Dictionary of the Christian Church*, 362.

51. Richardson and Bowden, *A New Dictionary of Christian Theology*, 192.

52. Bosch, *Witness to the World*, 13.

53. Khun, *The Structure of Scientific Revolution*.

Christians, and the meaning has broadened.⁵⁴ Now, "mission" is related to all ecclesiastical activities.⁵⁵ For Bosch, "mission" remains an indefinable subject: "it should never be incarcerated in the narrow confines of our own predilections. The most we can hope for is to formulate some approximations of what mission is all about."⁵⁶

For Bosch, the paradigm shift of the "mission" concept is related to serious challenges from a changing modern society towards the church and the Christian "mission." Bosch analyzes the challenges towards the Christian "mission" from the followings six aspects: (1) the advance of science and technology and the worldwide process of secularization; (2) the slow, but steady dechristianization of the West, traditionally conceived as the base of the entire modern missionary enterprise; (3) the fact that the modern world can no longer be divided into "Christian" and "non-Christian" territories; (4) the effect of imperialism and colonialism of western countries, leading to an inability or unwillingness among Western Christians for propagation of the gospel; (5) the crucial division between the rich and the poor, and the general concept of Christian circles as the rich and non-Christian circles as the poor, creating antagonism of poor non-Christians against rich Christians, and a reluctance among the Christians to propagate their faith; and (6) changes in attitude towards traditional theology and church authority. Younger churches are pursuing more "autonomy" rather than giving total dedication to tradition and the old ecclesiastical system. Also, new theologies for new circumstances emerge such as Third-World theology, liberation theology, black theology, contextual theology, *minjung* theology, African theology, Asian theology, and the like.⁵⁷

It is difficult to find any similarities between the term "mission" in the traditional and modern Protestant understanding of the word and that of the seventeenth-century puritans. John Eliot, unquestionably acknowledged

---

54. Bosch, *Transforming Mission*, 1.

55. According to Bosch, the broad application of the term "mission" reached its apex at the Fourth Assembly of the WCC (Uppsala, 1968). From the meeting, "mission" became involved in various aspects of human life such as health and welfare services, youth projects, activities of political interest groups, projects for economic and social development, constructive application of violence, combating racism, the introduction of the inhabitants of the Third World to the possibilities of the Twentieth Century, and the defense of human rights. Bosch, *Witness to the World*, 11. See also Kirk, *What is Mission?*, pt. II.

56. Bosch, *Transforming Mission*, 9.

57. Bosch, *Transforming Mission*, 4. For Walls, mission in our multicultural modern society is "the transmission of Christian faith across cultural frontiers." Walls, *The Missionary Movement in Christian History*, "Introduction," and ch. 19, "The Old Age of the Missionary Movement." See also Walls, *The Cross-Cultural Process in Christian History*.

as a puritan "missionary" by missiologists, did not use the term in his own writings, and the term is not found in any other seventeenth-century primary sources describing Eliot's work. One can conjecture that the reason the seventeenth-century puritans did not use the term is because they did not perceive "mission" in the same way as have modern missiologists. This may imply that the conception of the modern "mission" did not yet exist or had not settled conceptually with the puritans. Their understanding of conversion and pastoral ministry (considered in chapter 3) confirms this. For seventeenth-century puritans, Protestant pastoral ministry was the Word- and preaching-centered ministry, because they believed that the preaching of the gospel was the most significant task in their ministry. The ministry was mainly pursuing the conversion of the unconverted in their parishes, and ultimately pursuing the reformation of church and society.

It seems that seventeenth-century puritans did not have the concept of "mission" defined and understood by missiologists and ethnohistorians. However, it is evident that the propagation of the gospel was the most important and urgent ecclesiastical task for puritans. Therefore, one might argue that "mission" and "ministry" can be ultimately the same concept. However, for puritans, the main field for the gospel was their own local parish, and the object of the Word of God was the unconverted or ignorant in their "flock." In this sense, considering Bosch's distinction between "mission" and "evangelism," it would be true that puritans understood the concept of "evangelism." Yet, it is doubtful that seventeenth-century puritans, including John Eliot, in fact conceived of the term "mission" in the way it is defined by modern missiologists.

"Mission": Historical and Theological Interpretations

Along with the terminological understanding of "mission," it is also important to look at the theological and historical interpretation and application of the concept of "mission" by missiologists. First of all, missiologists and mission historians generally apply the concept of "mission" to every stage of Christian history, from the very beginning. For them, Christian history itself is the "mission" history. The spreading of the gospel and the establishment and development of churches are interpreted as the Christian mission history.[58] This interpretation of Christian history as a hermeneutical

---

58. See Latourette, *A History of the Expansion of Christianity*; Latourette, *A History of Christianity*; Robinson, *History of Christian Missions*; Glover, *The Progress of World-Wide Missions*; Neill, *A History of Christian Missions*; Kane, *A Concise Dictionary of the Christian World Mission*; Walls, *The Missionary Movement in Christian History*; Yates, *Christian Mission in the Twentieth Century*.

aspect reflects their "mission" perspective. Herbert Jedin says that historical research is based on the historians' "presuppositions and standards of value which cannot be derived from history itself."[59] Considering the importance of the historians' "presuppositions and standards of value," one of the most prominent historians to describe Christian history from the Christian "mission" perspective is Kenneth Scott Latourette (1884-1968), an American Orientalist, missiologist and historian of the expansion of Christianity.[60] Although Latourette, in his book *A History of Christianity*, argues that the expansion of Christianity is only one aspect of a whole history of Christianity,[61] it is clear that he understood Christian history from the "mission" perspective. For him, Christian history is the history of "expansion," as exemplified in his seven-volume work in *A History of the Expansion of Christianity*, and his attention to the nineteenth century as "the Great Century"[62] for Christian missions. Further, in relation to other historians such as W. von Loewenich, G. Ebeling, H. Bornkamm, K. D. Schmidt, J. Chambon, and Roland Bainton, Latourette's historical interpretation based on the mission perspective is clearly distinguishable.[63]

Second, the missiological interpretation of the Great Migration of puritans to New England, and of John Eliot and his work in New England, provide further examples of the hermeneutical aspect of the "mission." Many scholars related "mission" to the purpose of the Great Migration, drawing on Perry Miller's "errand into the wilderness" thesis, which argued that puritans migrated to New England to make a "city upon a hill" as a model society for England and other European countries to imitate. Scholars working from a mission perspective related the Great Migration to New

59. Jedin and Dolan, *Handbook of Church History*, 1:4.
60. Anderson, *Biographical Dictionary of Christian Missions*, 384.
61. Latourette, *A History of Christianity*, xxiv.
62. Latourette called the nineteenth century "The Great Century" in terms of Christian missions in his book, *A History of Christianity*, written in the Christian mission historical perspective. Latourette, *A History of Christianity*, 1063.
63. Jedin gives a brief introduction of several representative historians' hermeneutical perspectives of Christian history: "Church of the Word" (W. von Loewenich), "The history is the interpretation of Holy Scripture" (G. Ebeling), "The history of the Gospel and its effects in the world" (H. Bornkamm), "Christ continuing to work in the work, His Body which is led by the Holy Spirit to all truth and whose history is wholly God's work, but also wholly man's" (K. D. Schmidt), "the history of the Kingdom of God on earth" (J. Chambon). Jedin and Dolan, *Handbook of Church History*, vol. 1:3. Bainton describes a history of Christianity as the history of Western civilization. Bainton argues that Western civilization started from the appearance of Christianity and the formation and development of Christianity has been crucially related to those of Western civilization, and Christianity has been the origin, motive, and main source of Western civilization. Bainton, *Christendom*.

England Indian mission, because for them Indian conversion might be the most conspicuous sign of the "city upon a hill." Such scholars regarded the Great Migration as a missionary journey and enterprise.[64]

However, recent scholarship on motives for the Great Migration clearly argues that the main purpose of the Great Migration was not making a "city upon a hill" as a model society, but the pursuit of primitive purity in Christianity, and further reformation that puritans could not actualize under Laudian policy in 1630s England. This understanding revises previous arguments on the Great Migration based on Perry Miller's thesis of "errand into the wilderness," and makes it necessary to reconsider missiological arguments on the relationship between Indian mission and the Great Migration as a missionary journey.[65] This reconsideration is significantly related to reinterpretation of Eliot's preaching of the gospel to New England Indians.

Another example showing the hermeneutical aspect of the "mission" perspective is the understanding of "mission theology." Gerald H. Anderson defines the theology of mission as "a study of the basic presuppositions and underlying principles which determine, from the standpoint of the Christian faith, the motives, message, methods, strategy, and goals of the Christian world mission."[66] For Bosch, the theology of mission is about the "foundation, motive, and aim" of "mission," and for Kirk,

> the theology of mission is a disciplined study which deals with questions that arise when people of faith seek to understand and fulfil God's purposes in the world, as these are demonstrated in the ministry of Jesus Christ. It is a critical reflection on attitudes and actions adopted by Christians in pursuit of the missionary mandate. Its task is to validate, correct and establish on better foundations the entire practice of mission.[67]

Based on their definitions of the theology of mission, some scholars offer a missiological understanding of Reformation theology. In fact, this has been debated even among missiologists. The main point of the debate has been whether Reformation theology can be mission theology—whether Reformation theology in fact justifies mission. Some scholars believe that the

---

64. Miller, *Errand into the Wilderness*; Bosch, *Witness to the World*; Kane, *A Concise Dictionary of the Christian World Mission*; Jongeneel, "The Protestant Missionary Movement," 222–28; Carpenter, "The New England Puritans," 519–32.

65. Bozeman, *To Live Ancient Lives*; Hardman Moore, *Pilgrims*. The revisionist interpretation of the Great Migration will be discussed in detail in chapter 2.

66. Anderson, *Concise Dictionary of the Christian Mission*, 594. See also Kirk, *What is Mission?*, 21n25.

67. Bosch, *Witness to the World*, 21; Kirk, *What is Mission?*, 21.

reformers were not involved with missions, either theologically or practically. In 1906, Gustav Warneck, who was the father of missiology as a theological discipline, and one of the first Protestant scholars to consider the relationship between "mission" and the reformers, argued that the reformers did not engage in missionary activity, nor did they have the idea of missions that we understand today.[68] In 1978, Herbert Kane contended that Reformation theology was a critical reason for the delay of Protestant missions.[69]

In contrast, some missiologists argue a significant relationship between Reformation theology and the "mission" movement. For them, the Reformation was the root of the modern Protestant mission movement, and Reformation theology was the foundation of "mission theology" (even if the starting point of full-scale Protestant mission was William Carey, "the father of modern missions," and the previous Reformation period was "the dawn of the modern missionary era").[70] According to Robert Hall Glover, the Reformation was "a revival of apostolic faith" and a "necessary precursor of a revival of apostolic life and work." But Glover still acknowledged that the reformers' main concern was doctrine and theological correction, not the propagation of Christian faith to heathens.[71] Bosch also strongly argued for a significant connection between "mission" and reformers. Bosch cited other scholars, arguing that Luther, in particular, should be regarded as "a creative and original missionary thinker," and we must allow ourselves to read the Bible "through the eyes of Martin Luther the missiologist." For Bosch, Calvin was even more explicit, "particularly since his theology was one which took the believers' responsibility in the world more seriously than Luther's." According to Bosch, "for Calvin, the Christ who was exalted to God's right hand was pre-eminently the active Christ. He regarded the church as intermediary between the exalted Christ and secular order." Consequently, Bosch demonstrates that the reformers "pronounced an essentially missionary theology."[72] These serious debates on the relationship between Reformation theology and "mission" suggest not only differences

---

68. Warneck, *Outline of a History of Protestant Missions*, 9, quoted from Bosch, *Transforming Mission*, 244.

69. Kane, *A Concise History of the Christian World Mission*, 73–74.

70. Glover, *The Progress of World-Wide Missions*, 55, 58–59. See also Warren, *The Missionary Movement from Britain in Modern History*, 21–22; Robinson, *History of Christian Missions*, 42–60; Stanley, *The Bible and the Flag*, 56; Stanley, "Carey, William."

71. Glover, *The Progress of World-Wide Missions*, 45. See also Neill, *A History of Christian Missions*, 187–88.

72. Scherer, *Gospel, Church, and Kingdom*, 65–66; Oberman, *The Dawn of the Reformation*, 235–39. See Bosch, *Transforming Mission*, 244–45; Bosch, *Witness to the World*, 122.

of perspective in understanding theology, but also deep differences in theological understanding and interpretation. In other words, Reformation theology may or may not be a missiological theology. This has implications for considering Eliot's work with the Indians because, as Rooy argued in his book *The Theology of Missions in the Puritan Tradition* (1965),[73] Eliot's theological understanding of his Indian ministry can be understood as a "theology of mission," if approached from a modern missiological perspective. However, it is apparent from an analysis of puritan theology in its historical context that it was not a mission-orientated theology.[74]

My research does not ignore the contribution of the "mission" perspective adopted by missiologists and ethnohistorians in their scholarly research, but proposes a new perspective for understanding John Eliot better as a prominent puritan in seventeenth-century New England. Despite the significant scholarly contribution of previous John Eliot research (even with its modern missionary perspective), the seventeenth-century puritan theological and historical lens will be absolutely necessary to contextual and historical analysis and interpretation, and to discover significant puritan aspects in Eliot's Indian ministry which have not been explored well theologically: for example, Eliot's understanding of pastoral ministry, conversion theology and millenarianism and its relation to Indian pastoral ministry, the understanding of church and "visible saints," pastoral teaching and care, the practice of piety, and the relationship between reformation and Indian ministry in Praying Towns and Indian churches.

Methodology, Structure, and Resources

This book has started by suggesting a new perspective after historiographical analysis of previous researches and dominant scholarly angles to understand Eliot, and has offered an argument to justify a new perspective for Eliot research. The remainder of Part 1 develops the arguments introduced above for fresh attention to Eliot's context in puritan New England.

Chapter 2 seeks to understand the main motives for Eliot's Indian ministry. It will present new scholarship on puritanism in relation to the Great Migration and millenarianism, particularly focusing on the relationship between the motives for migration and Indian conversion. Based on this new scholarship, the chapter will explore Eliot's understanding of the millennium and of Indian origins, and how Eliot's thoughts on these themes were related to his Indian ministry. This chapter will pursue a historical and

73. See Rooy, *The Theology of Missions*.
74. See chapter 3.

circumstantial reconsideration of Eliot's contexts. In this sense, this chapter will be significant not only for its scholarly analysis, but also for its proposition of the necessity of and justification for a perspectival shift from missiological to seventeenth-century historical and theological perspectives.

Chapter 3 will examine puritan ministry in seventeenth-century Old and New England through literature by Old and New England puritans. In particular, this chapter will be framed by theological treatises of puritans such as Lewis Bayly, John Cotton,[75] Thomas Shepard, and Richard Baxter, all of whom significantly influenced Eliot inasmuch as he translated their literatures into the Algonquian Indian language.[76] Considering the intellectual relationship between Eliot and these puritans, their resources will be significant for investigating Eliot's thoughts. This chapter will provide an essential understanding of puritan pastorship and ministry, based on an understanding of puritanism as a pietistic Protestant reforming movement based on Reformed theology, particularly pursuing Word-centered, conversion-oriented, and parish-centered ministry, as well as primary ministerial tasks including pastoral teaching and care and the practice of piety in the seventeenth-century transatlantic context, as a background for Eliot's puritan ministry for the Indians. The research will suggest that conversion theology and pastoral theology were the most fundamental and lasting motives for Eliot's Indian ministry. Also, this chapter, from an examination of the materials in the Eliot Tracts, will propose Eliot's aspiration for reformation as another reason for Indian ministry. Eliot's belief in Indian conversion was a means for realizing the values of reformation. This chapter, along with chapter 2, will provide essential research for re-focusing perspectives on Eliot in Part 2.

Part 2 considers Eliot's pastoral activities with the Indians. Chapters 4–6 focus on what and how Eliot applied his puritan ideas to Indian ministry. Chapter 4 will investigate Eliot's theological and ministerial understanding of Praying Towns and Indian churches, and how he related them to the Kingdom of Christ. This chapter, first of all, will examine the process and motives of the establishment of Praying Towns, and the ideological foundations of the towns. After that, this chapter will research Indian churches as Congregational and Reformed churches reflecting Eliot's ecclesiastical vision. Through this, it will become clear that Praying Towns and native Indian churches were established in a certain order and process, based on Eliot's biblical and

75. Bremer, "Cotton, John."
76. Baxter, *A Call to the Unconverted* (1658); Bayly, *The Practice of Piety* (2nd ed., 1612); Shepard, *The Sincere Convert* (1640). John Eliot was also influenced by Richard Baxter's *The Saints' Everlasting Rest* (1650). John Eliot's letter to Richard Baxter, 16 October 1656, *CRBJE*, 154.

millenarian civil polity, puritan conversion theology, and congregationalist ecclesiology, all ultimately pursuing reformation. Also, this research will show how and in what degree Eliot applied his own ideology to the Praying Towns and Indian churches. The investigation, more importantly, will conclude that for Eliot, Praying Towns would only be complete through the establishment of Indian churches in the towns. The Praying Towns as the ideal biblical and covenanted Christian Indians' settlements, and Indian churches as reformed visible churches composed of "sincere converts," were ultimately pursuing Eliot's vision of the Kingdom of Christ.

Chapter 5 will answer the question of what and how Eliot taught the Indians and how he prepared them to become full church members, as "sincere converts" in the Praying Towns. This will be achieved through an examination of Eliot's practice of puritan ministry to New England Indians, focusing on puritan pastoral teaching and care and the practice of piety. Through this analysis, it will become apparent how Eliot applied and practiced his puritan theology and ministry, based on seventeenth-century Old and New England puritan traditions, to his specific ministerial activities in the New England Indian context. In addition, here Eliot's various ministerial activities, which have been considered as "mission," will be rediscovered and reinterpreted as puritan "ministry" from a seventeenth-century puritan theological and pastoral perspective. This will be the first investigation of its kind.

Chapter 6 will explore how Praying Indians understood Christianity, which they intellectually and empirically learned from Eliot, through the examination of the conversion narratives of both puritans and Indians. The comparative analysis of puritans' and Praying Indians' conversion narratives will provide an opportunity to hear at least an echo of Indians' unique voices. The chapter will consider what the narratives suggest about the Indians' understanding and knowledge of Christianity, based on Reformed theology through the teaching of Eliot, as well as from their own experience. Through the investigation of Praying Indians' own voices in this chapter, mainly derived from conversion narratives, it will become clear that not only was puritan conversion theology shared in common by puritans and Praying Indians, but also that the confessions of Praying Indians sound a distinctive note from their own context.

This book will draw from primary sources that were written by and about John Eliot, including the Eliot Tracts; *The Christian Commonwealth* (1659); *The Communion of Churches* (1665); *Indian Dialogues* (1671); "An Account of Indian Churches in New-England" (1673); and Eliot's personal letters, in particular, the correspondence between him and Richard

Baxter, 1656–82.[77] These writings will be tremendously important historical resources for the interpretation of Eliot, but also for the rediscovery and exploration of the significant puritan ministerial elements that Eliot practiced with the Indians. The Eliot Tracts, which have hitherto been treated by missiologists and ethnohistorians as missionary records and reports, are a collection of key documents written by Eliot and other figures describing Eliot's Indian ministry. There is no consensus on a complete list of the Eliot Tracts among scholars, but a core of eleven documents is generally accepted: Thomas Weld, Hugh Peter, and Henry Dunster, eds., *New Englands First Fruits* (1643); Thomas Shepard, ed., *Day-Breaking* (1647); Shepard, ed., *Clear Sun-Shine* (1648); Edward Winslow, ed., *Glorious Progress* (1649); Henry Whitfield, ed., *Light Appearing* (1651); Whitfield, ed., *Strength out of Weaknesse* (1652); John Eliot and Thomas Mayhew Jr., eds., *Tears of Repentance* (1653); John Eliot, ed., *Late and Further Manifestation* (1655); Eliot, ed., *Further Accompt* (1659); Eliot, ed., *Further Account* (1660); Eliot, ed., *Brief Narrative* (1671). The publications of the Eliot Tracts in about thirty years were not planned as a coherent series. They were published sporadically according to various necessities of Indian ministry. The overall purpose of the tracts was mainly to report on Indian ministry and to request support. Yet, one can find specific emphases of the contributors in each tract. For example, *Light Appearing* (1651), *Strength out of Weaknesse* (1652), and *Tears of Repentance* (1653) contain Eliot's understanding of the millennium and Indian origins. *Tears of Repentance* (1653), *Late and Further Manifestation* (1655), and *Further Account* (1660) offer significant resources of the test of Indian Christian faith, their conversion narratives, and the process of the establishment of Indian church. Also, *Strength out of Weaknesse* (1652) provides information of Natick as the first Praying Town. *Brief Narrative* (1671)

---

77. *The Christian Commonwealth* (written in 1651 and published in London, 1659); *The Communion of Churches* (1665). Eliot's *Indian Dialogues* (1671) was republished as a modern English version with introduction. See Bowden and Ronda, *John Eliot's Indian Dialogues*. For the text of *Indian Dialogues* (1671), this book refers to Bowden and Ronda's edition. Eliot's letters include the followings: Eliot's letters to Robert Boyle in Birch, *The Life of the Honourable Robert Boyle* (1744) in MHSC (1794), 3:177–88; "An Account of Indian Churches in New-England" (1673) in MHSC (1809), 124–29; CGTNEC; CJC; CRBJE, 138–76, 442–66. "An Account of Indian Churches" is a report of Indian ministry written as a letter form. The receiver of the letter is not clearly mentioned in the letter. See also Keeble and Nuttall, *Calendar of the Correspondence of Richard Baxter*. For the significance of epistolarity in the seventeenth-century transatlantic community, and in relation to New England Indian evangelization in particular, see Stevens, *The Poor Indians*, 62–83. According to Stevens, puritans' letters played an important role in creating a network between Old and New England in terms of not only sharing information, but also promoting an emotional bond of sympathy for Indian evangelization.

is the only resource in the tracts to describe the Praying Towns established by 1670. The materials in the Eliot Tracts had not been published together until the pamphlets were reprinted together in *MHSC* (1834) and *Sabin's Reprints* (1865). Michael P. Clark published a modern version in 2003.[78]

Indian Dialogues (1671), written by John Eliot, is noteworthy because it shows the contents and methodology of Eliot's pastoral teaching for the Indians. It is not a formal theological treatise, but it contains essential Reformed theological exposition and puritan ministerial teaching in a colloquial form. Also, it was used by Eliot for training native Indian pastoral leaders. Eliot said, "I find it necessary for me to instruct them (as in principles of art, so) in the way of communicating the good knowledge of God, which I conceive is most familiarly done by way of dialogues."[79] In fact, Eliot said that the book is "partly historical," but it was written based on what he actually said and did for the Indians. Eliot said:

> These dialogues are partly historical, of some things that were done and said, and partly instructive, to show what might or should have been said, or that may be (by the Lord's assistance) hereafter done and said, upon the like occasion. It is like to be

---

78. Clark's recent edition, *The Eliot Tracts: With Letters from John Eliot to Thomas Thorowgood and Richard Baxter* (2003) offers the whole texts of eleven Eliot Tracts and Eliot's letters to both Thomas Thorowgood and Richard Baxter, with a useful introduction to John Eliot and his works, including a historiography of research on John Eliot. See *ET*. This book refers to the texts in this edition. For further information of main contents and publication process of the Eliot Tracts, see *JEMI*, 66–67, 92, 113, 132, 133, 169, 207–8, 263; *ET*, 4, 31–34. *New Englands First Fruits* (1643) is still in controversy. Scholars such as Ola Elizabeth Winslow, Hilary Wyss, and Kristina Bross consider it as part of the Eliot Tracts (although it was published almost three years before Eliot's first preaching of the gospel to New England Indians in 1646) and so list eleven tracts. However, Cogley does not regard *New Englands First Fruits* (1643) as one of the Eliot Tracts. See *ET*, 4; *JEMI*, 4, 6, 7, 19–20, 21, 25, 263. See also Winslow, *John Eliot*, 201; Wyss, *Writing Indians*, 17–51, 190; Bross, "'That Epithet of Praying.'" Regarding the authorship of *New Englands First Fruits* (1643), Morrison, in his book, *The Founding of Harvard College*, clearly mentioned that Thomas Weld, Hugh Peter, and Henry Dunster were the authors of the tract. Morison, *The Founding of Harvard College*, 304–5. See also Kellaway, *The New England Company*, 9. Cogley also argued that Thomas Weld, Hugh Peter, and Henry Dunster were almost certainly the authors based on Stearns. *JEMI*, 4 and 268n6. Stearns, *The Strenuous Puritan*, 167. Milne acknowledged that Thomas Weld as a New England agent was the author of *New Englands First Fruits* (1643). Milne, "New England Agents and the English Atlantic." The author of *Day-Breaking* (1647) is anonymous. According to Kellaway, John Wilson, a minister in Boston and Thomas Shepard, a minister in Cambridge have been regarded as authors of the tract, but there is no clear evidence. Kellaway, *The New England Company*, 11. Cogley following Werge argued for Thomas Shepard's authorship of the tract. *JEMI*, 278n1; *ET*, 46n72. Werge, *Thomas Shepard*, 13, 121.

79. Eliot, *Indian Dialogues* (1671), 59.

one work incumbent upon our Indian churches and teachers, for some ages, to send forth instruments to call in others from paganry to pray unto God. Instructions therefore of that nature are required, and what way more familiar than by way of dialogues?[80]

Eliot also expressed this idea in his letter to Richard Baxter of 27 June 1671, "that great point of church work, to send out either officers, or brethren, to call in their kindred and countrymen unto Christ, as we are in the actual practice of it, so I have drawne up a few instructive dialogs which are also partly historical."[81] Therefore, it has the potential to provide a historical resource for understanding Eliot's Indian ministry.

Also, Eliot's contemporaries' literatures and correspondence will be significant sources to locate him in his own historical and ideological contexts. Lewis Bayly's *The Practice of Piety* (2nd ed., 1612), John Cotton's *The Way of the Churches of Christ in New England* (1645), Thomas Shepard's *The Sincere Convert* (1640) and *The Confessions* (1637–45), and Richard Baxter's *The Reformed Pastor* (1656) and *A Call to the Unconverted* (1658) are key sources for understanding Eliot's ideological background. Other historical records, such as Thomas Lechford's *Plain Dealing* (1642), *The Cambridge Platform* (1648), Daniel Gookin's *Historical Collections of the Indians in New England* (1674), Cotton Mather's biography of John Eliot, and the fragmentary records which survive from Eliot's Roxbury church, are also important for understanding the context and history of Eliot's Indian ministry.[82]

This book has a research limitation: the scarcity of primary sources by John Eliot. It is not easy to find resources for a profound investigation of his theology and ministerial ideas. For example, almost no sermon of Eliot remains in printed or published form. However, despite this limitation, this research, through intense reading and analysis of the surviving resources from a new perspective, will be helpful not only for viewing Eliot in a fresh light, but also for investigation of various aspects of Eliot and his Indian ministry which have not been properly explored before.

This introduction has shown how critical reflection on the missiological perspective in previous research prompts us to adopt a different angle from which to investigate John Eliot as a seventeenth-century puritan figure. Therefore, when considering Eliot as a puritan minister, a significant element of this book is the historical and contextual understanding of puritan

80. Eliot, *Indian Dialogues* (1671), 61.

81. CRBJE, 462.

82. Lechford, *Plain Dealing* (1642); *The Cambridge Platform* (1648) in CPC; HCINE; LJE; Thwing, *History of The First Church in Roxbury*.

ministry from a seventeenth-century transatlantic perspective. In relocating Eliot in his own historical contexts, this book ultimately pursues Eliot's understanding of pastoral activities with New England Indians (normally interpreted as "mission" in modern Protestant missionary perspective) through understanding Eliot's ideological background and how he applied and practiced those ideas in Indian ministerial fields. Consequently, Eliot's Indian "mission" can be reinterpreted and reanalyzed as a seventeenth-century puritan ministry, which pursued reformation as the fundamental motive for migration to New England, through a conversion-oriented and Word-centered ministry, Praying Towns and Indian churches, as well as pastoral teaching and care and the practice of piety.

2

Puritan Migration, Millenarianism, and Indian Conversion

Re-envisioning the Motives for John Eliot's Indian Ministry

THIS CHAPTER SEEKS TO understand the main motives for Eliot's Indian ministry through presenting a new interpretation of the relationship between puritan migration, millenarianism, and Indian conversion. In a tract printed in 1674, Daniel Gookin reported a conversation he had had with Eliot about the reasons for Indian ministry, around the time Eliot initiated preaching the gospel to the Indians in the mid-1640s:

> The truth is, Mr. Eliot engaged in this great work of preaching unto the Indians upon a very pure and sincere account: for I being his neighbour and intimate friend, at the time when he first attempted this enterprise, he was pleased to communicate unto me his design, and the motives that induced him thereunto; which, as I remember, were principally these three. First, the glory of God, in the conversion of some of these poor, desolate souls. Secondly, his compassion and ardent affection to them, as of mankind in their great blindness and ignorance. Thirdly, and not the least, to endeavour, so far as in him lay, the accomplishment and fulfilling the covenant and promise, that New England people had made unto their king, when he granted them their patent or charter, viz. that one principal end of their going to

plant these countries, was, to communicate the gospel unto the native Indians.[1]

Eliot's stated motives for Indian ministry need to be explored in relation to the mutual connection between puritan migration, the millennium, and Indian evangelization, which has been discussed by scholars from various perspectives. Missiologists, drawing on Perry Miller's "errand into the wilderness" theme, have regarded the Great Migration as a missionary enterprise. From this perspective, Indian conversion was an important sign of New England as a "city upon a hill." This idea was related to puritan millenarianism. Scholars have argued that puritans' strong belief in the advent of the millennium became the main motive for the Great Migration, in pursuit of a model society in New England. Indian conversion was also a signal phenomenon of the advent of the millennium. In these scholarly arguments, there is a clear ideological connection between motives for Indian ministry and interpretation of puritan migration and millenarianism. According to new scholarship, however, the purpose of the Great Migration to New England was not a missionary enterprise, but rather a pursuit of religious purity and ultimately reformation that the puritans could not actualize under Laudian policy in the England of the 1630s. Also, there is no clear evidence of millenarianism as a main motive for the puritans' migration.[2]

Based on recent scholarship, this chapter will seek a new understanding of the relationship between the Great Migration and the motives for Indian conversion. It will also introduce Eliot's thoughts on the millennium and Indian origins, and their relationship to his Indian ministry. The discussion will consider whether millenarianism was for Eliot the main motive for migration to New England, or if it was the initial reason for his preaching the gospel to the Indians. This analysis will be advanced by looking at how Eliot's own millenarianism was formed through his circumstantial interpretation of current religious and political upheaval when the Interregnum (1649–60) started, along with the influence of his contemporaries. Finally, through this investigation, which arises from recent scholarship's historical and circumstantial re-interpretation of puritanism, one can confirm the necessity of a perspectival shift—from the modern missiological to a seventeenth-century puritan theological and pastoral—for a new understanding of John Eliot and his work with the Indians.

---

1. HCINE, 170.

2. Details of the historiography will be provided in below (pp. 31–42). Milton, "Laud, William."

The Great Migration and Indian Conversion

In the past, many scholars have linked Indian conversion to the motives for puritan migration. Missiologists and mission historians have regarded "mission" as the primary reason for the Great Migration of puritans to New England. This missionary interpretation of the Great Migration has colored much of the literature about John Eliot. According to the nineteenth-century writer Joseph J. Kwait, "the first settlement of New England was a missionary enterprise," and the "pilgrims" were the pioneers of the Protestant world who attempted to convert "the heathen of foreign lands." For him, "the missionary designs of the colonies were never disavowed, and seldom forgotten."[3] In 1915, Charles Henry Robinson noted that, "the pilgrim fathers, who sailed for Massachusetts in the *Mayflower* (1620), were not unmindful of their obligation to Christianise the American Indians."[4] In 1964, Stephen Neill observed that while Anglicans were not actually good at the propagation of the Christian faith and civility to the Indians, John Eliot became the first figure to make a sustained attempt.[5] For David J. Bosch, John Eliot was "the real missionary pioneer" and for J. A. B. Jongenell, John Eliot was "one of the most important Protestant missionary figures of the Seventeenth Century."[6] More recently, John B. Carpenter not only argued about the missionary purpose of the Great Migration of the puritans, but also related the puritan experiment in New England and the puritan "mission" to the Indians in New England. Carpenter argues that "mission" had the "long-range target of demonstrating God's blessing upon the Puritan experiment." He says that the purpose of the puritan migration was clearly proclaimed in the "city upon a hill" language in John Winthrop's sermon, "A Modell of Christian Charity":

> We shall be as city upon a hill, the eyes of all people are upon us; so that if we shall deal falsely with our God in this work we have undertaken..., we shall be made a story and a by-word through the world, we shall open the mouths of enemies to speak evil of the ways of God..., we shall shame the faces of many of God's

---

3. Kwiat, *History of American Missions to the Heathen*, 11–12.

4. Robinson, *History of Christian Missions*, 369. See Glover, *The Progress of World-Wide Missions*, 53–54; Neill, *A History of Christian Missions*, 191–92; Carpenter, "The New England Puritans." Thompson and Johnson argued for the puritan movement as the cause of missionary enterprise in Great Britain. Thompson and Johnson, *British Foreign Mission*, 2.

5. Neill, *A History of Christian Missions*, 192.

6. Bosch, *Witness to the World*, 141; Jongeneel, "The Protestant Missionary Movement," 226.

worthy servants, and cause their prayers to be turned into curses upon us.[7]

Carpenter argues that this sermon shows the purpose of the puritans' mission-oriented migration. In other words, the puritan life as a "city upon a hill" would be so attractive that European churches would learn from it, and the Indians would go to the puritan churches to receive the gospel and Christian faith.[8] The "city upon a hill" theory was originally proposed by Perry Miller in the 1950s. Perry Miller argued that the primary purpose of the puritan's Great Migration was an "errand into the wilderness"[9] for the establishment of an ideal Christian society and the realization of the millennium in New England. Perry Miller says that puritans "did not flee to America; they went in order to work out that complete reformation which was not yet accomplished in England and Europe, but which would quickly be accomplished if only the saints back there had a working model to guide them."[10] Although Perry Miller did not directly relate the "city upon a hill" theme to Indian evangelization, the missiologists adopted the idea to argue for a missiological understanding of puritan migration to New England.

John Eliot was a puritan minister who initially worked with English settlers.[11] However, usually only his work with the Indians as "mission" has been emphasized. This may be because the records for the "Indian mission" were better documented than the records for his English ministry in Roxbury, Massachusetts. Also, as Cogley argues, "mission" was very important in New England society and history.[12] However, regardless of what documented resources have survived, it is evident that the historical perspective for understanding the main reason for the puritan migration is crucially related to the scholarly understanding of Eliot as a "missionary." For missiologists, the Great Migration itself was a missionary journey and enterprise, and Eliot, who preached the gospel passionately to the Indians, was

---

7. Winthrop, *The Winthrop Papers*, 2:295. For the whole text, see also Winthrop, *The Winthrop Papers*, 2:282–95. Heimert and Delbanco, *The Puritans in America*, 81–92. On Winthrop and his context, see Bremer, *John Winthrop*; Bremer, "Winthrop, John."

8. Carpenter, "The New England Puritans," 519.

9. This phrase came from Samuel Danforth's election sermon, "A Brief Recognition of New England's Errand into the Wilderness," delivered on 11 May 1670. See Miller, *Errand into the Wilderness*, 2. In chapter 1 of that book, Miller discusses the reason and purpose for the Great Migration as a new interpretation through the meaning of "errand into the wilderness."

10. Miller, *Errand into the Wilderness*, 11.

11. See Winslow, *John Eliot*, 21–40; Harling, "A Biography of John Eliot," 73–81; *ET*, 10; Hardman Moore, *Pilgrims*, 5, 7, 12.

12. Cogley, "John Eliot's Puritan Ministry," 1–2.

the quintessential "missionary" or, at least, "the real missionary pioneer" as Bosch calls him.[13]

Indian "mission" has probably been perceived as one of the most important elements of the "errand into the wilderness" and the creation of a model church and society. This idea has been supported by scholars such as J. F. Maclear and Philip F. Gura. Maclear understood that Eliot's Indian evangelization and Praying Towns were a model for England and European countries to imitate, to bring in the Kingdom of God based on the Bible.[14] Gura also related Praying Towns to the "city upon a hill" thesis. Gura argued that Eliot hoped that "his accomplishments with the unlettered Indians in Natick would provide the beacon for another, greater city on a hill."[15]

However, a consideration of recent research highlights a different understanding of the relationship between puritan migration and Indian conversion. For puritans, Indian conversion was not the primary reason for their migration. The Great Migration was for further reformation and a pure Christianity that they could not actualize under Laudian policy in the England of the 1630s. The reinterpretation of the relationship between puritan migration and Indian conversion is related to arguments against Perry Miller's idea of the "errand into the wilderness," and to different interpretations and ways of understanding the Great Migration. Theodore Dwight Bozeman, contradicting Perry Miller's idea of the "errand into the wilderness," argued that the main purpose of the puritans' Great Migration was the restoration of primitive Christianity. The puritans' most immediate concern was "archetypally enacted patterns of ecclesiastical polity and worship." Puritan emigrants sought liberty to enjoy "their primitive purity."[16] John Cotton, who migrated to New England and was one of the prominent puritan ministers in New England, demonstrated that puritan migration was for "the liberty and purity of his ordinances."[17] In this sense, as Bozeman argued, the Great Migration was "a restorationist campaign" and the primary purpose of the Great Migration was the restoration of primitive Christianity and purity.[18]

13. Bosch, *Witness to the World*, 141.
14. Maclear, "New England and the Fifth Monarchy," 247.
15. Gura, *A Glimpse of Sion's Glory*, 135.
16. Bozeman, *To Live Ancient Lives*, 113.
17. Cotton, *Gods Promise to His Plantations* (1630), 6.
18. Bozeman, *To Live Ancient Lives*, 114. For Bozeman's critique of Miller's "errand into the wilderness," see Bozeman, *To Live Ancient Lives*, ch. 3, "The Errand into the Wilderness Reconsidered." "[T]he history of Puritanism revealed the adaptation of Reformed ideas to a new situation. And once again the starting point for New England history became that portion of the brotherhood that valued purity the most." Hall, *The Faithful Shepherd*, 71.

Susan Hardman Moore, in her book *Pilgrims*,[19] offered a new understanding of the Great Migration through her examination of Old and New England historical circumstances from the 1630s to 1660s, with a historical exploration of remigration from New England to Old England, focusing on the reasons, purposes, and motives for puritans' migration and remigration. She argued that the puritans wanted to leave Old England because they perceived "a revitalisation of Catholic influence," as well as religious threats and enforcement in the 1630s. For Hardman Moore, the puritans' departure from Old England was not a bold or hasty decision, but rather a circumstantial and reluctant decision to seek God's providence. Unlike puritan migrants of the *Mayflower* in 1620, most emigrants in the 1630s did not identify themselves as separatists. Although they criticized their home church as tainted with "remnants of popery," and left their homes to pursue a purer church, they still declared their loyalty to the English church as a true church. Also, their migration, which was circumstantial and unpredicted, was part of English Reformation for pursuing "primitive purity" in the religious and political crisis of the 1630s in England.[20]

Following Bozeman's critiques of Perry Miller's "errand into the wilderness" theme, Hardman Moore highlighted that puritan migrants did not have "a sense of divine mission—an 'errand into the wilderness' to light a torch for purity that would show the way to a complete Reformation, to the millennial rule of Christ at the end of time." According to Bozeman and Hardman Moore, an understanding of the "errand into the wilderness" as the primary purpose for the Great Migration came from the second and third generations of emigrants, to portray the heroism of the first generation, in order to proclaim in their own time the strong and united agenda of the New England migration.[21]

For Winthrop's "city on a hill," discussed above, Hardman Moore proposed a corrected interpretation. According to Hardman Moore, "Winthrop's city upon a hill was not a 'world-redeeming beacon,' the 'hub of the universe,' and the 'New Jerusalem.'"[22] Winthrop's attitude in the sermon was defensive, and he was anxious about migration to New England.

---

19. Hardman Moore, *Pilgrims*.

20. Hardman Moore, *Pilgrims*, 30; Hardman Moore, "Popery, Purity, and Providence," 257–89; Hardman Moore, "New England Reformation," 143–58; Bozeman, *To Live Ancient Lives*; Bozeman, "Biblical Primitivism," 19–32.

21. Hardman Moore, *Pilgrims*, 30. Hardman Moore presents useful resources for the critique of Miller and Bozeman's view, "errand into the wilderness." See Hardman Moore, *Pilgrims*, 30n75.

22. Hardman Moore, *Pilgrims*, 31. Original quotations from Baritz, *City on a Hill*, 17; Bercovitch, *The Puritan Origins of the American Self*, 97.

Hardman Moore said: "Winthrop feared New England could become a byword for error, a cause for shame, the object of curses. A city on a hill is exposed. Winthrop wanted to be sure he and others would not be found in the wrong—either by the godly, or by God."[23] Bozeman, indicating that the Winthrop sermon was the most quoted but the least understood, argued: "having pondered the difficulties of establishing a colony in unfamiliar, unsettled territory, Winthrop foresaw a time of deprivation and hardship . . . the projected impact upon 'all people,' in other words, presupposed the failure of New England's enterprise."[24]

In light of these perspectives in recent research, it seems Eliot's initial reason for migration may not have been the conversion of New England's Indians, but rather puritan ministry for English settlers, ultimately pursuing reformation.[25] No evidence which reveals Eliot's own motives for migration, expressed in the 1630s or 1640s, has survived. However, his later biographer, Cotton Mather, gives a significant insight into Eliot's motives for migration. Mather said, "He came to New-England in the Month of November, A.D. 1631. among those Blessed old Planters, which laid the Foundations of a remarkable Country, devoted unto the Exercise of the Protestant Religion, in its purest and highest Reformation." After arrival at New England, Eliot joined the church of Boston and the church tried to appoint him as a teacher. However, Mather continued:

> Mr. Eliot had engaged unto a select number of his pious and Christian friends in England, that if they should come into these parts before he should be in the pastoral care of any other people, he would give himself to them, and be for their service. It happened, that these friends transported themselves hither the year after him, and chose their habitation at the town which they called Roxbury.[26]

Cotton Mather's account suggests that Eliot migrated to New England for further reformation and puritan ministry to English settlers. Eliot himself confessed his primary reason for migration in 1653. He migrated to New England to "have liberty to enjoy all the pure Ordinance[s] of Christ . . . to enjoy the holy worship of God, not according to the fantasies of man, but according to the Word of God, without . . . human additions and novelties."[27]

23. Hardman Moore, *Pilgrims*, 31.
24. Bozeman, *To Live Ancient Lives*, 92.
25. For reformation-centered puritan ministry, see chapter 3.
26. *LJE*, 5, 11–12.
27. Eliot, "The Learned Conjectures" in *ET*, 422, 423. "The Learned Conjectures" was Eliot's letter to Thomas Thorowgood which became the preface to Thorowgood's

Bozeman argued that Eliot's confession about his primary reason for the migration shows that the religious motive for the Great Migration was to pursue primitive Christian purity.[28] As Cogley has acknowledged, there is no mention or intention of the New England Indian "mission" in Eliot's confession of his purpose for emigration.[29] So, if Perry Miller's "errand into the wilderness" thesis is no longer persuasive to many scholars, this raises questions about a strong relationship between puritan migration and Indian conversion.

With the turn in recent scholarship against Miller's "errand into the wilderness" theme, the context of the first period of puritan migration will be significant for understanding the main reason for puritan migration. In fact, there are some early primary sources which relate puritan migration to Indian evangelization. The Charter of Massachusetts Bay (1629) proclaimed that "the principall Ende of this Plantacion" is to "wynn and incite the Natives of Country, to the Knowledg[e] and Obedience of the onlie true God and Saulor of Mankinde, and the Christian Fayth, which in our Royall Intencon, and the Adventurers free Profession."[30] Also, Winthrop, in his "General Observations" in 1629, said:

> [S]ince Christ's coming the church is to be conceived as universall without distinction of countryes, so as he that doth good in any one place serves the church in all places. . . . It is the revealed will of God that the gospell should be preached to all nations though we know not whether the Indians will receive it or not, yet it is a good worke to observe God's will in offering it to them; for God shall have glory by it though they refuse it.[31]

Although it is evident that Winthrop was concerned about Indian evangelization even before his migration to New England on the *Arbella*[32] in 1630, it is probably true that preaching the gospel to the Indians was not the puritans' primary reason for migration because, through Winthrop's words, one can realize that he regarded preaching the gospel as the will of God and universal duty of every church in the world, not as a unique task of the migrants. John Cotton also mentioned Indian evangelization in his

---

Jews in America (1660). See Thorowgood, *Jews in America* (1660), 1–22. Cogley, "Pagans and Christians on the New England Frontier," 97; Cogley, "Puritan Ministry," 3.

28. Bozeman, *To Live Ancient Lives*, 108.
29. Cogley, "Puritan Ministry," 3.
30. "The Charter of Massachusetts Bay."
31. Winthrop, "General Observations," in *The Winthrop Papers*, 2:119.
32. Winthrop, *The Winthrop Papers*, 2:230–31.

farewell sermon to the Winthrop's vessel to New England, *Gods Promise to his Plantation* (1630):

> [O]ffend not the poore Natives, but as you partake in their land, so make them partakers of your precious faith: as you reape their temporalls, so feede them with your spirituals: winne them to the love of Christ, for whom Christ died. They never yet refused the Gospell, and therefore more hope they will not receive it. Who knoweth whether God have reared this whole Planation for such an end?[33]

However, this reference also does not necessarily argue a direct relationship between the motives for puritan migration and Indian evangelization. Cotton's reference to the preaching the gospel to "poore Natives" was only a "course" with which puritans in New England should be concerned.[34] Thomas Lechford's reference, in his *Plain Dealing* (1642), gives us an important contextual understanding. Lechford criticized settlers for their lack of interest in Indian conversion in the early period after their migration: "And surely it is good to overthrow heathenisme by all good wayes and meanes. But there hath not been any sent forth by any Church to learne the Natives language, or to instruct them in the Religion."[35] Lechford's observation, in fact, reflects that there was a strong expectation on the part of English Christians in Old England to see conspicuous ministerial works for Indian conversion and evangelization by puritans after their arrival in New England. At the same time, Lechford's reference confirms the fact that puritans were not actually involved with the evangelization of Indians for at least a decade after their arrival in New England. It is true that after arriving in New England, the puritans' initial concern was to establish themselves in terms of life, government, and religion: "After God had carried us safe to New England, and wee had builded our houses, provided necessaries for our liveli-hood, rear'd convenient places for God's worship, and setled the Civill Government."[36] This situation reflects the fact that the puritans' priority in

---

33. Cotton, *Gods Promise to His Plantations* (1630), 19–20.

34. John Cotton argued that puritans in New England as a new plantation should have special care for God's ordinances, not to forget England as "our Ierusalem at home," having "publicke spirit," having a tender care to their children, and "offend not the poore Natives . . . and make them partakers of your precious faith." Cotton, *Gods Promise to His Plantations* (1630), 17–20.

35. Lechford, *Plain Dealing* (1642), 21; Dailey, "Lechford, Thomas."

36. *New Englands First Fruit* (1643), 67; *ID*, 22. Bowden and Ronda argue that puritans' Reformed theological understanding of predestination was one of the factors in their indifference to Indian evangelization in the early period of migration. *ID*, 24. This is a plausible idea, but there is no clear evidence from primary sources for it.

New England, at least in the early period from 1630 to the early 1640s, was not Indian conversion, but puritan ministry for puritans to secure the survival of fragile plantations. This can also be conjectured through the records in the Eliot Tracts (in the 1640s and 1650s). Thomas Mayhew of Martha's Vineyard[37] in his letter in *Glorious Progress* (1649) included a story about an Indian who lamented the Indians' ignorance of the knowledge of God for about thirty years, even after puritans' migration to New England via the *Mayflower* in 1620.[38] Also, an Indian Sachem, Towanquatick the Sagamore, after receiving the gospel from the puritans, mentioned that Indians were still in spiritual ignorance thirty years after the puritans had arrived in New England. He also highlighted the necessity of the gospel for the Indians.[39] The letter of Richard Mather in *Tears of Repentance* (1653) clearly shows puritans' lack of attention to Indian conversion, at least during the early period of their settlement in New England. Richard Mather said: "yea, and though there hath been Plantations of the English in the Country now 20. years and more, yea, some a matter of 30. years, or thereabout, yet of all this time . . . no considerable work of Grace hath appeared amongst the Indians till now of late."[40] This not only suggests puritans' indifference to Indian evangelization, but also reflects the fact that the main purpose of puritan migration was not Indian conversion. Although the puritans were actually connected with the Indians and had a kind of relationship with them, they did not actively try to preach the gospel to them and intentionally tried to keep their distance from them. The author of *New Englands First Fruits* (1643) said, "Yet (mistake us not) we are wont to keep them at such a distance, (knowing they serve the Devill and are led by him) as not to imbolden them too much, or trust them too farre; though we do them what good we can."[41] This also indicates the puritans' attitude towards the Indians in terms of evangelization in their early settlement period.

Edward Winslow in *Glorious Progress* (1649) reported that concrete Indian evangelization started from 1646:

37. Mandell, "Mayhew, Thomas"; Kellaway, *The New England Company*, 96–97. Kellaway argued that although Mayhew's concrete Indian evangelization work was begun just after Eliot's preaching of the gospel to Indians in 1646, his title as "the first Protestant missionary to the Indians in New England" should be shared with Eliot. Kellaway, *The New England Company*, 97.

38. *Glorious Progress* (1649), 149–50.

39. *Light Appearing* (1651), 179. For Indians, "Sagamore" meant their kings and governors. *Light Appearing* (1651), 177.

40. For Mather, minister in Dorchester, Massachusetts, see Hall, "Mather, Richard"; *Tears of Repentance* (1653), 264.

41. *New Englands First Fruits* (1643), 63. Thomas Weld, Hugh Peter, and Henry Dunster have been considered as the authors of the tract. See p. 26n78 above.

> In the year of our Lord, 1646. it seemed good to the most high God, to stirre up some reverend Ministers of the Gospel in New-England, to consider how they might be serviceable to the Lord Jesus, as well towards the Natives of that Countrey . . . in bringing them to a right understanding of God and themselves; and so by degrees to hold forth unto them that Salvation by Jesus Christ to all that should believe and obey his Commands.[42]

The phrase, "to consider how they might be serviceable to the Lord Jesus, as well towards the Natives of that Countrey," suggests that although Eliot started the task of Indian evangelization in 1646, the ministers still mainly focused on their own ministry for puritan settlers.[43] It also suggests that the Indian conversion issue had appeared later as a secondary concern. Eliot himself confessed that he was too busy taking care of his own ministry for puritans to translate the Bible into the Indian language: "I having yet but little skill in their language (having little leasure to attend it by reason of my continual attendance on my Ministry in our own Church)."[44] This implies that Eliot's main concern in relation to his early ministry in New England was not the Indians, but rather the English.

Finally, how are we to understand some references in the Eliot Tracts which seem to relate Indian conversion to the Great Migration, as if Indian conversion were the main reason for the migration? It is important to understand the context of the transatlantic world in the mid-1640s and 1650s. By the mid-1640s, puritan immigration had dried up, and William Laud had been overthrown. It is evident that, in these circumstances, New England puritans were looking for new ways to explain the providential purpose of settlement. Samuel Symonds's letter to John Winthrop of 6 February 1646/7 gives an important hint. Symonds said: "The scope of what I would expresse is to observe gods providences in mans motions at this tyme seeme plainly to tend to settle his people here. . . . Now to name what seemes to be gods ends in bringing his people hether." And then, Symonds stated that "To be hopefull Instruments in gods hand to gaine these Indians to Christs kingdome" was a providential purpose of migration and settlement in New England.[45] Puritans' understanding of Indian evangelization in relation to their

---

42. For Edward Winslow (1595–1655), colonial governor of Plymouth Colony, see Travers, "Winslow, Edward." *Glorious Progress* (1649), 147. *Day-Breaking* (1647) reported the first four meetings with the Indians in 1646. These meetings were mainly about sermons, catechizing, and the Indians' questions about the sermons and doctrinal teaching. See *Day-Breaking* (1647), 79–100. See also *JJW*, 632.

43. *Glorious Progress* (1649), 147.

44. *Light Appearing* (1651), 187.

45. Samuel Symonds to John Winthrop, 6 February 1646/7, *The Winthrop Papers*, 5:125–27.

new consideration of providential purposes of migration is also found in the materials in the Eliot Tracts in 1650s. John Endecott, in his letter in *Strength out of Weaknesse* (1652), seems to acknowledge that the puritan migration to New England was for the conversion of Indians: "[I]n the inlarging of the kingdome of his deare Sonne here amongst the Heathen Indians, which was one end of our coming hither."[46] In a letter in *Tears of Repentance* (1653), Eliot expressed a similar idea: "It is plainly to be observed, That one end of Gods sending so many Saints to New-England, was the Conversion of these Indians."[47] Edward Reynolds,[48] in his letter in *Further Accompt* (1659) also wrote, "How much those winds and shakings which carried many good men out of Old into New England have made way to the publishing of the name of Christ in those barbarous places."[49] As mentioned above, Eliot himself acknowledged that the accomplishment of the king's charter (proclaiming that "one principal end of their going to plant these countries, was, to communicate the gospel unto the native Indians") was a reason for his Indian ministry.[50] Yet, many references which seem to argue for the idea that puritans migrated to New England for the purpose of Indian conversion do not argue that Indian evangelization was their primary reason of migration, but are probably a circumstantial reinterpretation of the providential purpose of their migration in changed historical circumstances. Unfortunately there is no evidence of how New England puritans' new understanding of the providential purpose of migration influenced Eliot to initiate preaching the gospel to the Indians. However, it is probably true that after mid-1640s, Eliot reinterpreted Indian evangelization as a significant providential duty and task of puritan migrants in New England. In this sense, Eliot's relation of the accomplishment of king's charter—"to communicate the gospel unto the native Indians"—to his migration reveals Eliot's reinterpretation from the mid-1640s of the relationship between puritan migration and Indian evangelization. As will be shown later (in chapters 3–6), he would work out this vision on principles already established in his ministry in Roxbury, which drew on the puritan traditions of Old and New England.

In brief, the revised interpretation of the purpose of the puritans' Great Migration implicitly asks for a reinterpretation of missiologists' assumptions about the relationship between the Great Migration and Indian

---

46. *Strength out of Weaknesse* (1652), 242; Bremer, "Endecott, John."

47. *Tears of Repentance* (1653), 262.

48. Probably Edward Reynolds (1599–1676), Bishop of Norwich in the Church of England and author. See Atherton, "Reynolds, Edward."

49. *Further Accompt* (1659), 324.

50. *HCINE*, 170.

conversion. Puritan migration was for pure Christianity and further reformation, without the vision of the establishment of a model society in New England which involved the conversion of the Indians. Also, based on an understanding of the context of the Eliot Tracts, one can see that most of the references which seem to argue for the relationship between the Great Migration and Indian conversion in fact represented the settlers' circumstantial reinterpretation of their migration. In their rhetoric, this was proclaimed as a new reason that justified their migration from England to New England. The rapidly changing circumstances of the seventeenth-century transatlantic context seem to have shaped Eliot's understanding of his pastoral duty for New England Indians. This new interpretation confirms the necessity and significance of a historical and circumstantial perspective for John Eliot research. The understanding of the Great Migration has been significantly related to puritan millenarianism in relation to Indian conversion. The next section, based on new scholarship refuting previous interpretations, will examine Eliot's understanding of the millennium and Indian origins in relation to his motives for Indian ministry.

Millenarianism, Indian Origins, and Indian Conversion

In the past, many scholars have agreed that puritans' expectation of the imminent advent of the millennium in New England was a primary motive for the Great Migration of the 1630s, in order to make a model society and the Kingdom of God in New England. For such scholars, Indian conversion was not only an important indicator of the purpose, but also a primary reason for puritan migration. In this sense, previous research which gave a New England-centered understanding of the Great Migration made a crucial link between the Great Migration, the millennium, and Indian conversion. In other words, puritans migrated to New England to create a model society through reformation, and their strong belief in the imminence of the millennium was one of the main reasons for their migration. Based on this belief and expectation, for puritans, Indian conversion was a crucial factor in their decision to migrate, but it was also a major sign of the millennium.[51]

However, Bozeman has argued that there is no evidence that the puritans' apocalyptic prophetic understanding of their current situation and eschatological expectation became a crucial reason for the Great Migration.

---

51. Baritz, *City on a Hill*, 3–45; Maclear, "New England and the Fifth Monarchy," 229–31, 243–48, 253–55; Bercovitch, *The American Jeremiad*, 8–9; Jong, *As the Waters Cover the Seas*, 29–30; Gura, *A Glimpse of Sion's Glory*, 126–52; Zakai, *Exile and Kingdom*, particularly 120–206.

The assumption that puritan migrants, at least before the 1640s, were influenced by Brightman's millenarianism (demonstrating the imminent Middle Coming of Christ and the earthly Kingdom of God, symbolized as "New Jerusalem") stems from a misunderstanding of puritans' writings.[52] There is no clear evidence of millenarianism as a primary reason for the puritans' migration. Puritans' consciousness of the crisis was not because of calamities in England due to a realization of apocalyptic prophecy from the failure of reformation. Rather, it was due to a fear of "re-Catholicization" from this failure, which was compared to the violation of God's covenant in Deuteronomy. Puritans' major concern in writings which mentioned their awareness of the national crisis was not related to eschatological expectation, but to "the Deuteronomic structure of England's National Covenant." In this sense, eschatological expectation did not affect puritans who wanted to pursue further reformation in New England. For them, the primary reason for migration was the pursuit of purity in the Christian faith and the restoration of primitive Christianity.[53]

At this point the following questions are relevant: how did Eliot understand the millennium and how did he relate his millenarianism to the pursuit of Indian conversion and ministry? The following section will try to find an answer to these questions through an investigation of Eliot's own millenarianism. This section, like the previous one, will confirm the significance and necessity of understanding Eliot's Indian ministry in its historical context.

---

52. Scholars have argued that the writings of John Bale (1495–1563), John Foxe (1516/17–1587), Thomas Brightman (1562–1607), and John Cotton defended that the establishment of "New Jerusalem" was the motive of the Great Migration. Oh has argued that John Cotton was influenced by the idea of "the elect nation" for England in John Bale's *Image of Both Churches* (1547), John Foxe's *Actes and Monuments* (1563), and Thomas Brightman's writings such as *A Revelation of the Apocalyps* (1611), *A Most Comfortable Exposition of the Last and Most Difficult Part of the Prophecie of Daniel* (1635; repr., 1644), and *A Commentary on the Canticles* (1644). According to Oh, Cotton who related the concept of "the elect nation" to New England argued for New England as a chosen land and "New Jerusalem" in his *Gods Promise in His Plantation* (1630). Oh, "The Churches Resurrection," 47–74, 159–62. See also Maclear, "New England and the Fifth Monarchy," 228–29. Bozeman indicated that Haller related "the founding ideals of New Englanders" to the concept of "the elect nation" for England in his *Foxe's Book of Martyrs and the Elect Nation*. Bozeman, *To Live Ancient Lives*, 87. Freeman, "John Foxe"; King, "John Bale"; Bozeman, "Thomas Brightman." Zakai also argued that John Cotton's eschatological sermon and exposition such as *Gods Promise in His Plantation* (1634 [1630]) and *An Exposition upon the Thirteenth Chapter of the Revelation* (1655) revealed the ideas of New England as "New Jerusalem" and "the Land of Promise" for "God's chosen people." Zakai, *Exile and Kingdom*, 167–72.

53. Bozeman, *To Live Ancient Lives*, 193–236.

John Eliot and the Millennium

Eliot's millennial vision centered on the coming Kingdom of God, ruled by Christ, and based on the Word of God. Eliot wrote in his letter to Winslow of 29 December 1649:

> And when everything both Civil & Spiritual are done by the direction of the word of Christ, then doth Christ reigne, and the great Kingdome of Jesus Christ which we weight for, is even this that I do now mention; and by this means all Kingdomes and Nations shall become the Kingdomes of Christ, because he shall rule them in all things by his holy word.[54]

Eliot in *The Christian Commonwealth*—written in 1651 and published in 1659—also clearly expressed his millenarian vision: "his Kingdom is then come amongst us, when his will is done on earth, as it is done in heaven, where no Humane or Angelical Policy or wisdom doth guide anything, but all is done by Divine direction [Psalm 103.20]; and so it shall be on earth, when, and where Christ reigneth."[55] These references give us three main points of his millenarianism: the imminent Middle Coming of Jesus Christ, the advent of the millennium, and the establishment of the Kingdom of God which is ruled by Christ and based on the Scripture in the millennium.[56]

Eliot related his millenarianism to New England Indians. In a letter of 8 July 1649 printed in *Light Appearing* (1651), Eliot expected that the Kingdom of Christ would be installed among the Indians. He came to this conclusion when he considered the political upheaval of England which had

---

54. Eliot to Winslow, 29 December 1649, in *Light Appearing* (1651), 195. See also Eliot, "Preface," *The Christian Commonwealth* (1659); *Tears of Repentance* (1653), 260; Eliot, "The Learned Conjectures," in *ET*, 426.

55. Eliot, "Preface," in *The Christian Commonwealth* (1659). Eliot wrote this treatise as "a reply to a Lancashire Presbyterian manifesto, Edward Gee's *A Plea for Non-Scribers.*" Maclear, "New England and the Fifth Monarchy," 253–54. The reason for the delay in publication is not known. In his statement of 24 May 1661 for public renouncement of his antimonarchism in the tract, Eliot said that it had been "about nine or tenn yeares since" he sent the tract to be published. *RMB*, vol. IV, pt. II, 6. For Eliot's public renouncement of antimonarchism in the tract, see below.

56. Eliot's thoughts on the millennium and the origins of Indians are described in his letters, mainly from 1649 to 1653 in the Eliot Tracts and other correspondence, especially to Thomas Thorowgood (1653) and Richard Baxter (1663), and his own treatises, *The Christian Commonwealth* (1659) and *The Communion of Churches* (1665). See *Light Appearing* (1651), 184–207; *Strength out of Weaknesse* (1652), 224–30; *Tears of Repentance* (1653), 259–62; Eliot, "The Learned Conjectures," in Thorowgood, *Jews in America* (1660), 1–20, and *ET*, 409–27; Eliot to Baxter, 6 July 1663, in *ET*, 430–36. For John Eliot's millenarianism, Cogley provided a tremendously important investigation: "The Millenarianism of John Eliot"; *JEMI*, 76–104.

climaxed in the execution of Charles I in January 1649. He saw the beginning of the Commonwealth as the time of the Kingdom of Christ:

> Now this glorious work of bringing in and setting up the glorious kingdome of Christ, hath the Lord of his free grace and mercy put into the hands of his renowned Parliament and Army. ... And when the Lord Jesus is about to set up his blessed Kingdome among these poore Indians also, how well doth it become the spirit of such instruments in the hand of Christ to promote the work also being the same businesse in some respect which themselves are about by the good hand of the Lord.[57]

Eliot's words here confirm that he had a strong belief in the millennium and recognized a significant relationship between the millennium and Indian conversion and ministry. So, was millenarianism a crucial motive for Eliot's migration to New England and his Indian ministry? In order to answer this question, we need to understand how Eliot's millenarianism was formed.

Eliot's millenarianism was strongly influenced by his ideological, social, and political circumstances. It is evident that Eliot's millenarianism was strongly affected by John Cotton's eschatological ideas particularly as they appeared in Cotton's earlier lectures on Revelation and Canticles. Cotton had criticized human inventions in the divinely ordered political and ecclesiastical system. He argued for the advent of the millennium as the establishment of the Kingdom of Christ, marked by the restoration of primitive polity ruled by divine direction in the Kingdom. Cotton placed the Second Coming (Christ's final coming), the Resurrection of the Dead, and the Last Judgment as "three last things" in a distant future marking the termination of human history. Cotton's millenarian ideas show affinities in several respects with the ideas of Fifth Monarchists who "were a political and religious sect expecting the imminent Kingdom of Christ on earth, a theocratic regime in which the saints would establish a godly discipline over the unregenerate masses and prepare for the Second Coming."[58] Fifth Monarchists or Fifth Monarchy Men, whose name was taken from a biblical reference in the Book of Daniel to an expectation of four ancient kingdoms: Assyria (Babylonia), Persia, Greece, and Rome. These monarchies, Fifth Monarchists expected, would be followed by a fifth monarchy which was believed to be the Kingdom of Christ. The Fifth Monarchists argued for the laws of Moses until the prophecy was fulfilled, and considered the overthrow of the English monarchy as a sign of the imminent coming of

---

57. *Light Appearing* (1651), 186.
58. Capp, *The Fifth Monarchy Men*, 14.

the millennium.[59] There is no clear evidence to show how Eliot could be influenced by Fifth Monarchist millenarianism, but it is probably because of Cotton's influence. Eliot described Cotton as an advisor for his ministry. Cotton's influence and advice on the biblical polity of the millennium is evident. Eliot said that he consulted with Cotton and others: "Now dear Sir, it may be you will desire to know what kinde of Civil Government they shall be instructed in; I acknowledge it to be a very weighty consideration; and I have advised with Mr. Cotton and others about it."[60] Also, the case of the imminent Middle Coming of Christ and the advent of the earthly Kingdom of God in the millennium was similar to the idea of Thomas Brightman.[61] According to Bozeman, although Brightman's millenarianism did not affect the puritans before the 1640s and as the puritan migrants were not inspired by the millenarianism, the idea, in fact, was circulated and accepted by some of the puritans in part in the 1640s–50s. However, it was not as influential as scholars had expected it to be as they argued for the relationship between

59. Bozeman, *To Live Ancient Lives*, 263–80; Cogley, "John Eliot and the Millennium," 227–50; *JEMI*, 76–83. For bibliographical information of Cotton's lectures on Revelation and Canticles, see "Appendix One," in *JEMI*, 251–52. For the millenarianism of John Cotton and John Eliot, see Bozeman, *To Live Ancient Lives*, chs. 7–8; *JEMI*, ch. 4; Maclear, "New England and the Fifth Monarchy," 231–34. For Fifth Monarchist millenarianism, see Capp, *The Fifth Monarchy Men*; Maclear, "New England and the Fifth Monarchy," 236–40, 248–57; Gribben, *The Puritan Millennium*, 28, 51–52, 183. For recent scholarship on John Cotton's eschatology, see Chi, "'Forget not the wombe that bare you.'" Chi, in this dissertation, argued for the prominence of England in Cotton's eschatology. According to Chi, although Cotton defended New England Congregational way through his apocalyptic vision, he did not argue the exclusive role of New England in eschatological reformation, but demonstrated the support of New England for the reformation in England as his mother country. Eliot also acknowledged the influence of Henry Ainsworth (1571–1622) on his biblical interpretation. Eliot, *The Christian Commonwealth* (1659), 13, 18. Henry Ainsworth was a leader of a separatist congregation in Amsterdam and religious controversialist. Moody, "Ainsworth, Henry."

60. Eliot to Winslow, 29 December 1649, in *Light Appearing* (1651), 191. For more examples of Cotton's advice to Eliot, including written covenant rules for Praying Towns, see *Light Appearing* (1651), 201, 203; *Strength out of Weaknesse* (1652), 228. See also Maclear, "New England and the Fifth Monarchy," 247.

61. Maclear, "New England and the Fifth Monarchy," 227–29. Brightman, *A Revelation of the Apocalyps* (1611), *A Most Comfortable Exposition of the Last and Most Difficult Part of the Prophecie of Daniel* (1635; repr. 1644), and *A Commentary on the Canticles* (1644). For Brightman's millenarianism, see also Bozeman, *To Live Ancient Lives*, 198–217; Gribben, *The Puritan Millennium*, 40–42; Gribben, *Evangelical Millennialism*, 39. For the development and influence of the puritan eschatological interpretations, see Gribben, *The Puritan Millennium*, 21–58; Gribben, "The Church of Scotland and the English Apocalyptic Imagination," 48–52. See also Dawson, "The Apocalyptic Thinking of the Marian Exiles," 75–91.

puritan millenarianism and motives for the Great Migration.[62] Thomas Shepard's attitude is evidence of this. Thomas Shepard's reference to Brightman's millenarianism reveals the train of Brightman's thoughts at that time, but Shepard did not show any agreement with it:

> If Mr. Brightman's interpretation of Daniels prophesie be true, that Anno 1650. Europe will hear some of the best tidings that ever came into the world, viz. rumors from the Easterne Jews, which shall trouble the Turkish tyrant and shake his Pillars . . . but I have no skill in prophesies, nor do I beleeve every mans interpretation of such Scripture.[63]

Along with the influence of contemporary figures, Eliot was also strongly inspired by historical circumstances in England to have his own thoughts on the millennium. For Eliot, the execution of Charles I in January of 1649 and the beginning of the Commonwealth, which he regarded as the climax of the radical shift of the political situation in England, was a crucial influence which provoked him to develop his own millenarianism. The fact that Eliot's thoughts on the millennium were different before and after 1649 shows that his thoughts on the millennium were changed and clarified after the momentous events of 1649. Eliot wrote in his letter to Edward Winslow of 12 November 1648: "But that day of Grace is not yet come unto them. When Gods time is come, he will make way for it, & enable us to accomplish it. In the meane time, I desire to wait, pray, and believe."[64] This tells us that Eliot (in November 1648, at least) did not have a definite idea about the imminent coming of Christ and the millennium. However, after 1649 he expressed different eschatological ideas, particularly in relation to the advent of the millennium. In his letter of 8 July 1649 to Edward Winslow, Eliot revealed his interpretation of the millennium from the point of view of his circumstantial understanding of the political upheaval of England. For him, the regicide and the beginning of the Commonwealth were together an explicit sign of the advent of Christ and the establishment of the Kingdom of God. He said, after the regicide in January of 1649:

> [T]he peaceable summer beginning to arise out these distressed times of perplexity, all those signes preceding the glorious coming of Christ are accomplishing. . . . But notwithstanding all this black cloud, who seeth not the glorious coming of the Lord Jesus

---

62. Bozeman, *To Live Ancient Lives*, 193–236.
63. *Clear Sun-Shine* (1648), 133.
64. *Glorious Progress* (1649), 156–57.

breaking through this cloud, and coming with power and great glory?⁶⁵

Eliot in *The Christian Commonwealth*—written in 1651 and published in 1659—also stated that his belief in the coming of Jesus Christ and the advent of the Kingdom of Christ was strongly inspired and strengthened by the current political situation in Britain: "The late great changes, which have fallen out in great Britain and Ireland, have so amazed the most of men; and the black, and confused clouds, which have over-spread the whole land, have so darkened the way of those wheels of providence by which Christ is coming to set up his Kingdom."⁶⁶ For Eliot, the political and religious upheaval in England clearly showed that the arrival of the millennium was imminent. Eliot said, "It is the very reason why the Lord in this hour of temptation will bring Nations into distresse and perplexity, that so they may be forced to the Scriptures; the light whereof hath sole authority to extricate them out of their deep perplexities."⁶⁷ Eliot, considering civil war and regicide in England as "distresse and perplexity," strongly believed that God was involved with the situation to lead England to the Kingdom of Christ: "Now the time is come, to change Governments, and to cast down all at the foot of Christ, that he may Reign, and fill the Earth with the glory of his Government."⁶⁸

The establishment of the biblical Kingdom of God ruled by Christ premised the destruction of the Antichrist.⁶⁹ In *The Christian Commonwealth*, Eliot argued for the destruction of the Antichrist: "upon that text Dan.7.10 where is set forth the judgement of God executed upon Antichrist. . . . Therefore in the name of the Lord Jesus Christ, the King of Saints . . . I do beseech those chosen, and holy and faithful Saints, who by Councils at Home, or by Wars in the Field, have fought the Lords Battels against Antichrist."⁷⁰ For him, the Antichrist was not only Roman Catholics, collectively, but also the monarchy: "He is King of Kings and reigneth over Kings; for where Justice reignes . . . and that Antichristian principle for man to be above God, whether the Pope in the Church, or Monarches in the Common-wealth, is thrown to the ground."⁷¹ Eliot emphasizes the destruction of the monar-

65. *Light Appearing* (1651), 186.
66. Eliot, "Preface," in *The Christian Commonwealth* (1659); *JEMI*, 76–83.
67. Eliot to Winslow, 29 December 1649, in *Light Appearing* (1651), 192.
68. Eliot, "Preface," in *The Christian Commonwealth* (1659).
69. *Tears of Repentance* (1653), 260.
70. Eliot, "Preface," in *The Christian Commonwealth* (1659); Maclear, "New England and the Fifth Monarchy," 226.
71. Eliot to Winslow, 8 May 1649, in *Light Appearing* (1651), 186. See also Eliot, "Preface," in *The Christian Commonwealth* (1659).

chy, which is the political system of his mother country. For him, England's monarchical government was not only a human polity which should be overthrown in the millennium, it was also a "Government of Antichrist": "and he is now come to take possession of his Kingdom, making England first in that blessed work of setting up the Kingdom of the Lord Jesus: and in order thereunto, he hath cast down not only the miry Religion, and Government of Antichrist, but also the former form of civil Government."[72] Given Eliot's emphasis on the destruction and ruin of "Roman Religion" and "Roman-Image," and the general puritan understanding of the papacy as Antichrist, it is quite understandable why Eliot called the English monarchy in 1651 the "Government of Antichrist," which meant the English government mixed with "that dirty Roman Religion" that should be abolished in the Kingdom of God.[73] His emphasis on the destruction of the monarchy fully reflects his circumstantial understanding of the political upheaval in England. Eliot's strong anti-Catholicism in his millenarian vision strongly implies his aspiration for further reformation in England. In this sense, for Eliot, his millenarianism was not only his eschatological vision, but also at the heart of his vision for reformation in England.

Eliot, who strongly argued for the imminent advent of the millennium in the 1650s, revised his millenarianism again after the Restoration of 1660. His revised millennial ideas can be found in *The Communion of Churches*, published in 1665. The key points of revision were the absence of his argument about the imminent advent of the millennium, and his revision on political polity in the Kingdom of God. For Eliot, the Restoration of Charles II in 1660 was one of the crucial reasons that led him to reconsider the time of the millennium. The most serious problematic issue in his millenarianism was antimonarchism, as demonstrated in his letters in the Eliot Tracts and *The Christian Commonwealth* (1659), as argued above. After the Restoration of the monarchy, which he considered to be the Antichrist, Eliot had to retreat and revise his original idea. In fact, the Massachusetts General Court on 22 May 1661 declared the official prohibition indicating "sundry passages & expressions thereof is justly offensive, & in speciall relating to kingly government in England" and "Mr Elliot hath also freely & fully acknowledged to this Court, it is therefore ordered by this Court & the authority thereof, that the said booke be totally suppressed." Eliot publicly renounced his antimonarchism in *The Christian Commonwealth* (1659) through acknowledging his submission to the Court:

72. Eliot, "Preface," in *The Christian Commonwealth* (1659).

73. Eliot, "Preface," in *The Christian Commonwealth* (1659). *The Christian Commonwealth* (1659) was originally written in 1651.

> I doe hereby acknowledge to this honored court such expressions as doe too manifestly scandalize the government of England, by King, Lords, & Commons, as anti Christian, & justify the late innovators. . . . All forms of civil government deduced from Scripture, either expressely or by just consequence, I acknowledg[e] to be of God, & to be subjected unto for conscience sake; and whatsoever is in the whole epistle or booke inconsisting herewith, I doe at once for all cordially disoune.[74]

Also, in *The Communion of Churches* (1665), unlike *The Christian Commonwealth* (1659), Eliot retreated from his hostile attitude towards the monarchy and acknowledged that it is also a polity in the Kingdom of Christ: "When Christ shall rule all the World, both in Civil and Ecclesiastical affairs, by the Word of his mouth . . . by the hand of Saints, even holy and religious Kings, Princes, and chief Rulers."[75]

However, his desire for the millennium and his conviction in biblical polity were unchanged. What changed was that Eliot acknowledged that the monarchy could also be proper to establish biblical polity, although it was not clear whether he really accepted the monarchy or whether he acquiesced to conform because of the change in circumstances after 1660. A significant piece of evidence, which suggests that Eliot's main millennial idea had not changed, was a letter to Baxter in 1663. In this letter, Eliot still argued for the millennium and the establishment of biblical polity:

> [I]t may please the Lord to direct his People into a Divine Form of Civil Government, of such a Constitution, as that the Godly, Learned in all Places, may be in all Places of Power and Rule, this would so much the more advance all Learning, and Religion, and good Government; so that all the World would become a Divine Colledge. And lastly, when Antichrist is overthrown, and a divine Form of Church-Government is put in practice in all Places; then all the World would become divine.[76]

Eliot's continuing expectation of the Kingdom of Christ is shown in his vision of worship before Christ as the ruler of the millenial Kingdom in *The Communion of Churches*, published in 1665:

> Which Council may meet in Jerusalem, if the Lord will; and if that be so literal a meaning of sundry Texts that way looking.

---

74. *RMB*, vol. IV, pt. II, 5–6. See also Maclear, "New England and the Fifth Monarchy," 257; *ET*, 30; *JEMI*, 97–104.

75. Eliot, *The Communion of Churches* (1665), 17; *ET*, 30; *JEMI*, 97–104.

76. Eliot to Baxter, 6 July 1663, in *ET*, 433.

> And when that Council shall agree of Universal dayes of Fasting or Feasting before the Lord, upon just occasion; Oh! what glorious dayes will those be, when all the World shall appear together before the Lord in such acts of Worship![77]

Eliot in his letter to Baxter of 15 June 1669 acknowledged the delay of the second coming of Christ. However, he still showed his belief in the realization of the Kingdom of Christ:

> [T]his is one of the great remoraes why Christ delayeth that brightnesse of his coming which shall shine downe Anti-Christ into destruction—though withal the very sweet savor of the crosse, the spreadinge of the grace of Christ, the raising and exertinge of the faith and patience of the saints, and the multiplications of Gods Israel under these p[re]sent pressures and calamityes are no small beame of that glorious coming of Christ according to his owne Word 'then shall ye see the Son of Man coming in power and great glory.' . . . We stand by in a corner of the world, and admire at the grace of Christ which is so illustriously powered forth upon the Saints, and we see the word of Christ accomplished, [so] that the adversary standeth and beholdeth it what amazement and know not how to hinder it.[78]

In brief, through this section, one can understand that Eliot's strong millennial vision—formed through his circumstantial interpretation of the regicide and beginning of the Commonwealth in 1649, along with the influence of his contemporaries—was not the motive for his migration to New England in 1631, nor for the initiation of his Indian ministry which started in 1646.

So, it is important to ask the question: why did Eliot consider the millennium to be important in relation to Indian ministry? The reason becomes clearer through gaining an understanding of Eliot's ideas on the Indians' origins.

Indian Origins and Indian Conversion

Eliot, who argued for the imminent advent of the millennium, paid strong attention to the origin of New England Indians. For Eliot, the millennium was important not only for England, but also for the Indians. Eliot strongly believed that the Kingdom of Christ would be established among the

---

77. Eliot, *The Communion of Churches* (1665), 16.

78. Eliot to Baxter, 15 June 1668, in *CRBJE*, 171. The *Oxford English Dictionary* defines "remora" as "An obstacle, an impediment, a hindrance."

Indians, and that it was his work. He wrote in his letter to Winslow of 29 December 1649: "it is my desire and prayer; my work is to endeavour the setting up Christ Kingdome among the Indians ... for the furtherance of the Kingdome of Christ among these poor Indians, shall doubtlesse be had in remembrance before the Lord, not through merit, but mercie."[79] In another letter to Winslow of 21 October 1650, he wrote:

> I am perswaded that there be sundry such among them, whom the Lord will vouchsafe so far to favour and shine upon, that they shall become a Church, and a Spouse of Jesus Christ, and among whom the pure and holy Kingdome of Christ shall arise, and over whom Christ shall reigne, ruling them in all things by his holy word.[80]

The reason that Eliot related the millennium to New England Indians can be found in his ideas on Indian origins. It is true that the Indians were generally considered as Gentiles by the majority of puritans in seventeenth-century New England (except for some who believed "the lost ten tribes" theory, which will be discussed below). Puritans such as Thomas Shepard considered that the Indians were Gentiles, as the descendants of Tartars. According to Cogley, the Tartarian-origins view was probably the orthodox opinion in the seventeenth century.[81] Shepard said:

> It's some refreshing to thinke that there is ... the name of Christ sounding in those darke and despicable Tartarian Tents; the Lord can build them houses in time to pray in, when hee hath given unto them better hearts, and when perhaps hee hath cursed and consumed theirs who have disdained to give that worship and homage to Christ in their seiled houses, which poor Indians rejoyce to give to him in their poor Tents and Wigwams. I desire you to gather what stock of prayers you can for them.[82]

There is no evidence that Eliot agreed with this Tartarian-origins view. Indeed, he came up with what seems to be his own distinctive idea of the Indians as "Gentile Hebrews." His thoughts on Indian origins first

---

79. Eliot to Winslow, 29 December 1649, in *Light Appearing* (1651), 192, 194.
80. Eliot to Winslow, 21 October 1650, in *Light Appearing* (1651), 205.
81. *JEMI*, 15, 97.
82. *Clear Sun-Shine* (1648), 134–35. Tartars (or Tatars) are "a number of Central Asian peoples who, over the centuries, were a threat to civilized peoples in Asia and Europe. More specific names, for example Mongol, Turk, Kipchak, emerge for some of these peoples who were constantly moving, often over great distances, and who spoke a variety of related Turkic and Mongol languages." "Tartars," in Kerr and Wright, *A Dictionary of World History*. See also *JEMI*, 15–16, 84, 97.

appeared in his letter to Winslow of 8 July 1649, and later in a letter to Thomas Thorowgood in 1653, a fuller and more completed exposition which became "The Learned Conjectures," the preface of Thorowgood's *Jews in America* (1660).[83] Therefore, Eliot's ideas on Indian origins seemed to be formed in a similar period as the formation of his millenarianism. Eliot, when he received a letter from Winslow, said, "I had some thoughts in my heart to search the Original of this People." Where exactly his ideas on Indian origins came from is not clear, but the importance of his own study of the Bible and the influence of Hugh Broughton, a late Elizabethan Hebraist, is evident.[84] Eliot said: "Now this is I have thought, that it seemeth to me as clear in the Scripture . . . and learned Broughton put some of them over into America."[85] He also said in his letter to Thorowgood of 1653: "the Lord did put it into my heart to search into some Scriptures about that subject."[86] Eliot's letter to Winslow and Thorowgood gave an explanation of how the descendants of Noah were dispersed after the flood. He argued that after the cohabitation of thirty years of all the sons, "they beginning to grow numerous . . . need to disperse and spread themselves further upon the face of the earth and Shem's family were sent to eastern part and Japhet went to western part, and Ham went to southern part," so he said, "we believe Europe to be of Japhet, and Africa of Ham, we also believe all the East parts of the world to be peopled by the posterity of Shem." Eliot argued that the family of Joktan, as son of Eber as the line of Shem, went to eastern part and finally became "the first planters of America." So, following Hugh Broughton, he argued "it seemeth to me probable that these people are Hebrews, of Eber, whose sonnes the Scripture sends farthest East (as it seemeth to me) and learned Broughton put some of them over into America, and certainly this Country was people Eastward from the place of the Arks." He also said, "Hence therefore we may, not only with faith, but also with demonstration, say, that fruitful India are Hebrewes, that famous civil (though Idolatrous) nation of China are Hebrewes, so Japonia, and these naked Americans are Hebrewes, in respect of those that planted first these parts of the world."[87]

83. Eliot to Winslow of 8 July 1649, in *Light Appearing* (1651), 185; Eliot, "The Learned Conjectures," in *ET*, 409–27.

84. Winslow's letter has not survived, but it was probably written in late 1648 or early 1649. *JEMI*, 85; Jones, "Broughton, Hugh."

85. *Light Appearing* (1651), 185.

86. Eliot, "The Learned Conjectures," in *ET*, 411.

87. *ET*, 412, 417, 419, 420. For Eliot's full exposition on Indian origins, see *ET*, 410–20. See also Eliot to Winslow, 8 July 1649, in *Light Appearing* (1651), 185–86. Which book of Broughton Eliot referred to is not clear. However, Broughton, in *A Require of Agreement* (1611), considered the Indians in America as "Iocktanes sonnes" and related

It is important here to understand how Eliot distinguished the terms "Hebrews" and "Jews" or "Israelites." Cogley gives us clarification of the words, arguing that the line of Peleg, the eldest son of Eber, was the genealogical line of Abraham, Isaac, Jacob, and the twelve tribes of Israel which moved to the promised land with Moses and became the Israelites and the Jews. The line of Joktan, the younger son of Eber, was broadly considered as the descendants of Eber—not counted as Israelites or Jews, but Semites and Hebrews.[88] Therefore, according to Cogley's clarification, the descendants of Joktanites were considered as Gentiles although they were in Eber's line. So, Eliot, who argued that native Indians were the descendants of Joktan, son of Eber, considered the Indians to be Gentiles.

If Eliot distinguished "Hebrews" from "Jews" or "Israelites," how did he reconcile the conversion of the Jews or Israelites and the conversion of Indians as "Hebrews"? In order to answer this, one needs to know how Eliot understood the argument that "the lost ten tribes" moved and settled in America.[89] The arguments on the origin of native Indians as descendants of the lost ten tribes of Israelites, which caught the attention of Eliot, were made by Edward Winslow, John Dury, Thomas Thorowgood, and Menasseh ben Israel. Their ideas can be found in the Eliot Tracts, Eliot's correspondence, Thomas Thorowgood's *Jews in America* (1660), and Menasseh ben Israel's *The Hope of Israel* (1650).[90] They commonly agreed that the descendants of Israelites actually moved and settled in America, although the details of their arguments on the origin of Indians were different. Menasseh and John Dury believed that some of the descendants of the Israelites who settled in Asia moved to America, but Thorowgood thought that all the Israelites moved to America. Winslow's opinion was unclear on that issue. Menasseh

---

the prophecy of "the seventh trumpet" in Revelation to Indian conversion: "And with the seaventh Trumpet the last state shalbe to shew Gods mercy, to Iocktanes sonnes the Indians, and to you miserable Iewes." Broughton, *A Require of Agreement* (1611), 69, 77. See also Firth, *The Apocalyptic Tradition in Reformation Britain*, 161; *JEMI*, 86n18.

88. *JEMI*, 287n18. Cogley also gives us a helpful explanation of the distinction between "Jews" and "Israelites." The twelve tribes of Jacob were called the Israelites before the division of the monarchy after King Solomon. After the division of the monarchy, the term Israelites referred to the ten tribes settled in the northern kingdom of Israel and the descendants of the two tribes inhabited in the southern kingdom of Judah were called the Jews. After the Assyrian conquest of the northern kingdom in the eighth century BCE, the Israelites disappeared. For this reason, the disappeared Israelites were called "the lost ten tribes." *JEMI*, 286n14.

89. *Glorious Progress* (1649), 145.

90. Young, "Dury, John"; Katz, "Menasseh ben Israel." Thomas Thorowgood was a Presbyterian minister in Grimston, Norfolk. *JEMI*, 83. Thorowgood's *Jews in America* was originally published in 1650 and republished in 1660 with a letter form Eliot (1653) as a preface. *JEMI*, 86, 286n14.

argued that New England Indians were the descendants of Tartars who followed the lost tribes into the New World. However, Winslow, Dury, and Thorowgood all believed that Indians were the descendants of the lost tribes of Israelites.[91]

Cogley's explanation of the ideological relationship among Menasseh, Thorowgood, Dury, Winslow and Eliot is helpful. John Dury read Thorowgood's unpublished manuscript of *Jews in America* in late 1648 or early 1649 and contacted Menasseh for further information on the lost tribes theory. After that Dury also informed Edward Winslow of the theory, and Winslow expressed his ideas on it in his preface to *Glorious Progress* (1649). Also, Winslow wrote to Eliot about the theory in 1648 or 1649, and Eliot replied to Winslow about the issue in his letters in 1649. Eliot, who regarded New England Indians as descendants of Joktan, son of Eber, and Gentiles, did not give a clear answer to Winslow's question about Menasseh's idea that "some of the Israelites were brought into America, and scattered here" in his letter to Winslow of 8 July 1649.[92] Eliot wrote:

> I would intreat you to request the same godly Minister . . . to send to him to know his grounds, and how he came to that Intelligence, when was it done, which way were they transported into America, by whom, and what occasion, how many, and to what Parts first, or what steps of intimation of such a thing may there be.[93]

---

91. Edward Winslow's letter, *Glorious Progress* (1649), 144–46; John Dury, "An Appendix," in *Glorious Progress* (1649), 163–67; Thomas Thorowgood, *Jews in America* (1660). See also Maclear, "New England and the Fifth Monarchy," 245–46; *JEMI*, 83–97; Dury, "An Epistolicall Discourse"; Thorowgood, *Jews in America*, e-e2. Menasseh's *The Hope of Israel* (1650) was originally written in Spanish as *Esperança de Israel* (1650). For this book, see Israel, *The Hope of Israel* (1652). *JEMI*, 286n14. The idea of Indian origins was significantly related to the controversy of the readmission of Jews into England in seventeenth-century England. The readmission issue had already been debated in England before the arrival of Rabbi Menasseh ben Israel in London in 1655. The Jewish community, which already existed in an Eastern corner of London, was completely unknown to the English authorities before the arrival of Menasseh, who was a leader in the Dutch Jewish community and a key proponent of readmission along with John Dury. Menasseh played a vital role in Oliver Cromwell's approval of the readmission of Jews into England in 1656. For the readmission of Jews, millenarianism was a significant ideology. Many who believed in the imminent coming of Christ argued that the mass conversion of Jews should happen before the advent; in order to convert them it was absolutely necessary to bring and allow Jews into England to receive the Protestant faith. Katz, *The Jews in the History of England*, 107–44. See also Katz, *Philo-Semitism and the Readmission of the Jews to England*.

92. *JEMI*, 83–90.

93. Eliot to Winslow, 8 July 1649, in *Light Appearing* (1651), 185, 186.

However, after about five months, Eliot, in his letter to Winslow of 29 December 1649, expressed his agreement with the idea that the lost ten tribes were in America. He said, "Sir, you tell me of one that will publish reasons to prove (at least) some of the Ten Tribes are in America, it would be glad tidings to my heart."[94] And then, Eliot, in his letter to Thorowgood in 1653 which became the preface of *Jews of America* (1660), seemed to confirm that the lost ten tribes moved to America: "I thought, I saw some ground to conceive, that some of the Ten Tribes might be scattered even thus far, into these parts of America, where we are according to the Word of God, Deut.28.64."[95] In the latter part of the letter, Eliot more strongly confirmed his belief that the lost ten tribes moved to America:

> 1. That the Ten Tribes are dispersed and scattered into other Nations. 2. That they were scattered Eastward. 3. That it was for their sins, for which God did threaten them to be scattered to the utmost ends of the earth. 4. That they shall be found again, and called into Christ his kingdome. 5. Judah being scattered westward, and were scattered to the utmost ends of the Westerne world. Hence why ought we not to believe, that the ten Tribes being scattered Eastward, are scattered to the utmost ends of the Easterne world? and if so, then assuredly into America, because that is part of the easterne World, and propled by Easterne Inhabitants, as aforesaid.[96]

Although Eliot acknowledged that the lost ten tribes moved and settled in America, this did not mean that he believed that the Indians were the

---

94. Eliot to Winslow, 29 December 1649, in *Light Appearing* (1651), 192.

95. Eliot, "The Learned Conjectures," in *ET*, 410. Jong, *As the Waters Cover the Seas*, proposed 1655 or 1656 as the years that Eliot wrote "The Learned Conjectures" in a letter to Thorowgood, but Cogley argued that Eliot wrote the letter between March 1653 and February 1654. Cogley related Eliot's thoughts on Indian origins to the Praying Indians' confession of faith in 1652, contained in *Tears of Repentance* (1653), and argued for the Indian confessions as evidence to judge the composition year of the letter. Jong, *As the Waters Cover the Seas*, 70; Cogley, "The Millenarianism of John Eliot, 'Apostle to the Indians,'" 113–14; Cogley, "John Eliot and the Origins of the American Indians," 223n9. *Jews in America* (1660) contains nine letters of John Eliot to Thomas Thorowgood. Eight letters were written on 14 October 1650, 18 March 1653, 18 June 1653, 24 October 1653, 27 August 1654, 16 August 1655, 16 October 1656, and 7 October 1657 respectively, and "The Learned Conjectures," named by Thorowgood, which became the preface to *Jews in America* (1660), is undated in the treatise. Except for "The Learned Conjectures," all of the other letters appeared as paraphrased or in directly quoted forms. Thorowgood, "Introduction," in *Jews in America* (1660), 3; Thorowgood, *Jews in America* (1660), 32–34, 52–54. For Eliot's "The Learned Conjectures," see Thorowgood, *Jews in America* (1660), 1–22. See also *ET*, 409–27.

96. Eliot, "The Learned Conjectures," in *ET*, 421–22.

descendants of the Israelites. Eliot, in "The Learned Conjectures," after confirming the theory, strongly argued for the Indians as descendants of Joktan, son of Eber, and Gentiles.[97]

It is evident that Eliot changed his mind and renounced his belief that the lost ten tribes moved to America, sometime between 1653, when he wrote "The Learned Conjectures," and 1656. A letter to Thorowgood on 16 October 1656 revealed this. Eliot wrote:

> I doubt not, but the good Spirit of the Lord did set you on this work, and in this dark scrutiny, though your first arrows of Probabilities shot only at rovers to draw the hearts and eye of Gods people to look and search this way, to see if they can find them, did seem so improbable to some, as to say, it is not probable: This is but an act of the wise providence of God, to quicken and sharpen the work—and therefore dear Sir, go on, and the Lord will be with you; possibly it may be thought, that I might find out fairer Probabilities, by conversing with them, than you at such a distance by reading; and it may be, something might be said that way; but I have some reasons in my bre[a]st, which to me seem weighty, why I am herein so silent; I am called of God to labour among them, but not so far, as I yet see to be engaging in that point: your labours and letters have drawn me forth further that way, than otherwise I should have gone, but I desire you to spare me in this, and give me leave to hear and observe in silence, what the Lord will teach others to say in this matter.[98]

In this letter, Eliot retreated from his earlier conviction regarding the lost ten tribes theory, which he still held in 1653. As seen above, his attitude was not a total denial of Thorowgood's opinion; rather, Eliot expressed that he was not confident about the theory anymore, and that he needed more careful investigation and observation to find a better idea.[99]

Why then was John Eliot still concerned about Indian origins, and what was the relationship between Eliot's millenarian vision and his notions of Indian origins? Eliot's opinions tallied with the views of many who expected a great conversion of Jews and Gentiles before the millennium.

---

97. See *ET*, 410–20.

98. Thorowgood, *Jews in America* (1660), 34.

99. The reason he changed his mind regarding Indian origin is not clearly known. According to Cogley, Eliot's re-evaluation of biblical evidence for the Israelite-origins view might be the reason, or he might have come to agree with the Tartarian-origins view (probably the orthodox viewpoint in seventeenth-century Massachusetts). See *JEMI*, 96–97.

Edward Winslow related his current political circumstance to the conversion of not only Jews, but also Gentiles:

> Especially considering the juncture of time wherein God hath opened their hearts to entertain the Gospel, being no nigh the very years, in which many eminent and learned Divines, have from Scripture grounds according to their apprehensions foretold the conversion of the Jewes. However Right Honourable, the work of communicating and encreasing the light of the Gospel is glorious in reference to Jewes & Gentiles. And as God hath set a signall marke of his presence upon your Assembly . . . that as the Lord offered you (in this designe) a happy opportunity to enlarge and advance the Territories of his Sonnes Kingdom.[100]

Winslow's mention of "a signall marke of his presence" and "a happy opportunity to enlarge and advance the Territories of his Sonnes Kingdom" implicitly tells that he regarded England's political upheaval of 1649 as a sign of the advent of the millennium. Eliot likewise believed a massive conversion of Jews and Gentiles would occur before the millennium. Eliot argued in his letter to readers in 1652:

> In these times the Prophesies of Antichrist his down fall are accomplishing. . . . That the Gospel shall spread over all the Earth, even to all the ends of the Earth; and from the riseing to the setting Sun; all Nations shal[l] become the Nations, and Kingdoms of the Lord and of his Christ. Such words of Prophesie hath the Spirit used to stir up the servants of the Lord to make out after the accomplishment thereof: and hath stirred up a mighty Spirit of Prayer, and expectation of Faith for the Conversion both of the Jewes, (yea all Israel) and of the Gentiles also, over all the world. For this Cause I know every believing heart, awakened by such Scriptures, longeth to hear of the Conversion of our poor Indians, whereby such Prophesies are in part begun to be accomplished.[101]

---

100. *Glorious Progress* (1649), 145–46; *JEMI*, 85.

101. *Tears of Repentance* (1653), 261. See also *Tears of Repentance* (1653), 260. Eliot believed that the lost ten tribes would be converted with the Jews when the millennium was imminent. Eliot said, "And when the Lord inlarged the Promise to Jacob . . . he promised to make him a Nation and a multitude of Nations, which so farre as we regard a litteral accomplishment, is in part accomplisht in the Nation of Jewes, and the other part remaineth . . . to be accomplisht in the lost Israelites scattered in the world." Eliot's letter to Winslow, 8 July 1649, in *Light Appearing* (1651), 185.

Expectations of mass conversions before the millennium—Jews and then Gentiles—were commonly acknowledged in the seventeenth century.[102] Thomas Lechford argued that one of the reasons for the delay of Indian evangelization in New England was puritans' belief that Jews should be converted first. Lechford said, "some say out of Rev.15. last, it is not probable that any nation more can be converted, til[l] the calling of the Jews; till the seven plagues finished none was able to enter into the Temple, that is, the Christian Church, and the seventh Viall is not yet poured forth, and God knowes when it will bee."[103] Shepard, in *Day-Breaking* (1647), said that at least the year of 1647, was "not yet time for God to worke" because of the Jews-Gentile order of salvation, which was the first reason, with the uncivilizedness of Indians and spiritual barrenness in New England, which were the second and third reasons. He argued, "Three things have made us thinke (as they once did of building the Temple) it is not yet time for God to worke, 1. Because till the Jewes come in, there is a seale set upon the hearts of those people, as they thinke from some Apocalypticall places."[104] John Cotton also believed that the Jews should be converted first:

> It is true, there may be doubt that for a time there will be no great hope of any national conversion, till Antichrist be ruined, and the Jews converted . . . as now and then some proselytes were brought into the fellowship of the church of Israel, when there was a greater partition wall set up between Jews and Gentiles, than now there is between Christians and pagans. And the Lord shine upon them in mercy, in blessing the means of his grace to them in the Lord Jesus.[105]

Considering puritans' general recognition of first Jews and then Gentiles in the order of salvation, one can ask how Eliot reconciled the conversion of Jews and of the Indians in America, and how he argued for Indian conversion based on his understanding of Indian origin. A significant hint regarding Eliot's argument for the conversion of the Indians, considered as the descendants of "Hebrews," but not of "Jews" or "Israelites," can be found in his letter to Winslow of 8 July 1649:

> And when the Lord inlarged the Promise to Jacob . . . he promised to make him a Nation and a multitude of Nations, which so farre as we regard a litteral accomplishment, is in

---

102. Bozeman, *To Live Ancient Lives*, 218–19.
103. Lechford, *Plain Dealing* (1642), 21.
104. *Day-Breaking* (1647), 93.
105. Cotton, *The Way of Congregational Way Cleared* (1648), 274.

part accomplisht in the Nation of Jewes, and the other part remaineth (as it may seem) to be accomplisht in the lost Israelites scattered in the world, principally, if not wholly, amongst the sons of Japhet and Shem; and our God who can and will gather the scattered and lost dust of our bodies at the Resurrection, can and will finde out these lost and scattered Israelites, and in finding up them, bring in with them the Nations among whom they were scattered, and so shall Jacobs Promise extend to a multitude of Nations indeed; and this is a great ground of faith for the conversion of the Easterne Nations, and may be of help to our faith for these Indians.[106]

Here, we can understand that even though Eliot acknowledged that native Indians in America were the descendants of Shem who were not considered "Jews" or "Israelites," for him this was not a serious obstacle to envisioning Indian conversion, because of his conviction that the Indians would receive the grace of God for conversion, along with the "Jews" and "the lost Israelites scattered in the world," when the millennium was imminent. For Eliot, this belief was "a great ground of faith for the conversion of the Easterne Nations, and may be of help to our faith for these Indians."[107] For Eliot, the Indians' conversion should be regarded as a first step towards the advent of the millennium, in which all nations would receive the gospel and enjoy the rule of Christ. Eliot believed that Hebrew would be the universal language that all Christians could understand in the millennium.[108]

106. Eliot's letter to Winslow, 8 July 1649, in *Light Appearing* (1651), 185–86.

107. Eliot's letter to Winslow, 8 July 1649, in *Light Appearing* (1651), 186.

108. Eliot's letter to Winslow, 8 July 1649, in *Light Appearing* (1651), 186; Eliot, "The Learned Conjectures," in *ET*, 414, 421. Eliot to Baxter, 6 July 1663, in *ET*, 432. See also Breen, *Transgressing the Bounds*, 154; Gray, *New World Babel*, 24. Eliot's interest in the Christianization of other nations and peoples who had not heard the gospel appeared in his letter to John Cotton of 4 June 1651. Here, Eliot talked about John Jackson's book, *A Sober Word to a Serious People* (1651), sent to him by William Rogers. John Jackson, defending Seekers in the book, argued for the necessity to convert other nations that had not heard of Christianity. According to Jackson, "It were to be desired that the Lord would stir up the hearts of his people to cry mightily to him, and give him no rest, till he accomplish the work of gathering together his number out of all Nations, Kindreds, Tongues, and Peoples. . . . It must be done to full the Word of the Lord." Jackson, *A Sober Word to a Serious People* (1651), 38, 40, 41, cited in Cotton, *The Correspondence of John Cotton*, 446–47. Eliot expressed his appreciation for the book. Eliot's letter to John Cotton, 4 June 1651, in *CJC*, 447. Seekers were people who believed that there had not been a true church after Antichrist became uppermost in the church. During the Commonwealth period, the term "seekers" was used to describe people "dissatisfied with the existing religious sects." Cross, *The Oxford Dictionary of the Christian Church*, 1489. John Cotton partly agreed with the book, but argued for the validity of "the present ministry and present church" and criticized seekers' ideas and attitude. Cotton to Eliot, June 1651, in *CJC*, 449–52.

Eliot's hopes for universal redemption were related to his idea of the birthplace of the millennium. In fact, Eliot strongly believed that England would be a birthplace of the millennium. Eliot, in his letter to Winslow of 29 December 1649, argued that England's current upheaval was for change from polity based on human invention to biblical polity:

> England long since had happy experience of it, and it is often in my heart to desire they would pitch there in this present great change they are about; this is certaine, that all formes and Lawes of mans invention will shake, be unsettled; and many will doubt of subjecting to any way man can devise; and they will never rest till they come up to the Scriptures, and when they produce Scripture grounds for all they do, it will answer and satisfie all godly consciences, and awe the rest, and stop their mouths unlesse they will cavil against divine wisdome.[109]

Eliot confessed that "Oh my heart yearneth over distressed perplexed England, and my continual prayer unto the Lord for them is, that he would be pleased to open their hearts and eyes, and let them see their opportunity to let in Christ, and to advance his Kingdome over them."[110] For Eliot, although England was in serious national turmoil at that time, the situation was a blessing because the Kingdom of God based on the Word of God was coming. As he said: "Oh the blessed day in England when the Word of God shall be their Magna Charta [sic] and chief Law Book; and when all Lawyers must be Divines to study the Scriptures; and should the Gentile Nations take up Moses policie so farre as it is morall and conscionable, make the Scriptures the foundation of all their Lawes."[111]

Although Eliot believed that England was to be a birthplace of the millennium as stated above, he demonstrated new ideas on the birthplace of the millennium in 1653. In his letter to Thorowgood in 1653 which became the preface for *Jews in America* (1660), Eliot argued from Ezek 40–47 that New England as the "Easterne gate" was another birth place of the millennium:

> May it not be worthy of consideration, that when Ezekiels Gospel-temple . . . shall be measured, the Easterne gate is first measured, Ezek.40.6. again when the glory of the Lord cometh into that glorious Temple, he is upon his Westerne progresse, and first enters that Temple at the Easterne gate, Ezek.43.1,2,3. &c. again the frontispeece of that Temple is Eastward, Ezek.47. and those pretious waters of that Sanctuary, so wholesome,

---

109. Eliot to Winslow, 29 December 1649, in *Light Appearing* (1651), 192.
110. *Light Appearing* (1651), 195.
111. *Light Appearing* (1651), 195.

powerfull, and pretious, they run Eastward into the East land, and the further Eastward the more deep & wonderful they be: doth not all his shew, that there shall be a glorious Church in all the Easterne world?[112]

As stated above, Eliot talked about the establishment of the Kingdom of God among native Indians in his letters before 1653, when he explained the biblical polity in Praying Towns.[113] However, it is not certain whether Eliot, before 1653, considered New England to be another birthplace of the millennium. However, it seems likely that he was confident by 1653 about New England as a birthplace of the millennium, from the evidence in his letter to Thorowgood in 1653. In other words, Eliot, who confirmed the justification of the conversion of Indians as descendants of "Hebrews," finally thought that as there were native Indians living in New England it was therefore also a birthplace of the millennium. An important matter to consider is that although Eliot acknowledged that New England was an additional site for the millennium, he did not regard New England as a "New Jerusalem," which was the only place of the millennium according to many contemporary scholars.[114] After recognizing New England Indians as descendants of "Hebrews," and having confidence in this rationale for Indian conversion, Eliot added New England as another birthplace of the millennium. Eliot said: "And God grant that the old bottles of the Westerne world be not so uncapable of the new wine of Christ his expected Kingdom, that the Easterne bottles be not the only entertainers thereof for a season."[115] In this sense, for Eliot, England was the Western birthplace of the millennium and New England was the Eastern birthplace.[116] Consequently, although millenarianism was not the main motive for Eliot's Indian ministry, the reason that he considered the millennium important in relation to Indian ministry was that he believed that New England Indians could be converted with "Jews" and "lost Israelites" when the millennium was imminent. Perhaps this conviction was a strong motive for Eliot to push ahead his pastoral project for the Indians, at least until the Restoration (1660).

Then, what was the relationship between Eliot's thoughts on Indian origins and their relation to his Indian ministry after 1660? Unfortunately,

---

112. Eliot, "The Learned Conjectures," in *ET*, 420–21.

113. Eliot to Winslow, 8 July 1649, in *Light Appearing* (1651), 186. See also *Strength out of Weaknesse* (1652), 224–28.

114. See p. 42n52 above.

115. Eliot, "The Learned Conjectures," in *ET*, 421.

116. *JEMI*, 83. See p. 52n87 above for Eliot's conviction that the Indians reached America by a journey east from Israel.

there is no evidence to reveal Eliot's thoughts on Indian origins after 1660. However, one can surely suppose that regarding the crucial relationship between the millennium and Indian conversion, because of the Restoration (1660), which required Eliot to revise his ideas on the imminent advent of the millennium, he had to withdraw his belief in the imminent mass conversion of the Indians. Therefore, for Eliot, after 1660, his thoughts on the millennium and the mass conversion of New England Indians as the Hebrew descendants of Eber perhaps could no longer be a strong motive and stimulus for his Indian ministry, although he still had a vision of the millennium and Indian conversion in the future. In this sense, Cogley's indication that Eliot's millenarianism was an important part of his "mission," but it was not the "main story line," is absolutely right in terms of a fundamental motive for Eliot's Indian ministry.[117] However, Cogley (in light of the absence of evidence after 1660) is silent about what might have been the fundamental and lasting motive for Eliot's preaching of the gospel to New England Indians, and his pastoral work with them, even after 1660 and until his death in 1690.

Conclusion

In light of the revised interpretation of the purpose of the puritans' Great Migration, based both on new scholarship as well as on original sources describing the early period of puritan migration (mainly in the Eliot Tracts), it is apparent that the missiological understanding of Indian "mission" as the motive for the Great Migration based on Perry Miller's "errand into the wilderness" thesis needs to be revised. The primary reason for puritan migration, including John Eliot's decision to leave his homeland, was a search after pure Christianity and further reformation that could not be actualized under Laudian policy in England. Although we can find some references in Eliot's statements in the mid-1640s and the materials in the Eliot Tracts in 1650s, as if Indian conversion were the main reason for the migration, these references probably reflect a reinterpretation of puritan's providential purpose of migration in the changed historical circumstances of the mid-1640s and 1650s. This realization leads us to a new investigation of the fundamental motives for Eliot's Indian conversion and Indian ministry.

To reach this conclusion, this chapter, based on new scholarship, has provided a new interpretation of the relationship between millenarianism and Indian conversion. This chapter refutes previous research arguing that puritans migrated to New England under the strong influence of

117. *JEMI*, 103.

millenarianism in the seventeenth-century transatlantic world, in order to establish a model society in the imminently-coming millennium in New England as a "New Jerusalem." According to new scholarship, despite the millennial ideas which were circulating at that time, the puritans' main purpose of migration was not to establish a millennial ideal society in New England, but rather to pursue further reformation and purity within Christianity. Also, Eliot's millenarianism was formed not only by his contemporaries, but also in response to radically shifted circumstances which had climaxed in the execution of Charles I in 1649 and the beginning of the Commonwealth. This suggests strongly that millenarianism was not at the forefront of the original motives for puritan migration to New England in the 1630s. In addition, the circumstantial formation of Eliot's millenarianism after 1646, when he began preaching the gospel to the Indians, revealed that his millenarian vision was not the initial reason for his Indian ministry. However, it is clear that Eliot's thoughts on the millennium, and his expectation of it, became important stimuli for his Indian ministry. This can be well understood when we consider his thoughts on the origin of the New England Indians as the descendants of "Gentile Hebrews," and the possibility of their mass conversion in relation to the millennium. Yet, after 1660, despite his continuous vision of the Kingdom of Christ and Indian conversion, it is probably true that Eliot's millenarianism could not be a strong motive and stimulus for him to push ahead with his Indian ministry in quite the same way as it had been before. Lastly, through the reinterpretation of the relationship among puritan migration, millenarianism, and Indian conversion in Eliot's ministry, based on historical and circumstantial reconsideration of the seventeenth-century transatlantic world, one can realize the necessity and justification for a historical and circumstantial angle for understanding Eliot's Indian ministry.

If the original purpose of John Eliot's migration was not primarily for Indian evangelization, at least when he left England, why then did he preach the gospel to native Indians, and what encouraged him to do so? Also, if his thoughts on the millennium and Indian origin were not his initial motive, and could not be a strong stimulus after 1660 despite his continuous vision of the millennium and Indian conversion, what was the fundamental and lasting motive that pushed him to continue his ministry to the Indians? In order to answer this question, we need to return to the first and second reasons for Indian ministry that Eliot himself stated in the quotation cited at the start of this chapter: "First, the glory of God, in the conversion of some of these poor, desolate souls. Secondly, his compassion and ardent affection to them, as of mankind in their great blindness and ignorance."[118] How can we understand this reference and what kind of ideological foundation can we discover? This question will be answered in the next chapter, geared towards understanding seventeenth-century puritan pastoral theology and ministry as the ideological background of John Eliot's Indian ministry.

118. *HCINE*, 170.

3

The Historical and Theological Background

of Seventeenth-Century Puritan Ministry in Old and New England in Relation to the Motives for Indian Ministry

THE AIM OF THIS chapter is to understand the historical and theological background of John Eliot's Indian pastoral ministry through an examination of seventeenth-century puritan theological and ministerial ideas in Old and New England, focusing particularly on Lewis Bayly, John Cotton, Thomas Shepard, and Richard Baxter, all of whom significantly influenced Eliot's theology and ministry.[1] The ideological relationship between Eliot and the four puritans is evident. Lewis Bayly's thoughts on the practice of piety so strongly influenced Eliot that he translated Bayly's book, *The Practice of Piety* (2nd ed., 1612) into the Algonquian Indian language in 1665.[2] John Cotton's strong theological and ministerial influence on Eliot is not in

---

1. For Bayly, Cotton, Shepard, and Baxter, see Jones and Larminie, "Bayly, Lewis"; Bremer, "Cotton, John"; Jinkins, "Shepard, Thomas"; Keeble, "Baxter, Richard."

2. Lewis Bayly's *The Practice of Piety*, an "encyclopedic guide to godly living," was "one of the most frequently published and read of all puritan books throughout the seventeenth- century." It was continually published in at least fifty-seven editions in England between 1612 and 1743. It was translated into Welsh, French, Hungarian, Romanian, Italian, and Dutch. It was also translated into the Algonquian Indian language by John Eliot. Cambers, *Godly Reading*, 243–46. This book refers to the edition of 1695.

doubt either: Eliot described Cotton as his ministerial mentor. In particular, Eliot's millenarianism, his thoughts on biblical civil polity in Praying Towns, and congregationalist ecclesiology were strongly affected by John Cotton.³ Thomas Shepard was also a significant influence on Eliot. Shepard witnessed Eliot's Indian ministry and strongly supported it. Shepard's letters and reports of Eliot's Indian ministry in the Eliot Tracts, and his strong involvement with the publication of the tracts as one of their editors, prove his deep concern for Indian ministry.⁴ Shepard's theological influence on Eliot, in particular in the understanding of conversion, is evident in light of Eliot's translation of Shepard's treatise, *The Sincere Convert* (1640) into the Indian language in 1689. Also, the correspondence between John Eliot and Richard Baxter (1656–82) and Eliot's translation of Baxter's *A Call to the Unconverted* (1658) into the Indian language in 1664 clearly shows their mutual theological and ministerial relationship.⁵ The ideological relationships among Eliot and these four puritans signify Eliot's Old and New England puritan background. It is probably true that Eliot applied puritan traditions to his Indian ministry. In exploring these puritan traditions, this chapter provides an essential framework for the whole book.⁶

Among various aspects of puritanism, ministerial ideas and practices have been one of the main research subjects.⁷ Many scholars such as Patrick Collinson, David D. Hall, and Tom Webster have treated puritan ministerial ideas and practices as key issues in their comprehensive historical investigation of puritanism.⁸ Also, a good deal of research illuminates specific

3. *Light Appearing* (1651), 191, 201, 203; *Strength out of Weaknesse* (1652), 228. It is evident that John Cotton was also a strong supporter of Eliot's Indian evangelization work. Cotton described Eliot's Indian ministry: "And of late (through the grace of Christ) one of our fellow elders, Mr. Eliot, teacher of Roxbury, having gotten the knowledge of the Indian language preacheth to them every week: one week to one congregation on the fourth day, to the other on the sixth the week following. And to him they willingly give ear, and reform their vicious living according to this doctrine, and some of them offer themselves to be trained upon in English families, and in our schools: and there be of them that give good hope of coming on to the acknowledgement of the grace of Christ." Cotton, *The Way of Congregational Churches Cleared* (1648) in Ziff, *John Cotton on the Churches of New England*, 200. See also Cotton, *The Way of Congregational Churches Cleared* (1648), 273.

4. See *Day-Breaking* (1647); *Clear Sun-Shine* (1648).

5. *CRBJE*; Keeble and Nuttall, *Calendar of the Correspondence of Richard Baxter*.

6. Eliot's application of the puritan theological and ministerial ideology to his Indian ministry will be discussed in chapters 4–6.

7. For various scholarly aspects of puritanism with recent academic tendency and key bibliographies in puritan studies, see Coffey and Lim, *The Cambridge Companion to Puritanism*.

8. Collinson, *The Elizabethan Puritan Movement*; Collinson, *The Religion of Protestants*; Hall, *The Faithful Shepherd*; Webster, *Godly Clergy in Early Stuart England*.

ministerial issues such as pastorship, sacraments, preaching, conversion, the practice of piety or spirituality, and the church.[9]

Recently, significant research which pursued a more profound understanding of puritan pastoral ministry and pastorship, through the examination of specific puritan figures' ministerial ideology and practices, has been published. John H. Primus and J. William Black focused on Richard Greenham[10] and Richard Baxter respectively.[11] Paul C. H. Lim's work on Richard Baxter is also significant in terms of puritan pastoral theology and understanding of ministry. Although Lim mainly focused on Baxter's ecclesiology, he considered puritan ministerial elements, including conversion-oriented preaching and catechizing, baptism, and the Lord's Supper, as the essential factors not only for forming an ideal puritan church, but also for their practice of pastoral ministry.[12] Through these researches, one can rediscover the importance of the practice of pastoral ministry in puritan tradition.

More recently, scholars such as Arnold Hunt and Andrew Cambers provided a significant investigation on specific puritan practices of pastoral ministry and piety. Arnold Hunt has given a thorough examination of preaching in early modern England.[13] Hunt focused on how sermons were transmitted and how audiences reacted and responded to them. Through this research, Hunt provided important insights for understanding both puritanism as a religious practice, as well as English preaching culture itself. Andrew Cambers's recent work also shows similar tendencies. Cambers examined the meaning and role of reading in puritanism among many other religious practices, such as fasting and praying, psalm-singing, and meditation. Cambers argued that reading as a religious and cultural practice was vital to puritanism, and that this realization makes it possible to define puritanism as "a religious culture, rather than simply as doctrine and ideology."[14] Hunt's and Cambers's contributions have been their thorough

---

9. Nuttall, *The Holy Spirit in Puritan Faith and Experience*; Wakefield, *Puritan Devotion*; Morgan, *Visible Saints*; Pettit, *The Heart Prepared*; Holifield, *The Covenant Sealed*; Hambrick-Stowe, *The Practice of Piety*; Hambrick-Stowe, "III. Puritan Spirituality in America," 338–53; Stout, *The New England Soul*; Cohen, *God's Caress*; Rice, *Reformed Spirituality*; Bozeman, *To Live Ancient Lives*; Bozeman, *The Precisianist Strain*, 63–180; McGiffert, *God's Plot*; Chan, *Spiritual Theology*; Davies, *Worship and Theology in England*; Davies, *The Worship of the American Puritans*; Hinson, "Puritan Spirituality," 165–82; Lim, *In Pursuit of Purity, Unity, and Liberty*; Beeke, *Puritan Reformed Spirituality*.

10. Carlson, "Greenham, Richard."

11. Primus, *Richard Greenham*. See also Parker and Carlson, '*Practical Divinity*'; Black, *Reformation Pastors*.

12. See Lim, *In Pursuit of Purity, Unity, and Liberty*, 23–114.

13. Hunt, *The Art of Hearing*.

14. Cambers, *Godly Reading*, 1–33.

investigation of certain puritans' religious practice in relation to their social contexts; they have also provided a new understanding of puritanism as the more internalized and pietistic religious activity of an individual and of a certain community.

Reflecting the recent scholarship on puritanism, it will be necessary to provide another attempt to define "puritans" and "puritanism." In fact, the definition of "puritans," which was originally an opprobrious nickname applied by their enemies, has been seriously debated among scholars. The interminable scholarly debates and discourses on the term reflect puritans' complicated and multi-faceted experiences and ideologies in their own historical contexts. For this reason, many scholars have tried to define puritanism in a multi-dimensional fashion, from religious, theological, political, cultural, social, and moral perspectives.[15]

An understanding of puritans and puritanism focused on religious practices leads us into more practical, empirical, and spiritual aspects of puritanism. In fact, understanding puritanism from the perspective of piety or spirituality reflects the work of scholars such as F. Ernest Stoeffler, Howard L. Rice, and E. Glenn Hinson. Stoeffler, who emphasized the strong relationship between puritanism and pietism, argued for "pietistic puritanism."[16] Bozeman, who called Richard Greenham "the seminal pietist," also understood puritanism as a pietistic movement.[17] This understanding is also found in Rice:

> Puritanism was the British manifestation of continental Pietism, and as such it was also a protest against religious formalism, dogmatism, and lack of passion. The Puritans took their lively sense of a relationship with God seriously, and it led them to

---

15. Hill, *Society and Puritanism in Pre-Revolutionary England*, 15–30; Hall, "Puritanism," 283–96; George, "Puritanism as History and Historiography," 77–104; Collinson, "A Comment," 483–88; Wallace, *Puritans and Predestination*; Greaves, "The Puritan Non-Conformist Tradition in England," 449–86; Rohr, *The Covenant of Grace in Puritan Thought*; Lake, "Defining Puritanism—Again?," 3–29; Durston and Eales, "Introduction," in the *Culture of English Puritanism*, 1–31; Collinson, "Elizabethan and Jacobean Puritanism," 32–57; Spurr, *English Puritanism*, 1–58; Knoppers, "Introduction," in Knoppers, *Puritanism and Its Discontents*, 9–22; Morrill, "A Liberation Theology?," 27–48; Brautigam, "Prelates and Politics," 49–66; Lim, *In Pursuit of Purity, Unity, and Liberty*, 6–7n30; *PPEA*, 428–30; Hardman Moore, "Appendix I," in *Pilgrims*, 148–49; Coffey and Lim, "Introduction," in *The Cambridge Companion to Puritanism*, 1–15; Collinson, "Antipuritanism," 19–33; Lake, "The Historiography of Puritanism," 346–71; Cambers, *Godly Reading*, 10–16.

16. Stoeffler, *The Rise of Evangelical Pietism*, 24–108.

17. Bozeman, *The Precisianist Strain*, 63–180.

seek to purify the Church of England and also to reform the government of the nation.[18]

E. Glenn Hinson explicitly argued that "puritanism" was spirituality.[19] Through an understanding of puritanism as a pietistic movement or movement of piety or spirituality, one can maintain strong attention to the introspective and experimental tendencies in puritanism. As R. M. Hawkes indicated, "the essence of Puritanism was its piety, a stress on conversion, on existential, heartfelt religion."[20] Michael McGiffert argued in his book *God's Plot* (1972), that New England puritans' inward experience had not been focused on for a long period, during which Perry Miller's understanding dominated. Miller, in *The New England Mind*, published in 1939, argued for rationality, reason, and intellect as core aspects of puritan mentality, and ignored feeling, emotion, and empirical aspects:

> The Puritan conclusion from psychology was precisely what we have seen from the logic: man does nothing by compulsion, "nor by the force of instinct," but by rational determination, by intellectual comprehension. . . . Psychology thus reinforced the Puritans' unremitting insistence that all conduct be rational, that man yield not to instincts and blind emotions; it underlined this moral by describing the mechanism of behaviour so that the rule of reason became an inescapable factor in all actions, even the worst.[21]

Disputing Perry Miller, McGiffert argued for the experiential and emotional aspect of puritan piety and the serious inwardness of puritan religious life, based on Thomas Shepard's autobiography and journal.[22] This strong attention to inwardness and introspective piety has been followed by other scholars. Bozeman argued that "while the new Puritanism is variously described, its most noted characteristic is 'a move toward an inward, introspective

---

18. Rice, *Reformed Spirituality*, 12. According to Rice, the term "piety" is more preferred than "spirituality" in Reformed tradition. Rice said, "piety is nothing more than the pattern by which we shape our lives before God in grateful osingbedience to what God has done for us." Rice, *Reformed Spirituality*, 46. For Reformed spirituality focusing on puritans, see Beeke, *Puritan Reformed Spirituality*. For more resources for the understanding of piety in Reformed tradition, see Beeke, *Puritan Reformed Spirituality*, 28n200.

19. Hinson, "Puritan Spirituality," 165.

20. Hawkes, "The Logic of Assurance in English Puritan Theology," 247.

21. Miller, *The New England Mind*, 265.

22. McGiffert, *God's Plot*, 3–29. *God's Plot* has Thomas Shepard's autobiography, nearly 50 percent of the journal, and *The Confessions*. *The Confessions* was included in the revised edition in 1994. For puritan inwardness, see below.

piety.'" Hunt's latest research supports this realization. Hunt argued for inwardness and the emotional aspects of puritanism through his examination of English puritan preaching, which was not only logical and intellectual, but also "a direct appeal to the emotions." For him, learning how to listen to sermons, as "the art of hearing," was intended to make sermons a pivotal part of the godly life. Yet in doing so it created the conditions for a more private and internalized form of spirituality in which sermons played less of a part.[23]

Reflecting the focus in recent scholarship on aspects of puritan ministry and puritan piety, one can note scholars' high consideration of religious activity and practice of puritans, as well as the spiritual and aesthetic dimension of puritans' religious life. Also, recent scholarship's strong focus on the understanding of puritan ministry and pastorship is essential in terms of the strong relationship between puritan ministry and piety. Along with these considerations, we cannot ignore the general understanding of puritans who pursued "reforming the reformation" or "further reformation."[24] One can realize that in order to define puritanism there is necessarily a close connection between puritan piety, pastoral ministry, and reformation. For puritans, the most important means of realizing reformation was pastoral ministry in the pursuit of conversion as a total ontological change. For the ministry, pastoral teaching, including preaching and catechizing, pastoral care, and the practice of piety, were not only the key ministerial tasks, but also the essential means of pastoral ministry pursuing reformation. Also, puritan piety served as a sign of "visible saints": "the godly," as a result of internal change, were to be distinguished from "the ungodly," who needed to be converted and reformed. In this sense, puritan piety was also significant in whole scheme of puritan reformation. Therefore, the realization of the mutual relationship among puritan piety, puritan ministry based on pastoral teaching, practice of piety seeking intellectual knowledge, heartfelt religion and inwardness, and puritan pursuit of reformation are probably significant to re-define puritanism. Therefore, based on the scholarship on puritan piety and pastoral ministry, we can perhaps define puritanism as a pietistic Protestant reforming movement based on Reformed theology.

This chapter is heavily reliant on the writings of the four Old and New England puritans mentioned at the start—Bayly, Cotton, Shepard, and Baxter—who had a direct and indirect relationship with John Eliot.[25] Also, this

---

23. Bozeman, *The Precisianist Strain*, 65; Hunt, *The Art of Hearing*. 80–81. For emotionalism in puritanism, see Hunt, *The Art of Hearing*, 81–94.

24. Hardman Moore, *Pilgrims*, 1–34. See also Hardman Moore, "New England's Reformation," 143–58; Morrill, "The Puritan Revolution," 68–72.

25. Bayly, *The Practice of Piety* (2nd ed., 1612); Baxter, *The Reformed Pastor* (1656); Baxter, *A Call to the Unconverted* (1658), 45; Shepard, *The Sincere Convert* (1640), in

chapter, among various aspects of puritan ministry, will mainly investigate puritan understandings of the following: conversion and soteriology, pastoral teaching of the Word of God, pastoral care focused on pastoral counselling and spiritual direction, pastoral training for pastors, and puritan practice of piety. In chapter 2, we concluded that Eliot's millenarianism and his thoughts on Indian origins were not the initial motives for his preaching the gospel to the Indians, nor a lasting motive for him to press ahead with Indian ministry after 1660. So this leaves questions about Eliot's primary reason for initiating preaching the gospel to the Indians in 1646, and what the lasting motive for him was to continually push ahead his Indian ministry until his death in 1690. Eliot's own reference to the first two reasons for his Indian ministry, which he told Daniel Gookin in the mid-1640s, provides a crucial clue: "First, the glory of God, in the conversion of some of these poor, desolate souls. Secondly, his compassion and ardent affection to them, as of mankind in their great blindness and ignorance."[26] This chapter, based on the examination of seventeenth-century puritan ministry, will suggest that these two reasons reveal puritan theological and ministerial motives for Eliot to initiate preaching to the Indians and continually propel Indian ministry. This chapter will propose that puritan conversion theology played a vital role in relation to Eliot's ideological motive for Indian ministry. Moreover, the puritans' fundamental concern about conversion was related to their strong aspiration for reformation as their ultimate purpose in migration. This will be investigated in this chapter through examination of the puritans' thoughts on conversion and salvation as they appear in the Eliot Tracts. This chapter, therefore, will conclude that for Eliot, his puritan conversion theology and his puritan pastoral theology were not only the initial motives for preaching the gospel to Indians, but also the strongest and most lasting motives for his Indian ministry. Also, this chapter will suggest Eliot's aspiration for reformation as another reason for his Indian ministry, through the argument for Eliot's belief of Indian conversion as a means for realizing the values of reformation.

Along with chapter 2, this chapter provides the essential research for re-focusing perspectives on Eliot in chapters 4–6. Through the investigation, we will discover the theological foundations of Eliot's pastoral work with New England Indians, but also realize the justification for conversion as the theological motive for Eliot's Indian ministry. Also, the chapter will re-confirm the importance of historical and theological perspectives for

---

Albro, *The Works of Thomas Shepard*; Shepard, *The Sound Believer* (1645) in *The Works of Thomas Shepard*, 115–237. This book refers to the modern editions mentioned above.

26. HCINE, 170.

understanding Eliot as a seventeenth-century puritan figure, and how and on what basis we can define Eliot's pastoral work with the Indians, which has been normally understood as "mission."

A Ministry Oriented towards Conversion and Reformation

Puritans regarded conversion as a primary ministerial duty and divine command. Richard Baxter said, "We must labour, in a special manner, for the conversion of the unconverted. The work of conversion is the first and great thing we must drive at."[27] John Cotton also said, "we think it a principal (though not the only) work and duty of our ministry to attend the work of conversion, both of carnal English, and other nations, whether Christian, or pagan."[28] Also, puritans ultimately pursued reformation of church and society through a conversion-centered pastoral ministry. In this section, we will discuss the puritans' understanding of conversion and soteriology, which was a significant basis of their pastoral ministry and of the relationship between conversion-centered ministry and reformation. John Eliot pursued conversion-oriented ministry for the Indians and applied puritan conversion theology and soteriology to his Indian ministry. By exploring these themes, this section will provide an important ideological framework for Eliot's conversion-oriented Indian ministry.[29]

Puritan Understanding of Conversion and Soteriology

Puritan understanding of conversion was based on Reformed theology demonstrating human total depravity and God's absolute sovereignty on salvation.[30] Puritans held the same view as Calvin on the definition of conversion: "fundamental change; departing from ourselves and taking off our former mind" and "the real turning of our life to God."[31] In other words,

---

27. Baxter, *The Reformed Pastor* (1656), 94, 175–76. Baxter's reputation in pastorship and the significance of *The Reformed Pastor* (*Gildas Salvianus*, 1656) as an excellent pastoral manual has been well recognized. See Keeble, *Richard Baxter*, 83n28.

28. Cotton, *The Way of Congregational Churches Cleared* (1648), 268.

29. Chapters 5 and 6 will discuss John Eliot's puritan conversion theology and soteriology and conversion-oriented and reformation-centered Indian ministry.

30. Calvin, *Institutes of the Christian Religion*, II.i.5–8; II.iii.1; III.iii.9; III.xi. Calvin, *Commentaries*, I.26; III.6. Calvin, *The Bondage and Liberation of the Will*, 3.306; 5.350–54; 6.381.

31. Calvin, *Inst.*, III.iii.5.

puritans understood conversion as a total ontological change and the submission of one's whole being to God. Shepard argued that if someone is converted and accepts Christ:

> First. Give away thyself to him, head, heart, tongue, body, soul, and he will give away himself unto thee [Cant. Vi.3;]. . . . Secondly. Give away all thy sins to Christ . . . so as to receive power from him to forsake them. . . . Thirdly. Give away thine honor, pleasure, profit, life, for him; . . . Fourthly. Give away thy rags, forsake thine own righteousness, for him.[32]

Likewise, Baxter agreed that conversion is the whole change of a person's inner world along with their outer world in action. Baxter argued that conversion is

> to break the heart for sin, and make him flee for refuge unto Christ, and thankfully embrace him as the life of his soul: to have the very drift and bent of the heart and life to be changed. . . . He has a new understanding, a new will and resolution, new sorrows, and desires, and love and delight; new thoughts, new speeches, new company, if possible, and a new conversation.[33]

This understanding of conversion tells us that for puritans, conversion was actual and experiential rather than mere intellectual acceptance. The empirical understanding of conversion is related to the experimental nature of puritan theology, which is particularly found in William Perkins and William Ames.[34] The puritan experiential understanding of conversion and theology, and the importance of personal religious experiences in the

---

32. Shepard, *The Sincere Convert* (1640), 52.
33. Baxter, *A Call to the Unconverted* (1658), 17, 55–56.
34. Hambrick-Stowe, *The Practice of Piety*, 3; Hambrick-Stowe, "III. Puritan Spirituality in America," 304. Jinkins, "Perkins, William." William Perkins has been regarded as a puritan who "uniquely combined Continental Reformed theology with the indigenous tradition of English practical divinity and preaching." Hindmarsh, *The Evangelical Conversion Narrative*, 35. See also Tipson, "The Development of a Puritan Understanding of Conversion," 189–261; Pettit, *The Heart Prepared*, 62–65. For the mutual relationship between reformations on the European continent and in Britain, the following recent book gives significant resources. Ha and Collinson, *The Reception of Continental Reformation in Britain*. Sprunger, "Ames, William." Williams Ames's emphasis on empirical nature is found in his definition of theology in *Medulla theologica* (*The Marrow of Theology*) (1623). "Theology is the doctrine or teaching [*doctrina*] of living to God. . . . Since the highest kind of life for a human being is that which approaches most closely the living and life-giving God, the nature of theological life is living to God." Ames, *The Marrow of Theology* (1623), 77. *Medulla theologica* was translated as *The Marrow of Sacred Divinity* in English in 1643.

puritan faith, led to a strong emphasis on "intensity" and "inwardness."[35] For puritans, the emphasis on "inwardness" was important in their pursuit of conversion. Puritans initially seemed concerned for the human inner and spiritual situation, while focusing on external change and visibility as a result of conversion. Shepard's reference to sin of heart is a good example: "Sin is more abundantly in the heart than in the life. . . . Every actual sin is but as a shred broken off from the great bottom of sin in the heart."[36] This understanding also can be a significant example showing the puritan focus on inward experience in conversion theology.

So, what was the relationship between conversion and salvation for puritans? For Baxter, conversion is required for salvation and should be experienced first. He argued, "God has two degrees of mercy to show: the mercy of conversion first; and the mercy of salvation last" and "Indeed, if you will needs [sic] believe that you shall be saved without conversion, then you believe a falsehood."[37] Although puritans had a Calvinist understanding of predestination and God's absolute sovereignty over salvation, and acknowledged the impossibility of discerning whether someone is saved or not based on Calvin, for them conversion was perceived as an important measure for discerning human salvation.[38] For puritans, just belonging outwardly to the church was not enough to discern someone's possibility of salvation. Regardless of church involvement, puritans considered true conversion to be the most important issue. In this sense, puritan pastors were extremely concerned about the true conversion of their parishioners, because for them, "true" and "sound" conversion signified true Christians.[39]

Puritans explained the meaning of conversion or being "converted" especially through analysis of the difference between the "converted" and "unconverted," because they believed that true conversion could be discerned by certain visible and invisible signs or effects of faith.[40] The fact that an extreme antithesis between "converted" and "unconverted" commonly appeared in puritan devotional writings indicates their strong desire for the conversion of the unconverted. For puritans, the results of conversion were described as "salvation," "blessedness," "glory," "the kingdom of joy," and

---

35. Hambrick-Stowe, *The Practice of Piety*, 53; Hambrick-Stowe, "III. Puritan Spirituality in America," 306.

36. Shepard, *The Sincere Convert* (1640), 30.

37. Baxter, *A Call to the Unconverted* (1658), 23, 49.

38. Calvin, *Inst.*, III.xxi.1–2.

39. Baxter, *A Call to the Unconverted* (1658), 2, 6, 9, 17.

40. Shepard, *The Sincere Convert* (1640), 65–68, 77–78, 82–87; Baxter, *A Call to the Unconverted* (1658), 16–21; Hambrick-Stowe, "III. Puritan Spirituality in America," 304.

"peace with God."[41] Puritans called the unconverted "wicked" and "sinners" and said that they are in "the state of corrupted nature," "a state of death," and "a lamentable condition." In sinful life they are enslaved to their fleshly desires under the guilt of their sins and the wrath of God, and they justly deserve God's judgment and hell.[42] The more miserable the unconverted are, the more urgent it is for them to be converted in the minds of the puritans. This dialectical and paradoxical discourse can originally be found in Calvin. Calvin's definition of the corruption of human beings is that through sin, human beings have lost the image of God and of noble things that they already had. The depravity of human beings can be compared to the original condition as Calvin depicts the two conditions of human beings before and after the Fall and compares and contrasts them. These two aspects are on the one hand contradictory, but on the other hand they support each other. The emphasis on the human being's nobility paradoxically emphasizes his corruption, and vice versa. Calvin's strong emphasis on human beings' total depravity is not for its own sake, but its real purpose is the paradoxical emphasis on human being's nobility.[43] Roy W. Battenhouse says that, "anyone who examines Calvin's celebrated pessimism regarding man must realize that it reflects, actually, a most optimistic view of what man ought to be."[44] Francois Wendel says, "the weaker men had been, even before the Fall, the more disastrous was the condition of mankind after having sinned, and the more Calvin could magnify the immensity of the grace which had made their regeneration possible."[45] The more misery there is in human beings, the more Calvin accentuates human beings' original nobility. Likewise, for puritans, the stress on the hopeless miserable condition of the unconverted was the main reason for calling upon the ungodly to receive the gospel: "We must tell you of the wrath that is on you already, and the death that you are born under, for the breach of the law of works; but this is only to show you the need of mercy, and provoke you to esteem the grace of the Redeemer."[46] Shepard also said, "here is a matter of terror to all those that be of opinion

---

41. Baxter, *A Call to the Unconverted* (1658), 4, 17, 18, 56; Bayly, *The Practice of Piety* (2nd ed., 1612), 124–25.

42. Bayly, *The Practice of Piety* (2nd ed., 1612), 4, 28, 53, 95, 102, 122, 397; Baxter, *The Reformed Pastor* (1656), 94, 196, 245–46; Baxter, *A Call to the Unconverted* (1658), 2, 3, 6, 12–13, 15–17, 38, 44, 54–55. For Shepard's description of sin and the result of sin, see Shepard, *The Sincere Convert* (1640), 24–45.

43. Calvin, *Inst.*, I.xv.1–8; II.i.1–11.

44. Battenhouse, "The Doctrine of Man," 170.

45. Wendel, *Calvin*, 187.

46. Baxter, *A Call to the Unconverted* (1658), 21. See Baxter, *A Call to the Unconverted* (1658), 11–13.

that few shall be saved; and therefore, when they are convinced of the danger of sin by the word, they fly to this shelter."[47]

Puritans who proclaimed the need for conversion focused on how to be converted and saved. Puritans never de-emphasized God's sovereignty on conversion and Christ as the only means of redemption. Baxter said:

> [Y]ou must further know, that the mercy of God . . . provided a remedy, by causing his Son to take our nature, and being in one person God and man, to become a Mediator between God and man . . . but Christ has made a law of grace, or a promise or pardon, and everlasting life to all that by true repentance, and by faith in Christ, are converted unto God.[48]

For puritans, God who has sovereignty over salvation is also the one who now calls the unconverted. Baxter said, "I beseech you, I charge you, to hear and obey the Call of God, and resolvedly to turn, that you may live."[49] Puritans' description of the antithesis between death and life as the result of "converted" and "unconverted" signifies God's sincere calling to the unconverted: "You must ere long be converted or condemned, there is no other way but turn or die."[50]

However, interestingly, puritans seem to allow human beings to participate in conversion work, demonstrating that God's calling is a quest for human responsibility.[51] Although puritans were strongly based in Reformed theology on God's sovereignty and the total inability of human beings to achieve salvation, they seemed to acknowledge the necessity of

---

47. Shepard, *The Sincere Convert* (1640), 58.

48. Baxter, *A Call to the Unconverted* (1658), 15. See Baxter, *The Reformed Pastor* (1656), 188; Baxter, *A Call to the Unconverted* (1658), 6, 16, 21, 24; Shepard, *The Sincere Convert* (1640), 46, 101.

49. Baxter, *A Call to the Unconverted* (1658), 8. See Baxter, *A Call to the Unconverted* (1658), 3, 12, 29–30, 32; Shepard, *The Sincere Convert* (1640), 43.

50. Baxter, *A Call to the Unconverted* (1658), 13, 14.

51. Rohr has investigated the puritan understanding of the relationship between God's sovereignty on salvation and human responsibility. Rohr, who indicated puritans' strong belief in God's sovereignty on salvation, argued for "ultimate human destiny as divinely and unconditionally determined by God's eternal decree," as well as human accountability in "voluntarism inherent in Protestantism's call for faith and obedience as the believer's response to God's proclaimed Word." According to Rohr, for puritans, the notion of covenant of grace reconciled the tension in both directions. In other words, although only grace saves, a human being must receive the grace through his faith, and he is called upon to respond to grace in his faith and obedience. Rohr, *The Covenant of Grace in Puritan Thought*. See also Rohr, "Covenant and Assurance in Early English Puritanism," 195–203. Wallace also provided an essential research on Reformed doctrine of grace and predestination in puritans. Wallace, *Puritans and Predestination*.

human response toward God's calling of conversion.[52] For puritans, God's strong calling to the unconverted is asking for their immediate response to God's calling. A pastor's calling such as "Turn ye, turn ye; why will ye die?"[53] is a strong request for human response and action. That is to say that God's call for conversion is asking for voluntary determination by human beings with the use of human free will.[54] Baxter emphasized human will: "O poor sinners! It is a joyfuller life than this that you might live, if you were but willing, but truly willing to hearken to Christ and come home to God."[55] Baxter also said, "You may be condemned against your wills, because you sinned with your wills; but you cannot be saved against your wills. The wisdom of God has thought it meet to lay men's salvation or destruction exceedingly much upon the choice of their own wills."[56] Baxter argued that the principal cause of human corruption is not God, but human beings themselves.[57] In the same way, Baxter argued, if they were condemned, it was not because of "want of a call to turn and live, but because you will not believe and obey it."[58] In other words, for Baxter, human beings' disability is their "very unwillingness itself, which excuses not your sin, but makes it the greater." The greatest enemy to human beings is themselves, their own carnal hearts and wills.[59] Like Baxter, Bayly acknowledged the positive use of free will, especially of regenerated Christians, and urged them to use their will to practice good works and piety: "But as soon as a Man is regenerated, the grace of God freeth his will unto good, so that he doth all the good things he doth with a free-will: For so the Apostle saith, That God of his own good pleasure, worketh both the will and the deed in us. . . . And in this state every true Christian hath free-will."[60]

In addition to the use of free will, puritans acknowledged the positive use of means of grace.[61] Baxter strongly demonstrated the use of means of

52. Pettit, *The Heart Prepared*, chs. 3–4.

53. Baxter, *A Call to the Unconverted* (1658), 12, 29–30.

54. Baxter, *A Call to the Unconverted* (1658), 34; Shepard, *The Sincere Convert* (1640), 54–55.

55. Baxter, *A Call to the Unconverted* (1658), 4. See Baxter, *A Call to the Unconverted* (1658), 8.

56. Baxter, *A Call to the Unconverted* (1658), 54. See Baxter, *A Call to the Unconverted* (1658), 21–22, 31, 35, 37, 49.

57. Baxter, *A Call to the Unconverted* (1658), 10, 51, 53.

58. Baxter, *A Call to the Unconverted* (1658), 8.

59. Baxter, *A Call to the Unconverted* (1658), 49–50.

60. Bayly, *The Practice of Piety* (2nd ed., 1612), 112.

61. For the understanding of means of grace in Reformed tradition, see Rice, *Reformed Spirituality*, 187–99.

grace for conversion.⁶² The puritan understanding of the means of conversion can be found in God's calling in various ways. God's calling comes to the unconverted through various means: "every leaf of the blessed book of God. . . . It is the voice of every sermon. . . . It is the voice of many a motion of the Spirit. . . . It is the voice of your conscience. . . . It is the voice of the gracious examples of the godly. . . . It is the voice of all the works of God."⁶³ Bayly was against the argument for the meaninglessness of human will, efforts, and the use of means of grace because of "God's eternal predestination, and unchangeable Degree." He argued:

> [B]ut he should learn, that God hath predestinated to the means, as well as to the end. . . . If therefore upon thy calling thou conformest thy self to the Word and Example of Christ thy Master, and obeyest the good motions of the Holy Spirit, in leaving sin, and living a godly life; then assure thy self, that thou art one of those who are infallibly predestinated to everlasting salvation.⁶⁴

Likewise, Baxter argued that "you have the more cause to seek for that grace, and yield to it, and do what you can in the use of means, and not neglect it or set against it."⁶⁵ However, he never forgot God's initiative on conversion: "but we cannot convert ourselves till God converts us: we can do nothing without his grace."⁶⁶

The importance of the use of means of grace can be found in the relationship between stages of conversion, "morphology of conversion" or "pattern of regeneration," and the means of grace.⁶⁷ Based on the basic understanding of conversion, puritans provided a more concrete and systemized description of a standardized progression of conversion, known as *ordo salutis*, which was originally demonstrated by William Perkins, based on Calvin's thoughts.⁶⁸ In short, when human beings go towards

---

62. Baxter, *The Reformed Pastor* (1656), 252–53.

63. Baxter, *A Call to the Unconverted* (1658), 32–33.

64. Bayly, *The Practice of Piety* (2nd ed., 1612), 108–10.

65. Baxter, *A Call to the Unconverted* (1658), 49.

66. Baxter, *A Call to the Unconverted* (1658), 49. See Baxter, *A Call to the Unconverted* (1658), 6.

67. Pettit, *The Heart Prepared*, 7; Morgan, *Visible Saints*, 66.

68. Perkins, *Workes* (1608–31), 1:353–420, 635–44; 2:13. Ames, *Conscience with the Power and Cases thereof* (1643), Book II, in *Workes* (1643), cited in Morgan, *Visible Saints*, 66. As mentioned above, Shepard provided four stages of conversion. Shepard, *The Sound Believer* (1645), 115–37. However, in fact, not all puritans agreed with the "morphology of conversion." Baxter, in *Reliquiae Baxterianae* (1696), said, "Because I could not distinctly trace the workings of the Spirit upon my heart in that method which Mr. Bolton, Mr. Hooker, Mr. Rogers and other divines describe! nor knew the

conversion, at the preparatory stages, they initially experience inner contrition and humiliation with fear and terrors due to their sins, through stirring up of their heart led by the Holy Spirit. The use of means of grace is significant in order to open up and prepare their heart to receive God's grace. This understanding is conceptualized as the preparation of the heart for the grace of God.[69] This idea can be found in the puritans' arguments for self-examination and repentance in the process of conversion. Shepard emphasized self-examination as a preparation and a means of grace for conversion. Shepard's strong argument for self-examination was closely related to Antinomian controversy between 1636 and 1638 in New England. Shepard showed strong antagonism toward Antinomianism, which had been raised by Antinomianists such as Anne Hutchinson in 1630s.[70] The Antinomian controversy was related to the question of how believers might know if they were saved (or not). Orthodox opinion in New England was that believers can be changed through grace, and visible godly works would be signs of the change. However, others argued that this understanding was leading believers to be bound to works and laws for gaining assurance. The ideological difference between John Cotton and Thomas Shepard shows the key controversial issues in the Antinomian controversy. John Cotton argued that assurance of salvation can be known to believers instantly through a direct revelation from the Holy Spirit. The key antinomian figures following John Cotton's ideas—Anne Hutchinson, her brother-in-law the minister John Wheelwright, and the young aristocrat Sir Henry Vane, who had been elected as the colony's Governor in 1636—argued for "free grace" and direct revelation of the Holy Spirit, through which believers can have the assurance of salvation, and denigrated the role of work and law and sanctification as visible signs of grace. However, Shepard, who was strongly against Antinomianism, argued for believers' intense personal discipline and self-examination to prepare their hearts to receive the grace of God, and find

---

time of my conversion, being wrought on by the forementioned degrees. But since then I understood that the soul is in too dark and passionate a plight at first to be able to keep an exact account of the order of its own operations; and that preparatory Grace being sometimes longer and sometimes shorter." Baxter, *Reliquiae Baxterianae* (1696), 6.

69. Pettit, *The Heart Prepared*. On this, the puritans went beyond Calvin, who did not have the conception of preparation of heart to receive the grace of God and did not argue for the possibility of preparation of heart before the grace of God based on his strict demonstration on the absolute sovereignty of God and God's initiative in salvation. Pettit, *The Heart Prepared*, 39–44. For various theological discourses of continental reformers on the "preparation" which influenced puritan ideas, see Pettit, *The Heart Prepared*, 22–47.

70. Caldwell, *The Puritan Conversion Narrative*, 141.

godliness in their everyday life, as the sign of the grace through which they could confirm assurance of salvation.[71]

When he explained self-examination, Shepard considered "conviction of sin" and "compunction of sin" as the first and second acts of "a fourfold act of Christ's power in rescuing and delivering men out of their miserable state." This fourfold act played out as the four stages of conversion: "conviction of sin," "compunction of sin," "humiliation," and "faith."[72] For Shepard, "conviction of sin" was "the work of the understanding" and "compunction of sin" was the "sense and feeling of sin." He argued that "faith is wrought in us in that way of conviction and sorrow for sin" and "conviction which the Spirit works in the elect is ever accompanied with compunction, first or last."[73] Baxter beseeched his flock to examine themselves: "enter into an earnest search of your hearts, and say to yourselves, is it so indeed; must I turn or die? Must I be converted or condemned?"[74] During the preparatory stages, human beings experience continuous inner conflict and affliction related to despair, fear, and uncertainty of salvation. According to McGiffert, the puritans' concern for self-examination was crucially related to their serious and continuous doubts about the assurance of salvation.[75] Puritans experienced serious conflict between assurance and anxiety in seeking conversion. Interestingly, Shepard understood that the conflict was normal and could be solved through the dialectical and paradoxical relationship between assurance and anxiety. That is to say that assurance and anxiety are interrelated. If there is more anxiety, believers can experience more assurance.[76] Throughout the whole experience, they finally become ready to receive the grace of God and go towards the implantation of Christ in them. The implantation of Christ is also part of the ultimate salvation process. In

---

71. Hall, *The Antinomian Controversy*, 3–23; Bozeman, *The Precisianist Strain*, 211–331; Hardman Moore, *Pilgrims*, 6–7; Bremer, "The Puritan Experiment in New England," 134–36. Winship, "Hutchinson, Anne"; Winship, "Wheelwright, John"; Mayers, "Vane, Sir Henry, the Younger." John Cotton, in fact, was not considered as an Antinomian, but his ideas which were different from orthodox party were the key issues of Antinomian controversy. Hall, *The Antinomian Controversy*, 4. John Eliot and Thomas Weld, who served together as Roxbury's ministers, volunteered to testify against Hutchinson. Hardman Moore, *Pilgrims*, 7. For Antinomianism, see also Winship, *Making Heretics*; Como, *Blown by the Spirit*.

72. Shepard, *The Sound Believer* (1645), 115–237.

73. Shepard, *The Sound Believer* (1645), 117, 136; Pettit, *The Heart Prepared*, 18, 108–9.

74. Baxter, *A Call to the Unconverted* (1658), 20.

75. McGiffert, *God's Plot*, 10–12; Pettit, *The Heart Prepared*, 17; Morgan, *Visible Saints*, 70–71; Rohr, *The Covenant of Grace in Puritan Thought*, 170–74.

76. McGiffert, *God's Plot*, 19–26.

this sense, for puritans, their life in the world is the process of salvation, and their continuous practice of piety in their whole life is a significant means of grace towards the salvation of God.[77] Here, we can find an important relationship in puritan thought between the use of the means of grace and human responsibility. Shepard offered a puritan understanding of the relationship between salvation and the means of grace. Shepard strongly demonstrated salvation only through Christ[78] and the insufficiency of human duties.[79] Yet, Shepard acknowledged that salvation is not through religious duties, but through the means, so that people can be led to Christ as the fundamental cause of redemption. Shepard argued that this was different from Roman Catholic soteriology, which required human duties as a means of salvation.[80] Therefore, Shepard encouraged the use of the means of grace:

> Though thy good duties cannot save thee, yet thy bad works will damn thee. Thou art, therefore, not to cast off the duties, but the resting in these duties. Thou art not to cast them away, but to cast them down at the feet of Jesus Christ . . . hear a sermon to carry thee to Jesus Christ; fast and pray, and get a full tide of affections in them to carry thee to the Lord Jesus Christ. . . . Use duties as evidences of God's everlasting love to you when you be in Christ.[81]

For Shepard, the practice of the means of grace may honor God and the Lord Jesus Christ, although the means cannot save souls.[82] Puritans' stress on the use of the means of grace as a responsibility of human beings for salvation was related to their discourse on the harmony between God's initiative in conversion and human participation. Baxter argued that "you must know by what you must turn: and that is, by Christ as the only Redeemer and Intercessor; and by the Holy Ghost as the Sanctifier; and by his word as his instrument or means; and by faith and repentance as the means and duties, on your part to be performed. All this is of necessity."[83]

In addition, for puritans, the relationship between the use of means of grace and God's salvation is related to their ideas on predestination in relation to salvation. It seems that Baxter was more focused on the possibility of salvation rather than on the possibility of abandonment, while still

---

77. Hambrick-Stowe, "III. Puritan Spirituality in America," 303–4, 340–41.
78. Shepard, *The Sincere Convert* (1640), 101.
79. Shepard, *The Sincere Convert* (1640), 104.
80. Shepard, *The Sincere Convert* (1640), 99.
81. Shepard, *The Sincere Convert* (1640), 105–6.
82. Shepard, *The Sincere Convert* (1640), 107.
83. Baxter, *A Call to the Unconverted* (1658), 56.

acknowledging God's sovereignty: "We have indeed also a message of wrath and death, yea of a twofold wrath and death; but neither of them is our principal message."[84] God "takes no pleasure in the death of the wicked, but wants them to turn and live."[85] For Baxter, everyone who responds and accepts God's calling can be converted and can go to the way of salvation: "But if you will turn and come into the way of mercy, the mercy of the Lord is ready to entertain you. . . . But if they will not come in, it is owing to themselves. His doors are open; he keeps none back: he never sent such a message as this to any of you."[86] In this sense, the most important issue for Baxter is "converted or not" rather than "predestined or not." It is also worth considering Shepard's thoughts on this topic. Shepard's answer to the question about whether redemption is only appointed for some or it is not intended for all was that "though Christ be not intended for all, yet he is offered unto all, and therefore unto thee."[87] Shepard called the offer of Christ for all "the universal offer of Christ" and said that the offer was not from "Christ's priestly office immediately, but from his kingly office," which was given by the Father giving Christ all power and dominion in heaven and earth to command all men to gather unto him and "to go and preach the gospel to every creature under heaven [Matt. xxviii.18, 19]."[88] For Shepard, therefore "the Lord Jesus is offered to every particular person."[89] Here, once again, the key issue is not whether the person was predestined as one of the elect or not, but whether the person would determine to accept God's calling or not. Bayly also argued that God's power of salvation is for everyone who believes, while acknowledging "the preaching of the Gospel is the chief ordinary means" for the conversion of the souls predestined to be saved by God.[90] For Baxter, God's door of salvation is open to anybody who is converted:

> [T]hink not to extenuate it by saying, that it was only for his elect; for it was your sin, and the sin of all the world, that lay upon our Redeemer; and his sacrifice and satisfaction are sufficient for all, and the fruits of it are offered to one as well as another; but it is

---

84. Baxter, *A Call to the Unconverted* (1658), 21.

85. Baxter, *A Call to the Unconverted* (1658), 25. See Baxter, *A Call to the Unconverted* (1658), 27.

86. Baxter, *A Call to the Unconverted* (1658), 23. See Baxter, *A Call to the Unconverted* (1658), 22.

87. Shepard, *The Sincere Convert* (1640), 49.

88. Shepard, *The Sincere Convert* (1640), 49.

89. Shepard, *The Sincere Convert* (1640), 49, 50.

90. Bayly, *The Practice of Piety* (2nd ed., 1612), 116.

true, that it was never the intent of his mind to pardon and save any that would not by faith and repentance be converted.[91]

In this sense, for puritans, human beings should not give up their efforts and should undertake responsibility to respond and accept God's calling for conversion and salvation, because nobody knows who is predestined and who will be converted.[92] For puritans, human beings' responsibility is to desire and take actions for redemption given by God: "If I was willing to receive Christ, I might have Christ offered to me; but will the Lord offer him to such a one as desires not to have Christ? . . . God can make us a willing people."[93] Therefore, puritans demonstrated the preaching of the gospel to everybody. Baxter said, "Sure I am, it is most like to the spirit, and precept, and offers of the gospel, which requireth us to preach Christ to every creature, and promiseth life to every man, if he will accept it by believing."[94]

In sum, although puritans like Shepard and Baxter believed in God's sovereignty and predestination, signifying God's initiative in redemption, they still considered human responsibility and response towards conversion and salvation to be important. This does not mean that salvation depends on human beings, but it does demonstrate the significance of human desire and response to God's calling for human salvation. In conversion and salvation, puritans emphasized positivism, arguing for the importance of human responsibility, rather than negativism, which is based on passivity and inability from the assumption of predestined destiny.

Conversion, Ministry, and Reformation

The puritans' concern about conversion reflects the poor ministerial conditions in seventeenth-century Britain. The urgent ministerial problems were a serious lack of ministers, their lack of training, and the perceived ignorance and immorality of parishioners. The persistence of "popish customs" in each area was also an issue in the seventeenth century. This phenomenon was severe in "the dark corners of the land" as remote and isolated places, particularly in the western and northern parts of Britain.[95] Baxter describes the poor situation of pastoral ministry in his youth:

91. Baxter, *A Call to the Unconverted* (1658), 26. See Baxter, *A Call to the Unconverted* (1658), 23, 27.

92. Shepard, *The Sincere Convert* (1640), 54.

93. Shepard, *The Sincere Convert* (1640), 51.

94. Baxter, *The Reformed Pastor* (1656), 188.

95. Hill, *Change and Continuity in Seventeenth-Century England*, 6–9, 18; Collinson, *The Elizabethan Puritan Movement*, 128.

> We lived in a country that had but little preaching at all. In the village where I was born there were four readers successively in six years time, ignorant men, and two of them immoral in their lives, who were all my schoolmasters. In the village where my father lived there was a reader of about eighty years of age that never preached, and had two churches about twenty miles distant.[96]

Baxter criticized the serious ministerial inability and lack of qualification of his contemporary church and ministers for the reformation of church and ministry.[97] For him, the ministry of his contemporary church was "unreformed" and "corrupted ministry."[98] This led to pastoral neglect of the "unconverted," or "old, ignorant, dead-hearted sinners," as Baxter put it.[99] For puritans, the reformation of ministry meant the urgent pursuit of converting the unconverted. Considering the poor pastoral situation of the seventeenth century, "the salvation of souls" was the fundamental purpose of ministry, and in this sense, puritan ministry was a conversion-centered ministry: "The ministerial work must be carried on purely for God and the salvation of souls, not for any private ends of our own."[100] Puritans understood that ministers were sent by God to call to the unconverted and proclaim the gospel for the saving of souls.[101] Therefore, a pastor's chief duty was the conversion of the unconverted through ministerial means, especially the preaching of the gospel.[102]

For puritans, their conversion-centered ministry was ultimately pursuing the reformation of church and society. Puritans considered conversion to be the fundamental element for the accomplishment of reformation, because reformation is not about the change of visible forms, but the fundamental existential change of human beings:

> Alas! can we think that the reformation is wrought, when we cast out a few ceremonies, and changed some vestures, and gestures, and forms! Oh no, sirs! It is the converting and saving of souls that is our business. That is the chiefest part of reformation,

---

96. Baxter, *Reliquiae Baxterianae* (1696), 1.
97. Baxter, *The Reformed Pastor* (1656), 46, 54, 70–71, 136.
98. Baxter, *The Reformed Pastor* (1656), 136.
99. Baxter, *The Reformed Pastor* (1656), 46.
100. Baxter, *The Reformed Pastor* (1656), 111.
101. Baxter, *A Call to the Unconverted* (1658), 45. See Baxter, *The Reformed Pastor* (1656), 112, 175–76.
102. Baxter, *A Call to the Unconverted* (1658), 2. See Shepard, *The Sincere Convert* (1640), 44.

that doth most good, and tendeth most to the salvation of the people.[103]

The reformation that puritans pursued was not only about personal and ecclesiastical godliness, but also concerned the holiness of all towns and nations. Baxter's vivid description tells us about his vision of the reformation of church and society:

> One would have thought that, after all this light . . . the people of this nation should have joined together as one man, to turn to the Lord, and should have come to their godly teacher and lamented all their former sins, and desired him to join with them, in public humiliation, to confess them openly, and beg pardon of them from the God . . . there should not be an ungodly person left among us, nor a worldling, nor a drunkard, or a hater of reformation, or an enemy to holiness, to be found in all our towns and countries.[104]

This reference reflects the "reformation of manners" which was a puritan campaign from the late sixteenth-century to mid-seventeenth-century ("Manners" here means "morality" and personal behaviour rather than politeness.). The main target of this "reformation" was swearing, drunkenness, alehouse-haunting, idleness, sexual immorality, absence from church, dancing, football, sports, and other pastimes on a Sunday afternoon, particularly among the poor, the young, and the marginal, and particularly in "the dark corners of the land" signifying the northern and western regions of Britain. This puritan campaign led not only by ministers but also magistrates, was pursued through various educational means based on puritans' religious and social standards. For puritans, the moral devastation was related to serious ministerial desolation as mentioned above. In this sense, for puritans, among educational tools, a conversion-oriented and preaching-centered pastoral ministry was a significant means for the "reformation of manners."[105] Puritans believed that reformation could be accomplished through their pastoral ministry based on the preaching and propagation of the gospel as the key

---

103. Baxter, *The Reformed Pastor* (1656), 211.
104. Baxter, *A Call to the Unconverted* (1658), 5.
105. Hill, *Change and Continuity in Seventeenth-Century England*, 3–47; Collinson, *The Religion of Protestants*, 220–41; Wrightson, "The Puritan Reformation of Manners,"; Wrightson, *English Society 1580–1680*, 183–221; Ingram, "Reformation of Manners in Early Modern England," 47–88; Webster, "Early Stuart Puritanism," 53–54; Walsham, "The Godly and Popular Culture," 279–82. See also Wrightson and Levine, *Poverty and Piety in an English Village*.

task of their ministry.[106] Through Word-centered pastoral teaching, puritans aimed for the conversion of the unconverted in their own parishes, and through the conversion of their "flock," they ultimately pursued the reformation of the church and society. Also, for puritans, catechizing and personal instruction as key elements of pastoral teaching were ultimately related to reformation. Baxter argued that catechizing and personal instruction were not only "the chief part of Church reformation," but also "the chief means" of the reformation.[107] Baxter demonstrated that "The design of this work is, the reforming and saving of all the people in our several parishes. For we shall not leave out any man that will submit to be instructed; and though we can scarcely hope that every individual will be reformed and saved by it."[108] Also, for puritans, the practice of piety was ultimately to seek reformation. As conversion and pastoral teachings were significant foundations and crucial means of reformation, puritans pursued the purity of the Christian faith through the reformed practice of piety.[109] For puritans, the purity of the Christian faith meant not only the "simplicity," but also the "pristine purity" of the purely biblical ancient church.[110] Bayly, for instance, argued for the prayer that was practiced by zealously devotional Christians in the primitive church: "Call to mind the zealous devotions of the Christians in the Primitive Church, who spent many whole nights and vigils in watching and praying for the forgiveness of their sins; and that they might be found ready at the coming of Christ."[111] For puritans, Christian purity was the value of the reformation of church and society, based on Reformed tradition. Puritan piety was strongly based on Reformation theology and Biblicism, which was distinguishable from the Roman Catholic understanding of spirituality, despite some of the similarities in style.[112] In this sense, the reformed practice of piety was not only the expression of the puritan Christian faith, but also a serious effort to achieve a pure Christianity and church. In sum, for puritans, conversion was not only the fundamental ministerial concern, but also the

---

106. Black, *Reformation Pastors*, 51, 105.

107. Baxter, *The Reformed Pastor* (1656), 189.

108. Baxter, *The Reformed Pastor* (1656), 188. See Baxter, *The Reformed Pastor* (1656), 175, 190.

109. Davies, *The Worship of the American Puritans*.

110. Baxter, *The Reformed Pastor* (1656), 123, 162; Davies, *The Worship of the American Puritans*, 1–2.

111. Bayly, *The Practice of Piety* (2nd ed., 1612), 155.

112. Hambrick-Stowe, *The Practice of Piety*, 43; Hambrick-Stowe, "III. Puritan Spirituality in America," 301; Davies, *The Worship of the American Puritans*, 17–18. For the relationship between puritan piety and Catholic spirituality, see Hambrick-Stowe, *The Practice of Piety*, 25–39; Hambrick-Stowe, "III. Puritan Spirituality in America," 318–19.

starting point to actualize reformation through the establishment of a pure reformed church and society. Furthermore, for puritans, their faithful pastoral ministry, seeking the conversion of the unconverted, was an essential means of reformation. Baxter, in *A Call to the Unconverted* (1658), explicitly showed his ultimate ministerial aim for churches—the conversion of the "unconverted," that is, the reformation of the church.[113]

The significance of the puritan understanding of conversion-oriented and reformation-centered ministry emerges when we consider Eliot's application of the puritan traditions to his Indian ministry. In the next sections, we will discuss key elements of puritan pastoral ministry in detail.

Puritan Ministry and Pastoral Teaching and Care

This section will focus on puritan pastoral teaching and care as the core ministerial task and duty. Eliot's pastoral practice to the Indians was based on puritan traditions. The understanding of seventeenth-century puritan pastoral teaching and care which will be discussed in this section will provide an essential background to understand Eliot's pastoral teaching and care for the Indians.[114]

Puritan Pastoral Teaching and the Word of God

Puritans acknowledged that fundamentally ministry is operated by God through the Holy Spirit. At the same time, they argued the importance of the means of ministry and urged the proper use of it. Baxter demonstrated:

> [A]nd though I know that we have a knotty generation to deal with, and that it is past the power of any of us to change a carnal heart without the effectual operation of the Holy Ghost; yet it is so usual with God to work by means, and to bless the right endeavours of his servants, that I cannot fear but great things will be accomplished.[115]

For puritans, the most important means of ministry was pastoral teaching focused on the Word of God, because the proclamation of the Word was crucially related to conversion.[116] The teaching of the Word meant not

---

113. Baxter, "Preface," in *A Call to the Unconverted* (1658).

114. For Eliot's pastoral teaching and care, see pp. 159–78 below.

115. Baxter, *The Reformed Pastor* (1656), 231. See Baxter, *The Reformed Pastor* (1656), 43, 129–30.

116. Baxter, *The Reformed Pastor* (1656), 120–21, 178; Bayly, *The Practice of Piety* (2nd ed., 1612), 116.

only the Bible itself, but also "truths of religion," "principles of religion," or "grounds of Christian Religions" as the right Christian doctrines based on the Bible.[117]

Puritans' emphasis on the role of ministers as teachers of God's Word came from their perception that contemporaries neglected the Word; they severely criticized this as "corrupted ministry."[118] For puritans, one of the most serious problems was the ignorance of the flock from want of faithful ministers to teach rightly. Shepard lamented that "there is no faithful minister, no compassionate Lot, to tell them of fire and brimstone from heaven for their crying sins; . . . they have either no minister at all to teach them, either because the parish is too poor, or the church living too great to maintain a faithful man."[119]

Pastoral teaching was basically for the unconverted, because the teaching of the Word was primary pursuing conversion and salvation.[120] However, in puritan ministry, the converted were also very important objects of pastoral teaching. Baxter cited the various kinds of parishioners who needed pastoral teaching as the following: "the young and weak," "those who labour under some particular corruption," "the declining Christians" and "the strong."[121] This indicates the fact that puritan pastors tried to implement continuous pastoral teaching for various kinds of parishioners.

Among the various ways of pastoral teaching, preaching was the primary ministerial task.[122] The recognition of the importance of preaching the gospel since the Reformation began in sixteenth-century continental Europe is significant for understanding puritan ministry. For zealous protestant preachers, the propagation of the gospel was the most important ministerial task.[123] John Cotton argued, "How shall men (ordinarily) be

117. Baxter, *The Reformed Pastor* (1656), 42, 113; Bayly, *The Practice of Piety* (2nd ed., 1612), 118; See Baxter, *A Call to the Unconverted* (1658), 4. Bayly, Baxter, and Shepard commonly considered the knowledge of God and man and doctrinal issues as key topics for pastoral teaching. Bayly, *The Practice of Piety* (2nd ed., 1612), 1-104. For Bayly, one of the hindrances of piety was the misunderstanding of the Scripture and doctrines: Bayly, *The Practice of Piety* (2nd ed., 1612), 118.

118. Baxter, *The Reformed Pastor* (1656), 136.

119. Shepard, *The Sincere Convert* (1640), 69-70. See Baxter, *The Reformed Pastor* (1656), 200. See also Morgan, *Visible Saints*, 7.

120. Davies, *The Worship of the American Puritans*, 81-82.

121. Baxter, *The Reformed Pastor* (1656), 97-100. See Baxter, *A Call to the Unconverted* (1658), 9.

122. Baxter, *The Reformed Pastor* (1656), 196.

123. Ford, "Preaching in the Reformed Tradition," 66-68; Carlson, "The Boring of the Ear," 250-51, 254-60. For the understanding of preaching in the Reformed tradition, see Ford, "Preaching in the Reformed Tradition," 65-88.

converted to the faith without hearing? And how shall they hear without preaching? And how shall they preach, unless they be sent? And who are now sent, but pastors and teachers?"[124] The puritan idea of the propagation of the gospel was closely related to their understanding of ministry and pastorship based on Reformed theology.[125] At the same time, for puritans, their Reformed ministry was the process of reformation. Due to the Reformation in sixteenth-century continental Europe, a new understanding of pastoral ministry and the identity of ministry emerged in England. Although there were similarities between Roman Catholic priests and Protestant pastors in terms of basic ministerial duties, their means and ultimate ends were completely different.[126] For the Roman Catholic Church, the key role of priests was as a mediator between God and humanity in the Mass representing Christ. However, for puritans, under the influence of Reformed theology, the most important ministerial duty was to preach, and their basic role as a minister was to be a preacher.[127] The difference was not about degree, but about kind, because the difference was a fundamental change in theological emphasis from Scripture and tradition to only Scripture as the source of authority.[128] In this sense, the importance of preaching in puritan ministry was crucially related to *sola scriptura* as the quintessence of the Reformed theology, and it was also obligatory for Protestant ministers.[129] Calvin offered a theological basis for the relationship between the Word of God and the obligation of pastors. While he basically considered discipline, administering the sacraments, and warnings and exhortations in church as important duties of pastors, he clearly stated that the propagation of the gospel is the most important and glorious duty.[130] Calvin said that Paul "contends that there is nothing more notable or glorious in the church than the ministry of the gospel, since it is the administration of the Spirit and of righteousness and of eternal life [II Cor.4:6; 3:9.]."[131] Calvin's emphasis on preaching as a pastor's main duty is closely connected to his idea about the Word of God. For Calvin, the Word of God is the absolute authority and standard:

124. Cotton, *The Way of Congregational Way Cleared* (1648), 269.
125. Hall, *The Faithful Shepherd*, 71.
126. Black, *Reformation Pastors*, 22–23.
127. Hall, *The Faithful Shepherd*, 3–20; Webster, *Godly Clergy in Early Stuart England*, 95–121; Black, *Reformation Pastors*, 17–51.
128. Webster, *Godly Clergy in Early Stuart England*, 95–97; Black, *Reformation Pastors*, 23.
129. Hall, *The Faithful Shepherd*, 3–20.
130. Calvin, *Inst.*, IV.iii.4, 6. For Calvin's understanding of preaching, see Parker, *Calvin's Preaching*.
131. Calvin, *Inst.*, IV.iii.3.

> Accordingly, we must here remember that whatever authority and dignity the spirit in Scripture accords to either priests or prophets, or apostles, or successors of apostles, it is wholly given not to the men personally, but to the ministry to which they have been appointed; or (to speak more briefly) to the Word.[132]

Calvin demonstrated that "the only authorized way of teaching in the church is by the prescription and standard of his Word."[133] Based on his special emphasis on the Word of God as the absolute authority, Calvin said that maturity and growth for believers in church comes through the preaching of pastors:

> We see how God, who could in a moment perfect his own, nevertheless desires them to grow up into manhood solely under the education of the church. We see the way set for it: the preaching of the heavenly doctrine has been enjoined upon the pastors. We see that all are brought under the same regulation, that with a gentle and teachable spirit they may allow themselves to be governed by teachers appointed to this function.[134]

For Calvin, preaching was not just propagation of the gospel, but also a crucial means of teaching and instruction of the Word of God:

> So today he not only desires us to be attentive to its reading, but also appoints instructors to help us by their effort. . . . Let us accordingly not in turn dislike to embrace obediently the doctrine of salvation put forth by his command and by his own mouth. For, although God's power is not bound to outward means, he has nonetheless bound us to this ordinary manner of teaching.[135]

In sum, for Calvin, the main duty of pastors is to propagate and teach the Word of God as the absolute authority and standard for believers' faith and life. Through Calvin's ideas, we can discover the original form of the Word-centered and preaching-centered Protestant ministry which significantly

---

132. Calvin, *Inst.*, IV.viii.2.
133. Calvin, *Inst.*, IV.viii.8.
134. Calvin, *Inst.*, IV.i.5.
135. Calvin, *Inst.*, IV.i.5.

influenced puritans.[136] For William Fulke,[137] "the primary pastoral task is to teach people the Bible, or, in biblical terms, to feed the flock of God," and teaching the Bible "is the chiefe & principall office that is in the church."[138] For William Perkins, "the prince of puritan theologians," preaching was the most important duty of pastors.[139] Richard Bernard,[140] in *The Faithfull Shepheard* (1607), which is considered one of the most substantial works for puritan ministry in the sixteenth and seventeenth century, argued that preaching is the fundamental ministerial task and duty of pastors. The entire contents of the book are about the minister as preacher.[141] William Ames also emphasized the preaching of ministers as the key pastoral task, stating that, "Here the preaching of the Word is of utmost importance, and so it has always been of continuous use in the church."[142] Therefore, it is evident that the main difference between pre-and post-Reformation was the emphasis on preaching as the most important task in ministry.[143] The ministry based on Reformed theology that the puritans were pursuing was exclusively focused on preaching. Thus, it could be called "preaching ministry" and ultimately "a pulpit-led reformation,"[144] because, as Hardman Moore indicated, "parish pulpits" were "the way to secure and build up England's Reformation."[145]

Puritans pursued the conversion and salvation of the unconverted or ignorant through a "preaching ministry," because preaching was the most

---

136. The theological and ministerial influence of Calvin and other reformers on the puritans is well explored by J. William Black's book, *Reformation Pastors*. Black argues that Richard Baxter practiced parish ministry for the conversion of the ignorant, ultimately pursuing reformation through multi-dimensional pastoral approaches and strategies, which are well described in his *Gildas Salvianus (The Reformed Pastor*, 1656). For Black, Baxter's pastoral theology and practice were established and developed based on Martin Bucer (1491–1551). See Black, *Reformation Pastors*, chs. 2–4.

137. Bauckham, "Fulke, William."

138. Fulke, *A Brief and Plaine Declaration* (1584), 35, 45, 15, cited in Black, *Reformation Pastors*, 29.

139. Perkins, *Of the Calling of the Ministerie* (1605), 8, 24, 56. See Black, *Reformation Pastors*, 36; Hall, *The Faithful Shepherd*, 4–5; Collinson, *The Elizabethan Puritan Movement*, 125; Collinson, "Shepherds, Sheepdogs, and Hirelings," 194.

140. Greaves, "Bernard, Richard."

141. Bernard, *The Faithfull Shepheard* (1607), chs. 1–2. See also Collinson, "Shepherd, Sheepdogs, and Hirelings," 196; Black, *Reformation Pastors*, 38–39.

142. Ames, *The Marrow of Theology* (1623), 191.

143. Hall, *The Faithful Shepherd*, 6; Collinson, *The Elizabethan Puritan Movement*, 26; Collinson, "Shepherds, Sheepdogs, and Hirelings," 195.

144. Hall, *The Faithful Shepherd*, 49; Collinson, "Shepherd, Sheepdogs, and Hirelings," 195; Black, *Reformation Pastors*, 17–18, 41–42; Webster, *Godly Clergy in Early Stuart England*, 96.

145. Hardman Moore, *Pilgrims*, 19.

important and the chief means of grace.[146] For Calvin, faith can only be obtained by hearing the gospel: "God breathes faith unto us only by the instrument of his gospel, as Paul points out that 'faith comes from hearing' [Rom 10:17]. Likewise, the power to save rests with God [Rom 1:16]; but (as Paul again testifies) He displays and unfolds it in the preaching of the gospel [Rom 1:16]."[147] Based on Calvin, puritans argued for a direct and critical relationship between preaching and teaching the Word of God and the salvation of people. Puritans believed that there was no salvation without the preaching and hearing of the gospel.[148] Richard Bernard argued for the relationship between human salvation and preaching. For him, a pastor's preaching of the Word of God is absolutely necessary for people's faith and salvation: "And heerein ordinarily God shew his power to save all that shall be saved. It was from the beginning Preaching and Prophecying . . . how can people call on him in whom they beleeved? How can they beleeve of whom they have not heard? And how can they hear without a Preacher?"[149] For Baxter, who considered conversion not only as the primary purpose of ministry, but also as the most joyful and glorious thing,[150] propagation of the gospel and the Word of God is crucially related to conversion.[151] Baxter argued that the instruction of the Word "is a most hopeful means of the conversion of souls" and "it is about the most necessary things, the principles or essentials of the Christian faith."[152] Puritans understood that God calls the unconverted not by prophets or apostles receiving and proclaiming the message through immediate revelation, but "by his ordinary ministers, who are commissioned by him to preach the same gospel which Christ and his apostles first delivered."[153] In this sense, a preacher's duty was "an excellent privilege" of pastors as "the ambassadors of God and the instruments of men's conversion."[154]

---

146. Hall, *The Faithful Shepherd*, 16, 53.

147. Calvin, *Inst.*, IV.i.5.

148. Collinson, "Shepherd, Sheepdogs, and Hirelings," 195.

149. Bernard, *The Faithfull Shepheard* (1607), 1–2.

150. Baxter, *The Reformed Pastor* (1656), 94, 176.

151. Baxter, *The Reformed Pastor* (1656), 103–4. For Baxter's understanding of preaching and catechizing in relation to church reformation through conversion-oriented ministry, see Lim, *In Pursuit of Purity, Unity, and Liberty*, 23–52.

152. Baxter, *The Reformed Pastor* (1656), 174.

153. Baxter, *A Call to the Unconverted* (1658), 1. See Bayly, *The Practice of Piety* (2nd ed., 1612), 116.

154. Baxter, *The Reformed Pastor* (1656), 127, 128.

For puritan preachers, the "doctrine, reason and use" structure was the traditional puritan way of preaching.[155] According to Lisa M. Gordis, among various sermon manuals and rhetorics that New England ministers used, William Perkins's *The Arte of Prophecying* (1592) and Richard Bernard's *The Faithfull Shepheard* (1607), based on Perkins's manual, were the most influential.[156] William Perkins stated "The Order and Summe of the Sacred and Onely Method of Preaching" in his treatise, *The Arte of Prophecying*:

> 1. To reade the Text distinctly out of the Canonical Scriptures. 2. To give the sense and understanding of it being read, by the Scripture it selfe. 3. To collect a few and profitable points of doctrine out of the natuall sense. 4. To apply (if he have the gift) the doctrines rightly collected, the life and manners of men in a simple and plaine speech.[157]

In preaching, the puritans valued plainness along with Biblicism.[158] According to Horton Davies, puritans pursued wholly Bible-centered and plain preaching: "the Puritans did not cultivate pulpit oratory, but the exegesis and application of Scripture. Their aim was not primarily to delight and amuse, but to instruct the congregation."[159] Also, puritans' plain style of preaching was strongly related to their conversion-oriented ministry. Lim's observation of the relation between Richard Baxter's plain style of preaching and conversion is noteworthy. According to Lim, the puritans' plain style of preaching focused on the conversion of listeners. The reason that Baxter avoided "the florid, eloquent style of pulpit discourse" was because of the urgency of conversion and salvation.[160]

For puritans, preaching was not the only means for pastoral teaching. Baxter developed and pursued various pastoral skills and duties for parish

---

155. Davies, *The Worship of the American Puritans*, 87–89; Haller, *The Rise of Puritanism*, 134; Morgan, *Godly Learning*, 121; Bremer, *The Puritan Experiment*, 187. The puritan way of preaching was strongly based on the Reformed tradition. For exegesis, structure, and style in Reformed preaching, see Ford, "Preaching in the Reformed Tradition," 69–76. See also Hunt, *The Art of Hearing*, 95–96.

156. Gordis, *Opening Scripture*, 16.

157. Perkins, *The Arte of Prophecying* (1607), 148. *The Arte of Prophecying* was translated in English from *Prophetica* (1592).

158. Haller, *The Rise of Puritanism*, 129–33; Morgan, *Godly Learning*, 121–22; Bremer, *The Puritan Experiment*, 25, 188; Gordis, *Opening Scripture*, 13–15; Davies, *The Worship of American Puritans*, 85; Ford, "Preaching in the Reformed Tradition," 73–74.

159. Davies, *The Worship of American Puritans*, 85; Bremer, *The Puritan Experiment*, 188; Ford, "Preaching in the Reformed Tradition."

160. Lim, *In Pursuit of Purity, Unity, and Liberty*, 40–44.

ministry, such as catechizing, visitation, and counselling.[161] Although he acknowledged that "preaching the gospel publicly is the most excellent means,"[162] for him it was not enough, and he argued for other means of effective teaching.[163] For puritans, aside from preaching the most effective means of teaching was catechizing.[164] This was effective not only for the salvation of the unconverted, but also for the reformation of church.[165] Baxter indicated the want of catechizing in the church as a serious problem.[166] Also, puritan pastors believed that catechizing was valuable to help parishioners achieve maturity of Christian faith.[167] For them, the right pastoral education through catechizing was laying the foundations for the Christian faith. If the foundations were neglected, the whole ministry would be frustrated.[168]

Puritans used various methods for catechizing. Baxter regarded personal or private instruction of catechism very highly. Baxter said to his contemporary colleagues, "now, brethren, the work is before you. In these personal instructions of all the flock, as well as in public preaching, doth it consist."[169] For a detailed methodology of personal instruction, Baxter suggested private conference for catechism: "As to the manner of it: it will be by private conference, when we may have an opportunity to set all home to the conscience and the heart."[170] Visitation was another effective way of personal teaching for Baxter: "As to the delivery of them, the best way is for the minister first to give notice in the congregation, that they shall be brought to their houses, and then to go himself from house to house and deliver them, and take the opportunity of persuading them to the work."[171]

161. For Baxter's various pastoral methodologies, Baxter, *The Reformed Pastor* (1656), 87–111, 178.

162. Baxter, *The Reformed Pastor* (1656), 196.

163. Baxter, *The Reformed Pastor* (1656), 59–60, 196–97.

164. Ian Green, in his book, provides helpful investigation of catechizing in sixteenth to eighteenth-century England in terms of definition, methodologies, functions, and contents of catechisms and catechizing. Green, *The Christian's ABC*.

165. Baxter, *The Reformed Pastor* (1656), 175, 188–89. Baxter provided fourteen benefits of catechizing. See Baxter, *The Reformed Pastor* (1656), 174–89. For Baxter's understanding of catechizing, see Lim, *In Pursuit of Purity, Unity, and Liberty*, 44–51. For discussion on catechism for reformation, see below.

166. Baxter, *The Reformed Pastor* (1656), 184.

167. Baxter, *The Reformed Pastor* (1656), 176–77.

168. Baxter, *The Reformed Pastor* (1656), 238.

169. Baxter, *The Reformed Pastor* (1656), 211. See Baxter, *The Reformed Pastor* (1656), 41, 174–89, 195, 197, 199, 228, 232.

170. Baxter, *The Reformed Pastor* (1656), 174. See Baxter, *The Reformed Pastor* (1656), 200, 255.

171. Baxter, *The Reformed Pastor* (1656), 235. See Baxter, *The Reformed Pastor* (1656), 103–4. See also Green, *The Christian's ABC*, 93–229.

Puritan teachings can also be divided into text- and oral-based teachings. Adam Fox has argued in his book, *Oral and Literate Culture in England 1500–1700*, that orality and literacy in reciprocity were a strong means of communication not only for the literate, but also for the unlettered in sixteenth- and seventeenth-century England.[172] Puritan pastors who focused on the content of pastoral teaching also stressed how to teach. It has been generally recognized that pastoral teaching in the Reformed tradition was textually-based. This idea has been supported by reformers' Biblicism and Word-centered reformation, through the emphasis on teaching the Bible and the translation of it into native languages, and instructing a Protestant understanding of Christian doctrines. In this sense, for Protestants, including puritans, literacy was a significant means to pastoral teaching, and writings and publication of a literature were crucially related to their further reformation.[173] The centrality of Scripture reading and meditation on Scripture in the puritan practice of piety points to the importance of literacy in puritan ministry.[174] According to Hambrick-Stowe, New Englanders were "relatively literate and book-orientated Protestants." So, for them reading was a crucial means of practicing piety not only at public worship, but also for private and individual devotional life.[175] As Andrew Cambers argued, "reading was a central part of devotional practice and remained so throughout the seventeenth-century."[176] Puritan personal writings as an important devotional practice which definitely required literacy also reflect the relationship between literacy and puritan practice of piety. Puritans kept diaries and journals that contained self-examination and spiritual experiences in the communion with God. These literary outputs of their devotional life were not only for their own spiritual growth, but also for other believers who wanted to follow their example.[177] In these circumstances, the publi-

---

172. Fox, *Oral and Literate Culture in England*.

173. Hambrick-Stowe, "III. Puritan Spirituality in America," 300–301. Ian Green, in *Print and Protestantism*, argued for the spread and impact of Protestantism in early modern England by means of print through the examination of "best-sellers and steady sellers" of English religious literature published from 1530 to 1700. Green, *Print and Protestantism in Early Modern England*, particularly 553–90.

174. Bayly, *The Practice of Piety* (2nd ed., 1612), 143–47. See also Wakefield, *Puritan Devotion*, 14–16.

175. Hambrick-Stowe, *The Practice of Piety*, 157.

176. Cambers, *Godly Reading*, 80. Cambers, in this book, argued for the strong relationship between reading and puritanism. For him, "godly reading" was a core aspect of puritan practice of piety and "a crucial strand of puritan self-identity." In this sense, for him, "reading was vital to the practice of puritanism." See Cambers, *Godly Reading*, 1–38.

177. Hambrick-Stowe, *The Practice of Piety*, 5–7, 186–90; Hambrick-Stowe, "III.

cation of puritan theological writings and sermons was significant for the church and became immensely popular, taking advantage of the development of publication in the sixteenth- and seventeenth-century transatlantic World.[178] The popularity of devotional literature such as Lewis Bayly's *The Practice of Piety* (2nd ed., 1612), Richard Baxter's *The Saints' Everlasting Rest* (1650) and *A Call to the Unconverted* (1658), and Thomas Shepard's *The Sincere Convert* (1640), and *The Sound Believer* (1645) in the transatlantic world clearly reflects the importance of text-based pastoral education for puritans.[179] Baxter offered the examples of text-based pastoral teachings in his book. He stressed the importance of teaching and studying the Scriptures,[180] catechisms,[181] and other religious books that were relevant for pastoral education.[182] This underlines the fact that puritan pastors in many cases relied on texts for pastoral teaching.[183]

In addition to text-based teaching, oral education was also used in pastoral teaching.[184] Considering the significance of preaching in puritan ministry, it is evident that oral communication was a still powerful means of pastoral teaching.[185] In fact, many sermons were published in written form for pastoral education. However, it is important to notice that the published sermons were the revised sermon notes from orally proclaimed

---

Puritan Spirituality in America," 351–52. See also Gordis, "The Conversion Narrative in Early America," 373, 383.

178. Haller, *The Rise of Puritanism*, 82, 85; Amory, *Bibliography and the Book Trades*, 105–45; Keeble, "Puritanism and Literature," 309–24.

179. Hambrick-Stowe, *The Practice of Piety*, 38, 49–50. See also Green, *Print and Protestantism in Early Modern England*, 328, 332, 335–37, 348–51, 371, 598, 599, 656.

180. Baxter, *The Reformed Pastor* (1656), 59–60, 100.

181. Baxter, *The Reformed Pastor* (1656), 101.

182. Baxter, *The Reformed Pastor* (1656), 101.

183. Baxter, *The Reformed Pastor* (1656), 236.

184. David D. Hall and Alexandra Walsham, in a joint article, provided a new interpretation refuting previous understandings of the relationship between literacy and print culture and Protestantism: the dominance of literacy and print culture in religious communication and education for reformation. They argued that in addition to printed books, there were other mediums for communication and "orality" was still as powerful a means of religious communication and education as "literacy" was in the seventeenth-century transatlantic world. See Hall and Walsham, "'Justification by Print Alone?,'" 334–85.

185. Hunt, *The Art of Hearing*, 19–59. Here Hunt argued for preaching as a fundamentally oral activity. According to Hunt, who provided significant investigation into how sermons were transmitted and how sermon listeners interacted and responded towards sermons in various ways, sermon "note-taking" was a crucial source to understand the response of audience toward preaching in the early modern England. Hunt, *The Art of Hearing*, 94–114.

preaching.[186] Pastoral teaching based on oral communication can clearly be found in puritans' question- and answer-based teachings. Catechizing is a good example. Catechizing was conducted by doctrinal questions and organized answers. It was based on a text and implemented in a dialogical method between pastors and parishioners. Here, one can find oral-based education. Although puritan pastors chiefly used the written and published texts, they had to implement them orally. For puritan ministers, parishioners' answers and reactions told how and what the pastors were teaching them. Pastors selected and revised the questions according to the answers telling the degree of levels and growth of parishioners. Also, parishioners' levels and understanding of doctrines were a standard of pastoral educational methodology and contents.[187] In sum, for puritan pastors, text- and oral-based educational methodologies were harmonized for effective pastoral teaching.

Puritan Pastoral Care: Counselling and Spiritual Direction

Puritan pastoral counselling and spiritual direction were important ministerial tasks practiced by puritan ministers in the Reformed tradition.[188] One of the best examples is the ministry of Richard Greenham, who pursued multi-dimensional pastoral practices. Greenham pursued puritan parish ministry at Dry Drayton, a small farming village five miles from Cambridge, from 1570 to 1591. Although he supported the reformation for purer worship under Elizabeth I, he was more concerned about parish ministry and pastoral care rather than active participation in theological and ecclesiastical controversy for further reformation. For Greenham, who was also known as "the model puritan," "the foremost architect of the first great awakening of Protestant piety," "Practical theologian," "the first organizer of the science of Protestant spiritual counselling," and "the seminal pietist," preaching was not the only means of ministry despite his emphasis on its importance. He used various pastoral means and strategies to take care of his parish, including pastoral counselling for "wounded consciences."[189]

   186. Hambrick-Stowe, *The Practice of Piety*, 117–18.
   187. Baxter, *The Reformed Pastor* (1656), 240–51.
   188. Pastoral counselling and spiritual direction have been strongly emphasized in Reformed tradition. Rice, *Reformed Spirituality*, 131–35.
   189. Haller, *The Rise of Puritanism*, 25–28; Knappen, *Tudor Puritanism*, 382–86; Collinson, *The Elizabethan Puritan Movement*, 128, 349, 369; Collinson, *The Religion of Protestants*, 119; Collinson, "Shepherd, Sheepdogs, and Hirelings," 199–200; Primus, *Richard Greenham*; Parker and Carlson, *'Practical Divinity'*; Bozeman, *The Precisianist Strain*, 63–83; Black, *Reformation Pastors*, 33. Despite Greenham's emphasis on various

Baxter, like Greenham, considered counselling to be a role of the minister.[190] Baxter said, "We must be ready to give advice to inquirers, who come to us with cases of conscience. . . . A minister is not to be merely a public preacher, but to be known as a counsellor for their souls."[191] For Baxter, the duty of ministers of the gospel is not only to instruct, but also to "pronounce the absolving words of peace" to parishioners and to pray for them.[192] This shows the key work of ministers as counsellors. For puritans, personal catechizing instruction and pastoral visitations were not only related to the teaching of the Word, but also to spiritual counselling and direction. For Baxter, visitations of the sick were a good example of pastoral care, and he argued that diligent visiting and helping the sick was the duty of a minister.[193] For Baxter, through personal catechizing and instruction, a minister "shall come to be better acquainted with each person's spiritual state, and so the better will know how to watch over them."[194] In this sense, personal visitations and instruction accompanying better personal acquaintance and attention were functionally connected to spiritual counselling and direction. In addition, spiritual direction can also be found in Baxter as part of the role of the puritan pastor. It is similar to counselling. The following directions from Baxter for the unconverted who seek conversion implied the role of pastor as a spiritual director, guiding parishioners to spiritual examination and training:

> First, that you will seriously read over this small Treatise. Secondly, when you have read over this book, I would entreat you to go alone, and ponder a little what you have read. . . . And withall that you will go to your Pastors (that are set over you to take care of the health and safety of your souls, as Physitians do for the health of your bodies) and desire them to direct you what course to take, Thirdly, When by Reading, Consideration, Prayer and Ministerial Advice, you are once acquainted with your sin and misery, with your Duty and Remedy, delay not, but presently forsake your sinful company and courses, and turn to God, and obey his Call.[195]

---

ministerial means and strategies, it is clear that preaching was Greenham's most important pastoral concern. Carlson, "The Boring of the Ear," 255–60.

190. Rice, *Reformed Spirituality*, 132. For Baxter's understanding of pastoral duties, see Baxter, *The Reformed Pastor* (1656), 94–111.

191. Baxter, *The Reformed Pastor* (1656), 96.

192. Baxter, *A Call to the Unconverted* (1658), 31.

193. Baxter, *The Reformed Pastor* (1656), 44, 102.

194. Baxter, *The Reformed Pastor* (1656), 178.

195. Baxter, *A Call to the Unconverted* (1658), 7. See Baxter, *A Call to the Unconverted* (1658), 20–21.

The puritan understanding of a pastor as a counsellor and spiritual director is connected to the puritan parish-centered ministry. For puritans, if pastors were counsellors and spiritual directors overseeing parishioners, parish-centrism would be absolutely necessary. Baxter said, "If the pastoral office consists in overseeing all the flock . . . Will God require the blood of so many parishes at one man's hands."[196] Baxter also tells us that his primary ministerial target was the "flock" in his own parish. Black has argued that parish-centered ministry was one of the similarities between the ministry of Martin Bucer and that of Richard Baxter.[197] Calvin hinted towards a parish-centered ministry:

> Although we assign to each pastor his church, at the same time we do not deny that a pastor bound to one church can aid other churches. . . . But to keep peace in the church, this order is necessary . . . this arrangement ought to be observed as generally as possible: that each person, content with his own limits, should not break over into another man's province.[198]

Following Calvin's idea, writing in the 1650s Baxter demonstrated parish-centered ministry. For Baxter, "every flock should have its own pastor, and every pastor his own flock . . . so it is the will of God, that every church should have its own pastor, and that all Christ's disciples 'should know their teachers that are over them in the Lord.'"[199] Also, he mentioned that "flocks must ordinarily be no greater than we are capable of overseeing, or 'taking heed to.'"[200] This statement shows us that for Baxter, the argument for parish-centered ministry was very practical. In sum, puritan pastors perceived themselves not only as preachers, but also as counsellors and spiritual directors in a parish-based ministry. This self-understanding implicitly reflects the circumstances of the puritan ministry in the seventeenth century.

Pastoral Training for Pastors

Pastoral training and education for pastors was considered to be a significant part of puritan ministry. Greenham's regular teachings and conversations with young pastors are a good example of this. Many young generations of Protestant ministers regularly visited from Cambridge and learned from

196. Baxter, *The Reformed Pastor* (1656), 88.
197. Black, *Reformation Pastors*, 53–79.
198. Calvin, *Inst.*, IV.iii.7.
199. Baxter, *The Reformed Pastor* (1656), 88.
200. Baxter, *The Reformed Pastor* (1656), 88.

Greenham, paying great attention to his practical ministry and pastoral skills.[201] Puritans' concern for the education of pastors was not only related to the aim of having a successful ministry through the development of pastoral skills, but it was also connected to the serious recognition of the inability and unfitness of the pastors. Baxter seriously indicated the problems of "imperfectly qualified" pastors and "unsanctified" preachers and teachers in the church.[202] For Baxter, unqualified pastors could not manage the ministry with "old, ignorant, dead-hearted sinners" in their parish[203] and their untrained and unskilled preaching became the object of jeering and disappointment of parishioners.[204] Baxter lamented that the sins and misery of "troubled ministers" are "the greatest grief and trouble" to parishioners in the world.[205] Shepard indicated that because of the want of faithful and compassionate ministers to teach well, parishioners are so ignorant in the poor parish which is the reason for their collapse.[206]

Based on this recognition, Baxter urged pastors to take heed of them first.[207] For the education and training of pastors, Baxter emphasized not only intellectual and spiritual training, but also the need for the right manners and mentality, such as a mature and faithful pastoral attitude, diligence, and integrity etc.[208] Also, Baxter urged pastors to acquire a ministerial "holy skill" for more effective preaching and teaching of God's truths to their parishioners.[209] For the development of pastoral skills, Baxter argued, "O, therefore, brethren, lose no time! Study, and pray, and confer, and practise; for in these four ways your abilities must be increased . . . lest you are weak through your own negligence, and lest you mar the work of God by your weakness."[210] In

201. Collinson, *The Elizabethan Puritan Movement*, 128, 349, 369; Collinson, *The Religion of Protestant*, 119; Collinson, "Shepherd, Sheepdogs, and Hirelings," 199–200; Primus, *Richard Greenham*; Parker and Carlson, *'Practical Divinity'*; Bozeman, *The Precisianist Strain*, 63–83; Black, *Reformation Pastors*, 33.

202. Baxter, *The Reformed Pastor* (1656), 46, 54, 60.

203. Baxter, *The Reformed Pastor* (1656), 46.

204. Baxter, *The Reformed Pastor* (1656), 70–71. See Baxter, *The Reformed Pastor* (1656), 60, 203.

205. Baxter, *A Call to the Unconverted* (1658), 5.

206. Shepard, *The Sincere Convert* (1640), 68, 70.

207. Baxter treated this issue in chapter 1, "Oversight of Ourselves," in *The Reformed Pastor* (1656).

208. For the intellectual and spiritual training of pastors, see Baxter, *The Reformed Pastor* (1656), 58–59, 61–62, 70–71, 72–86, 111–12, 122; Baxter, *A Call to the Unconverted* (1658), 2. For the right manners and attitude of pastors, see Baxter, *The Reformed Pastor* (1656), 46, 53, 61, 63–65, 111–12, 116–21, 133–34, 146, 192–93, 201–4, 229–31.

209. Baxter, *The Reformed Pastor* (1656), 70.

210. Baxter, *The Reformed Pastor* (1656), 71.

addition, Baxter emphasized meetings and conferences of pastors: "I bless the Lord that hath placed me in such a neighbourhood, where I may have the brotherly fellowship of so many able, faithful, humble, unanimous, and peaceable men."[211] In Baxter's mind, the "brotherly meetings" were not only for the improvement of their edification and effectual carrying out of the ministry, but also for unity and concord in the church.[212] Lastly, for Baxter, the reformation of church leaders is an essential element of the further reformation of the church and society. Baxter argued, "how can we more effectually further a reformation, than by endeavouring to reform the leaders of the Church? . . . because of faithful endeavours are of so great necessity to the welfare of the Church, and the saving of men's souls."[213]

This examination of puritan pastoral teaching and care presents a significant background for Eliot's Indian ministry, through which one can understand what and how Eliot applied puritan ministerial ideals about a Word-centered ministry with various methodologies, including pastoral counselling and spiritual direction, in a parish-centered ministerial system, with pastoral education for pastors in his Indian ministry (which will be discussed in chapter 5).

Puritan Ministry and the Reformed Practice of Piety

The practice of piety, as an essential element of puritan ministry, was applied to Eliot's Indian ministry. The examination of puritan Reformed piety in this section will be another important framework for investigating Eliot's ministerial application of puritan piety in Praying Towns.[214]

One can say that puritan practice of piety based on Reformed tradition had two principles: the pursuit of conversion, and Biblicism.[215] For puritans, the practice of piety was not only a visible sign of their conversion, but also a means of conversion and a lifelong duty, ultimately towards salvation.[216] As Hambrick-Stowe indicated, puritans' conversion-oriented

211. Baxter, *The Reformed Pastor* (1656), 136.
212. Baxter, *The Reformed Pastor* (1656), 47.
213. Baxter, *The Reformed Pastor* (1656), 39.
214. For Indian practice of piety, see pp. 178–88 below.
215. For the understanding of piety or spirituality in Reformed tradition, see Rice, *Reformed Spirituality*; Hageman, "Reformed Spirituality," 60–72. For Calvin's understanding of piety, see Battles, *The Piety of John Calvin*; Battles, "True Piety according to Calvin," 289–306; Bouwsma, "The Spirituality of John Calvin," 318–33; Jones, *Calvin and the Rhetoric of Piety*; Lee, "Calvin's Understanding of Pietas," 225–39; McKee, *John Calvin*; Beeke, *Puritan Reformed Spirituality*, 1–33; Beeke, "Calvin on Piety," 125–52.
216. Hambrick-Stowe, *The Practice of Piety*, ix, 53, 93.

practice of piety can be found in their stress on conversion in their devotional books. Lewis Bayly, who introduced a detailed manual of spiritual exercises in his book *The Practice of Piety*, never forgot to mention his main pastoral concern—human salvation. Bayly said that one of the purposes of his book, *The Practice of Piety*, was "the salvation of inward soul,"[217] and he discussed the knowledge of God and human beings in relation to salvation first before giving the description of the actual practices.[218] Puritans' strong concern for conversion in the practice of piety reminds us of Calvin's belief that the union with Christ through regeneration was the starting point of the spiritual life.[219]

Puritan's concern for conversion and salvation is reflected in their actual practice of piety. For puritans, for example, the administration of sacraments was "the seals of the covenant" and reflects "the two stages of the redemptive cycle, preparation and growth in grace."[220] The puritan understanding of the Sabbath also reflects their conversion-centered understanding of the practice of piety. The Sabbath as a key puritan practice of piety seriously signifies not only God's rest after creation, but also God's redemption through the resurrection of Christ, which brought a new creation.[221] Also, puritans' continuous exercises of repentance and renewal through regular practice of meditation and prayer every morning and evening reminded them of the fact that they experienced death, resurrection, and redemption in God's grace, and that this process is still continually going on in their life. For puritans, this "cycle of the redemptive drama" is re-emphasized and re-experienced through the practice of piety as a means of grace.[222]

The second principle of the puritan practice of piety is Biblicism. For puritans, Scripture as the Word of God was not only the absolute authority and standard of Christian life, but also an important means of grace.[223] Puritans strictly adhered to a Reformed theological understanding of God's

---

217. Bayly, *The Practice of Piety* (2nd ed., 1612), A6.

218. Hambrick-Stowe, "III. Puritan Spirituality in America," 303; Bayly, *The Practice of Piety* (2nd ed., 1612), 4–104.

219. Calvin, *Inst*.II.iii.6; III.i.1. Rice, *Reformed Spirituality*, 31; Hinson, "Puritan Spirituality," 169.

220. Hambrick-Stowe, *The Practice of Piety*, 123; Hambrick-Stowe, "III. Puritan Spirituality in America," 346.

221. Bayly, *The Practice of Piety* (2nd ed., 1612), 222–67; Hambrick-Stowe, *The Practice of Piety*, 96–98.

222. Hambrick-Stowe, *The Practice of Piety*, 150. Bayly, *The Practice of Piety* (2nd ed., 1612), 138–43, 185–98.

223. Wakefield, *Puritan Devotion*, 11–14.

sovereignty in salvation. Therefore, they denied not only "the Catholic doctrine of the efficacy of forms in themselves," but also "the Arminian doctrine of human capability of salvation through self-willed use of forms." However, they believed that God uses "ordinary means" and is present in ecclesiastical and ritual activities as means of grace.[224] For puritans, God offers not only the content of the exercise in Scripture, but also the will to practice it through grace, while acknowledging that there is no role for human ability to play.[225] For puritans who were strongly based on Biblicism as a central heritage of Reformed tradition, the Bible as the Word of God was the true and only standard and rule of life.[226] Scripture, for puritans, was the most important devotional book, providing guidance for godliness in every aspect of life.[227] Based on Biblicism, puritans considered reading and hearing the Word of God, and constantly attending public preaching of the Word to be significant means of grace for salvation.[228] In sum, puritans' fundamental concern for conversion, and strong belief in the Scripture as the Word of God in the Reformed tradition, were the essential base for forming their devotional life.

Puritan piety, based on the two principles, is related to the concept of "visible saints." Bayly, who defined "saints" as "the Regenerate in respect of their Zealous endeavour to serve God in unfeigned holiness" and "True Christians,"[229] demonstrated a sincere and diligent practice of piety: "This all God's Saints (whilst they here lived) knew well: when with so often fastings, so earnest prayers; so frequent hearing the Word, and receiving the Sacraments and with such abundance of tears they devoutly begged at the hands of God for Christ's sake to be received into his Kingdom."[230] In this sense, for puritans, piety was not only a duty of "visible saints," but also an outward sign identifying being "saints."

Baxter argued that conversion "must be a total change, and you must be holy, and new creatures, and born again."[231] This means that for puri-

---

224. Bayly, *The Practice of Piety* (2nd ed., 1612), 108; Hambrick-Stowe, *The Practice of Piety*, 94; Hambrick-Stowe, "III. Puritan Spirituality in America," 343.

225. Hambrick-Stowe, *The Practice of Piety*, 45.

226. Baxter, *The Reformed Pastor* (1656), 123; Baxter, *A Call to the Unconverted* (1658), 57. Rice, *Reformed Spirituality*, 95–119.

227. Hambrick-Stowe, *The Practice of Piety*, 8; Hambrick-Stowe, "III. Puritan Spirituality in America," 308.

228. Baxter, *A Call to the Unconverted* (1658), 57.

229. Bayly, *The Practice of Piety* (2nd ed., 1612), 107.

230. Bayly, *The Practice of Piety* (2nd ed., 1612), 138.

231. Baxter, *A Call to the Unconverted* (1658), 37.

tans, "visible saints" as "sincere converts" must show sanctified life.[232] For a sanctified life of "visible saints," repentance in everyday life was a significant practice of piety for puritans.[233] For puritans, the starting point of piety was repentance and humility or humiliation.[234] Bayly stressed that although God is merciful, the mercy is only for the repentant: "Joyful assurance to a Sinner that repents; no comfort to him that remains impenitent. God is infinite in mercy, but to them only, who turn from their sins to serve him in holiness, without which no man shall see the Lord, Heb. 12. 14."[235] Bayly argued for penitence in the devotional practice every morning:

> Therefore before thou prayest, let God see that thy heart is sorrowful for thy sin: and that thy mind is resolved (through the assistance of his grace) to amend thy faults... shut thy chamber-door, and kneel down at thy bed-side, or some other convenient place, and in reverent manner lifting up thy heart, together with thy hands and eyes, as in the presence of God, who seeth the inward intention of thy soul, offer up unto God from the Altar of a contrite heart, thy prayer as a morning-sacrifice, through the mediation of Christ, in these or the like words.[236]

According to Charles E. Hambrick-Stowe, puritans' strong concern for piety was related to "a devotional revival" which appeared in Europe in the late sixteenth- and early seventeenth-century. Hambrick-Stowe defines puritanism as "a devotional movement dedicated to the spiritual regeneration of individuals and society."[237] For puritans, piety was "heart religion," pursuing inner and spiritual experience, especially in the encounter and experience of God.[238] Puritan piety as "heart religion" can be frequently found in their practice of reading, meditation, and prayer, as the three major activities of individual piety. These activities were conducted together

---

232. Baxter, *A Call to the Unconverted* (1658), 18.

233. Bayly, *The Practice of Piety* (2nd ed., 1612), 112. See Bayly, *The Practice of Piety* (2nd ed., 1612), 108, 114, 137.

234. Hambrick-Stowe, *The Practice of Piety*, 34.

235. Bayly, *The Practice of Piety* (2nd ed., 1612), 123.

236. Bayly, *The Practice of Piety* (2nd ed., 1612), 147.

237. Hambrick-Stowe, *The Practice of Piety*, 23. See Hambrick-Stowe, *The Practice of Piety*, 53; Hambrick-Stowe, "III. Puritan Spirituality in America," 338.

238. Hambrick-Stowe, *The Practice of Piety*, 43, 44; Hambrick-Stowe, "III. Puritan Spirituality in America," 338. White, *English Devotional Literature*, 56, cited in Hambrick-Stowe, "III. Puritan Spirituality in America," 300. In addition to "piety," puritans used other expressions; "devotion," "godly or heavenly conversation," "spiritual exercises," "pilgrimage of the souls," and "spiritual warfare." Hambrick-Stowe, "III. Puritan Spirituality in America," 338.

in daily life.[239] For puritans, reading, meditation, and prayer were basically connected through Scripture, because puritans' exercise of mediation and prayer started from Scripture reading: "But for as much, that as faith is the soul, so reading and meditating of the Word of God, are the Parents of Prayers: therefore before thou prayest in the Morning, first, read a Chapter in the word of God; then meditate a while with thy self how many excellent things thou canst remember out of it."[240] For puritans, Scripture reading was the primary practice in puritan devotional reading, a significant practice of piety, and a means of grace.[241]

Puritan meditation as "a comprehensive method for Puritan devotion—a biblical, doctrinal, experiential, and practical art"—was basically conducted about a Bible reading, but the range of subjects for meditation was wide.[242] Bayly provided a multi-dimensional understanding of meditation. He said, meditation was not only focused on the Scripture, but also that it was related to every area of Christian life. Also, meditation was regularly practiced in the morning and evening, and extra exercises were a significant part of the preparation for Sabbath and sacraments.[243] For puritans, meditation mainly focused on self-examination. Through the examination, puritans tried to prepare themselves as much as possible so that they could attain the proper spiritual condition to be accepted by God. The meditation for self-examination can commonly be found in meditations for the morning, evening, Sabbath, Holy Communion, fasting, and in times of sickness.[244] Meditation mainly focused on self-examination, but it was expanded to other areas such as the work of Christ, forgiveness of sins, blessing and glorification of Christians, birthdays, and the turning of the

---

239. Hambrick-Stowe, *The Practice of Piety*, 50; Hambrick-Stowe, "III. Puritan Spirituality in America," 348. See Bayly, *The Practice of Piety* (2nd ed., 1612), 138–43.

240. Bayly, *The Practice of Piety* (2nd ed., 1612), 143.

241. Bayly, *The Practice of Piety* (2nd ed., 1612), 143–47, 158–60; Hambrick-Stowe, "III. Puritan Spirituality in America," 348; Rice, *Reformed Spirituality*, 109–17; Cambers, *Godly Reading*, 2, 16–24. Cambers has provided significant investigation of devotional reading as a practice of piety divided into private or individual reading, and family reading as social and communal reading. For the individual and family godly reading as a practice of piety, see Cambers, *Godly Reading*, 39–117.

242. Beeke, *Puritan Reformed Spirituality*, 95.

243. Bayly, *The Practice of Piety* (2nd ed., 1612); Hambrick-Stowe, "III. Puritan Spirituality in America," 348.

244. Bayly, *The Practice of Piety* (2nd ed., 1612), 143–47, 185–88, 267, 278–79, 292–96, 306, 308, 329, 364; Hambrick-Stowe, *The Practice of Piety*, 168, 170; Hambrick-Stowe, "III. Puritan Spirituality in America," 348–49; Beeke, *Puritan Reformed Spirituality*, 95–97.

year. Also, creatures were the objects of meditation, and public and private crises were important occasions for the practice of meditation.[245]

For puritans, prayer was connected with meditation, because meditating was a kind of preparation of heart for prayer as conversation with God. Bayly provided a combined form of meditation and prayer in his *The Practice of Piety* (2nd ed., 1612).[246] Considering Bayly's manual, prayer, especially private or "secret prayer" starts from Scripture reading and meditation.[247] For puritans, the primary purpose of prayer was as a means of union with God.[248] As Hambrick-Stowe has explained, prayers in puritan traditions mainly divided into prayer in public worship service, and private or "secret prayer." Regardless of public or private practice, the common ground of the prayers was spiritual conversation with God.[249] Shepard said, "Holy prayers . . . are such desires of the soul left with God, with submission to his will, as may best please him."[250] Bayly stated that prayer is the "spiritual sacrifice": "prayer is thy spiritual sacrifice, wherewith God is well pleased. . . . Bend therefore thy Affections . . . to so holy an exercise; assuring thy self, that it doth by so much the more please God."[251] These references show how puritans' major concern for prayer was spiritual communion with God. For pursuing communion with God, puritans practiced regular prayer. Puritans prayed every morning, evening and Sabbath.[252] But, for them, special prayers at irregular times were also important. These were for special occasions such as sacraments, times of sickness, death, and when visiting the sick.[253] The various occasions of prayers reflect puritans' diligent practice of prayer with various contents based on their strong belief in the efficacy

245. Hambrick-Stowe, *The Practice of Piety*, 32, 162, 164, 169, 171–74. For puritan meditation tradition, see Wakefield, *Puritan Devotion*, 85–89; Chan, *Spiritual Theology*, 164, 168; Beeke, *Puritan Reformed Spirituality*, 73–100.

246. Bayly, *The Practice of Piety* (2nd ed., 1612), 139–61, 185–89; Hambrick-Stowe, *The Practice of Piety*, 161, 163.

247. Bayly, *The Practice of Piety* (2nd ed., 1612), 143. See also Rice, *Reformed Spirituality*, 89–92.

248. Hamtrick-Stowe, *The Practice of Piety*, 175, 179. For the understanding in Reformed tradition, see Rice, *Reformed Spirituality*, 71–94.

249. Wakefield, *Puritan Devotion*, 67–84; Hambrick-Stowe, *The Practice of Piety*, 104–9, 175–86; Davies, *The Worship of American Puritans*, 146–75.

250. Shepard, *The Sound Believer* (1645), 265. See also Davies, *The Worship of American Puritans*, 146; Hambrick-Stowe, *The Practice of Piety*, 176.

251. Bayly, *The Practice of Piety* (2nd ed., 1612), 154.

252. Bayly, *The Practice of Piety* (2nd ed., 1612), 147–62, 183, 189–98, 282–86; Hambrick-Stowe, *The Practice of Piety*, 177.

253. Bayly, *The Practice of Piety* (2nd ed., 1612), 353–63, 365–76, 399–402, 418–21; Hambrick-Stowe, *The Practice of Piety*, 184.

of prayer.[254] Puritan prayers were not only for self-examination and repentance, but also for petition and intercession for themselves and for others in their community, and for thanksgiving.[255]

In terms of the style of prayer, puritans were not limited to meditative prayer. Cotton argued for prayer based on Scripture from a sincere heart led by the Holy Spirit. Cotton's definition of prayer, which is considered to be one of the earliest New England definitions of prayer, clearly shows the puritan style of prayer: "Lawfull prayer is a lifting up (or pouring out) of the desired of the heart unto God, for Divine blessings, according to his will, in the name of Jesus Christ, by the helpe of the Spirit of Grace."[256] For Cotton, the prayer restrained by a prayer book was "unlawful": "Wee conceive it also to be unlawful to bring in ordinarily any other Bookes into the publique worship of God, in the Church, besides the Book of God."[257] Based on this idea, puritans also argued for extempore prayer, an "outburst of prayer" or "ejaculatory prayer."[258] The essential point in puritans' understanding of prayer was that they pursued prayer not from formal written texts, but from a sincere heart oriented towards communion with the living God. This is why Bayly asked believers to pray earnestly with "the inward mourning of the heart, by the outward means of the voice, and tears of the eyes." For Bayly, "such filial earnestness and importunity in prayer, is our heavenly Father well pleased."[259]

For puritans, fasting cannot be omitted as a key practice of piety, especially in the relation to "heart religion" for communion with God. For Bayly, through fasting, believers pursued not only repentance, but also amendment of life in devout prayer and good works. The ultimate purpose of fasting, according to Bayly, was intended to be helpful for the worship of God: "The true Ends of Fasting are not to merit God's favour, or eternal life (for that we have only of the gift of God through Christ) nor to place Religion in bodily abstinence (for Fasting in itself is not the worship of God, but an

---

254. Hambrick-Stowe, *The Practice of Piety*, 176.

255. Baxter, *A Call to the Unconverted* (1658), 57; Hambrick-Stowe, *The Practice of Piety*, 180–83; Hambrick-Stowe, "III. Puritan Spirituality in America," 350.

256. Cotton, *A Modest and Cleare Answer to Mr. Balls Doiscours of Set Formes of Prayer* (1642), 1, cited in Davies, *The Worship of American Puritans*, 146.

257. Cotton, *A Modest and Cleare Answer to Mr. Balls Doiscours of Set Formes of Prayer* (1642), 5, cited in Davies, *The Worship of American Puritans*, 42.

258. Hambrick-Stowe, *The Practice of Piety*, 185; Hambrick-Stowe, "III. Puritan Spirituality in America," 350.

259. Bayly, *The Practice of Piety* (2nd ed., 1612), 294.

help to further us the better to worship God)."²⁶⁰ For Bayly, "true Ends of Fasting" are the following:

> First, To subdue our Flesh to the Spirit. . . . Secondly, That we may more devoutly contemplate God's holy Will, and fervently pour forth our Souls unto him by prayer. . . . Thirdly, That by our serious humiliation, and judging of ourselves, we may escape the judgment of the Lord; not for the merit of our Fasting . . . but for the mercy of God, who hath promised to remove his judgments from us, when we by Fasting do.²⁶¹

The final goal of fasting clearly shows that the puritan practice of piety pursues "heart religion" seeking communion with God.

Another example of the puritan practice of piety is singing psalms. For puritans, singing psalms was not only a significant means of grace, but also a means of communion with God. Cotton stated:

> Singing was a means of grace, a well-established way that one might communicate with God. As with all means of grace, singing was a natural phenomenon, a human activity through which God chooses to work. . . . That is, all persons have within them the duty and the means to sing praises. The act of singing, then, could bring a soul into harmony with God. . . . Singing was what Puritans called a converting ordinance.²⁶²

Psalm-singing was seriously practiced both in public worship and private devotional meetings. *The Bay Psalm Book* (1640) reflected the liturgical and devotional meaning and role of singing psalms in puritan Christian communities.²⁶³

---

260. Bayly, *The Practice of Piety* (2nd ed., 1612), 301.

261. Bayly, *The Practice of Piety* (2nd ed., 1612), 301. See also Davies, *The Worship of American Puritans*, 61–66.

262. Cotton, *Singing of Psalmes a Gospel-Ordinance* (1647), 5–6, 48, cited in Hambrick-Stowe, *The Practice of Piety*, 113.

263. Cotton, *The Way of the Churches of Christ in New England*, 67, cited in Davies, *The Worship of American Puritans*, 47; Cotton, *Singing of Psalmes* (1647), 2; Hambrick-Stowe, *The Practice of Piety*, 111–16. For the practice of psalm-singing in the early modern England, see Green, *Print and Protestantism*, 503–52. *The Bay Psalm Book* (1640) was the first book printed in North America. It is recognized that John Eliot was one of the writers and publishers of the book. Eliot et al., *The Whole Book Psalmes Faithfully Translated into English Metre* (1640); Haraszti, *The Enigma of the Bay Psalm Book*, 12, 13, 16, 36; Winslow, *John Eliot*, 65–70; Bozeman, *To Live Ancient Lives*, 139–50; Davies, *The Worship of American Puritans*, 126–27. The book, in fact, was "the third output" from the press at Cambridge, Massachusetts, but it was the first printed document called a book in North America. For the publication history of *The Bay Psalm Book*, see Winship, *The Cambridge Press*, 21–34, 94–104. See also Amory, "'Gods Altar Needs Not Our Pollishings,'" 34–57.

For puritans, Sabbath keeping was significant as a key practice of piety and also as a means of grace. Based on Reformers' thoughts on the Sabbath, puritans innovated Sabbath as a key devotional practice and regulated Sabbath more strictly than reformers.[264] For puritans, the Sabbath was not only for divine rest in God, but it was also the most important time to worship God through gathering all together in church. For puritans, the gatherings in church on the Sabbath meant the union of individual Christians and the divine community pursuing the same goal towards God:

> Almighty God will have himself worshipped, not only in a private manner, by private Persons and Families; but also in a more publick sort, of all the godly joyned together in a visible Church: that by this means he may be known not only to be the God and Lord of every singular Person; but also of the Creatures of the whole universal World.[265]

According to Bayly, puritans' Sabbath keeping was practiced in harmony between the public worship service of the whole community and personal and private devotional exercises. It was particularly based on family devotional practice before and after worship, including morning and evening prayer, self-examination, singing psalms, and reflections on sermons, scriptures, and catechism. Here, we can notice that the puritan family practice of piety shows the ideal harmonization of communal practice and personal practice because the preparation and reflection for Sabbath were mainly practiced through the family practice of piety. For puritans, family was the smallest community for piety and a bridge between a person and the church community.[266]

Lastly, puritans also considered sacraments as a significant practice of piety. Following Calvin, for puritans, sacraments were not only a significant practice of piety, but also seals and outward signs of being "saints."[267] Bayly said, "the Sacraments do not only signifie and offer, but also seal and exhibit

---

264. Bayly, *The Practice of Piety* (2nd ed., 1612), 222–86; Hambrick-Stowe, *The Practice of Piety*, 96; Hambrick-Stowe, "III. Puritan Spirituality in America," 307. See also Wakefield, *Puritan Devotion*, 59–63.

265. Bayly, *The Practice of Piety* (2nd ed., 1612), 222, 259; Hambrick-Stowe, *The Practice of Piety*, 96–98; Davies, *The Worship of American Puritans*, 43.

266. Bayly, *The Practice of Piety* (2nd ed., 1612), 200–203, 265–86; Baxter, *The Reformed Pastor* (1656), 101, 186; Wakefield, *Puritan Devotion*, 55–8; Davies, *The Worship of American Puritans*, ix; Hambrick-Stowe, *The Practice of Piety*, 143–50; Hambrick-Stowe, "III. Puritan Spirituality in America," 347; Hinson, "Puritan Spirituality," 167.

267. Calvin, *Inst.*, IV.xiv.1–6; IV.xv.1–6; Wendel, *Calvin*, 312–18; Wakefield, *Puritan Devotion*, 37–39; Holifield, *The Covenant Sealed*, 14; Rohr, *The Covenant of Grace in Puritan Thought*, 178–79.

indeed, the inward spiritual grace." Bayly considered baptism as "the washing of Regeneration, and the renewing of the Holy Ghost" and the Lord's Supper as "the communion of the body and blood of Christ."[268] John Cotton also said, "For we receive the Lord's Supper, not only as a seal of our communion with the Lord Jesus, and with his members in our own church, but also in all the churches of the saints."[269]

The understanding of sacraments as a sign and seal of "visible saints" led puritans to make strict regulations for the practice of sacraments. Strict regulation can be found in the practice of the Lord's Supper in particular. In New England, puritans restricted the admission to Holy Communion to church members who had passed a test of faith through a test on doctrinal knowledge and a public profession of conversion experience.[270] Although the public testimony of conversion experience was not required for church membership in Old England,[271] it is evident that strict regulation of admission to Holy Communion was practiced by puritan ministers like Baxter in Old England. Baxter emphasized the necessity of strict regulations and a test of faith for the Lord's Supper.[272] Baxter delineated repentance, church discipline, and catechizing of parishioners as essential for preparing for the sacrament: "Is it not God's ordinance that they should be personally rebuked and admonished, and publicly called to repentance, and be cast out if they remain impenitent?"[273] Baxter also argued for strict regulations for baptism. Although Baxter argued for infant baptism, he did not allow the baptism of

---

268. Bayly, *The Practice of Piety* (2nd ed., 1612), 117. See Bayly, *The Practice of Piety* (2nd ed., 1612), 309, 316, 320, 448. See also Wakefield, *Puritan Devotion*, 39–42.

269. Cotton, *The Keys of the Kingdom of Heaven* (1644), 109. See also Wakefield, *Puritan Devotion*, 33–37.

270. Hambrick-Stowe, *The Practice of Piety*, 123, 125; Davies, *The Worship of American Puritans*, 188.

271. According to Patricia Caldwell, although public confession of faith as a requirement of church membership was a unique aspect of New England puritan churches, the exact origin of the tradition is not clear. For the origin of puritan conversion narratives, see Caldwell, *The Puritan Conversion Narrative*, ch. 1, "Origins." See also Morgan, *Visible Saints*, 65–66. D. Bruce Hindmarsh argued that William Perkins's conversion theology offered an ideological base for conversion narratives. Hindmarsh considered the works of Richard Kilby (or Kilbye, *d.* 1617), a puritan, were the beginning of conversion narratives: Kilby, *The Burthen of a Loaden Conscience* (1608); Kilby, *Hallelu-iah: Praise Yee the Lord, for the Unburthening of a Loaden Conscience* (1614). See Hindmarsh, *The Evangelical Conversion Narrative*. Hindmarsh, in this book, provided a significant research on English conversion narratives mainly in the eighteenth century. Chapter 1 is a good source to understand seventeenth-century puritan conversion narratives. See Hindmarsh, *The Evangelical Conversion Narrative*, 33–60.

272. Baxter, *The Reformed Pastor* (1656), 109–11, 163.

273. Baxter, *The Reformed Pastor* (1656), 164.

children whose parents were not qualified in terms of the Christian faith.[274] In sum, for puritans, the concept of "visible saints" was crucially related to the practice of piety. The practice of piety, for puritans, was not only a sign and seal of "visible saints," but also showed the self-identity of Christians. Through actual visible practice of piety, they not only confirmed their visible and external identity, but also confirmed their invisible and spiritual identity as true Christians deserving ultimate salvation. In this sense, for puritans, the practice of piety was also ultimately to seek reformation. As conversion and pastoral teachings were significant foundations and crucial means of reformation, puritans pursued the purity of the Christian faith through the reformed practice of piety. So, the reformed practice of piety was not only the expression of the puritan Christian faith, but also a significant means of realization of pure Christianity and church. Therefore, it is true that the practice of piety was "what made a puritan a puritan."[275]

Through the understanding of seventeenth-century puritan ministry, one can finally realize the main motive for Eliot's Indian ministry. The next section, based on the puritan background, will propose puritans' keen concern for conversion-oriented and reformation-centered pastoral ministry in their historical contexts as John Eliot's fundamental and lasting motive that led him to continue his ministry to the Indians.

Conversion, Reformation, and the Motives for Indian Ministry

The investigation of seventeenth-century puritan ministry suggests that conversion was Eliot's fundamental theological and ministerial concern. Although the puritans did not get involved with Indian evangelization and ministry soon after their arrival in New England, one of the main reasons for their decision regarding Indian evangelization was due to their primary concern for conversion. Cogley said that the main reason for Eliot's decision to get involved with Indian evangelization was because Eliot "learned to appreciate their humanity and to sympathize with their problems" after encountering native Indians in 1646. In other words, for Cogley, Eliot's motive of spreading the gospel was his compassion toward the physically and spiritually poor unconverted.[276] In fact, as mentioned earlier, Gookin reported that Eliot's "compassion and ardent affection to them" was one of the

---

274. Baxter, *The Reformed Pastor* (1656), 253.
275. Hambrick-Stowe, *The Practice of Piety*, viii.
276. *JEMI*, 171, 249.

two first reasons for initiating preaching to the Indians in 1646.[277] However, Eliot's "sympathy" needs to be reconsidered in terms of puritan pastorship which considers conversion to be a fundamental concern.

Puritans' deep concern for conversion can be found in the description of the Indians' situation in the materials published in the Eliot Tracts. For the puritan authors of the Eliot Tracts, the Indians were so savage, and they did not have any civilization. Also, the Indians displayed a spiritually "poor" existence. From a Christian perspective they needed conversion and salvation. The Eliot Tracts describe the Indians as having a spiritual existence that was the target for conversion. In the Eliot Tracts, the Indians were considered to be "miserable Captives,"[278] "miserable Heathen,"[279] "these poor captivated men,"[280] and "the poor, naked, ignorant Indians."[281] This is mainly because for the puritans, the Indians were miserable souls who deserved to go to hell. "Heaven and Hell" was a main focus of Eliot's teaching to the Indians. In his letter in *Glorious Progress* (1649), Eliot said:

> And when I had done preaching, they began to propound questions, and one of them propounded this; If it be thus as you teach, then all the world of Indians are gone to hell to be tormented for ever, until now a few may goe to Heaven and be saved; Is it so? These principles of a twofold estate after this life, for good and bad people, Heaven and Hell, I put amongst the first questions that I instruct them in, and catechise the children in; and they doe readily embrace it for a truth, themselves by their own traditions having some principles of a life after this life, and that good or evill, according to their demeanour in this life.[282]

For the puritans, the Indians were in the "darke corners of the earth" and "these poor out-casts, who have thus long been estranged from him, spilt like water upon the ground and none to gather them."[283] The authors of dedicatory epistle to *Strength out of Weaknesse* (1652) said:

> The Lord hath manifested that there is a seed according to the Election of grace, even amongst these also as well as other Gentiles, that the Lord hath visited them to take out of them a people for his Name . . . the great Love of God, is Love to Soules,

277. HCINE, 170. See also pp. 29-30, 71 above.
278. *Strength out of Weaknesse* (1652), 238.
279. *Tears of Repentance* (1653), 254.
280. *Tears of Repentance* (1653), 254.
281. *Late and Further Manifestation* (1655), 302.
282. *Glorious Progress* (1649), 153.
283. *Clear Sun-Shine* (1648), 107.

and our tenderest compassion should be manifested in pittying of Soules.[284]

The expression, "pittying" of Indians, travels beyond human sympathy. It conveys a strong puritan pastoral concern for Indian conversion. Waban, a Praying Indian, demonstrated in his sermon based on Matt 9:12–13 that Indians were in "soul sicknesse" and Christ was the "Physitian of souls."[285] Waban's sermon suggests that Praying Indians also recognized that they were the objects of pastoral and spiritual concern.

Puritans' recognition of the Indians as the object of conversion was related to their pastoral responsibility for them. Eliot expressed his strong desire and expectation for Indian conversion and Christianization as his fundamental pastoral concern:

> [W]e shall finde them to grow in knowledge of the principles of Religion, and to love the wayes of the Lord the better, according as they come to understand them, and to yield obedience to them, and submit to this great change, to bridle lust by lawes of chastity, and to motifie idlenese by labour, and desire to traine up their children accordingly.[286]

Eliot, in *The Indian Grammar Begun* (1666), expressed his strong compassion toward native Indians as "poor souls": "God first put into my heart a compassion over their poor souls, and a desire to teach them to know Christ, and to bring them into his kingdome."[287] For Eliot, compassion drove his pastoral concern for Indian conversion. For the puritans, "soul-saving worke" for Indians was definitely their pastoral duty and obligation as puritan ministers.[288]

Based on the recognition of pastoral responsibility for Indian conversion, the puritans who were involved with the Indians' conversion regarded evangelization as the providence of God. In his prefatory epistle of *Tears of Repentance* (1653), Eliot expressed his firm conviction that Indian

---

284. "To the Reader," in *Strength out of Weaknesse* (1652), 217. The puritans who supported the publication of *Strength out of Weaknesse* (1652) through their co-authorship of the letter "To the Reader" as the preface of the tract were the following: W. Gouge, Edm[und]: Calamy, Simon Ashe, Wil[liam]: Spurstowe, Jer[emiah]: Whitaker, Lazarus Seaman, George Griffith, Phillip Nye, William Bridge, Henry Whitfeld, Sidrach Simpson, William Strong, Joseph Caryl, and Ralph Venning. *Strength out of Weaknesse* (1652), 218.

285. *Further Accompt* (1659), 333.

286. *Light Appearing* (1651), 205.

287. Eliot, *The Indian Grammar Begun* (1666), 65.

288. *Strength out of Weaknesse* (1652), 241. See *Clear Sun-Shine* (1648), 107–10.

evangelization was God's will and providence which required support from England.

> Beloved Reader, I have no more to say as necessary to Prepare for the following Matter, only to beg, yea earnestly to beg the continuance of all your Prayers; by the power whereof. . . . I beleeve this wheele of Conversion of these Indians, is turned: and my Heart hath been always thereby encouraged, to follow on to do that poor little I can, to help forward this blessed Work of Spreading and Exalting the Kingdom of our dear Savior Jesus Christ.[289]

In sum, although Indian conversion was not the main reason for New England migration, the reason that Eliot became actively involved with Indian ministry sprang from a fundamental puritan pastoral concern for "soul-saving worke."

Eliot's unquenchable desire for reformation also became a strong motive for his continuous Indian ministry. As argued earlier, Eliot's primary reason for migration was to "enjoy the holy worship of God, not according to the fantasies of man, but according to the Word of God, without . . . human additions and novelties."[290] In this sense, for Eliot, Indian conversion was crucially related to reformation as his ultimate reason for migration to New England. As argued above, for Eliot, conversion was the most important task of pastoral ministry, and the ministry was an essential means for the realization of reformation. Therefore, Eliot's strong desire for reformation was probably another reason for Indian ministry. This can be found in the rhetoric for reformation in the Eliot Tracts. Thomas Shepard, in *Clear Sun-Shine* (1648), argued that because of "the present troubles" and "those destructive designes which were on foot, and carried on for the Introduction of so great evils both into Church and State" under Laudian policy, New England puritans "were content to sit downe, and pitch their tents in the utmost parts of the Earth, hoping that there they might be out of the reach of their malice" in order to "enjoy the liberties of the Gospel."[291] Eliot and his colleagues who proclaimed reformation as their main reason for migration strongly urged the reformation in England.[292] Their argument for

---

289. *Tears of Repentance* (1653), 260, 262.

290. Eliot, "The Learned Conjectures," in *ET*, 423.

291. *Clear Sun-Shine* (1648), 104.

292. Laura M. Stevens, in *The Poor Indians*, argued for the important role of the rhetorical effect of English missionary writings such as the Eliot Tracts in creating a social and emotional network between Old and New Englanders in ultimate pursuit of the constitution of British identity. Regardless of whether one accepts Stevens's focus on

reformation was not mainly in New England, but in fact in England. Unlike New England-centric interpretations of the Great Migration,[293] the authors of the materials in the Eliot Tracts implicitly and explicitly argued for further reformation in England. Characteristic of the rhetoric is that Eliot and his colleagues in the Eliot Tracts related their migration, ultimately pursuing reformation, also to Indian conversion. For puritan migrants, Indian conversions were a visible example for justifying their migration, but also an effective means for urging the reformation in England. The circumstantial reinterpretation of their migration, and Indian conversion in the relation to the migration of the authors of the Eliot Tracts, can be understood as persuasive rhetoric for urging the reformation of England.

The authors of the Eliot Tracts seemed to try to stimulate the English through the introduction of Indian conversion. Shepard, in *Day-Breaking* (1647), clearly compared Indians and English in terms of religious attitudes. He said, "that none of them slept Sermon or derided Gods messenger: Woe unto those English that are growne bold to doe that, which Indians will not, Heathens dare not."[294] He also said, "If English men begin to despise the preaching of faith and repentance, and humiliation for sinne, yet the poore Heathens will bee glad of it, and it shall doe good to them.... Indians shall weepe to heare faith and repentance preached, when English men shall mourne, too late, that are weary of such truths."[295] Eliot also said that Indian evangelization and Praying Towns was a model as a stimulus to England and European countries. He said, "These things being so, the worke which wee now have in hand will be as a patterne and Copie before them, to imitate in all the Countrey."[296] Maclear implied that this understanding of Eliot reflected the idea of Indian conversion as a sign of the "city upon a hill" as Miller argued.[297] However, Eliot's mention of "a patterne and Copie" was not arguing for New England as a model society, but signified that Indian conversion and Praying Towns based on the Bible were a strong stimulus to England to pursue further reformation.

The contrast between Indians and Englanders in terms of Christian faith was extended to severe criticism of Englanders. John Durie [Dury][298]

British identity, a certain rhetorical function of the Eliot Tracts' targeting Old England was evident. See Stevens, *The Poor Indians*.

293. See pp. 31–34 above.
294. *Day-Breaking* (1647), 94.
295. *Day-Breaking* (1647), 94.
296. *Strength out of Weaknesse* (1652), 226.
297. Maclear, "New England and the Fifth Monarchy," 247.
298. Young, "Durie [Dury], John."

criticized Englanders that "The converted Heathens in New-England, goe beyond you, O ye, Apostate Christians in England!"[299] William Leveri[t]ch,[300] in his letter in *Strength out of Weaknesse* (1652), said, "it pleaseth God to help some of these poore Creatures to looke over and beyond the Examples of some of our looser sort of English."[301] These criticisms of Englanders were ultimately aimed at urging reformation in England. This intention can be found in Joseph Caryl's letter as the preface of *Further Account* (1660). He compared the relationship between Jews and Gentiles with the relationship between Indians and English:

> I may, not unfitly, make use of those Prophesies of Moses and Esaias concerning the Jewes and Gentiles . . . in this present case between us in England and Indians. The Lord hath begun to provoke us to Jealousie by them that were no people, and by a foolish Nation hee hath angred us, hee is found of them that sought him not, hee is made manifest to them that asked not after him, but all the day long hath hee stretched out his hands unto us a disobedient and gainsaying people.[302]

These references significantly indicate that the authors of the Eliot Tracts seriously urged Englanders to pursue pure reformed Christianity through conversion and the reformed Protestant faith.

Lastly, if the rhetoric of the Eliot Tracts was aiming ultimately at the reformation of England, how can we understand Eliot's ministry for Indian conversion in New England? What was the relationship between Indian conversion and ministry and reformation in New England? For Eliot, the reformation was not limited to a certain region. In fact, Eliot and his colleagues expressed a strong desire for reformation in England (as noted above). For them, England their mother country should be reformed further. They believed that the Protestant churches and ministry in New England, and the Indian conversion phenomenon, were a strong stimulus to the Christians and churches in England for pursuing further reformation. However, at the same time, for Eliot, New England was also a place for realizing the reformation. After encountering Indians and experiencing their conversion and religious changes, Eliot's convictions about Indian conversion and evangelization as a new vision in New England were strengthened. In this sense, the

---

299. *Glorious Progress* (1649), 166.

300. William Leverich is probably William Leveritch. He does not appear in *ODNB* and *ANB*. According to Hardman Moore, William Leveritch (1603–77) was a minister in New England. Hardman Moore, "Appendix 3," in *Pilgrims*, 194.

301. *Strength out of Weaknesse* (1652), 235.

302. *Further Account* (1660), 359.

rhetoric of the Eliot Tracts for Indian conversion and urging reformation was also targeting New England puritans who were indifferent to Indian conversion.[303]

Conclusion

For puritans, conversion was the primary task and purpose of ministry. Under poor ministerial conditions, including a serious lack of ministers, their pastoral inability, and the ignorance and immorality of parishioners, conversion was a fundamental and urgent issue for a puritan minister. For puritans rooted in Reformed theology, conversion brought a fundamental ontological change not only of invisible heart, but also of visible life. Puritans' special concern for inner change and examination for conversion implicitly reflects the fact that conversion was an actual and experimental phenomenon rather than an intellectual agreement or acceptance, but also the strong inwardness in puritan conversion and piety. For puritans, conversion experience was essential for salvation and for them, conversion was a significant measure for human salvation. Puritans' vivid description of the contrast between the "converted" and the "unconverted" shows puritans' urging conversion upon the unconverted. Also, their strong emphasis on God's calling for conversion requested human determination and response. Puritans argued for human response and responsibility by using free will and the means of grace toward the calling of God for salvation. Although puritans were strongly based in Reformed theology on the total depravity of human beings and God's absolute sovereignty over salvation, they highlighted human determination and active response towards God for conversion as their fundamental spiritual concern.

For puritans, the most important means of ministry was pastoral teaching focusing on the Word of God, because the proclamation of the Word is crucially related to conversion as puritans' fundamental concern. Puritans' emphasis on pastorship as teachers of God's Word came from their current poor ministerial situation neglecting the teaching of the Word. For puritans, preaching was a primary task and duty of pastors. However, they also emphasized other ways of pastoral teaching. Another important pastoral method of teaching was catechizing. For effective pastoral teaching, puritans highlighted various methodologies such as personal or private instruction, and visitations based on text-based and oral education. Also, puritans developed counselling and spiritual direction as a significant aspect of pastoral teaching

---

303. For New England puritans' indifference with Indian evangelization, see pp. 35–39 above.

and pastorship. In addition, puritan pastors took heed of both parishioners and pastors themselves. As seen in the example given by Richard Greenham, pastoral teaching for pastors was also an important area of puritan ministry.

Puritans considered the practice of piety not only as a visible sign of conversion, but also as a means of conversion and a lifelong duty, ultimately toward salvation. The two key issues in puritan piety were conversion and Biblicism based on Reformed tradition. For puritans, the practice of piety was the pursuit of "heart religion"; seeking inner spiritual experience and communion with God through meditation, prayer, fasting, and singing psalms. Also, for puritans, piety was not only a duty of "visible saints," but also a sign of being "visible saints." Because of this concept, puritans considered visible sanctified life to be of great importance.

In addition, it is worth mentioning that the ultimate pursuit of the puritan ministry was the reformation of both church and society. Conversion was not only the fundamental concern of puritans, but also the starting point to actualize reformation through the establishment of the pure reformed church and society. Puritans pursued the reformation through their faithful conversion-oriented ministry.

Lastly, this chapter tried to answer the questions: for Eliot, what was the fundamental reason to initiate his preaching to the Indians, and what was the lasting motive for him to continually push ahead his ministry to them in the New England wilderness? In pursuit of a possible answer, this chapter has argued for puritan conversion theology as plausible motive. Although Eliot did not have a vision for Indian conversion when he left England in 1631, one of the primary reasons that he finally became involved with Indian ministry was the puritans' fundamental ministerial concern for "soul-saving worke." The Eliot Tracts provide significant resources for understanding puritan thought on conversion and salvation, which became an ideological motive that led Eliot to push ahead with Indian ministry as his new pastoral vision in New England. In this sense, Eliot's first two reasons for Indian ministry—"the glory of God, in the conversion of some of these poor, desolate souls" and his "compassion and ardent affection to them"—reflect his puritan theological and ministerial motives for Indian conversion and ministry.[304]

Through the rhetoric urging the reformation in England and New England via arguing for Indian conversion, one can understand a significant point: (as mentioned above) puritans conceived that true conversion is a sign and process of reformation. This is a crucial hint, to realize that one of the reasons Eliot was eagerly involved with Indian conversion was his conviction that Indian conversion was a means for realizing the values of

---

304. *HCINE*, 170.

reformation. For Eliot, as for England, the phenomenon of Indian conversion was a visible and effective means not only for fundraising, but also for urging further reformation in England. At the same time, for New England, Indian conversion was not only a means of evoking interest and support for Indian ministry, but also for the process and actualization of the values of reformation in New England.

In the following chapters, we will examine how Eliot pursued his pastoral ministry to the New England Indians in the ideological communication with his puritan background in the seventeenth-century transatlantic world. In chapter 4, we will, first of all, investigate Praying Towns and Indian churches as examples of Eliot's pastoral field which fulfilled his puritan vision.

Part 2

John Eliot and the Indians

4

Praying Towns and Indian Churches

JOHN ELIOT, WHO FIRST started preaching the gospel to New England Indians in 1646, finally began to establish Praying Towns from 1650 on. Eliot established Natick as the first Praying Town in 1651, and by 1675, thirteen more Praying Towns were established by Eliot. The first official Indian church was established at Natick in 1660, and five more churches were established by 1675.[1] John Eliot's short summary of a letter of Mr. John Wilson, the pastor of the church of Christ at Boston in New England, who visited Natick, is as follows:

> The next Letter good Reader ... is one that came from Mr John Wilson ... who accompanying the Governour, together with Mr Eliot and sundry others to their new Towne built by the Converted Indians, where they purpose by Gods permission to cohabit together, that so they may enjoy all those Ordinances the Lord Jesus hath left unto his Church.[2]

John Wilson, as Eliot described in the letter, witnessed what Eliot as a puritan pastor was doing and how the Indians of Natick responded and lived under the pastoral direction of Eliot in their special town. For Eliot, the Praying Town was not only a civilized cohabitation of Praying Indians, but

---

1. For the explanation of the term, "Praying Indians," see p. 4n6 above.
2. *Strength out of Weaknesse* (1652), 230. Bremer, "Wilson, John (c.1591–1667)"; Hardman Moore, "Appendix 3," in *Pilgrims*, 186–201.

also a place for practicing Christian faith. The ideal Christian community that Eliot dreamed about was a biblical community covenanted with God; not only an ecclesiastical, but also a civil community governed by Christ. That would be the "Kingdome of our Lord Jesus." John Wilson provided Eliot's profession about the town: "he professed unto mee that upon all his best observation, there was a very hopefull beginning amongst them of the Grace & Kingdome of our Lord Jesus. The Lord vouchsafe to be the Omega among them as well as the Alpha of this blessed change."[3]

There has not been much research into Eliot's theological understanding of the establishment of the Praying Towns and Indian churches. However, there are a few studies that investigate the theological and ministerial meaning of the Praying Towns and Indian churches in relation to the Kingdom of Christ. Ola Elizabeth Winslow provided a description of the establishment of the Praying Towns and Indian churches as significant missionary achievements in her biography.[4] Alden T. Vaughan argued for the sincerity of puritan mission in relation to the social and political context of the English puritans and native Indians, and treated the Praying Towns as Eliot's missionary result, but without serious theological consideration.[5] Theodore Dwight Bozeman's work on the Praying Towns has been important, but mainly focused on the realization of primitivism in the towns, based on Scripture.[6] Sydney H. Rooy, unlike other researchers, provided theological analysis of the three communities which Eliot pursued—the Praying Towns, the church, and the Kingdom of God. However, Rooy's discussion was framed by a modern understanding of "mission" and "missionary works," and focused on the process of the establishment of Praying Towns and Indian churches as the development and achievement of Eliot's missionary works. Also, Rooy did not consider the puritans' own theological and ministerial analysis of Praying Towns and Indian churches.[7] Richard W. Cogley, who offered the most thorough description of Eliot's missionary work in New England, analyzed the detailed process of the establishment of the Praying Towns and Indian churches. However, he did not address Eliot's ecclesiology in depth.[8]

This chapter seeks to answer some major questions: how Eliot in his theology and ministry understood Praying Towns and Indian churches, and

3. *Strength out of Weaknesse* (1652), 233.
4. Winslow, *John Eliot*, 122–36, 148–59, 160–6.
5. Vaughan, *New England Frontier*, ix–lxv, 235–308.
6. Bozeman, *To Live Ancient Lives*, 153, 267–76.
7. Rooy, *The Theology of Missions*, 156–241.
8. *JEMI*, 1–171.

what the relationship between the two Christian communities was. These are topics which have not been explored well, to date.

For a theological investigation of Praying Towns and Indian churches, the records and reports in the Eliot Tracts are essential resources, not only for the process of the establishment of the towns and churches but also for theological ideas about the communities. Eliot's two treatises on civil polity and church polity—*The Christian Commonwealth* (1659) and *The Communion of Churches* (1665)—are also significant writings for understanding Eliot's ideological foundations for the two communities. Although *The Communion of Churches* (1665) mainly focuses on ecclesiastical polity, it is also useful for investigating Eliot's theological and ministerial understanding of the church itself. In addition, the correspondence between John Eliot and Richard Baxter, 1656-82, is a tremendously important source for understanding Eliot's ecclesiology.[9]

Praying Towns

Eliot acknowledged that he first preached to the Indians at Nonantum on 28 October 1646. Daniel Gookin also confirmed this.[10] After this, Eliot visited Nonantum a further three times, on 11 and 26 November and 9 December 1646.[11] After 1646, Eliot's Indian ministry progressed rapidly. During his

---

9. In the correspondence between Eliot and Baxter, we can see serious ecclesiological debates between them, alongside other issues such as ministerial reports, personal affairs and thanks, and requests for financial and personal help. This correspondence is an essential resource for understanding the ecclesiological ideas of Eliot and Baxter and similarities and differences between them. See *CRBJE*, 138–76, 442–66; Keeble and Nuttall, *Calendar of the Correspondence of Richard Baxter*. Through the ecclesiastical argument with Baxter in their correspondence, in particular, between 1667 and 1670, Eliot strongly expressed his ideas on congregationalism. See *CRBJE*, 161–76, 442–62. Eliot's argument for congregationalism and Baxter's refutation of it is main contents of the correspondence in the period.

10. *Day-Breaking* (1647), 83; *Clear Sun-Shine* (1647), 124; *HCINE*, 168. In fact, before he preached at Nonantum, Eliot preached at Dorchester mill, which was Neponsitt, with the aid of an interpreter. Yet, he was not welcomed by the Indians and he also did not consider it his first preaching to the Indians. *Clear Sun-Shine* (1648), 124. See also *ET*, 10; *JEMI*, 49.

11. *Day-Breaking* (1647), 79–100; *JJW*, 673–74, 682–84; Rooy, *The Theology of Missions*, 179–86; Morrison, *A Praying People*, 37–38, 44, 50–53. Nonantum was the first Indian town to obtain legal status from the General Court in 1646. *Day-Breaking* (1647), 97; *Clear Sun-Shine* (1648), 114, 117, 120, 134, 136, 137, 120; *Further Account* (1660), 365, 373, 382, 389; *JEMI*, 52. According to Shepard in *Day-Breaking* (1647), the meaning of Nonantum in English is rejoicing. He connected the meaning of the town's name with the joy felt by Christians who enjoy God and his word. *Day-Breaking* (1647), 97.

Indian ministry from 1646 to 1649, Eliot realized the necessity for a separate and stable place for effective pastoral teaching and ministry.

Natick, recognized as the first Praying Town and the "chief town,"[12] was established shortly after the Society for the Propagation of the Gospel in New England was established in 1649 (the society had been formed by the Long Parliament to promote the conversion of New England Indians).[13] Eliot searched "for a fit place" and finally through his "sundry journeyes and travels to severall places" he chose Natick, a place on the north side of the Charles River. Natick was granted 2000 acres by the General Court of Massachusetts in October 1651, along the Charles River near the town of Dedham. The Praying Indians who moved to the new settlement at Natick mainly came from Nonantum. For a while the Indians lived in wigwams. In addition to these there were soon also various sizes of English-style buildings built of wood. Along with private houses, a large meetinghouse was built for worship services and as a school room. The place for worship and schooling was the lower floor, and storage was on the second floor. In one corner on the second floor, Eliot also had a room which he used for overnight stays when he visited to do pastoral teaching. The Praying Indians also built a footbridge over the Charles River, and created a fort made of whole trees.[14]

The population of Natick is not known, but through some comments in the Eliot Tracts and other resources we can conjecture that there were approximately one hundred Praying Indians, including children.[15] John Endecott reported "the Indians which were in number men & women about one hundred."[16] Eliot said that "because we cannot have competent

12. *Late and Further Manifestation* (1655), 304; *Brief Narrative* (1671), 402; Winslow, *John Eliot*, 122–36; *JEMI*, 105–39.

13. The Society is also known as The New England Company. It was given this name in 1660 and was the oldest English Protestant missionary society. *HCINE*, ch. XI; Winship, "Introduction," in *The New England Company of 1649 and John Eliot*; Kellaway, *The New England Company*. For the history of Natick Praying Town before 1800, see O'Brien, *Dispossession by Degrees*. O'Brien, in his book, argued that Natick Indians were not erased or made extinct by diseases and war, but actually survived in their land, which was becoming a Euro-American society, while the Natick were slowly and steadily being displaced by the English. For the Praying Town of Natick in Eliot's lifetime, see O'Brien, *Dispossession by Degrees*, 31–90.

14. *Light Appearing* (1651), 201–2; *Strength out of Weaknesse* (1652), 231–32, 243; "A Brief Narration," in *Late and Further Manifestation* (1655), 303; *HCINE*, 180–83; *LJE*, 89; Byington, "John Eliot," 126–27; Winslow, *John Eliot*, 122–36; *JEMI*, 106–11; *ET*, 15; Morrison, *A Praying People*, 76–99. For the map of Natick area, see *JEMI*, 108, map 2.

15. According to John Wilson, "there were I thinke not fewer then [sic] a hundred men women and young ones." *Strength out of Weaknesse* (1652), 232.

16. *Strength out of Weaknesse* (1652), 242.

accommodations at Natick, for those that be there, which are about fifty lots, more or less."[17]

By 1675, thirteen further Praying Towns had been established. Each town had its own land (between two thousand and seven thousand acres), its own place of worship, a school and a teacher. Also, each town had its own native pastoral leaders who were trained by Eliot. According to Gookin, there were eleven hundred Praying Indians in the Praying Towns in 1674.[18]

The Praying Towns were not just a simple place of cohabitation for the Praying Indians' new life. The towns were established based on a well-organized ideological paradigm. Eliot's purposes and ideological foundations for the towns will be discussed below.

"Civility" and "Religion": The Purpose of the Towns

For Eliot, one of his most important ministerial projects was to establish the Praying Towns. The towns were not only civilized ministerial fields, but also the place where he could actualize the values of the Kingdom of Christ to help to usher in the millennium. Eliot mentioned two specific purposes of the towns: "civility" and "religion." Eliot said, "I finde it absolutely necessary to carry on civility with Religion."[19] For Eliot, Praying Towns were not only places of civility, but also places for effective pastoral teaching.

Civilizing the Indians was a significant task in Eliot's Indian ministry, because of the function of civilization as an essential means for the effective practice of puritan pastoral teaching. In other words, the civilization of native Indians was a prerequisite for Eliot's puritan ministry to native Indians, or a key task that had to be pursued simultaneously with the preaching of the gospel. According to the Eliot Tracts, the English did not perceive the Indians to be civilized enough, and for puritan ministers, the Indians' uncivilizedness hindered the spreading of the gospel. The authors of *New Englands*

---

17. *Late and Further Manifestation* (1655), 304.

18. The Praying Towns after Natick were the following: Punkapoag, Wamesit, Hassanamesit, Okommakamesit, Nashobahh, and Magunkog which were considered as "old towns"; Quantisset, Pakachoog, Chabanakongkomun, Wabquisset, Manchage, Maanexit, and Waeuntug, which were considered as "new towns" by Gookin. For detailed information about the other Praying Towns including the name of each town and leaders, see *Brief Narrative* (1671), 402–6; *HCINE*, ch. VII; Byington, "John Eliot," 129–30; Winslow, *John Eliot*, 160–66; *JEMI*, 140–71; *ID*, 40. Against Gookin's description of old Praying Towns, Cogley argued that Magunkog (established in 1669) hardly qualified as "old." *HCINE*, 180–89; *JEMI*, 145. For Gookin's description of new Praying Towns, see *HCINE*, 189–93.

19. *Glorious Progress* (1649), 158.

First Fruits (1643) argued that the foremost reason that made native Indians' "coming into the gospel the more slow" was their uncivilizedness, from an English perspective: "First, their infinite distance from Christianity, having never been prepared thereunto by any Civility at all."[20] It is important to understand that when we see the term "civility" in the Eliot Tracts, the term needs to be understood from the perspective of seventeenth-century English puritan authors. That is to say, when the authors argued the necessity of "civility" or "civilization" in native Indians, they meant the English style of "civility," consciously or unconsciously. Scholars today stress that Indians had their own political and economic system and cultural and religious life, and therefore modern writers do not judge the relationship between Indian and English civilization to be a matter of inferiority or superiority to others.[21] The judgement of civilizedness or uncivilizedness and inferiority or superiority in the Eliot Tracts reveals a seventeenth-century English-centered perspective.

The aspects of "civilization" mentioned in the Eliot Tracts can be broadly divided into two parts.[22] The first is civilized life and culture supported by civilized elements, such as an English style of clothes, gardening, building, and literacy. Eliot expressed his strong concern for (as he saw it, from his English perspective) the Indians' uncivilized life. He wrote to Edward Winslow that "they have not meanes of Physick at all, onely make use of Pawwawes when they be sick, which makes them loath to give it over."[23] In another letter, he seemed to imply that the provision of suitable apparel for the Indians and "imployment of them in planting Orchards and Gardens" were important. He also mentioned teaching them English-style gardening skills and how to use tools, as a form of "project" for the Indians. This clearly reflects his English view of the "uncivilizedness" of the native Indians.[24]

The rules for moral and ordered life, among the Praying Indians, encouraged and expected by the puritans, was expressed in a code of conduct or order which was made by the Indians themselves in August 1646, based on English standards. This order not only includes a general social code of conduct, such as regulations for change of apparel and hair style and against

---

20. *New Englands First Fruits* (1643), 58.

21. See Kupperman, *Settling with the Indians*; Kupperman, *Indians and English*; Wilbur, *The New England Indians*; Calloway, *New Worlds for All*; Hoffer, *Sensory Worlds in Early America*.

22. The lexical definition of the term "civilization" is "The stage of human social development and organization which is considered most advanced." *Oxford Dictionary of English*, s.v. "civilization," http://www.oxfordreference.com.

23. Eliot to Winslow, 12 November 1648, in *Glorious Progress* (1649), 154.

24. Eliot to Winslow, 13 November 1649, in *Glorious Progress* (1649), 157–58.

crimes such as stealing, fornication, lying, adultery, and murder (with penalties), but also orders for conduct in religion such as Sabbath-keeping and household prayer meetings.[25] From one perspective, the Praying Indians' rules for ordered and moral life can be understood simply in terms of social and civilized life in an English fashion. However, from another perspective, the desire shown in the rules for a changed or reformed life can be seen as the result of a puritan ministry that emphasized visible signs of "sincere converts" in their ordinary life. Thomas Shepard understood the "Conclusions and Orders" made and agreed to by native Indians "as fruits of the ministry of the Word."[26] For Shepard, the reason that native Indians created the "Conclusions and Orders" as their code of conduct, based on English standards, was partly because "they see and heare of their great distance from others of the English" as much as they called themselves "poore Creatures" but "the chiefe cause seemes to be the power of the Word, which hath been the chiefe cause of these Orders."[27]

Secondly, civility in the Eliot Tracts signifies well-organized settlements. In fact, civilized life and well-organized settlements were a prerequisite for New England puritans as well. However, the difference between Indians and puritans in terms of the necessity of civilized life and settlements was that the former needed both of them while the latter needed only firm and well-arranged settlements in New England (since they brought their own civilization from England). Eliot's emphasis on Indian civility can be found in his argument for the establishment of Praying Towns as well-systemized settlements. In a letter to Winslow, Eliot argued that the establishment of Praying Towns was for the Indians' civility. He stated that through the formation of a government based on this civility, the Indians "might have a Church and the Ordinances of Christ among them."[28] For Eliot, the establishment of the Praying Towns was urgent: "I dayly still see more evidence that this is the very way which the Lord would have us take at present."[29]

Although Eliot said that civility should be established first before the practice of the ordinances of Christ, this probably did not mean that civility was more important, but rather that he believed civility was required for Christian religious life. For him, one of the reasons for this urgency

25. "Conclusions and Orders made and agreed upon by divers Sachims and other principall men amongst the Indians at Concord, in the end of the eleventh moneth, Au. 1646." *Clear Sun-Shine* (1648), 115–16.
26. *Clear Sun-Shine* (1648), 116.
27. *Clear Sun-Shine* (1648), 116.
28. Eliot to Winslow, 8 July 1649, in *Light Appearing* (1651), 186.
29. *Light Appearing* (1651), 187.

regarding the civility of Indians was because Eliot believed that a civilized political and social system was essential for the establishment of a puritan ecclesiastical system for puritan ministry. For Eliot, from his puritan ministerial perspective, the "unfixed," "confused," "ungoverned," "uncivilized," and "unsubdued" Indian society was not appropriate for the paradigm of puritan Christianity and ministry.[30]

One of the most serious problems Eliot perceived with regards to the Indians' "uncivilizedness" was their illiteracy. Eliot expressed his hope for native Indians' literacy. In a letter to Winslow of 21 October 1650, he said: "If the Lord please to prosper our poor beginnings, my purpose is . . . to have schoole exercises for all the men by daily instructing of them to read and write, &c."[31] The importance he placed on literacy was not only for civility, but also ultimately for the teaching of the Bible, which was the puritan ministers' primary task: "If the Lord bring us to live in a Towne and Society, we must have special care to have Schools for the instruction of the youth in reading, that they may be able to read the Scriptures at least."[32] Eliot's ultimate goal was to make it possible for the Indians to read the Bible in their own language: "my desire therefore is to teach them all to write, and read written hand, and thereby with pains taking, they may have some of the Scriptures in their own Language."[33] In this sense, for Eliot, literacy was not an option but a prerequisite for the puritan pastoral teaching of the Word of God as the center of puritan ministry.

Eliot mentioned various reasons for the establishment of the Praying Towns in the documents printed in the Eliot Tracts. It is evident that effective pastoral teaching based on the Word was one of the primary reasons. Eliot in his letter to Winslow of 12 November 1648 said:

> A place must be found . . . where they must have the word constantly taught, and government constantly exercised, meanes of instructing them in Letters, Trades, and Labours, as building, fishing, Flax and Hemp dressing, planting Orchards, &c. Such a project in a fit place, would draw many that are well minded together.[34]

30. *Glorious Progress* (1649), 159; *Light Appearing* (1651), 201; *Late and Further Manifestation* (1655), 303.

31. Eliot to Winslow, 21 October 1650, in *Light Appearing* (1651), 206.

32. Eliot to Winslow, 8 July 1649, in *Light Appearing* (1651), 187. For Eliot's educational activity for the literacy of Indians, see *Clear Sun-Shine* (1648), 132; *Strength out of Weaknesse* (1652), 223, 225, 231, 243; *Tears of Repentance* (1653), 257; *Brief Narrative* (1671), 401.

33. Eliot to Winslow, 21 October 1650, in *Light Appearing* (1651), 206.

34. *Glorious Progress* (1649), 152. For the purposes and reasons of the establishment

Eliot's strong aspiration to found the towns for pastoral reasons is also clearly shown in a letter of 29 December 1649, which cited the argument of an Indian who was the chief Sachem of Pautuket for the necessity of constant and regular pastoral teaching. This signalled a need for puritan residential pastors in the Indian community. Eliot said:

> [M]y coming thither but once in a yeere, did them but little good, because they soone had forgotten what I taught, it being so seldome, and so long betwixt the times. . . . That he had many men, and of them many nought, and would not beleeve him that praying to God was so good, but if I would come and teach them, he hoped they would beleeve me; He farther added . . . as if one should come and throw a fine thing among them, and they earnestly catch at it, and like it well. . . . But they cannot look into it to see what is within it . . . they cannot tell whether . . . it may be a precious thing; but if it be opened, and they see what is within it, and see it precious, then they should beleeve it (so said he) you tell us of praying to God, (for so they call all Religion).[35]

According to Eliot, the Indians' desire for constant and regular pastoral care convinced him that Praying Towns were necessary: "such elegant arguments as these did he use, with much gravity, wisdom and affection; and truly my heart much yearneth towards them, and I have a great desire to make our Indian Towne that way."[36]

Eliot's purpose in founding Praying Towns, especially for the pastoral ministry for the Indians, illuminates the relationship between Praying Towns and parish-centered puritan ministry. For Eliot, the Praying Towns were not only an effective place for pastoral teaching, but also a kind of parish. That is to say that for Eliot, the Praying Towns were ministerial fields where he could effectively teach the Gospel and train up the Indians as mature and good Christians, not only in terms of knowledge of God, but also in a practical Christian life. This aspiration conformed to what other puritan pastors tried to do in their own parishes in New and Old England.

Eliot argued that civility should go hand in hand with the gospel. Eliot, in a letter to Shepard, wrote: "That which I first aymed at was to declare & deliver unto them the Law of God, to civilize them, Which course the Lord

---

of the Praying Towns that Eliot argued, see *Glorious Progress* (1649), 152, 158–59; *Light Appearing* (1651), 186–87, 189; *Strength out of Weaknesse* (1652), 226, 230; *Late and Further Manifestation* (1655), 303.

35. Eliot to Winslow, 29 December 1649, in *Light Appearing* (1651), 189.
36. *Light Appearing* (1651), 189.

took by Moses, to give the Law to that rude company because of Transgression, Gal. 3.19. to convince, bridle, restrain, and civilize them, and also to humble them."[37] Eliot also wrote, "I finde it absolutely necessary to carry on civility with Religion."[38] Here, it is evident that Eliot believed civilization and evangelization should be simultaneous. For Eliot, civility was necessary in order to understand the puritan way of life. With regards to the issue of cultural conflict between the Indians and the English, scholars described puritan ministers as the destroyers of Indian traditions and cultural oppressors who had transplanted English civilization in the native Indians' community.[39] However, for Eliot, considering the primary sources of Eliot's Indian ministry from the perspective of puritan ministry, it is probably true that the main purpose for emphasizing the Indians' civilization was not just transplantation of English civilization itself, but rather the Indians' conversion and evangelization through the preaching of the gospel. Therefore, civilizing the Indians was a form of preparation for puritan ministry. In fact, the Indians, at first, did not fully agree with or follow the English style of culture and civilization. Eliot in his letter to Shepard wrote, "But when I first attempted it, they gave no heed unto it, but were weary, and rather despised what I said." However, following this the Indians changed their minds and attitude towards English culture and civilization and instead wanted to accept it. For Eliot, the Indians' open-mindedness and acceptance of English civilization was a step towards receiving the Word of God:

> A while after God stirred up in some of them a desire to come into the English fashions, and live after their manner, but knew not how to attain unto it, yea despaired that ever it should come to passe in their days, but thought that in 40. Yeers more, some Indians would be all one English, and in an hundred yeers, all Indians here about, would so bee . . . my heart moved within mee, abhorring that wee should sit still and let that work alone, and hoping that this motion in them was of the Lord, and that this mind in them was a preparative to imbrace the Law and Word of God.[40]

In sum, for Eliot and the native Indians, civility was not the main purpose, but rather a means for successful evangelization. Civility was absolutely necessary for the pastoral teaching of the Word of God and for puritan ministry

37. Eliot to Shepard, 24 September 1647, in *Clear Sun-Shine* (1648), 124.

38. Eliot to Winslow, 13 November 1649, in *Glorious Progress* (1649), 158.

39. Jennings, *Invasion of America*. For more bibliography for this argument, see pp. 7–9 above.

40. Eliot to Shepard, 24 September 1647, in *Clear Sun-Shine* (1648), 124.

itself. In this sense, the simultaneous pursuit of civility and evangelization was one of Eliot's effective pastoral strategies for his native Indian ministry.

Biblicism and Millenarianism: The Ideological Foundations of the Towns

For Eliot, Praying Towns were based on his vision of biblical and millenarian civil polity. Along with the materials in the Eliot Tracts, Eliot's *The Christian Commonwealth*—written in 1651 and published in 1659—is a significant source that can be used to understand Eliot's thoughts on civil polity and its relation to his vision of the Kingdom of Christ in the millennium.[41] This treatise, composed of eight chapters, was written with Biblicism and millenarianism as its ideological foundations. For Eliot, Praying Towns were not only a well-organized cohabitation for "civility," but also a pastoral field for "religion" based on the Bible: "The present work of the Lord that is to be done among them, is to gather them together from their scattered kinde of life; First, unto Civil Society, then to Ecclesiastical, and both by the Divine direction of the Word of the Lord; they are still earnestly desirous of it."[42] *The Christian Commonwealth* (1659) also provides an argument which focused on the presentation of biblical civil polity, mainly through literal exposition and adaptation from the Scripture, especially Exodus 18.[43] For Eliot, Scripture was the standard and basis: "There is undoubtedly a forme of Civil Government instituted by God himself in the holy Scriptures, whereby any Nation may enjoy all the ends and effects of Government in the best manner. . . . We should derogate from the sufficiency and perfection of the Scriptures."[44] Eliot also said: "The written Word of God is the perfect Systeme of Frame of Laws, to guide all the Moral actions of man, either towards God or man: the Application whereof to every Case according to its

41. Maclear, "New England and the Fifth Monarchy," 253–55.

42. *Light Appearing* (1651), 201. See Eliot, *The Christian Commonwealth* (1659), 5. See also Morrison, *A Praying People*, 90–99.

43. Chapter I is about the foundation of the polity of the Kingdom of Christ: Covenant of God as membership requirement of the polity and the Bible. Chapter II provides detailed regulations of the division of polity. Chapter III is about the role of rulers, the functional manual of each division, the cohabitation and superintendence regulations, and ruler meetings. Chapter IV explains the regulations and process of judgement in each division including the appeal or transmission of certain difficult or weighty issues to higher courts. Chapters V and VI mainly treat the roles and duties of rulers. Chapter VII is about the detailed regulation and multiplication of the divisions. Lastly, chapter VIII re-emphasizes the Scripture as the fundamental foundation and the only law of the polity.

44. Eliot, "Preface," in *The Christian Commonwealth* (1659).

circumstances, must be by the wisdom and discretion of the Judges, guided by the light of the Scriptures."[45] Eliot attributed his vision for the Praying Towns to his own study of the Bible rather than to any other resources, including political theory. He said, "This occasion did first put me upon this Study, who am not Statesman, nor acquainted with matters of that nature; but only spend time in the Study of the holy Books of God."[46]

Millenarianism was also an essential foundation of civil polity. As has already been argued in chapter 2, Eliot expressed his millenarian vision after 1649, when he was seriously concerned about the situation in England, and expressed his strong desire for the realization of the Kingdom of God ruled by Christ, based on Scripture, in England. Eliot had a strong aspiration for the establishment of the Kingdom of Christ in the Indian community of New England. He stated that "it is my desire and prayer; my work is to endeavour the setting up Christ Kingdome among the Indians."[47] For Eliot, the millenarian concept of the Kingdom of Christ in the Indian Praying Towns embraced not only civil, but also religious areas. Eliot said: "Touching the way of their Government, I also intimated the purpose of my heart, that I intend to direct them according as the Lord shall please to help and assist to set up the Kingdome of Jesus Christ fully, so that Christ shall reigne both in Church and Common-wealth, both in Civil and Spiritual matters."[48] To do this, a biblical political structure was essential:

> We will ... fly to the Scriptures, for every Law, Rule, Direction, Form, or whatever we do. And when everything both Civil & Spiritual are done by the direction of the word of Christ ... and by this means all Kingdomes and Nations shall become the Kingdomes of Christ, because he shall rule them in all things by his holy word.[49]

The Christian Commonwealth (1659) introduced additional features of Eliot's civil polity. Eliot's ideal civil polity was a representative system.[50]

45. Eliot, *The Christian Commonwealth* (1659), 35.

46. Eliot, *The Christian Commonwealth* (1659), 6.

47. Eliot to Winslow, 29 December 1649, in *Light Appearing* (1651), 192. Eliot also expressed this idea in his letter to Jonathan Hanmer, 19 July 1652. See *JEI*, 8.

48. Eliot to Winslow, 29 December 1649, in *Light Appearing* (1651), 195. See *Light Appearing* (1651), 192.

49. Eliot to Winslow, 29 December 1649, in *Light Appearing* (1651), 195. See Eliot, "An Account of Indian Churches in New-England" (1673), 129.

50. Eliot's strong support for a representative system can not only be found in *The Christian Commonwealth* (1659) for his civil polity, but also in *The Communion of Churches* (1665) for his ecclesiastical polity. The representative system in Eliot's church polity will be discussed below.

Eliot, in *The Christian Commonwealth* (1659), patterned his form of polity on Scripture:

> The particular form of Government, which is approved of God [Exod. 18.23], instituted by Moses [Exod. 18. 24.] ... they choose [Exod.18.21] unto themselves Rulers of thousands [Exod. 18.25; Deut. 1.15], of hundreds, of fifties and of tens, who shall govern according to the pure, holy, righteous, perfect and good Law of God [Deut. 1.17], written in the Scriptures of the Old and New testament.[51]

For Eliot, this representative system was of "Divine Institution": "And adding to this, above all considerations and commendations, that it is a Divine Institution, sprung from heavenly wisdom commanded in Scripture, filled with the Spirit of God, which is able to carry on the wheels of this Government, with a most irresistible and successful force and power."[52] He argued that even "the Angels of Heaven are governed by this Order of Government" and "the Saints in heaven seem to be in the same order; for when Christ cometh to judgement, and all the Saints with him, I Thes.4.13. they shall come in this order."[53] Eliot argued that a representative council system would operate in the Kingdom of Christ because God would commit the management to the people that He chooses: "Now therefore by these preparations made by the naked Arm of the Lord Jesus to set up his Kingdom in England, he calleth upon those Wortheies into whose hands he hath betrusted the managing of this great work, now to advance Christ, not man; not themselves, but Christ."[54]

Also, Eliot pursued the harmonization of civil and ecclesiastical functions in the polity. That is to say, civil and ecclesiastical functions were separate but complementary jurisdictions, and each had its own God-given rule. Eliot, in *The Christian Commonwealth*, argues that rulers have duties in relation to religious affairs, including the practice of all the commandments of God. They also have to maintain the purity of religion and piety, but also public and juridical affairs including a sound social life based on the commandment of God, legal judgment, punishment, education of youth, trade, fishing, and tillage.[55] Eliot discussed the duties and roles of rulers as representatives not only in religious affairs, but also in public affairs.[56]

---

51. Eliot, *The Christian Commonwealth* (1659), 3–4.
52. Eliot, *The Christian Commonwealth* (1659), 6.
53. Eliot, *The Christian Commonwealth* (1659), 6, 7.
54. Eliot, "Preface," in *The Christian Commonwealth* (1659).
55. Eliot, *The Christian Commonwealth* (1659), 23–27.
56. Eliot, *The Christian Commonwealth* (1659), 15–27.

Eliot applied his biblical and millenarian civil polity to the Praying Towns. On 6 August 1651, Eliot held a large meeting with Praying Indians who gathered from diverse areas. He read and expounded Exodus chapter 18 to the Indians as the biblical standard for the political and social structure of the Praying Towns. He had already explained this biblical social structure to the Praying Indians several times. Now, Eliot reported that the Indians chose their rulers for each part within the town:

> [A]nd finally they did solemnly choose two Rulers among themselves, they first chose a Ruler of an Hundred, then they chose two rulers of Fifties, then they chose Ten or Tithing Men. ... And lastly, for that dayes worke every man chose who should be his Ruler of ten, the Rulers standing in order, and every man going to the man he chose, and it seemed into mee as if I had seene scattered bones goe, bone unto his bone, and so lived a civill politicall life, and the Lord was pleased to minister no small comfort unto my spirit, when I saw it.[57]

Eliot fully acknowledged the important role of Indian rulers in Praying Towns and considered them to be a significant medium for God's management of the Christian communities.

After about one month, the Praying Towns were proclaimed to be a biblical civil covenantal community on 24 September 1651. Eliot reported:

> After this worke was ended, they did enter into Covenant with God, and each other, to be the Lords people, and to be governed by the word of the Lord in all things. ... Thus have I briefly descried that blessed day wherein these poore soules solemnly became the people of the Lord: this was on the 24th day of the 7th Moneth, 1651.[58]

The Indian civil covenant reflects seventeenth-century civil covenants in English settlements. According to David A. Weir, who analyzed the contents of all the surviving civil and church covenants in New England from 1620 to 1708, the terms "civil covenant" and "church covenant" signify written documents that are "relatively brief and that spell out the initial vision for a New England community or religious body." While "church covenants" primarily focused on "the divine-human relationship," "civil covenants" "were more secularized and concerned with this world." Weir argued that the covenants as "axiomatic templates" were utilized as "an instrument of formation" of

---

57. *Strength out of Weaknesse* (1652), 226–27. For Gookin's description of the civil polity of Praying Towns, see *HCINE*, 177, 181.

58. *Strength out of Weaknesse* (1652), 227, 229. 24 September 1651.

the community, as they had functioned as the reformational instrument in Europe. The civil and church covenants, which provided a strong base for New England society, show how New England puritans sought an ordered social structure on which to establish their settlements. According to Weir, there are approximately 101 civil covenants that survive, and these civil covenants can be categorized into four types: combination or compact, charter, patent, and legislative action. Also, the civil covenants had a great variety of forms, and there is no uniform model. The broad spectrum of New England civil covenants reveals "the heterogeneity of early New England attitudes toward civil government, and the flexibility that could be found in the arrangements of church, state, religion, and society." Some covenants, such as the New Haven Plantation, emphasized federal theology, biblical social structure and civil government as a holy and sacred institution, and the establishment and maintenance of the church of Christ and its ordinances. In contrast, other covenants, such as the covenants of Woburn and Medfield, Massachusetts Bay Colony, were not theocentric or christocentric although they were not totally secular.[59]

For Eliot, Praying Towns as biblical civil covenantal communities included the traditional biblical concept of covenant which was recognized as the key communal identity of ancient Israel as God's people. The covenant as biblical civil covenant includes not only the testament of people's faith and the Ten Commandments, but also social orders and a code of conduct based on the covenant and commandments.[60] Eliot, in *Strength out of Weaknesse* (1652), provided a statement of the biblical civil covenant that the Praying Indians should follow:

> Wee are the sonnes of Adam, wee and our forefathers have a long time been lost in our sinnes, but now the mercy of the Lord beginneth to finde us out againe; therefore the grace of Christ helping us, wee doe give ourselves and our Children, &c. Wee doe give ourselves and our Children unto God to be his people, Hee shall rule us in all our affaires, not onely in our Religion, and affaires of the Church (these wee desire as soone as wee can, if God will) but also in all our workes and affaires in this world, God shall rule over us. Isa.33.22. The Lord is our Judge, the Lord is our Law-giver, the Lord is our King, Hee will save us; the Wisedome which God hath taught us in his Booke, that shall guide us and direct us in the way. Oh Jehovah, teach us wisedome to finde out they wisedome in thy Scriptures, let the grace of Christ helpe us, because Christ is the wisedome of God,

---

59. Weir, *Early New England*, 2, 6, 74, 87–103, 103–7, 125, 135.
60. Weir, *Early New England*, 1–23.

> send they Spirit into our hearts, and let it teach us, Lord take us
> to be thy people, and let us take thee to be our God.⁶¹

Except for the opening part of the covenant about the sins of the Indians as "the sonnes of Adam," which was apparently included by Cotton's advice, it is likely that all the contents of the covenant were created by Eliot himself.⁶² According to Eliot, for Praying Indians, the covenant was "an Act of knowledge and faith" and "this Act of forming themselves into the Government of God, and entering into this Government is the first publique Record among the Indians."⁶³ According to Weir, among fourteen Praying Towns established by Eliot, only Natick had a civil covenant.⁶⁴

It is not easy to compare Natick's Indian civil covenant to English civil covenants directly. However, it is evident that Indian civil covenant reveals the puritan aspiration for a theocentric and ordered civil society based on the Bible. As we can see above, the core themes of the Indian civil covenant were total submission to God, the sovereignty and ruling of God in ecclesiastical and civil affairs, the authority of the Bible, christological statements, and trinitarian understanding through emphasizing the works of God, Christ, and the Holy Spirit in the community. According to Weir, the strong christological statements of the native Indians' civil covenants drafted by John Eliot and Thomas Mayhew were unusual in English civil covenants.⁶⁵ If, for example, we compare the Natick civil covenant with a church covenant in seventeenth-century New England, it seems the Indian civil covenant was not dissimilar to a church covenant in New England. The church covenant of Boston First Church published by John Cotton in 1641 is a good model. John Cotton provided the church covenant of Boston First Church in his *A Coppy of a Letter of Mr. Cotton of Boston, in New England* (1641):

> I am to require of you in the name of the Lord, and of his Church, before you can be admitted there unto, whether you be willing to enter a holy Covenant with God, and with them and by the grace and helpe of Christ be willing to deny your selfe, and all your former polutions, and corruptions, wherein in any sort you have walked, and so to give up your selfe to the Lord Iesus, making him your onely priest and attonement, your onely profit, your

---

61. *Strength out of Weaknesse* (1652), 227. See HCINE, 181; LJE, 90. Mayhew also provided a platform of covenant in *Tears of Repentance* (1653). See the letter of Thomas Mayhew, 22 October 1652, in *Tears of Repentance* (1653), 256–57.
62. *Strength out of Weaknesse* (1652), 227–28. See JEMI, 112–13.
63. *Strength out of Weaknesse* (1652), 227.
64. Weir, "Appendix I," in *Early New England*, 243–66.
65. Weir, *Early New England*, 10, 73–135.

onely guide and King, and Lawgiver, and to walke before him in all professed subjections unto all his holy Ordinance, according to the rule of the Gospell, and to walke together with his Church and the members thereof in brotherly love, and mutuall edification and succor according to God; then doe I also promise unto you in the name of this Church, that by the helpe of Christ, we likewise will walke towards you in all brotherly love and holy watchfulnesse to the mutuall building, up one of another in the fellowship of the Lord Iesus, Amen, Amen.[66]

In Boston's church covenant, the stress on repentance of sins, total submission to God, believing God as king, lawgiver, and ruler, the authority of the Bible, and christocentric understanding are similar to the emphases of the Natick civil covenant.

Although Praying Towns became biblical and civilized Christian societies soon after their establishment, it is striking that no covenanted church appeared in any of the towns until 1660. It was usual for puritans in New England to proclaim their civil covenants first before establishing a church. However, the delay of nine years was unusual.[67] Why was the formation of an Indian church delayed for nine years? There were significant theological and ministerial reasons for the delay, probably related to Eliot's ecclesiology, which will be discussed below.

Indian Churches

Eliot's next project after establishing the Praying Towns was to establish the visible church of Christ based on New England's congregationalist ecclesiology.[68] An official Indian church was not established until 1660, although Natick as the first Praying Town (formally established in 1651) had a puritan ministry, including worship, pastoral teaching, and the practice of piety, from the start.[69] After Natick's covenanted Indian church was established in 1660, five more churches were established; one at Hassanemest, one at Mashpege, two at Martha's Vineyard, and one at Nantucket.[70] It is not clear how many church members there were. Eliot frankly said, "I have not number[e]d them, nor can I, though all baptized both adult and infants, are

66. Cotton, *A Coppy of a Letter of Mr. Cotton* (1641), 6.
67. Weir, *Early New England*, 92–93, 99.
68. *Strength out of Weaknesse* (1652), 227.
69. *Light Appearing* (1651), 201; *Strength out of Weaknesse* (1652), 221, 229, 231; *Late and Further Manifestation* (1655), 304.
70. Eliot, "An Account of Indian Churches in New-England" (1673), 124.

regist[e]red in the church at Natick; as also burials of such as are baptized, yet I know not if any of the other churches do so."[71] However, one can find approximate numbers of Natick church in 1670 through his report in *Brief Narrative*: he said, "we have betwixt forty and fifty Communicants at the Lord's Table."[72]

Eliot constantly strove towards establishing covenanted churches in the Indian Praying Towns, although he recognized that the essential first steps—introducing worship, pastoral education, and the practice of piety—could take a substantial time. Eliot, in his letter in *Light Appearing* (1651), shows his strong desire for the Indian church in the towns:

> By former Letters sent by Mr. Saltonstall; I informed you of the present state of the Indian work, and though I might adde farther matters, yet I shal[l] forbear, only this, still they continue constant, and earnestly desire to set upon the way of cohabitation & prepare for their enjoyment of that great blessing to gather a Church of Christ among them.[73]

Through Eliot's record of a speech made by an old Indian, Wamporas, "one of our first and principall men," we can glimpse Eliot's keen desire for the establishment of the Indian church:

> [W]hen I visited him the last time that I saw him in this world ... one of his sayings was this: now I dye, I strongly intreate you ... that you would strongly intreate Elder Heath ... and the rest, which have our Children, that they may be taught to know God, so as that they may teach their Countrymen ... because such an example would doe great good among them, his heart was much upon our intended worke, to gather a Church among them, I told him I greatly desired that he might live ... to be one in that worke, but if he should now dye he should goe to a better Church.[74]

The Indian expressed his wish for an Indian church: "I now shall dye, but Jesus Christ calleth you that live to goe to Naticke, that there the Lord might rule over you, that you might make a Church, and have the Ordinance of

---

71. Eliot, "An Account of Indian Churches in New-England" (1673), 124–25.

72. *Brief Narrative* (1671), 403; Byington, "John Eliot," 131–32. Eliot repeated in a letter to Robert Boyle, the Governor of New England Company of 6 July 1669, "there be betwixt 30 & 40 communicants at the Lord's table." *CGTNEC*, 27.

73. Eliot to Winslow, 29 December 1649, in *Light Appearing* (1651), 195. See also *Light Appearing* (1651), 198.

74. *Strength out of Weaknesse* (1652), 222–23.

God among you, believe in his Word, and doe as hee commandeth you."[75] The Indian's speech, as recorded by Eliot, was a brief but well-described vision of the ideal of Praying Towns. The formation of a church was an essential part of this vision. Furthermore, it is probably true that Wamporas' desire for the Indians' own church reflects Eliot's strong aspiration for there to be Indian churches in Praying Towns. For Eliot, the establishment of Praying Towns would only be complete through the establishment of Indian churches. In his letter of August 1651, Eliot said that he was, in fact, preparing for the establishment of the Indian church in the Praying Town: "Moreover, wee were in preparation for a Church-state, and that was a great matter to seeke the Lord in."[76]

In the light of the process of the towns' establishment, as mentioned above, and the role and function of the Praying Towns as Christian settlements, the following questions might be asked: How did Eliot understand the universal church? What are the differences and relationship between the two Christian communities: covenanted Praying Towns and covenanted Indian churches? Was the fact that Eliot distinguished between Praying Towns and the churches related to his own ecclesiology? The next two sections will try to answer these questions through investigation of Eliot's ideas on the church and its application to Indian churches. The next section will focus on the key elements in Eliot's understanding of the church which were directly related to Indian churches.

John Eliot's Congregational Ecclesiology

The Indian churches were established by John Eliot based on his own ecclesiology. Cotton Mather, in *The Life and Death Of The Renown'd Mr. John Eliot* (1691) presented Eliot as a stalwart supporter of New England's congregationalist ecclesiology:

> [H]e justly espoused that way of Church-Government which we call the Congregational; he was fully perswaded, that the Church state which our Lord Christ hath instituted in the New Testament, is, In a Congregation or Society of Professed Believers, Agreeing and Assembling together, among themselves, with Officers of Divine Appointment, for the Celebration of Evangelical Ordinances, and their own mutual Edification.[77]

---

75. *Strength out of Weaknesse* (1652), 223.
76. *Strength out of Weaknesse* (1652), 227.
77. *LJE*, 58.

John Eliot's ecclesiology can be summarized as a biblical and millenarian congregationalism, intended to bring further reformation.[78] Like *The Cambridge Platform*, he strongly affirmed the biblical foundation of ecclesiastical polity.[79] For Eliot, the Scripture was the standard of ecclesiastical polity. He said in *The Communion of Churches* (1665) that the "Foundation, Formation, and Constitution" of churches "is deducible from the Word of God."[80] Millenarianism was another ideological foundation for his understanding of the church. Eliot pursued Indian churches in the Praying Towns based on his millenarian vision. Eliot expressed his vision in *Light Appearing* (1651): "there be sundry such among them, whom the Lord will vouchsafe so far to favour and shine upon, that they shall become a Church, and a Spouse of Jesus Christ, and among whom the pure and holy Kingdome of Christ shall arise, and over whom Christ shall reigne, ruling them in all things by his holy word."[81] This statement explicitly shows that for Eliot, the ideal Indian community was ultimately pursuing the values of the Kingdom of Christ ruled by Christ, based on Scripture, established and operated by the harmonization of Praying Towns as a cohabitation of God's covenanted people and the church in the community. That is to say, for Eliot, Praying Towns and Indian churches were not only the essential Christian communities comprising the Kingdom, they also characterized the Kingdom of Christ in his millenarian vision. As argued in chapter 2, Eliot had to abandon his belief in the imminent coming of the millennium after the Restoration of 1660. However, it is probably true that his ideal of Indian churches was still related to his millenarian vision even after 1660. The evidence can be found in Eliot's *The Communion of Churches* (1665) in which he still showed his millenarian understanding of church polity.[82] Eliot strongly expected the

---

78. *The Cambridge Platform* (1648) as the standard and authoritative statement of congregationalism as "a dominant church-system" in New England proclaimed "the autonomy of the local church, the dependence of the churches upon one another for counsel, the representative character of the ministry" as the key principles of the polity. CPC, 166–67, 186. For the background of The Cambridge Synod and Platform in 1646–1648, see CPC, 157–88. For the text of *The Cambridge Platform* (1648), see CPC, 194–237.

79. *The Cambridge Platform* (1648), ch. 1, in CPC, 203–4.

80. Eliot, *The Communion of Churches* (1665), 12.

81. Eliot to Winslow, 21 October 1650, in *Light Appearing* (1651), 205.

82. Eliot's *The Communion of Churches* (1665) is composed of eight chapters. Eliot in chapter I discusses the definition and functions of councils as the essential components of ecclesiastical polity. Chapters II and III are about the way each council is composed in the whole hierarchical structure. Chapter IV explains the regulation of council meetings, including the duration and places of the meetings. Chapters V–VII discusses the role, function, detailed regulations of "ecclesiastical councils." Chapter VIII talks about the maintenance of the councils, especially in terms of financial operation and the necessary attitude and quality of council representatives. Some aspects of his church polity

perfect church polity which can be realized "When Christ shall rule all the World, both in Civil and Ecclesiastical affairs, by the Word of his mouth by the hand of Saints, even holy and religious Kings, Princes, and chief Rulers."[83] Eliot, in contrast with his earlier tract (*The Christian Commonwealth*), did not mention the imminence of the advent of the Kingdom of Christ, and his hostile voice toward the monarchy disappeared. However, he did not hide his expectation of the Kingdom of God.[84] That is to say, although Eliot did not expect the imminent coming of the millennium after 1660, he still expected the Kingdom of Christ in the millennium, and his ideal of the church was based on the millenarian vision.

For Eliot, the church is "a company of visible Saints," and "the Visible Church of Christ" composed of "visible saints" "is builded upon a lively confession of Christ."[85] This understanding reminds us of *The Cambridge Platform* (1648), which declared New England congregationalist ecclesiology. The platform defines "saints" of the church as follows:

> The matter of a visible church are Saints by calling. By Saints, wee understand, Such, as have not only attained the knowledge of the principles of Religion, & are free from gros & open scandals, but also do together with the profession of their faith & Repentance, walk in blameles obedience to the word, so as that in charitable discretion they may be accounted Saints by calling.[86]

This definition signifies that visible saints should not only confess to Christ and profess their faith, but should also show their visible sanctification in

---

were never touched on in the practice of the Indian churches—notably the system of hierarchically-ordered councils. Eliot offered four kinds of councils in church polity: "church council," "provincial council," "national council," and "oecumenical council." Through the introduction of hierarchical four kinds of council system, Eliot presented his church polity as a harmonized form of Congregational and Presbyterian polity. This is noticeable difference between Eliot's church polity and *The Cambridge Platform* (1648) although he heavily relied on *The Cambridge Platform* (1648) which mentioned only Synods as "spirituall & ecclesiasticall assemblyes" composed of "elders and other messengers" from churches. Eliot strongly argued that this hierarchical system was different from Episcopal polity and unlike Episcopal polity was based on the Scripture. Eliot was against the idea that his church polity might strengthen the Episcopal polity. Eliot, *The Communion of Churches* (1665), "preface," chs. II–III, 22; *The Cambridge Platform* (1648) ch. XVI, in CPC, 233–34.

83. Eliot, *The Communion of Churches* (1665), 17.

84. Eliot, *The Communion of Churches* (1665), "Preface," and ch. III. For the development and revision of Eliot's millenarianism, see pp. 41–50 above.

85. *Strength out of Weaknesse* (1652), 227; Eliot, *The Communion of Churches* (1665), 1.

86. *The Cambridge Platform* (1648), in CPC, 205–6.

their life. Eliot argued that the approval of participation in the Sacraments and voting in the church, as the privilege of full church members as "visible saints," should be based "upon the due evidence of some hopeful reall work and change of heart by Faith and Repentance, duely manifested to the Church."[87] This tells that Eliot strongly supported for strict church membership regulation through public confession of faith judged by church members. Eliot's correspondence with Baxter is helpful to understand his idea of church membership regulation. For Baxter, Eliot "is too p[ar]ticular and strict in describing the Qualification of churches or church-members." Baxter also noted "we that have justly blamed the Congregationall men for shutting out others by too strict conditions."[88] Baxter argued that only "the profession of repentance for sins past, and of assent and consent to the baptismall covenant is required for church membership."[89] Baxter refuted the judgement of a certain person's faith by other people for church membership:

> The people have no Ruling power in the Admission of members nor in Judging of fellow Communicants. Nor are they obliged to take any p[ar]ticular cognizance of the satisfactorynes of mens professions and qualifications. . . . Never did any Apostle or other minister of Christ in Scripture . . . ask the consent of the people before they baptized any. Nor did they ever examine any before they were admitted into their particular communions.[90]

However, Eliot clearly argued, in his correspondence with Baxter, for public confession of conversion and Christian faith which is judged by church members:

> [B]elievers are not like ordinary people, they are kings and priests and princes in all lands. . . . No man on earth is [so] fitt ecclesiastically to judge, according to his measure and manner, in a spiritual cause, as a believer. . . . God and man will have more respect to the judgment of a sound believer than of an ungodly officer.[91]

As *The Cambridge Platform* (1648) declared, Eliot, in his letter of 15 June 1668, argued for the relationship between the public confession of faith

---

87. Eliot, *The Communion of Churches* (1665), 36.
88. Baxter to Eliot, End of 1667, in *CRBJE*, 162.
89. Baxter to Eliot, End of 1667, in *CRBJE*, 162.
90. Baxter to Eliot, 27 March 1668, in *CRBJE*, 169–70. See Baxter to Eliot, 5 February 1670 (?), in *CRBJE*, 458, 460. The year of this letter is not clear.
91. Eliot to Baxter, 10 January, 1667/8, in *CRBJE*, 165. See Eliot to Baxter, 28 October 1668, in *CRBJE*, 175.

judged by church members, and church membership: "Againe, touching the covenant there is the invisible covenant of faith, whereby we are all united to Christ; by w[hic]h we are invisibly united together, also, in the mystical body of Christ, and this state is made visible by our visible p[ro]fession of relig[ion] and confession."[92]

Eliot's emphasis on sincere conversion as the requirement for church membership was crucially related to reformation. For Eliot, the primary task in the reformation of parishes was parishioners' sincere conversion and confession of a change of heart as evidence of their sincere Christian faith: "The first act of a Parish in giving themselves up unto the Lord in the way of reformation and submitting to be ordered by the councils, doth bring all the members into a state of confirmation, or confirmed members of the Church."[93] The relationship between sincere conversion and reformation argued by Eliot reminds us of Baxter's core ministerial agenda, that is, conversion-oriented ministry and church reformation.[94]

Eliot's congregational church polity is significant in his understanding of the church. For understanding Eliot's church polity, *The Communion of Churches* (1665) is an essential resource. One can say that Eliot's ideal ecclesiastical polity, like his civil polity, is a representative system.[95] Eliot said: "When Political Bodies, whether Civil or Ecclesiastical, are multitudinous, and remote from the place of action, either all cannot act, or if they do, it must be by Representatives."[96] He explained teaching and ruling elders, both of which represent the whole church: "The persons sent ought to be Elders, of both Orders, Teaching and Ruling to represent the whole Church; or in defect of Ruling Elders to represent the people, Faithful Brethren eminent in holiness and wisdom, who are as Elders."[97]

Autonomy is another significant aspect of Eliot's congregational church polity, well described in *The Communion of Churches* (1665). Congregational autonomy is found in the election of church officers by individual

92. Eliot to Baxter, 15 June 1668, in *CRBJE*, 172. *The Cambridge Platform* (1648), ch. XII, in *CPC*, 221–24.

93. Eliot to Baxter, 28 October 1668, in *CRBJE*, 175.

94. Baxter, *The Reformed Pastor* (1656), 111, 112, 175–76, 189, 190, 211; Baxter, "Preface," in *A Call to the Unconverted* (1658).

95. Eliot's strong support for a representative system can not only be found in his two treatises—*The Christian Commonwealth* (1659) and *The Communion of Churches* (1665)—but also in his argument for the ruling elder system which is found in his correspondence with Baxter.

96. Eliot, *The Communion of Churches* (1665), 11.

97. Eliot, *The Communion of Churches* (1665), 4. Cotton Mather witnessed that Eliot was a strong supporter of the ruling elder system in the church. *LJE*, 62. See also *The Cambridge Platform* (1648), chs. VI–VII, in *CPC*, 210–14.

churches. Eliot argued that representatives should be elected by the vote of church members, a system derived from the Bible. The representative system in which church members participate in the vote for electing their representatives signifies the value of equality in congregationalism, which strongly reveals the independence and autonomy of congregationalism (as *The Cambridge Platform* declared).[98] Eliot argued in *The Communion of Churches* (1665) that "A company of such Confessors, or a company of these confessing Believers" as "A Church of Believers . . . have power to call Officers, by whom they become an Organick Body, and sitted to administer and enjoy all instituted Worship."[99] This idea is also found in his letter to Baxter. Eliot, in his letter of 20 June 1669 to Baxter (who criticized the authority of the individual church to elect church officers), refuted the criticism, and argued that his idea about the authority of individual church to select church officers was biblical, and that the authority came from Christ:

> [I]f your meaning be that there should not be a concurrence and consent of the Fraternity, the vulgus of the Church, in an ecclesiastical mission of such a man, to that I cannot consent, because the Script[ure] seemeth to me to hold forth the concurrence and consent of the whole Church in the election of such officers as we are now speaking off. [Instances the Acts i, 15, 16, 23—the case of Matthias and, xiii, 1, 2, 3—the case of Paul and Barnabas.] . . . I yet see not but a Council of Churches may, what great authority from Christ and acceptance to all the saints, give such a call and mission.[100]

In sum, Eliot pursued the formation of churches which were reformed in the congregational way, and composed of "sincere converts" who professed a Christian faith which could be publicly and doubtlessly acknowledged. Based on this outline of Eliot's understanding of the church and church polity, the extent to which he applied his ecclesiology to Indian churches will now be discussed.

---

98. Eliot, *The Communion of Churches*, 1–5. *The Cambridge Platform* (1648), in *CPC*, ch. IIX (VIII), X. See also *CPC*, 166–67, 186, 210.

99. Eliot, *The Communion of Churches* (1665), 2.

100. Eliot to Baxter, 20 June 1669, in *CRBJE*, 449–50. For Baxter's criticism, see Baxter to Eliot, end of 1667, in *CRBJE*, 160. This letter is not dated. Baxter to Eliot, 22 September 1668, in *CRBJE*, 443.

The Establishment of the Congregational Indian Churches

Indian churches were established based on Eliot's congregationalist ecclesiology. Eliot said in "An Account of Indian Churches in New-England" (1673): "They both consent unto and practise the same discipline and ordinances as we practise in the English congregational churches, they studiously endeavour to write after the English copy in all church order."[101] Also, he ministered to Indian churches in the same way as to an English church. Eliot answered the question, "what is the man[n]er usually of their inchurching?" with "The same (so near as we can) that is practised in gathering churches among the English."[102]

Eliot clearly distinguished Indian churches from Praying Towns. The two most noticeable ecclesiastical aspects that Eliot applied to Indian churches were church membership regulations and church polity. First of all, Eliot practiced the congregational way of church membership regulation for Indian churches. This implicitly reflected his puritan conversion theology and understanding of the church. That is to say, Eliot distinguished Praying Towns as Indian Christians' settlements and pastoral parishes from the church, based on his own conversion theology and ecclesiology. Eliot delayed the establishment of the Indian church and the conferring of church membership on Praying Indians until after the establishment of the Praying Towns, although some Praying Indians enquired about "Church-Estate, Baptism and the rest of the Ordinances of God" even before the establishment of the Praying Towns. Eliot said: "but I shewing them how uncapable they be to be trusted therewith, whilst they live so unfixed, confused, and ungoverned a life, uncivilized and unsubdued to labor and order; they begin now enquire after such things."[103] Eliot also needed to be cautious when implementing the church establishment project even after the official establishment of the Praying Towns. In fact, Eliot thought that the year 1652, after the establishment of Natick in 1651, was the appropriate time to consider the Praying Indians' church membership. Eliot said, "now" after the official establishment of the Praying Town, "my argument of delaying them from entering Church-Estate, was taken away."[104] However, the establishment of the first Indian church was delayed for eight years. Richard Mather, in his letter of 13 October 1652 contained in *Tears of Repentance* (1653), explained several reasons for the delay. Richard Mather said that someone

---

101. Eliot, "An Account of Indian Churches in New-England" (1673), 125.
102. Eliot, "An Account of Indian Churches in New-England" (1673), 124.
103. *Glorious Progress* (1649), 159. See *Tears of Repentance* (1653), 268.
104. *Tears of Repentance* (1653), 268.

might ask "If there be such a Work of God amongst them, Why were they not combined and united into Church-Estate, when there was that great Assembly at Natick." Mather argued that it was not surprising for it to take a long time to establish the church, like the Temple in the days of Solomon. For Mather, the establishment of Natick Praying Town in such a short time was remarkable:

> Such an one many do well to consider, that the material Temple was many yeers in building, even in the daies of Solomon, who wanted no helps and furtherances thereunto, but was abundantly furnished therewith, and longer in Re-edifying after the Captivity; and therefore no marvel if the building of a Spiritual Temple, an holy Church to Christ, and a Church out of such rubbish as amongst Indians, be not begun and ended on a sudden; It is rather to be wondered at, that in so short a time, the thing is in so much forwardness as it is.[105]

Mather also indicated that absence of pastoral leadership for the Indian church was a factor. He said that Praying Indians "are not furnished with any to be an able Pastor and Elder over them, by whom they might be direct and guided in all the Affairs of the Church, and Administrations of the House of God."[106] Thus Mather anticipated and deflected possible criticism from his English audience about the delay in forming Indian churches.

For Eliot, along with the reasons for delay stated by Richard Mather, one of the main reasons that he felt he could not push ahead with establishing the Indian church, despite his strong desire, was the uncertainty of Praying Indians' Christian faith. For Eliot, sincerity of conversion and Christian faith was the most important requirement for Indian churches. In New England, certainty and profession of Christian faith was not just a simple statement. Personal testimony was crucially related to the requirement of official church membership. Thomas Lechford, who was "an unfriendly but extremely judicious witness who left us the best detailed account of day-to-day New England church procedures," wrote that public confession of Christian faith and conversion experience judged by church representatives was strictly practiced in the seventeenth-century New England puritan community:

> When a man or woman commeth to joyne unto the Church so gathered, he or shee commeth to the Elders in private, at one of their houses, or some other place appointed, upon the weeke

---

105. *Tears of Repentance* (1653), 265.
106. *Tears of Repentance* (1653), 265.

dayes, and make knowne their desire, to enter into Church-fellowship with that Church, and then the ruling Elders, or one of them, require, or ask him or her, if he bee willing to make known unto them the worke of grace upon their soules, or how God hath beene dealing with them about their conversion. . . . And if they satisfie the Elders, and the private assembly . . . that they are true beleevers, that they have beene wounded in their hearts for their originall sinne, and actuall transgressions, and can pitch upon some promise of free grace in the Scripture, for the ground of their faith, and that they finde their hearts drawne to beleeve in Christ Jesus, for their justification and salvation, and these in the ministerie of the Word, reading or conference: and that they know competently the summe of Christian faith. . . . Then afterwards, in co[n]venient time, in the publique assembly of the Church, notice is given by one of the ruling Elders, that such a man, or woman, by name, desireth to enter into Church-fellowship with them.[107]

It is true that the test of Christian faith for church membership for the establishment of Indian church was one of the most important elements in Eliot's Indian ministry. Eliot talked about his plan to examine Indians' confessions of Christian faith for church membership in a letter to Jonathan Hanmer of 7 October 1652:

> The present state of our busynesse, is through the grace of Christ, come up to this, that upon the 13th day of this month . . . we have a day of fasting and prayer, wherin we shall call forth sundry Indians to make confession of Jesus Christ his truth and grace. Whose confessions, if they, to charity, appear to be such as were not revealed to them by fresh and blood, but by the father, then we shall proceed to build them into a visible constituted church, for the Injoyment of Christ and all his holy ordinances.[108]

The church membership process began from the summer of 1652 at Natick, through the trial of conversion narratives and test of Christian doctrinal knowledge. Eliot reported:

> I did this Summer call forth sundry of them in the dayes of our publick Assemblies in Gods Worship; sometimes on the

---

107. Caldwell, *The Puritan Conversion Narrative*, 67. Lechford, *Plain Dealing* (1642), 4–5. For more detailed description of the process of church membership approval, see Lechford, *Plain Dealing* (1642), 4–11. Cotton Mather also provided Eliot's idea on the regulation of church membership. *LJE*, 59–62.

108. Eliot to Jonathan Hanmer, 7 October 1652, in *JEI*, 12.

> Sabbath Sometimes on Lecture daies, to make confession before the Lord of their former sins, and of their present knowledge of Christ, and experience of his Grace . . . which having done, and being in my own heart hopeful that there was among them fit matter for a Church . . . it pleased God to give their Confessions such acceptance in their hearts.[109]

For Eliot, the conversion narratives and presentation of Christian knowledge was "to give them acceptance the Saints, into the fellowship of Church-Estate, and enjoyment of those Ordinances which the Lord hath betrusted his Churches withal."[110]

The first examination of the Praying Indians' conversion narratives, and the test of their Christian doctrinal knowledge by "the reverend Elders" of neighbor churches of Roxbury, who were invited by Eliot, was held on 13 October 1652 at Natick.[111] Eliot asked whether the examiners "would ask them Questions touching the fundamental Points of Religion" first and then listen to the conversion experiences of the Praying Indians. The examiners decided that Praying Indians "should first make confession of their experience in the Lords Work upon their hearts, because in so doing, it is like something will be discerned of their knowledg[e] in the Doctrines of Religion."[112] The examination of the Praying Indians' doctrinal knowledge, which in the event did not happen in October 1652 at Natick because of limited time, was conducted on 13 June 1654 at Roxbury. It was originally planned to take place in 1653. However, there were several reasons for the delay. Copies of *Tears of Repentance* (1653), containing Praying Indians' conversion narratives which Eliot had sent to Old England for publication, returned to New England late. In fact, Eliot wanted the "Confessions" to be published in England, desiring "to hear what acceptance the Lord gave unto them, in the hearts of his people there who daily labour at the Throne of grace, and by other expressions of their loves, for an holy birth of this work of the Lord, to the praise of Christ, and the inlargement of his Kingdome." Eliot also wanted "the knowledge of their Confessions," after returning to New England, "might be spread here, unto the better and fuller satisfaction of many, then the transacting thereof in the presence of some could doe." Also, groundless circulated rumours about Praying Indians' "conspiracy with others, and with the Dutch, to doe mischief to the English," because

---

109. *Tears of Repentance* (1653), 268.
110. *Tears of Repentance* (1653), 268.
111. *Tears of Repentance* (1653), 268.
112. *Tears of Repentance* (1653), 269; *JEMI*, 127.

at that time the English were at war with Holland.[113] Despite the situation, Eliot eagerly tried to have the examination of Praying Indians' faith through his proposition of the examination to the attendees of "a great meeting at Boston in 1653." He said in the proposition:

> That they having now seen their confessions, if upon further triall of them in point of knowledge they be found to have a competent measure of understanding in the fundamentall points of Religion; and also, if there be due testimony of their conversation, that they walke in a Christian manner according to their light, so that Religion is to be seen in their lives; whether then it be according to God, and acceptable to this people, that they be called up unto Church-estate?[114]

Eliot also persuaded elders to have an examination meeting for Praying Indians. Finally, the examination was conducted on 13 June 1654. The contents of the examination, including the questions and answers, are contained in *Late and Further Manifestation*, published in 1655.[115] After this examination meeting in 1654, there was no further meeting for doctrinal examination and test of faith until 1659. Although puritan ministers and elders examined the Praying Indians' faith and doctrinal knowledge from 1652 to 1654, one question still remained: "What shall we further doe? And when shall they enjoy the Ordinances of Jesus Christ in Church-estate?" The main reason for the puritans' hesitancy to push ahead with the establishment of an Indian church seems to have been uncertainty about Praying Indians' Christian faith. In fact, Eliot believed he knew "more of the sincerity of some of them, then other doe, and are better satisfied with them." However, he was "well content to make slow hast in this matter" because he remembered "that word of God, Lay hands suddenly upon no man." Eliot thought that "Gods works among men, doe usually goe on slowly, and he that goeth slowly, doth usually goe most surely, especially when he goeth by counsell . . . the greater proof we have of them, the better approbation they may obtain at last."[116]

Eliot, who reported the uncertain capacity of the Indians for "church-estate" in *Glorious Progress* (1649) and *Tears of Repentance* (1653), still could

---

113. *Late and Further Manifestation* (1655), 304–5; *JEMI*, 130–31.

114. *Late and Further Manifestation* (1655), 305. Eliot said about the meeting that "there being a great meeting at Boston, from other Colonies as well as our owne, and the Commissioners being there." However, there is no clear information of the meeting.

115. *Late and Further Manifestation* (1655), 311–17. Eliot talked about the examination in his letter to Jonathan Hanmer, 29 August 1654. See *JEI*, 22.

116. *Late and Further Manifestation* (1655), 318.

not fully trust Praying Indians' Christian faith as "sincere converts" who should show true conversion expression and proper doctrinal knowledge, with visible signs of their conversion.[117] He worried about "such danger of polluting and defiling the name of Christ among their barbarous friends and Countrey-men."[118] In fact, there was a serious scandal among Praying Indians in 1654. Eliot reported that "three of the unsound sort of such as are among them that pray unto God" were seriously involved with four "sins": "1. The sin of Drunkennesse, and that after many former Punishments for the same. 2. A willfull making of the Child drunk, and exposing him to danger also. 3. A degree of reproaching the Rulers. 4. Fighting." Eliot confessed that this scandal among the Praying Indians "sunk my spirit extreamly, I did judge it to be the greatest frowne of God that ever I met withall in the work, I could read nothing in it but displeasure, I began to doubt about our intended work." One of the offenders was Eliot's interpreter who participated in the translation of the Scripture into the Indian language. He also did "some other acts of Apostacy at this time."[119]

In addition, Eliot in 1655 cited several realistic reasons that made the process of examination of faith and the establishment of an Indian church slow. The reasons were "many other great occasions" which hindered meetings for examination, and the difficulty of finding interpreters who could attend the meeting. Also, "the dayes also will soon grow short, and the nights cold, which will be an hindrance in the attendance unto the accomplishment of that work, which will most fitly be done at Natick." The most serious issue was the lack of pastoral leaders to train and instruct Praying Indians who were "living in sundry Towns and places remote from each other." Because of these reasons, Eliot and other puritans leaders wanted to "make the slower hast to accomplish this work among them."[120]

Finally, on 15 April 1659, seven Praying Indians had a meeting about a trial of conversion narratives at Roxbury church, with Roxbury church members, for "a private preparatory Confession." Almost three months later, on 5 July, eight Praying Indians had an official meeting about their conversion narratives and a test of their doctrinal knowledge with John Eliot, elders of Roxbury church, and "Messengers" from ten neighbor churches near Roxbury who were invited by Roxbury church to attend the meeting. The conversion narratives from both meetings are included

---

117. *Glorious Progress* (1649), 159; *Tears of Repentance* (1653), 268.
118. *Late and Further Manifestation* (1655), 318.
119. *Late and Further Manifestation* (1655), 306-7.
120. *Late and Further Manifestation* (1655), 318-19.

in *Further Account* (1660).[121] The eight Praying Indians were admitted to membership of the church at Roxbury and soon after the elders of Roxbury allowed the confessed Praying Indians to have their own church at Natick Praying Town in 1660.[122]

The reasons for the delay of faith and doctrinal examination, and the serious carefulness and hesitancy that Eliot showed in the process, clearly signify how much Eliot wanted to be cautious about the establishment of Indian churches and giving Indians official church membership. This hesitancy in practice is reminiscent of Eliot's puritan conversion theology and his thoughts on the relationship between church membership and "sincere converts"—who should show not only true conversion experience, but also visible signs of their conversion. Reviewing the long drawn-out Indian church membership procedure from 1652 to 1659, for Eliot, it is clear that the conversion narrative and test of Christian doctrinal understanding, as the requirements for church membership, were a vital pastoral issue because of his understanding of the church as a visible church of sincere converts. Eliot mentioned the ecclesiastical importance of the requirements. The test was a confirmation of the genuine Christian faith of the Praying Indians who had so recently been in "great depth of darkness":

> It is a great matter to betrust those with the holy priviledges of Gods house, upon which the name of Christ is so much called, who have so little knowledge and experience in the ways of Christ, so newly come out of that great depth of darknesse, and wild course of life ... as to give sufficient proof and experience of their ste[a]dfastnesse in their new begun profession.[123]

Also, the test of faith was not only for themselves, but also for the next generations. As Eliot said, "Being also the first Church gathering among them, it is like to be a pattern and president of after proceedings, even unto following Generations." In this sense, for Eliot, it was "very needful that this proceeding of ours at first, be with all care and warinesse guided, for the most effectuall advancement of the holinesse and honour of Jesus Christ among them."[124]

121. The Praying Indians were Nishohkou, Antony, Ponampiam, John Speen, Wutasakompauin, Monotunkquanit, Piumbuhhou, Waban. Among them Waban could not attend the meeting of preparatory conversion narrative in April 15 because of his sickness, but later he also went to Roxbury to have a trial conversion narrative. *Further Account* (1660), 360–95; *JEMI*, 133. About Waban's absence, see *Further Account* (1660), 374.

122. *HCINE*, 181; Byington, "John Eliot," 131; Kellaway, *The New England Company*, 90; *JEMI*, 136.

123. *Late and Further Manifestation* (1655), 318.

124. *Late and Further Manifestation* (1655), 318.

Eliot applied his ideas on church polity to the formation of individual Indian churches in the Praying Towns. To what degree Eliot applied his wider thoughts on church polity, demonstrated in *The Communion of Churches* (1665), is not clear. However, through the materials published in the Eliot Tracts, we can confirm that some aspects of congregational church polity were applied to Indian churches. It is clear that there was at least a teaching and ruling elder system in place in individual Indian churches. Eliot's description of Indian churches in Plymouth and Martha's Vineyard mentioned the ordination of teaching and ruling elders, and also provision for deacons in Indian churches (as *The Cambridge Platform* of 1648 had acknowledged).[125] Eliot said that when he attended

> a Meeting at Mak{?}epog {i.e., Mahshepog, or Mashpee} near Sandwich in Plimouth-Pattent, to gather a Church among the Indians ... one of the Indians, named Jude, should have been ordained Ruling-Elder, but being sick at that time, advice was given that he should be ordained with the first opportunity, as also a Deacon to manage the present Sabbath day Collections, and other parts of that Office in their season.[126]

Eliot also mentioned the elders and deacons of the Indian church at Martha's Vineyard:

> From them we passed over to the Vinyard.... On a day of Fasting and Prayer, Elders were ordained, two Teaching-Elders, the one to be a Preacher of the Gospel, to do the Office of a Pastor and Teacher; the other to be a Preacher of the Gospel, to do the Office of a Teacher and Pastor.... Also two Ruling-Elders, with advice to ordain Deacons also, for the Service of Christ in the Church.[127]

Congregational autonomy is also found in the Indian churches. The autonomous test of Christian faith in Praying Towns was a good example of it. After the establishment of the first Indian church at Natick, the test of Christian faith was controlled by the Praying Indians themselves. Eliot described the Indian church's autonomous practice of church membership regulation in his letter to Robert Boyle, the Governor of New England Company of 6 July 1669:

> The 2nd Towne is Pakeunit ... in this towne are 8 or ten more or lesse upon theire p[ro]bational confession, & because some of them are very ancient, not able to go to Natick; therefore the

---

125. *The Cambridge Platform* (1648), in *CPC*, ch. VII.
126. *Brief Narrative* (1671), 400.
127. *Brief Narrative* (1671), 401.

Church have appoynted a meeting at this Towne this Autumne, to heare theire confessions of Christ, & to receive such into the Church as (through grace) shall be approved.[128]

Evidence of how members were admitted also survives in "An Account of Indian Churches in New-England" (1673). Eliot answered about the question, "What is the manner of their admission of any new converts into the churches?":

> They are diligently instructed and examined both publickly and privately in the catechism; their blaimless and pious conversation, is publickly testified, their names are publickly exposed as desireing to make confession and join unto the church. The teachers and chief brethren do first hear their preparatory confessions, and when they judge them meet they are called publickly to confess, confederate and be baptised, both themselves and their children, if not up grown; the up grown are called upon to make their own confession, and so to be baptized as their parents were.[129]

Based on the autonomy of church membership, the pastors of Indians churches ministered Sacraments in their own church.[130]

The election of church officers through voting of church members was also a significant example of congregational autonomy that Eliot applied to Indian churches. In fact, this congregational way was in fact applied to the election of Praying Towns' rulers. As mentioned above, Praying Indians chose their own rulers of their towns by themselves.[131] Likewise, Eliot applied the congregational way to Indian churches for electing church officers. Eliot's reference to equality in Indian churches in *Indian Dialogues* (1671) is a good indication that Eliot tried to apply his own church polity to Indian churches. Eliot's commitment to introducing the congregational way of electing church officers in Indian churches is revealed by his record of Indians' conversation. When Philip Keitasscot, an Indian sachem, said, "I perceive that in your praying to God, and in your churches, all are brought to an equality. Sachems and people are all fellow brethren in your churches ... The vote of the lowest of the people hath as much weight as the vote of the sachem." Anthony, a Praying Indian, answered: "There is such a rule in the gospel way of the churches, as equality of vote among believers in the matters

---

128. *CGTNEC*, 27–29. In this letter, Eliot introduced eight Praying Towns and their autonomy. See *Brief Narrative* (1671).

129. Eliot, "An Account of Indian Churches in New-England" (1673), 126.

130. Eliot, "An Account of Indian Churches in New-England" (1673), 125.

131. *Strength our of Weaknesse* (1652), 226–27.

of Jesus Christ. And herein is a great point of self-denial in sachems and chief men, to be equal to his brethren in the things that appertain to Christ."[132]

Conclusion

Eliot's Indian ministry was practiced initially through the formation of Praying Towns. The towns, based on the Bible and millenarian ideology, were Indian Christian settlements and pastoral fields for pursuing civilized life and Christian religious life through puritan pastoral ministry.

For Eliot, the Praying Towns were not the same as the "visible church." Although Eliot considered Praying Towns as Christian settlements in which Praying Indians "may enjoy all those Ordinances the Lord Jesus hath left unto his Church,"[133] he cautiously tried to establish gathered churches on the New England model within the towns. Eliot's aspirations for native Indian Christians meant that he distinguished between the towns and the churches, on the basis of his congregationalist ecclesiology. For Eliot, although Praying Towns were Christian settlements and a pastoral field for ministry and the practice of piety, not all Praying Indians were "sincere converts." Eliot tried to establish reformed visible Indian churches composed of "sincere converts" in the towns. The church was established based on Eliot's conversion- and reformation-centered puritan ministry, following the congregational way. In this sense, for Eliot, the Indian churches were an actualized form of his ecclesiastical vision, just as the settlers' churches of Massachusetts Bay were—including his own at Roxbury.

Eliot believed that Praying Towns would only be complete through the establishment of Indian churches in the towns. The Praying Towns and Indian churches had their own identity and role in Eliot's ministry and, in fact, the communities were ultimately pursuing in a tangible form, in spite of its imperfection, his vision of the Kingdom of Christ. What and how Eliot taught the Indians and prepared them to become full church members, as "sincere converts" in the Praying Towns, will be discussed in the next chapter.

---

132. Eliot, *Indian Dialogues* (1671), 127. Philip Keitasscot is the Wampanoag sachem, Metacom which is known as King Philip. *ID*, 166n40; *ET*, 22.

133. *Strength out of Weaknesse* (1652), 230.

5

John Eliot's Practice of Indian Ministry

THIS CHAPTER WILL ANSWER the question of how, in practice, Eliot and his colleagues prepared the inhabitants of Praying Towns to become church members. Thomas Shepard, in the preface of *Clear Sun-Shine* (1648), argued for the significance of pastoral ministry for Indian conversion through describing the changes in Praying Indians when they had received the gospel:

> Here thou mayst see, the Ministry is precious, the feet of them who bring glad tidings beautifull, Ordinances desired, the Word frequented and attended, the Spirit also going forth in power and efficacy with it, in awakening and humbling of them, drawing forth those affections of sorrow, and expressions of tears in abundance . . . we read here, their leaving of sinne, they forsake their former evill ways, and set up fences never to returne. . . . They set up prayers in their families morning and evening, and are in earnest in them. . . . They rest on the Lords day, and make laws for the observation of it, wherein they meet together to pray & instruct one another in the things of God, which have been communicate to them.[1]

---

1. *Clear Sun-Shine* (1648), 107.

These changes in native Indians can probably be considered as the result of Eliot's Indian ministry. Thirteen years after Eliot started preaching the gospel to Indians, Monotunkquanit, a Praying Indian, in his own conversion narrative, confessed how and what made him change and become a Praying Indian. His change ultimately came from his minister's pastoral ministry for conversion:

> After I went to Dorchester Indians, the praying Indians; and they that were my friends, did say it was good to pray to God; and said, Tomorrow is our Lecture, and the Minister cometh to teach us; then my heart desired to see the Minister, and hear what he said: next day he came, and taught the Indians: I went and desired to see: when I came, my son Sam came with mee; the Minister call'd my son, and set him afore, and asked him, Who made him? And he was taught to answer, God. Then he commended my son, and asked whose son he was; they said, Mine. The Minister gave him two apples: then the Minister said to me, Do you pray to God? You see your childe saith, God made him; and therefore it is your duty to pray to God.[2]

The purpose of this chapter is to examine John Eliot's practical pastoral ministry, which will be considered in two parts: pastoral teaching and care, and the practice of piety. This chapter will answer the following questions: how Eliot understood and practiced pastoral teaching and care in Indian ministry, and what the content, means, and methodology were. It will also examine how Praying Indians understood the puritan practice of piety, and the continuity and discontinuity between their own understanding of piety and traditional puritan way. Through the investigation, we will understand how Eliot prepared the Praying Indians to become church members.

It is not easy to find thorough investigations of Eliot's pastoral ministry to Praying Indians, although there are important works which have briefly addressed the topic. Many studies, however, have regarded Eliot's ministerial work with the Indians as a missionary achievement, without sufficient theological analysis of it in terms of its context in seventeenth-century Old and New England puritanism.[3]

Through investigation of the materials published in the Eliot Tracts, Eliot's other writings, including personal letters, and related puritan literature on puritan pastoral ministry, it can be shown that, for Eliot, pastoral

---

2. *Further Account* (1660), 372.

3. Harling, "A Biography of John Eliot"; Rooy, *The Theology of Missions*; Winslow, *John Eliot*; Vaughan, *New England Frontier*; *JEMI*. For more information, see pp. 5–14 above.

teaching and care and the practice of piety were significant means of Indian conversion and evangelization. In addition, Eliot's pastoral activities for native Indians can be analyzed and reinterpreted in more detail from the perspective of seventeenth-century puritan theology and ministry. This is a perspective which has not often been adopted in previous research. Furthermore, this chapter will argue that Eliot's Indian ministry not only had strong ideological continuity with Eliot's contemporary puritan tradition, but also that Indian ministry showed its own uniqueness because of the contextual difference between puritans and Indians.

Pastoral Teaching and Care

Pastoral Teaching and the Word of God

Eliot pursued Bible-centered and Reformed theological-oriented pastoral teaching, which can be glimpsed in the Eliot Tracts, *Indian Dialogues* (1671), letters written by Eliot and his colleagues, catechisms, and Praying Indians' sermons and confessions.

For Eliot, pastoral teaching of the Word of God as a primary task was the most important means of puritan ministry.[4] Eliot said, "The Bible, and the Catechism drawn out of the Bible, are general helps to all parts and places about us, and are the ground-work of Community amongst all our Indian-churches and Christians."[5] How Eliot considered the importance of teaching the Word of God is found in the catechism for Indians: "[1. Quest] How may wee come to know Jesus Christ? [Answ.] [1] Our first answer was, That if they were able to read our Bible, the book of God, therein they should see most cleerely what Jesus Christ was."[6] The Praying Indians' understanding of the Bible as the Word of God is significant evidence of what Eliot taught them about the Bible. Piumbukhou, a Praying Indian, is recorded in *Indian Dialogues* (1671) as saying this:

> The Book of God is no invention of Englishmen. It is the holy law of God himself, which was given unto man by God, before Englishmen had any knowledge of God; and all the knowledge which they have, they have it out of the Book of God. And this

---

4. Baxter, *The Reformed Pastor* (1656), 231. See Baxter, *The Reformed Pastor* (1656), 43, 129–30.

5. *Brief Narrative* (1671), 402.

6. *Day-Breaking* (1647), 84.

> book is given to us as well as to them, and it is as free for us to search the scriptures as for them.[7]

Anthony, another Praying Indian, defined the Word of God thus: "It is the will of God written in the Bible, whereby he rightly guideth man, in everything in this world, and whereby he bringeth us to eternal salvation."[8] Anthony also defined scripture as:

> The word and will of God written in a book, whereby we not only hear it with our ears, when it is spoken by others, but we may see it without eyes, and read the writing ourselves.... For a word spoken is soon gone, and nothing retaineth it but our memory, and that impression which it made upon our mind and heart. But when this word is written in a book, there it will abide, though we have forgotten it. And we may read it over a thousand times.... We do therefore call the Word of God scripture, because it is written in a book.[9]

The Praying Indians' strong Biblicism reflects Eliot's puritan pastoral teaching based on Reformed theology.[10] William, a Praying Indian, used Biblicism to criticize the Roman Catholic Church:

> I have heard that in the other part of the world there be a certain people who are called Papists, whose ministers and teachers live in all manner of wickedness and lewdness, and permit and teach the people so to do. And these wicked ministers will not suffer the people to read the Word of God.... And they are so cruel, that if they find anyone that readeth the Word of God, they will kill him. They choose rather to lead all their people with them to hell, than to suffer them to see the light whereby they may be saved.[11]

This not only reminds us of *sola scriptura* as a core of Reformed theology, but also of Eliot's reformation-centered Indian ministry.

As mentioned in chapter 3, preaching was one of the most important means of Eliot's pastoral teaching.[12] However, and unfortunately, it is almost

---

7. Eliot, *Indian Dialogues* (1671), 71. See Eliot, *Indian Dialogues* (1671), 92.
8. Eliot, *Indian Dialogues* (1671), 139.
9. Eliot, *Indian Dialogues* (1671), 139–40.
10. Calvin, *Inst.*, IV.iii.4; IV.viii.2. See also Hall, *The Faithful Shepherd*, 3–20; Webster, *Godly Clergy in Early Stuart England*, 95–97; Black, *Reformation Pastors*, 23.
11. Eliot, *Indian Dialogues* (1671), 136. See Eliot, *Indian Dialogues* (1671), 138, 141.
12. Cotton, *The Way of Congregational Way Cleared* (1648), 269; Baxter, *The Reformed Pastor* (1656), 196. For seventeenth-century puritan understanding of preaching, see pp. 87–93 above.

impossible to examine Eliot's preaching by studying his own sermonic texts because of their absence—nothing appears to survive, in print or in manuscript. Nevertheless, the Praying Indians' own sermons can perhaps provide important clues to gain an understanding of Eliot's preaching. *Further Accompt* (1659) contains significant examples of six short sermons by Praying Indians, translated from their own language by Eliot. According to Eliot, those "exhortations" were delivered by Waban, Nichokhou, Anthony, John Speene, Piumbubbon, and Wutasakompavin on "a late day of fasting and prayer at Natick," 15 November 1658.[13] Although those sermons were prepared and delivered by the Praying Indians themselves, it is evident that Eliot taught them how to preach. Eliot, in a letter to Henry Whitfield, acknowledged this:

> Whereby you may observe the manner of my teaching them, for they imitate mee, as for our method of preaching to the English by way of Doctrine, reason, and use, neither have I liberty of speech, for that way of teaching being very unskil[l]full in their Language, nor have they sufficient abilitie of understanding to profit by it, so wee as by this way, whereof you have herein a little Taste.[14]

Thus through the Indians' sermons, which appear in print in Eliot's translation, it is possible to examine the characteristics of how Eliot taught them to preach in the puritan tradition. The Praying Indians' sermons in *Further Accompt* (1659) commonly followed this puritan sermonic structure which was "doctrine, reason and use" as Eliot mentioned.[15] One such example is Nichokhou's sermon, which was based on Gen 8:20–21.[16] When he had

---

13. *Further Accompt* (1659), 332. For more examples of Praying Indians' sermon texts, see Eliot, *Indian Dialogues* (1671), 91–94, 117–19.

14. Eliot to Henry Whitfield, October 1651, in *Strength out of Weaknesse* (1652), 230. This letter's exact date is unknown. Henry Whitfield [Whitfeld] (1590/91–1657) was a minister of Guilford church in New England and a parish minister at Winchester in England. He supported New England Indian evangelization and published *Light Appearing* (1651). Bremer, "Whitfield [Whitfeld], Henry." See also Hardman Moore, "Appendix 3," in *Pilgrims*, 196.

15. Haller, *The Rise of Puritanism*, 134; Davies, *The Worship of the American Puritans*, 87–89; Morgan, *Godly Learning*, 121; Bremer, *The Puritan Experiment*, 187. The puritan way of preaching was strongly based on the Reformed tradition. For exegesis, structure, and style in Reformed preaching, see Ford, "Preaching in the Reformed Tradition," 69–76. See also Hunt, *The Art of Hearing*, 95–96.

16. "Genesis. 8:20. Noah built an Altar unto Jehovah, and took of every clean Beast, and of every clean fowle, and offered burnt offerings on the Altar. 21. And the Lord smelled a sweet Savour; and the Lord said in his heart, I will not againe curse the ground any more for mans sake; for the imaginations of mans heart is evill from his

read the main text, in the first part of the sermon, he described and interpreted the meaning of the verses, "In that Noah sacrificed to God he shewed himself thankfull; in that he worshipped God, he shewed himselfe godly; in that he sacrificed clean beasts, he shewed that God is an holy God, pure and clean." Following this he said "and all that come to God, and worship him, must be pure and clean: and know that we must by repentance purge ourselves, and cleanse our hearts from all sin; which is a work we are to doe this day."[17] Praying Indians also learned puritans' plain style of preaching.[18] Following the puritan style used by Eliot, the Praying Indians' sermons began from biblical interpretation and concluded with biblical application in a plain style. The Praying Indians' profound theological and ministerial understanding of the Bible is suggested by the report of Piumbubbon's sermon on the Beatitudes in Matt 5:1–10.[19] They made frequent use of biblical citations from other parts of the Scripture to support their sermons.[20]

In brief, preaching was one of the most significant means of pastoral teaching in Eliot's Indian ministry. The examples of the puritan pattern and style of preaching, which appeared in Praying Indians' sermons, implicitly reveal Eliot's understanding of puritan preaching and his teaching about preaching to Indian converts who became teaching elders.

Along with preaching, for Eliot, catechizing was also an essential means of puritan pastoral teaching.[21] Eliot thought that Indians should constantly practice catechism.[22] Eliot's description of his work for Indians on the Sabbath day in his letter to Shepard, 24 September 1647, offers a vital clue to understanding his thoughts on catechizing for Indians. Eliot explained how he practiced "foure things"—catechizing, preaching, admonition and censure, and teaching through questions and answers.[23] Eliot exercised catechizing first:

---

youth, neither will I again smite any more everything living as I have done." I cited this text as appeared in *Further Accompt* (1659). See *Further Accompt* (1659), 334.

17. *Further Accompt* (1659), 334.

18. Haller, *The Rise of Puritanism*, 129–33; Morgan, *Godly Learning*, 121–22; Bremer, *The Puritan Experiment*, 25; Gordis, *Opening Scripture*, 13–15.

19. *Further Accompt* (1659), 338–39.

20. Nishokhou's citation of Gen 22:12 in his sermon based on Gen 8:20–21 and Anthony's citation of Matt 3:8 and 25:51 for his sermon based on Matt 6:16–18 are good examples. *Further Accompt* (1659), 334–36.

21. Baxter, *The Reformed Pastor* (1656), 175–77, 188–89.

22. Eliot to Winslow, 12 November 1648 and 13 November 1649, in *Glorious Progress* (1649), 151, 158.

23. Eliot to Shepard, 24 September 1647, in *Clear Sun-Shine* (1648), 126–30.

> In my exercise among them . . . wee attend foure things, besides prayer unto God, for his presence and blessing upon all we doe. First, I catechize the children and youth . . . they can readily say all the Commandements, so far as I have communicated them, and all other principles about the creation, the fall, the redemption by Christ, &c. wherein also the aged people are pretty expert, by the frequent repetition thereof to the children, and are able to teach it to their children at home, and do so.²⁴

Thus catechizing was one of the primary tasks of Eliot's ministry for Indians. Also, it is evident that Eliot encouraged them to teach catechism in their own private meetings. According to Ian Green, the church was not the only place for catechizing. Another place for catechizing was the home, which in the English context meant usually "a household unit of parents and children or masters and servants, but occasionally with a minister or chaplain present or with a number of like-minded families gathered for some kind of 'conference.'" Green has argued that although "relatively few works were designated as being for use in households only" and "we have no institutional records to help us decide how far or in what ways the duty was actually performed," it is evident that daily home catechizing was encouraged, since parents knew their children better than ministers. Also, home catechizing was the duty of parents and a spiritual or moral one, so it was a support to ministers and reinforced church catechizing.²⁵ In this sense, Eliot's emphasis on catechizing in private meetings reflects the tradition of catechizing in seventeenth-century England. In addition, Eliot's accounts of his catechetical practice shows that the content of his catechism for the Indians was not only the story of the Bible itself, and a Protestant understanding of Christian doctrines, but also the practice of piety and Christian ethics based on the Bible and Christian doctrines.²⁶

---

24. *Clear Sun-Shine* (1648), 126–27.

25. Green, *The Christian's ABC*, 204. See Green, *The Christian's ABC*, ch. 4, "Catechizing in School and at Home."

26. *Day-Breaking* (1647), 84–91; Eliot to Winslow, 12 November 1648, in *Glorious Progress* (1649), 155–56; Eliot to Winslow, 2 December 1648, in *Glorious Progress* (1649), 160–61; Thomas Allen to Henry Whitfield, 8 January 1651/2, in *Strength out of Weaknesse* (1652), 244–45; "Some Helps for the Indians," in *Further Accompt* (1659), 341–53. See Green, *The Christian's ABC*, Part II, "The Message." Green offers the analysis of the contents of catechisms in chs. 6–12 (Part II) focusing on "Catechetical Structures," "The Apostle's Creed," "Predestination," "Assurance, Justification, and the Covenant of Grace," "The Ten Commandments," "The Lord's Prayer," and "Sacraments" respectively.

For Eliot and the Praying Indians, following puritan tradition, the aim of catechizing was conversion.[27] In this sense, for Praying Indians, the pastoral teaching of the Bible and catechizing were significant means of grace.[28] Poquanum, a Praying Indian, confessed that "when the Children were Catechized, and taught the ten Commandments, I hearkened, and by them I came to know that there was a God, and that there was sin against God; and hereby God made me to see all my sins."[29] According to Wutasakompauin's confession, their understanding of the process of repentance and conversion came from their catechizing: "Again, I learned in a catechism, that Christ sendeth his Spirit into my heart, to break it, to make it repent, to convert me, to cause me to believe: my heart said, therefore I desire to pray to God, and to believe for pardon, and adoption, and peace with God."[30] This explicitly shows that the Indians did not simply consider catechizing to be an intellectual teaching of the Bible and Christian doctrines, but that they also thought of it as a means of grace primarily to pursue conversion and salvation.[31] In this sense, Praying Indians' references to catechisms in their confessions and sermons suggests the significance of catechizing for the formation of their Christian faith. Waban, a Praying Indian, confessed:

> Again, I learn in the Catechize, Q. What hath Christ done for us? A. He dyed for us, hee was buried, he rose again for us, and by his resurrection hee raiseth our souls unto grace, and also at the last day: And my heart said, Oh let it be so in me. . . . Again it is said in Catechism, Why is Christ a Prophet? A. To teach me the way to heaven: therefore my heart desireth that Christ may ever lead me by his Word.[32]

Waban's confession signifies not only the importance of catechizing for the Indians' Christian faith, but also the fact that catechizing for the Indians was crucially related to their test of faith for church membership. Along with the Praying Indians' references to catechisms in their confessions and sermons, the comparison between the contents of catechism, which Eliot introduced in some parts of the materials published as the Eliot Tracts, especially in "The Examination of the Indians at Roxbury, The 13th Day of the 4th Month, 1654" in *Late and Further Manifestation* (1655), is a significant

---

27. Baxter, *The Reformed Pastor* (1656), 1–34, 174. See also Lim, *In Pursuit of Purity, Unity, and Liberty*, 23–52.

28. Baxter, *A Call to the Unconverted* (1658), 57.

29. *Tears of Repentance* (1653), 290.

30. *Further Account* (1660), 393.

31. Green, *The Christian's ABC*, 25–29.

32. *Further Account* (1660), 376. See *Further Accompt* (1659), 337.

source to understand Eliot's practice of catechizing.[33] Eliot, after the Indians' test of faith on 13 April 1654, wrote that he actually wanted the elders who had tested the Indians' faith to test them further with more doctrinal and biblical questions, but the elders acknowledged that "they did perceive that they were instructed in points of Catechisme, by what they had heard from them."[34] This clearly demonstrates the relationship between catechizing and the test of faith.

In terms of catechizing methodology, along with public catechizing, pastoral visitation and private instruction were also significant in Eliot's puritan ministry for the Indians.[35] In light of Ian Green's findings about the great variety of catechisms and methods of catechizing,[36] it is evident that catechizing was practiced in various forms in Eliot's Indian ministry. Eliot's pastoral visitation as a way of teaching the Indians is described in the Praying Indians' confession: Waban said, "Now I will pray, because the Minister is come to my house, now I heard the Word of God."[37] In fact, pastoral visitation to the Indians was suggested by Eliot himself after he realized that the evangelization of the Indians was progressing much more slowly than he had expected. Eliot, in a letter to Thomas Shepard, 24 September 1647, wrote:

> [T]hey said they did not know God, and therefore could not tell how to pray I told them if they would learn to know God, I would teach them: unto which they being very willing, I then taught them (as I sundry times had indeavored afore) but never found them so forward, attentive and desirous to learn till this time, and then I would come to their Wigwams, and teach them, their wives and children, which they seemed very glad of; and from that day forward I have not failed to doe that poore little which you know I doe.[38]

Pastoral visitation was not only necessary for effective teaching, but also because of the distance between Indian and puritan settlements. Eliot,

---

33. "The Examination of the Indians at Roxbury, the 13th Day of the 4th Month, 1654," in *Late and Further Manifestation* (1655), 311–20.

34. "The Examination of the Indians at Roxbury, the 13th Day of the 4th Month, 1654," in *Late and Further Manifestation* (1655), 317.

35. Baxter, *The Reformed Pastor* (1656), 87–111, 178, 235.

36. Green, *The Christian's ABC*, 5.

37. *Further Account* (1660), 394. See *Further Account* (1660), 382.

38. Eliot to Shepard, 24 September 1647, in *Clear Sun-Shine* (1648), 124. Wigwams were "Indians houses or tents made of barks or matts," and "the fire is in the midst, over which they leave a place for the smoak [sic] to go out at." *Day-Breaking* (1647), 83; *Light Appearing* (1651), 178.

in a letter to Edward Winslow of 12 November 1648, included the story of a female Praying Indian who was "a diligent hearer; and out of desire to live where the Word of God was taught, they fetched all the corne they spent, sixteen miles upon their backes from the place of their planting."[39] Eliot also mentioned that he sometimes visited Indian places which were about forty miles away from his own place: "I have been foure times their this Summer, and there be more people by far, then be amongst us; and sundry of them do gladly hear the word of God, but it is neer 40.miles off, and I can seldom goe to them; whereat they are troubled, and desire I should come oft[e]ner, and stay longer when I come."[40] These references show how Eliot believed that visitations for the purpose of pastoral teaching were essential for Indian ministry.

Private pastoral teaching was also conducted when Praying Indians visited Eliot. Shepard introduced the story of a family of Praying Indians that came to Eliot: "I shall speake a little more of the old man who is mentioned in the story now in print; this old man hath much affection stirred up the Word, and comming to Mr. Eliots house (for of him I had this story) Mr. Eliot told him that because he brought his wife & all his children constantly to the Lecture."[41] The pastoral work with the Indians conducted in Eliot's settlement, Roxbury, is mentioned in a confession made by a Praying Indian known as Anthony. His confession suggests that the Praying Indians visited or stayed there temporarily: "My brother said, Go dwell with the English, and learn their manners; I yielded, because I loved my brother: I dwelt here at Roxbury, and came to this meeting house."[42]

For Eliot, following puritan tradition,[43] both text- and oral-based teaching were significant methods for pastoral teaching with native Indians. At first, for Eliot, text-based education was essential. This methodology was closely related to his emphasis on the Indians' level of literacy. As mentioned in chapter 4, literacy was required for effective pastoral teaching, and the ultimate reason for literacy was to be able to read the Bible.[44] But literacy was important not only to puritan Biblicism, but also to text-based pastoral teaching. According to Fox, literacy and print-based culture had

39. Eliot to Winslow, 12 November 1648, in *Glorious Progress* (1649), 151.
40. Eliot to Winslow, 12 November 1648, in *Glorious Progress* (1649), 152.
41. *Clear Sun-Shine* (1648), 121.
42. *Further Account* (1660), 382.
43. Wakefield, *Puritan Devotion*, 14–16; Hambrick-Stowe, *The Practice of Piety*, 5–7, 38, 49–50, 186–90; Fox, *Oral and Literate Culture in England*. Hall and Walsham, "'Justification by Print Alone?,'" 334–85; Hunt, *The Art of Hearing*, 19–59. For puritan understanding of text- and oral-based pastoral teaching, see pp. 95–97 above.
44. See p. 130 above.

increasingly influenced the means and content of communication, and its impact had been powerful in sixteenth- and seventeenth-century England.[45] Eliot carried this emphasis over to New England with him. His understanding can be illustrated by a letter written in 1651:

> I know not whether I have yet mentioned our Schoole . . . wee have two men in some measure able to teach the youth with my guidance, and inspection. And thus we order the Schoole: The Master daily prayeth among his Schollers, and instructeth them in Catechisme for which purpose I have compiled a short Catechisme, and wrote it in the Masters booke, which he can reade, and teach them; and also all the Copies he setteth his Schollers when he teacheth them to write, are the Questions and Answers of the Catechisme, that so the Children may be the more prompt and ready therein: wee aspire to no higher learning yet, but to spell, reade, and write, that so they may be able to write for themselves such Scriptures as I have already, or hereafter may . . . translate for them . . . my chief care is to Communicate as much of the Scriptures as I can by writing.[46]

In addition to his emphasis on literacy, Eliot's translation work indicates the importance of text-based pastoral teaching. His work to translate the Bible, catechisms and puritan literatures into the Algonquian Indian language was one of the most important pastoral tasks for Indian evangelization.[47] Eliot expressed his strong desire for the translation of the Bible and catechism into the Indians' language: "I do very much desire to translate some parts of the Scriptures into their language, and to print some Primer in their language wherein to initiate and teach them to read, which some of the men do much also desire."[48] Eliot translated the Bible into the Indian language under the name of *The New Testament of Our Lord and Saviour Jesus Christ* (Cambridge, 1661, 1685) and *The Holy Bible: Containing the Old Testament and the New* (1663, 1685). The Indian Bible published in 1663 was "the first complete Bible printed in the Western Hemisphere, the first complete Bible printed in a non-European tongue for evangelical purposes, and the first printed Bible for which an entire phonetic writing system was devised." Also the Bible "would remain the only complete Bible in an indigenous New World tongue until 1862, when missionaries translated the Old and

---

45. Fox, "Introduction," in *Oral and Literate Culture in England*.
46. Eliot to Henry Whitfield, October 1651, in *Strength out of Weaknesse* (1652), 225.
47. For "Algonquian," see p. 4n6 above.
48. Eliot to Winslow, 8 May 1649, in *Light Appearing* (1651), 187.

New Testament into Western Cree."[49] The Indian Bible translated by Eliot with his native Indian helpers was "the most visible artifact of the emerging bicultural community of Christian Indians in New England" because before the Bible the Indian language did not exist in written form.[50] Eliot also translated and printed a primer and catechism for Indians in 1654, which was reprinted in 1662, 1669, and 1686 or 1687. However, only the third edition of *The Indian Primer* printed in 1669 is extant. He also published *The Logick Primer* (1672). Eliot's translation of puritan literature into Indian language is significant. He translated Richard Baxter's *A Call to the Unconverted* (1658), Lewis Bayly's *The Practice of Piety* (2nd ed., 1612), and Thomas Shepard's *The Sincere Convert* (1640) in 1664 (reprinted in 1688), 1665, and 1689 respectively.[51]

For Eliot, the translation of the Bible was a primary means of Indian evangelization.[52] In his letter to Richard Floyd [Lloyd], a treasurer of the New England Company, Eliot said: "I shall not trouble you with anything at present save this one businesse of moment, touching the Printing of the Bible in the Indian Language, touching which businesse sundry of the Elders did petition unto the Commissioners, moving them to further it, as a principall means of promoting Religion among them."[53] Edward Reynolds also described the translation and printing of the Scripture as a significant work for promoting the gospel to the Indians: in addition to improving the natural reason of the Indians: "The other work which is set about in order to

---

49. Gray, *New World Babel*, 56.

50. Wyss, *Writing Indians*, 1.

51. For the history and process of Eliot's publications, see James Constantine Pilling, *Bibliography of the Algonquian Languages*, 127–84; Winship, *The Cambridge Press 1638-1692*, 150–244, 349–57; Kellaway, *The New England Company*, 122–47; Winslow, "Appendix: Legacy in Print," in *John Eliot*, 195–204; *JEMI*, 119–24 and "Appendix Five: Eliot's Massachusetts Publications." For the background of the early New England printing and bookselling, see Amory, "Printing and Bookselling in New England," 105–45.

52. Gray argued that unlike Jesuits who complained that "the Native American lexicon was not fit for Christian discourse" and they "lacked the words needed to convey Christian abstractions," puritans, particularly John Eliot, became actively involved with the translation of the Bible into Indian language. It was mainly because for puritans, reading and understanding the Bible was the primary method of Indian evangelization. Gray, *New World Babel*, 35, 41, 49, 50. For the comparison of Jesuit missionaries and puritans toward Indian languages in relation to evangelization, see Gray, *New World Babel*, 28–55.

53. Eliot to Richard Floyd, 28 December 1658, in *Further Accompt* (1659), 329–30. Richard Floyd [Lloyd], a member and treasurer of New England Company, does not appear in *ODNB* and *ANB*. According to Hardman Moore, he was probably a merchant who migrated to New England by 1642 and returned to England by July 1649. Hardman Moore, *Pilgrims*, 108; Hardman Moore, "Appendix 2," in *Pilgrims*, 161.

the premoting of the Gospel amongst the poor Indians is the translating of the Scripture into their tongue, and Printing it for their use, which as it is a necessary and an excellent worke, and a work of great labour."[54]

It is evident that the translation of puritan literature was also important to Eliot. In a letter to Baxter of 6 July 1663, Eliot explained his reason for translating one of his books:

> My Work about the Indian Bible being . . . finished . . . they having no Books for their private use, of ministerial composing. For their help . . . I have therefore purposed in my heart . . . to translate for them a little Book of yours, intituled [sic], [*A Call to the Unconverted*] . . . that the Call of Christ by your holy labours shall be made to speak in their Ears, in their own Language, that you may preach unto our poor Indians.[55]

Through the letter, one can understand that Eliot appreciated the value of puritan theological and ministerial writings as useful resources for his pastoral ministry in English settlements and in the Indian community.

In fact, the difficulty of the Algonquian Indian language was one of the reasons for the delay in the Indians' evangelization, along with "their infinite distance from Christianity." This is highlighted by the authors of *New Englands First Fruits* (1643), who stated that "Secondly, the difficulty of their Language to us, and of ours to them. . . . Thirdly, the diversity of their owne Language to it selfe; every part of that Countrey having its own Dialect, differing much from the other."[56] For Eliot, this was also a serious issue that he had to overcome before he could effectively preach the gospel to the Indians. The English puritans found it extremely hard to learn the Indians' language, as it was completely different from the English linguistic system.[57] William Leveri[t]ch[58] described this:

> [T]he Indian tongue be very difficult, irregular, and anomalous, and wherein I cannot meete with a Verbe Substantive as yet, nor any such Particles, as Conjunctions, &c. which are essentiall to the severall sorts of axioms, and consequently to all rationall

---

54. Edward Reynolds, "To The Christian Reader," in *Further Accompt* (1659), 327–28.

55. Eliot to Baxter, 6 July 1663, in *ET*, 430. See also Baxter, *Reliquiae Baxterianae* (1696), 115; Keeble and Nuttall, *Calendar of the Correspondence of Richard Baxter*, 2:39–40.

56. *New Englands First Fruits* (1643), 58.

57. Kellaway, *The New England Company*, 83–84.

58. See p. 116n300 above.

and perfect discourses, and . . . their words are generally very long.[59]

In fact, Roger Williams,[60] who wrote and published *A Key into the Language of America* (1643) criticized New England ministers' inactivity in learning the Indians' language:

> I believe that none of the Ministers of New England, nor any person in the whole Countrey is able to open the Mysteries of Christ Jesus in any proprietie of their Speech or Language, without which proprietie it cannot be imagined that Christ Jesus sent forth his first Apostles or Messengers, and without which no people in the World are long wil[l]ing to heare of difficult and heavenly matters.[61]

However, it is evident that Eliot, who was involved with Indian evangelization from 1646, had a serious concern for Indians' language and tried to learn and overcome the linguistic barrier in various ways. It is probably true that Eliot started to study the Indian language about 1643 or perhaps earlier.[62] He expressed the difficulties he had been having when learning the Indians' language several times in his letters. He had needed the help of native Indians to learn the language and to translate the Bible:

> I having yet but little skill in their language (having little leasure to attend it by reason of my continual attendance on my Ministry in our own Church) I must have some Indians, and it may be other help continually about me to try and examine Translations, which I look at as a sacred and holy work, and to be regarded with much fear, care, and reverence.[63]

This reference shows Eliot's strong concern for learning the language. Eliot's personal helper for learning Indians' language also tells of Eliot's positive efforts to learn the language. Eliot introduced an Indian who was his personal Indian language teacher and interpreter in his letter to Winslow:

59. William Leveri[t]ch to Henry Whitfield, 22 September 1651, in *Strength out of Weaknesse* (1652), 235.

60. Bremer, "Williams, Roger."

61. Williams, *The Bloody Tenent yet More Bloody* (1643), 219, cited in *ET*, 35n2. See also Williams, *The Bloody Tenent yet More Bloody* (1643), 371–72; Williams, *A Key into the Language of America* (1643). According to Wyss, Roger Williams's book contains a list of Algonquian words, but it was more like "a phrase book than any systematic attempt to 'convert' the language into a written form." Wyss, *Writing Indians*, 1n1.

62. Tooker, *John Eliot's First Indian Teacher and Interpreter*, 12; Thwing, *History of the First Church in Roxbury*, 25–27; *ID*, 27.

63. Eliot to Winslow, 8 May 1649, in *Light Appearing* (1651), 187.

> There is an Indian living with Mr. Richard Calicott of Dorchester, who was taken in the Pequott Warres, though belonging to Long Island; this Indian is ingenious, can read; and I taught him to write, which he quickly learnt, though I know not what use he now maketh of it: He was the first that I made use of to teach me words, and to be my Interpreter.[64]

Eliot, in *The Indian Grammar Begun* (1666), confessed that only through the help of an Indian interpreter could he finish his Indian grammar book and translate the Commandments, the Lord's Prayer, and many texts of Scripture.[65]

Finally, Eliot started to overcome the obstacle of the language, and by 1646 could teach and preach. Over the years, as has been shown, he published a variety of religious texts in the Indian language. In 1666 he even published an Indian language grammar book.[66] In sum, Eliot's serious involvement with translations and publications for the Indian ministry shows that, for Eliot, text-based education was a significant method of pastoral teaching. In this he followed puritan tradition.

Along with text-based education, orality was also an important means of pastoral teaching for Eliot. Although literacy had become a strong vehicle of communication, orality was still the primary means of communication in sixteenth- and seventeenth-century England. Orality was not radically replaced by literacy, but spoken and written forms of communication were in mutual and complementary relationship.[67] The function of orality as a

---

64. Eliot to Winslow, 2 December 1648, in *Glorious Progress* (1649), 160. According to Tooker, the Indian interpreter was Cockenoe-De-Long Island. Tooker, in his book, investigated the career of Cockenoe-De-Long Island as an Indian interpreter of English language based on various historical records of New England. Tooker, *John Eliot's First Indian Teacher and Interpreter*. John Eliot mentioned another Indian interpreter. *Light Appearing* (1651), 206. According to Daniel Gookin's *HCINE*, he was Job Nesutan who took the place of Cockenoe-De-Long Island. See also Tooker, *John Eliot's First Indian Teacher and Interpreter*, 16; Byington, "John Eliot," 116. Pequot War (1636–37) was "the first major armed conflict between Puritans colonists and Native Americans in New England." See Luder, "Pequot War," 477.

65. Eliot, *The Indian Grammar Begun* (1666), 66. See also Pickering, *A Grammar of the Massachusetts Indian Language*; Tooker, *John Eliot's First Indian Teacher and Interpreter* 12; Byington, "John Eliot," 117; Thwing, *History of the First Church in Roxbury*, 26.

66. *Day-Breaking* (1647), 84, 85, 88; *Clear Sun-Shine* (1648), 118; *Strength out of Weaknesse* (1652), 232–33, 242. Eliot, *The Indian Grammar Begun* (1666). John Winthrop mentioned Eliot's preaching in Indian language. Winthrop, *The Journal of John Winthrop*, 673, 683, 688.

67. Fox, *Oral and Literate Culture in England*, 5–6, 11, 50. See also Fox and Woolf, *The Spoken Word*, 8.

means of communication can be easily found in Indian ministry. Eliot's oral pastoral education is clearly demonstrated in his preaching and catechizing. As Green indicated, catechizing was "an essentially oral exercise." The pattern of questions and answers in pastoral teaching was a primary methodology for catechism. The dialogue between Eliot and the Indians described in Eliot's letter to Edward Winslow of 21 October 1650 clearly shows the prototype for oral pastoral education.[68] Also, the fact that the confession of conversion experiences and the examination of faith based on the catechism were completely oral-based reflects the significance of orality in Eliot's pastoral teaching.[69] One of the most commonly used expressions by the Praying Indians when they were confessing, especially when they talked about pastoral teaching was "I heard" certain words of God in the minister's preaching.[70] This is understandable if we take the publication year of the Indian Bible, which was 1663, into consideration. It is evident that until the publication of the Indian Bible, Eliot's Bible lessons were delivered orally for at least seventeen years after his first preaching of the gospel to the Indians in 1646. As David D. Hall and Alexandra Walsham have argued,[71] there were not enough texts and books in New England. In fact, Eliot, in a letter to Edward Winslow of 29 October 1649, pleaded for books and money for himself and Mayhew:

> Mr. Ma[y]hew, who putteth his hand unto this Plough at Martins Vineyard, being young, and a beginner here, hath extreme want of books; he needeth Commentaries and Common Places for the body of Divinity. . . . [I]f therefore the Lord bring any meanes into your hand, I desire you would . . . send him over such books as may be necessary for a young Scholar. . . . And for myself I have this request (who also am short enough in books)

---

68. Eliot to Winslow, 21 October 1650, in *Light Appearing* (1651), 199–200. For the examples of puritan oral teaching in question-and-answer form, see *Day-Breaking* (1647), 86–87, 88, 91; *Clear Sun-Shine* (1648), 120, 126–27; *Glorious Progress* (1649), 151, 153; *Light Appearing* (1651), 199–200; *Strength out of Weaknesse* (1652), 233. For the examples of Praying Indians' questions and puritans' answers, see *Day-Breaking* (1647), 84–86, 88–91; *Clear Sun-Shine* (1648), 117, 120–22, 128–30; *Glorious Progress* (1649), 151, 155–56, 160; *Light Appearing* (1651), 193–94, 196–97, 199–200; *Strength out of Weaknesse* (1652), 226, 233. Green, *The Christian's ABC*, 8. Green, however, argued that written forms of catechisms were also given to literate catechumens to help their illiterate fellow to memorise the contents of catechisms. Green, *The Christian's ABC*, 8.

69. See *Tears of Repentance* (1653), 268–95; "The Examination of the Indians at Roxbury, the 13th Day of the 4th Month, 1654," in *Late and Further Manifestation* (1655), 311–20; *Further Account* (1660), 360–96.

70. *Further Account* (1660), 357–95.

71. Hall and Walsham, "'Justification by Print Alone?,'" 334–85.

that I might be helped to purchase my brother Weld his books, the summe of the purchase is ({£}34.). I am loth they should come back to England when we have so much need of them here, and without ready money there I cannot have them. . . . I wrote likewise by my last to intreat for some encouragement to Master Mahu who preacheth to the Indians, and that some monies may be laid out in books for him; for young Scholars in New-England are very poor in books, as he is in extreme want.[72]

This letter not only shows that the supply of printed texts was insufficient, but also explicitly indicates that oral pastoral education was absolutely necessary and was still a significant means of ministry in addition to written texts.

Puritan Pastoral Care: Counselling and Spiritual Direction

In Eliot's puritan ministry for the Indians, the pastor was not only a teacher of the Word of God, but also a ministerial counsellor and director.[73] For Eliot, private meetings and visitation as means of pastoral teaching were related to pastoral counselling and spiritual direction. Eliot told the story of a female Indian who traveled sixteen miles for pastoral teaching: "I severall times visited her, prayed with her, asked her about her spiritual estate? She told me: she still loved God, though he made her sick, and was resolved to pray unto him so long as she lived, and to refuse powwowing."[74]

As mentioned above, Indians' questions and puritan ministers' answers were a significant part of pastoral teaching. Among Indians' questions, there were many practical ones that imply the role of pastor as spiritual director and counsellor. The Indians' questions that Thomas Shepard printed in *Clear Sun-Shine* (1648) are good examples. After teaching the gospel in an Indian lecture at Noonanetum, "a wife of one Wampooas a well affected Indians" asked, "whether do I pray when my husband prayes if I speak nothing as he doth, yet if I like what he saith, and my heart goes with it?" Another question raised by "the wife of one Totherswampe" was "whether as husband should do well to pray with his wife, and yet continue in his passions, & be angry

---

72. Eliot to Winslow, 29 October 1649, in *Light Appearing* (1651), 192–93, 196. Kellaway, *The New England Company*, 91–92. For Weld's catalogue of the books (patristic, puritan and continental Reformed texts), see Bodleian, MS. Rawl. D. 934, fols 34r–38v, cited in Hardman Moore, *Pilgrims*, 134n76. Eliot talked about the book supply from England in his letter to Jonathan Hanmer, minister of Barnstaple, 19 July and 7 October 1652. See *JEI*, 6–10, 11–12.

73. Baxter, *The Reformed Pastor* (1656), 94–111; Baxter, *A Call to the Unconverted* (1658), 7, 20–21. See also Rice, *Reformed Spirituality*, 131–35.

74. *Glorious Progress* (1649), 151. For "powwowing," see below, 186–87.

with his wife?"[75] These questions reveal Indians' interest in Christian faith and piety, and their gradual change. At the same time, the questions show that Indians' questions were not only about Christian doctrines and the Bible, but also, sometimes more seriously, about their Christian life itself. In other words, for Indians, being Christian was about how to know and understand God and the Bible, and also how to live actually as a Christian. The practical question of an aged Indian that Thomas Shepard introduced shows an example of puritan ministerial counselling, and what could happen often in their ministry. Shepard said that "there was an aged Indian who proposed his complaint in propounding his question concerning an unruly disobedient son" and he asked "what one should do with him in case of obstinacy and disobedience, and that will not hear Gods Word, though his Father command him, nor will nor forsake his drunkennesse, though his father forbid him?" Shepard also said that "there were many answers to set forth the sinne of disobedience to parents." Mr. Wilson,[76] especially, issued a strong rebuke, but the young Indian did not accept the teaching and harshly resisted it:

> Mr. Wilson was much inlarged, and spake so terribly, yet so graciously as might have affected a heart not quite shut up, which this young desperado hearing (who well understood the English tongue) instead of humbling himself before the Lords Word, which touched his conscience and condition so neare, hee was filled with a spirit of Satan, and as soone as ever Mr. Wilsons speech was ended hee brake out into a loud contemptuous expression; So, saith he: which we passed by without speaking againe, leaving the Word with him, which we knew would one day take its effect one way or other upon him.[77]

This story illustrates the conflict between puritans and Indians when puritans taught the gospel and Christian way of life. At the same time, this story clearly shows what Indians asked, and what help they needed from puritan ministers, and how the ministers approached the questions. Here, one finds an example of pastoral counselling and direction for Indians who had begun to understand Christianity and a Christian life.

Pastoral counselling by John Speen, a Praying Indian and pastoral leader in Natick Praying Town, is another good example of pastoral counselling and spiritual direction in Indian ministry. Eliot described the counselling Speen provided for Penitent, a native Indian, in *Indian Dialogues*

---

75. *Clear Sun-Shine* (1648), 117.
76. Probably John Wilson (c. 1591–Aug. 1667). See p. 123n2 above.
77. *Clear Sun-Shine* (1648), 118.

(1671).⁷⁸ Penitent said, "My heart is broken with grief. I am ready to sink into the ground because of my distressed mind. . . . It may be you may give me counsel what I shall do in my distress, and advise me if there be any way or means to comfort this distressed soul of mine."⁷⁹ John said:

> Alas, your sorrowful countenance doth indeed discover that your mind is oppressed with grief, and in such cases men are miserable comforters. . . . My first counsel therefore is, that you would pray unto God, and believe in Jesus Christ, and he will surely give you rest. But as for man, especially such a poor creature as I am, I cannot help you, nor is there any help for you in the hand of man.⁸⁰

Penitent said, "But the words of a true-hearted loving friend may minister some comfort, and I do already feel that your words have relief in them, in that you tell me Jesus Christ is so tender-hearted towards those that are of an afflicted spirit." And then John Speen said:

> I am very weak, but I am willing to help your afflicted soul to go to Jesus Christ, who will not fail to comfort you. Seeing therefore it is your desire, let me hear your griefs and troubles. It may please God to put a word into my mouth, whereby the good spirit of God may speak comfort to your sorrowful heart.⁸¹

These examples suggest what the Praying Indians had learned about pastoral counselling and spiritual direction from John Eliot in his Indian ministry.

Pastoral Education for Indian Pastoral Leaders

Eliot, in a letter to Henry Whitfield of August 1651, wrote of the necessity to train up Indian ministerial leaders: "and further, my scope so to traine up both men and youths, that when they be in some measure instructed themselves, they may be sent forth to other parts of the Countrey, to traine up and instruct others, even as they themselves have been trained up and

---

78. Eliot provided an example in a separate section in "Dialogue III" in *Indian Dialogues* (1671). This is helpful to understand puritan pastoral counselling and spiritual direction in Indian ministry. See Eliot, *Indian Dialogues* (1671), 149–62. The conversation between Penitent and John Speen is a part in their whole dialogue.

79. Eliot, *Indian Dialogues* (1671), 149–50.

80. Eliot, *Indian Dialogues* (1671), 150.

81. Eliot, *Indian Dialogues* (1671), 150. For other practical examples of pastoral care in *Indian Dialogues* (1671), see Eliot, *Indian Dialogues* (1671), 133–34.

instructed."[82] John Wilson, in a letter of 27 October 1651, reported: "among the Indians there be some greater proficients in knowledge, and of better utterance by farre then their fellows, Grave and serious men, whom Mr Eliot hath trained up . . . to instruct and exhort the rest of the Indians in their Lords day and other meetings, when he cannot come to them himself."[83] Almost twenty years later, Eliot wrote that the trained native Indian pastoral leaders were sent for pastoral teaching of other Indians, and their works were successful: "God hath in mercy raised up sundry among themselves to a competent ability to teach their countrymen. Many have been sent forth by the church this winter to divers places, and not without good success, through the grace of God."[84] Piumbukhou, a Praying Indian, in *Indian Dialogues* (1671), described the training for Indian pastoral leaders and their work for other Indians: "our hope is the greater, because the Lord hath raised up sundry of our young men . . . unto good knowledge in the scriptures, and are able to teach others the good knowledge of God, and are fit to be sent forth unto all parts of the country, to teach them to pray unto God."[85]

Following puritan tradition, Eliot emphasized education for Indian ministerial leaders. This related to the efficiency of Indian ministry.[86] First of all, in terms of the puritan pastoral and ecclesiastical structure, Eliot had to carry out his Indian ministry while acting as a minister to the English settlers at Roxbury. In other words, for Eliot, English ministry was his full-time job, and Indian ministry was only part-time despite its significance. This circumstance reflects not only the Indian ministerial situation in New England (in terms of the lack of ministers for Indians), but also implicitly reveals the understanding of pastorship and pastoral structure in seventeenth-century puritan society. That is to say, pastorship was crucially related to parish-centered ministry, which meant that a certain pastor was for a certain parish, so a pastor who was supposed to work for his own

---

82. Eliot to Whitfield, October 1651, in *Strength out of Weaknesse* (1652), 225.

83. John Wilson to Whitfield, 27 October 1651, in *Strength out of Weaknesse* (1652), 232.

84. Eliot, "To the Right Worshipful," in *Indian Dialogues* (1671), 59. Eliot said this in his letter to Henry Ashurst, the treasurer of the New England Company of 30 November 1670. CGTNEC, 39. Gauci, "Ashurst, Henry."

85. Eliot, *Indian Dialogues* (1671), 80.

86. Richard Greenham showed a good example of pastoral training for pastors. See Collinson, *The Elizabethan Puritan Movement*, 128, 349, 369; Collinson, *The Religion of Protestant*, 119; Collinson, "Shepherd, Sheepdogs, and Hirelings," 199–200; Primus, *Richard Greenham*; Parker and Carlson, '*Practical Divinity*'; Bozeman, *The Precisianist Strain*, 63–83; Black, *Reformation Pastors*, 33. Richard Baxter also strongly emphasized pastoral training for pastors. Baxter, *The Reformed Pastor* (1656), 46, 54, 60, 70–71, 203. See also pp. 100–101 above.

parish church should not go elsewhere to undertake pastoral activity. This continued in New England settlements.[87] In Eliot's context, as primarily a pastor to English settlers, it is evident that he absolutely needed pastoral helpers to sustain Indian ministry. The remoteness of Indian settlements was also a factor. Eliot said:

> But above all other Reasons this is greatest, that they living in sundry Towns and places remote from each other, and labourers few to take care of them, it is necessary that some of themselves should be trained up, and peculiarly instructed, unto whom the care ruling and ordering of them in the affaires of Gods house may be committed, in the absence of such as look after their instruction.[88]

A second reason for Eliot's emphasis on the training of Indian pastoral leaders was because he expected their work would have a better pastoral effect: "There be severall providences of God appearing to worke, which make mee thinke that the most effectuall and generall way of spreading the Gospel will be by themselves."[89] Eliot indicated that this was mainly because of language problems:

> when so instructed as I have above mentioned; as for my preaching, though such whole hearts God hath bowed to attend, can picke up some knowledge by my broken expressions, yet I see that it is not so taking, and effectuall to strangers, as their owne expressions be, who naturally speake unto them in their owne tongue.[90]

In this sense, Eliot argued for the necessity of training up Indian pastoral leaders for the effective preaching of the Gospel, and described how he actually trained them. He said:

> To the end therefore that they may be the better able to teach others, I doe traine them up, and exercise them therein: when I am among them on the Lords dayes, appointing two, each Sabboth to exercise, and when they have done, then I proceed, and assuredly I finde a good measure of abilitie in them, not only in prayer . . . but in memory to rehearse such Scriptures as

---

87. Bowden and Ronda argued that one of the reasons of puritans' indifference to Indian evangelization in the early period of migration was puritan understanding of parish-centered pastorship. *ID*, 24–25.

88. *Late and Further Manifestation* (1655), 318.

89. Eliot to Whitfield, October 1651, in *Strength out of Weaknesse* (1652), 225.

90. Eliot to Whitfield, October 1651, in *Strength out of Weaknesse* (1652), 225.

> I have read unto them and expounded: to expound them also as they have heard mee doe, and apply them.[91]

To educate the Indian leaders, Eliot not only taught the Bible and doctrines, but also provided a general education, including an introduction to liberal arts and science. Eliot said in *Brief Narrative* (1671):

> for which cause I have begun to teach them the Art of Teaching . . . Liberal Art and Science, how to analyze, and lay out into particulars both the Works and Word of God; and how to communicate knowledge to others methodically and skil[l]fully, and especially the method of Divinity. . . . The Bible, and the Catechisms drawn out of the Bible, are general helps to all parts and places about us, and are the ground-work of Community amongst all our Indian-Churches and Christians.[92]

Eliot not only trained up Indian teachers for pastoral teaching, but also appointed other officers to serve the churches. Through Eliot's *Brief Narrative* (1671), one can realize that there were not only Indian teachers and pastors, but also ruling elders and deacons as well in Indian churches.[93] In sum, following the puritan tradition of pastoral education for pastors, Eliot eagerly tried to train up selected Indian leaders. This training was not only for Eliot himself to have ministerial helps from Indians, but also for ministerial efficiency from the pastoral activity of Indians in their own language.

Praying Indians' "Praying to God": Indian Practice of Piety

Henry Whitfield, who edited *Light Appearing* (1651), provided his reflection on the Christian religious life of Praying Indians in comparison to English Christians. This is noteworthy because of his observation of the Praying Indians' actual exercise of Christianity. Also through his observations, one can glimpse what the puritans actually wanted to see from Praying Indians—who were expected to have changed according to puritan standards. Whitfield presented Praying Indians' religious life as Christians in five aspects:

> These Indians are found . . . to prize Ordinances. . . . These Indians are plain-hearted seek for Christ to enjoy him for himself.

---

91. Eliot to Whitfield, October 1651, in *Strength out of Weaknesse* (1652), 225. See *Brief Narrative* (1671), 402.
92. *Brief Narrative* (1671), 402.
93. *Brief Narrative* (1671), 400–401. See also pp. 154–56 above.

... These Indians are industrious and pursue the things of their salvation.... These mourn and weep bitterly, and are pained under the sight and sense of their sins, when convinced of them. ... They are careful and constant in duties of worship, both in private and family prayer, hearing the Word, observation of the Sabbath, meet often together, and will pray together as occasion serves, converse lovingly together, are teachable, patient, and contented.[94]

Henry Whitfield seemed to understand that the actual practice of piety was not only a duty of Christians, but also a sign of Christian identity. The practice of piety, along with puritan pastoral teaching and care, was one of the key tasks that Eliot taught in Indian ministry.

For the Indians, repentance was the starting point to become Praying Indians. For them, repentance was for salvation, and it strongly signified a changed and reformed life as "godly Indians."[95] Piumbukhou, a Praying Indian, said: "We now call you to repent of your evil ways, and to reform your lives to serve the true and living God, to seek for pardon of your sins, and mercy to appease his wrath which is kindled against you."[96] For Praying Indians, the abandonment of their traditional life was significant in terms of their practice of repentance. Lindford D. Fisher, who argued for "hybridised indigenous Indian Christianity," demonstrated that the Indians did not abandon their traditional religious cultures entirely while they followed and adopted "certain forms, rituals, and beliefs of European Christianity."[97] In fact, according to Daniel Gookin's observations, the Praying Indians continued to live in wigwams as their traditional house in the Praying Towns, because an English house "was more chargeable to build and not so warm, and cannot be removed so easily their wigwams ... and themselves being generally artists in building and finish their own wigwams: for these and like reasons, they do incline to their old fashioned houses." Also, they continued to hunt and fish while learning and developing English husbandry. So, Eliot seemed to allow the Indians' living in wigwams and their traditional husbandry.[98] However, the Praying Indians should show their transformation

94. *Light Appearing* (1651), 208.
95. *Brief Narrative* (1671), 404.
96. Eliot, *Indian Dialogues* (1671), 88.
97. Fisher, "Native Americans, Conversion, and Christian Practice in Colonial New England," 101–24. Fisher's article provides a rare substantial research on the practice of piety of New England Indians particularly of Eliot's time period. However, despite its contribution, Fisher did not provide an investigation of puritan traditions as the crucial basis of the Indian Christian practice.
98. HCINE, 181, 188; *JEMI*, 107–8.

through their changed lifestyle, from heathens to Christians. In particular, they must abandon their pagan religious customs which were contradictory to Christianity. One can find this understanding in Waban's description of himself as a Praying Indian:

> I am a praying Indian. I have left our old Indian customs, laws, fashions, lusts, pauwauings, and whatever is contrary to the right knowledge of the true God, and of Jesus Christ our redeemer. I repenteth me of all my fore-past life. . . . All the works of darkness in which I was wont to take pleasure, I do now forsake and abandon.[99]

Among native Indians' former religious customs, "Pawwaws" was a representative Indian traditional religious custom which was most seriously considered and frequently appears in the Eliot Tracts. According to "Conclusions and Orders" (a conduct code made by Indians in August, 1646), "Pawwows are Witches or Sorcerers that cure by help of the devil."[100] Piumbukhou, a Praying Indian, explained "Pawwaws" to Praying Indians. For them, "Pawwaw" is worshiping the devil: "Your prayers and powwowings are worshipping of the Devil, and not of God, and they are among the greatest of your sins."[101] Thomas Mayhew offered a detailed explanation of Indian "Pawwaws" in a letter "To the much Honored Corporation in London" in *Tears of Repentance* (1653):

> [T]hey had many meetings with their Pawwaws . . . to pacifie the Devil by their Sacrifice, and get deliverance from their evil. . . . The Pawwaws counted their Imps their Preservers, had them treasured up in their bodies, which they brought forth to hurt their enemies, and heal their friends; who when they had done some notable Cure, would shew the Imp in the palm of his Hand to the Indians; who with much amazement looking on it, Deified them, then at all times seeking to them for cure in all sicknesses, and counsel in all cases.[102]

---

99. Eliot, *Indian Dialogues* (1671), 95–96.

100. *Clear Sun-Shine* (1648), 115. In the Eliot Tracts, "Pawwaw," "Pauwau," "Powwow," or "Pawwawnomas" appears as the same meaning and "Pawwaw" is used as verb and noun indicating the person who does "Powwaws." New England Indian's religiosity can be mainly described as Shamanism and pantheism. For native Indians' "Pawwaw" and religiosity, see *ID*, 13–21; Cohen, "Conversion among Puritans and Amerindians," 239–44; Morrison, *A Praying People*, 10–17. For Thomas Mayhew's description of Indian religiosity, see *Tears of Repentance* (1653), 253.

101. Eliot, *Indian Dialogues* (1671), 88.

102. *Tears of Repentance* (1653), 253–54.

According to Eliot, the most serious difficulty that Indian ministry faced was "Pawwaws" and Sachems' hindrance:

> This businesse of praying to God ... has hitherto found opposition only from the Pawwawes and profane spirits; but now the Lord hath exercised us with another and a greater opposition; for the Sachems of the Countrey are generally set against us, and counter-work the Lord by keeping off their men from praying to God as much as they can.[103]

Eliot reported that the first effect of the preaching of the Word was Indians' immediate decision to forsake "all their Powwaws": "The effect of the Word which appears among them, and the change that is among them is this: First, they have utterly forsaken all their Powwaws, and given over that diabolicall exercise, being convinced that it is quite contrary to praying unto God."[104] Although native Indians found it "hard to get from under the yoake of cruelty that they and their forefathers had so long groaned under."[105] The converted Indians confessed that they renounced "Pawwaws" as one of the most serious sins that they had to repent and renounce.[106]

For Praying Indians who abandoned their former religious customs, reading and meditation on the Bible were essential practices of piety in Praying Towns. Eliot said, "The Bible, and the Catechism drawn out of the Bible, are general helps to all parts and places ab[o]ut us, and are the groundwork of Community amongst all our Indian-Churches and Christians."[107] In Eliot's Indian ministry, Bible learning was not only a means of pastoral teaching, but also a pious practice:

> [W]e wisht them to thinke, and meditate of so much as had been taught them; and which they now heard out of Gods booke, and to thinke much and often upon it, both when they did lie downe on their Mats in their Wigwams, and when they rose up, and to goe alone in the fields and woods, and muse on it, and so God would teach them.[108]

---

103. Eliot to Winslow, 21 October 1650, in *Light Appearing* (1651), 202. See *Light Appearing* (1651), 179–80.

104. Eliot to Shepard, 24 September 1647, in *Clear Sun-Shine* (1648), 125.

105. *Light Appearing* (1651), 181.

106. *Light Appearing* (1651), 183; *Strength out of Weaknesse* (1652), 238–40; *Further Account* (1660), 364. See also Eliot, "An Account of Indian Churches in New-England" (1673), 126.

107. *Brief Narrative* (1671), 402. For puritan understanding of Biblicism in the practice of piety, see p. 103 above.

108. *Day-Breaking* (1647), 84–85.

This reflects the regular practice of Bible meditation in puritan tradition as it appears in Bayly's *The Practice of Piety* (2nd ed., 1612).[109] Also, it is evident that for Praying Indians, learning the Bible was not just an intellectual practice of piety, but the practice of "heart religion" that brings about inner and spiritual experience. Piumbukhou, a Praying Indian, said: "Our joys in the knowledge of God, and of Jesus Christ, which we taught in the Book of God, and feel in our heart, is sweeter to our soul, than honey is unto the mouth and taste."[110]

Prayer was one of the integral parts of the practice of piety in the puritan tradition.[111] For the Indians, "praying to God" signified their Christian identity. This understanding is interestingly found in the Indians' own definition of prayer: "praying to God" was "their general name of Religion."[112] Eliot provided a more detailed explanation of what the Indians meant by prayer:

> Their frequent phrase of Praying to God, is not to be understood of that Ordinance and Duty of Prayer only, but of all Religion, and comprehendeth the same meaning, with them, as the word [Religion] doth with us: And it is observable, because it seemeth to me, That the Lord will make them a Praying people: and indeed, there is a great Spirit of Prayer pow[e]red out upon them, to my wonderment; and you may easily apprehend, That they who are assisted to express such Confessions before men, are not without a good measure of inlargement of Spirit before the Lord.[113]

Based on the Indians' understanding of "praying to God" as their religious identity as Christians,[114] prayer was also emphasized as an act of piety in *Indian Dialogues* (1671). Piumbukhou, a Praying Indian, explained about his practice of prayer before and after meals and before sleep, which is similar to what was taught in Bayly's *The Practice of Piety* (2nd ed., 1612).[115] First of all, Piumbukhou mentioned saying a prayer before a meal: "Therefore God hath taught us, and it is our custom, among all that are godly, to pray

---

109. Bayly, *The Practice of Piety* (2nd ed., 1612), 143–47.

110. Eliot, *Indian Dialogues* (1671), 69–70.

111. Bayly, *The Practice of Piety* (2nd ed., 1612), 139–61, 185–89; Hambrick-Stowe, *The Practice of Piety*, 161, 163. For puritan understanding of prayer, see pp. 106–7 above.

112. *Light Appearing* (1651), 202; *Tears of Repentance* (1653), 261.

113. *Tears of Repentance* (1653), 261–62.

114. Fisher, "Native Americans, Conversion, and Christian Practice in Colonial New England," 108.

115. Bayly, *The Practice of Piety* (2nd ed., 1612), 209–22.

to God for a blessing before we eat and therefore I entreat you to have so much patience and compliance, as to give me the quiet liberty to pray to God before we eat."[116] This was what Eliot recorded as Piumbukhou's actual prayer before a meal:

> Let us lift up our eyes and hearts to God in heaven, and say, almighty, glorious, merciful and heavenly Father. . . . Bless us at this time, and this food which is set before us . . . make us wise to receive it at thy hand, to sue the strength we get by it to the glory of thy name, through Jesus Christ. And bless all our souls, feed them by thy word and truth . . . help us all to rejoice in the Lord through Jesus Christ. Amen.[117]

Eliot recorded how Piumbukhou also explained about prayer after a meal: "Our Lord Jesus Christ did so before meat, as it is written of him in many examples, and we are not to doubt but he did the same after meat, because the Lord hath commanded the same so expressly, saying, when thou hast eaten and art full, then beware lest thou forget the Lord [Deut. 6:11–12]."[118] Eliot recorded how Piumbukhou gave an example of the prayer after a meal: "O Lord our God, for our life, health, food, raiments, and for the present food whereby we are refreshed . . . We do pray for a blessing upon both, that our food may strengthen our bodies, and our discourse may do good to our souls."[119]

Like puritans in England who practiced ejaculatory prayer, Praying Indians had an understanding of ejaculatory prayer.[120] As Waban in *Indian Dialogues* (1671) was reported to have said:

> [C]rying is an earnest manner of praying. And the matter of our cry is to say Abba, Father, that is, to call God our father, and to ask him a child's portion in the name of Jesus Christ, it shall be surely granted. . . . For we are foolish children, and know not what is best for our selves, but the father doth. And therefore when we make our prayers and request unto God, we must leave the matter to his love and wisdom, to give us what, and when, and how he will. And because we are ignorant what to pray for, therefore the spirit of God who dwelleth in our heart, he is called the spirit

---

116. Eliot, *Indian Dialogues* (1671), 73. See Eliot, *Indian Dialogues* (1671), 82.

117. Eliot, *Indian Dialogues* (1671), 73–74. See Eliot, *Indian Dialogues* (1671), 76.

118. Eliot, *Indian Dialogues* (1671), 77. The Bible passages were originally in footnote 13 in Bowden and Ronda's edition of *Indian Dialogues* (1671).

119. Eliot, *Indian Dialogues* (1671), 76.

120. Bayly, *The Practice of Piety* (2nd ed., 1612), 294. See also Hambrick-Stowe, *The Practice of Piety*, 185; Hambrick-Stowe, "III. Puritan Spirituality in America," 350.

of grace and supplication; and Rom. 8:26, 27, Likewise the Spirit also helpeth our infirmities.... And this is the condition of every true converted believer, that he can pray, and desires to pray, and is ever lifting up his heart to God in prayer.[121]

Public fasting and thanksgiving were also significant aspects of the puritan piety promoted by Eliot in Indian ministry. According to his biographer Mather, Eliot said: "we have many Days for both Fasting and Thanksgiving in our Pilgrimage."[122] Eliot, in his "An Account of Indian Churches in New-England" (1673), said, "All days of publick fasting and thanksgiving which are exercised among us, they do religiously observe, even as they doe the Sabbaths, and sometimes we have fasting days among ourselves."[123] Days of fasting and prayer for repentance were regularly kept and practiced not only on ecclesiastically special days, such as the days for covenanting and church membership approval, but also during a certain difficult periods because of various reasons such as natural disasters and diseases. Exhortations by Praying Indians, delivered at a fast day on the 15 November 1658, provide important sources for understanding the practice of repentance and fasting in Eliot's Indian ministry. This particular fast day was not only for "preparation for gathering a Church," but also because of "much rain, and sicknesse and other tryalls" in the Praying Towns.[124] Through the Praying Indians' exhortations, one can notice that repentance was considered and practiced seriously by the Praying Indians under Eliot's pastoral direction and fasting was also an important practice of piety in relation to repentance. Waban, one of the Praying Indians, said in an exhortation (based on Matt 9:12–13), "we are all sick of that sicknesse in our souls, but we know it not: we have many at this time sick in body, for which cause we do fast and pray this day." Waban described human sins as "sicknesse in souls." He urged that humans should repent to Christ, and the fasting day was the day of repentance: "Therefore what should we doe this day? Goe to Christ the Phisitian; for Christ is a Physitian of souls . . . therefore let all sinners goe to him. Therefore this day know what need we have of Christ, and let us goe to Christ to heale us of our sins."[125] Nishokhou, a Praying Indian, understood in his exhortation (based on Gen 8:20–21) that repentance is a "spiritual sacrifice": "we must by repentance purge ourselves. . . . These are

---

121. Eliot, *Indian Dialogues* (1671), 107.

122. LJE, 20. See also Bayly, *The Practice of Piety* (2nd ed., 1612), 301; Davies, *The Worship of American Puritans*, 61–66.

123. Eliot, "An Account of Indian Churches in New-England" (1673), 126.

124. *Further Accompt* (1659), 332–33.

125. *Further Accompt* (1659), 333.

true and spirituall sacrifices which God requireth at our hands. Sacrifice of Righteousnesse."[126] The exhortation by Anthony (based on Matt 6:16–18) presented repentance and fasting as doctrine that Christ taught and Christians should practice: "The Doctrine that Christ teacheth us in these words, is the Doctrine of fasting and prayer; and the duty we doe this day, is to practise this Doctrine, for God calleth us this day to fasting and prayer." Anthony related fasting to repentance. He said, "But why must we fast? Answ. That we might the more effectually mourn for sin . . . so that fasting is an help to mourning. Now this day is a day of mourning . . . we must mourn for our sins." He repeated, "This is a day of Repentance, we must therefore fast this day, so as becometh Repentance, therefore we must confesse our sins, and we must mo[u]rn for our sins, and we must forsake our sins, for these are works meet for Repentance."[127]

Psalm-singing was also an essential puritan practice of piety in ministry to the Praying Indians.[128] Eliot, who was actively involved with the publication of *The Bay Psalm Book* (1640), also translated the psalms into a metrical version in the Indian language.[129] The Eliot Tracts contained a description of Praying Indians' psalm-singing, which was regularly practiced. Eliot's personal letters and the Eliot Tracts show that psalm-singing was practiced publicly, and privately at home. John Wilson's description in the Eliot Tracts is helpful. He visited a Praying Town in 1651 and mentioned the psalm-singing. Wilson provided a detailed description of Praying Indians' use of psalms after Eliot's preaching, by reading and also singing:

> Then Mr Eliot prayed and preached in the Indian Language for some houre more, about coming to Christ, and bearing his yoake. This Text was translated by him from the Scripture into English, speaking with much authoritie, and after his latter prayer the Indian Schoole Master read out of his Booke one of the Psalmes in meter, line by line, translated by Mr Eliot into Indian, all the men and women, &c. singing the same together in one of our ordinary English tunes melodiously.[130]

---

126. *Further Accompt* (1659), 334.

127. *Further Accompt* (1659), 335–36.

128. For the significance of psalm-singing in puritan tradition, see Cotton, *Singing of Psalmes* (1647), 2; Hambrick-Stowe, *The Practice of Piety*, 111–16; Green, *Print and Protestantism*, 530–33.

129. Eliot, *The Psalter* (1658 or 1659, 1663 or 1664, 1682). See Cogley, "Appendix Five," in *JEMI*, 260. For *The Bay Psalm Book* (1640), see p. 108n263 above.

130. *Strength out of Weaknesse* (1652), 233. See *Strength out of Weaknesse* (1652), 242.

Eliot's later description of a Sunday service for the Praying Indians, in a letter of 1684 to Robert Boyle, the Governor of New England Company, also showed that psalm-singing was an essential part of public worship: "When the chapter is read, a psalm is sung, which service sundry are able to manage well. . . . When that service is done, they sing a psalm, according to the pattern of Christ; then he blesseth the church, and so finisheth the morning service."[131]

Sabbath-keeping was perhaps the most important puritan public practice of piety of Praying Indians.[132] Cotton Mather, in his biography of Eliot, emphasized Eliot's Sabbath-keeping:

> I must not omit his exact Remembrance of the Sabbath-day, to keep it holy. It has been truly and justly Observed, That our whole Religion fares according to our Sabbaths; that poor Sabbaths make poor Christians; and that a strictness in our Sabbaths inspires a vigour into all our other Duties. Our Eliot knew this, and it was a most Exemplary zeal that he acknowledged the Sabbath of our Lord Jesus Christ withal.[133]

Eliot himself is said to have expressed this idea about the Sabbath: "The Observation of it in Holy Duties unto the utmost of the strength for them, which God should be pleased to give us, I have pleaded for; the necessity also of a serious preparation for it in sundry previous Duties, I have declared."[134] Based on Eliot's idea about the Sabbath being in keeping with puritan tradition, it is true that it was urged that the Sabbath should be kept in Indian ministry. Praying Indians also well understood the importance of the worship service on the "Lord's day," and Sabbath-keeping as a significant practice of piety. In the Praying Indians' confession cited in *Tears of Repentance* (1653), Sabbath-keeping and worship on that day were frequently mentioned as a significant Christian duty. Nishohkou, a Praying Indian, said: "I heard of that good way, to keep the Sabbath, and not to work on that day, and I did so: but yet again I sinned in it, because I did not reverence the Word of God; yea, and sometimes I thought that working on the Sabbath was no great matter. . . . Now I desire truly to pray; now I desire to reverence the Word every Sabbath day."[135] For Praying Indians, the Sabbath

---

131. Eliot to Boyle, 22 April 1684, in Birch, *The Life of the Honourable Robert Boyle* (1744), 443.

132. Bayly, *The Practice of Piety* (2nd ed., 1612), 222–86; Hambrick-Stowe, *The Practice of Piety*, 96; Wakefield, *Puritan Devotion*, 59–63.

133. *LJE*, 22.

134. *LJE*, 25–26.

135. *Tears of Repentance* (1653), 287–88. See *Tears of Repentance* (1653), 284. For the description of Praying Indians' Sabbath-keeping, see Eliot, *Indian Dialogues* (1671), 91.

was spiritually beneficial. The day was for "communion with God": as the Praying Indian Piumbukhou said, "We enjoy the Lord's Sabbath days for our souls good, and communion with God."[136] This completely reflects the puritan understanding of Sabbath.[137] Piumbukhou is also quoted as saying: "Six days God hath given us, wherein to do all our own business and works. Every seventh day God hath commanded us to give unto him, to rest from our own works, and to do his work, to pray unto him, to hear his word, to talk and speak of heavenly matters, for the good of our souls."[138] Anthony, another of the Praying Indians, observed:

> The doctrine of the sabbath is a great point in religion. It is one of the ten moral, universal commandments of God, which are required of all mankind; and the fourth command, a chief hinge of all the rest. By a religious keeping of the sabbath, we act our obedience to all the commands. By profaning the sabbath, we turn all religion and good order out of doors, and set open a door unto all sin and wickedness, so weighty a matter is the good keeping of the sabbath day.[139]

Eliot, in his letter to Boyle of 22 April 1684, described how Praying Indians kept Sabbath: "They do diligently observe and keep the Sabbath, in all the places of their public meetings to worship God. . . . So that the sanctifying of the Sabbath is a great and eminent part of their religion."[140] In this letter, Eliot provided a detailed explanation of the public worship service as the most important part of the Sabbath in Indian churches. Praying Indians had two public worship services, in the morning and afternoon, on the "Lord's day":

> The acts of worship, which they perform in their public meetings, are as followeth. The officer beginneth with prayer, and prayeth for all men, rulers, ministers, people, young, old, sick, well, English or Indians, & according to that word, 1:Tim:ii:12. I will that first of all prayers be made, &c. I say, the officer beginneth with prayer, *viz.* where they have an officer ordained, as it is almost in all the churches. . . . There is not yet a church gathered in every place, where they meet to worship God and keep the Sabbath; but where it is so, they chuse some able godly

---

136. Eliot, *Indian Dialogues* (1671), 81. Eliot confirmed Praying Indians' Sabbath-keeping. Eliot, "An Account of Indian Churches in New-England" (1673), 125.

137. Bayly, *The Practice of Piety* (2nd ed., 1612), 222, 259.

138. Eliot, *Indian Dialogues* (1671), 91.

139. Eliot, *Indian Dialogues* (1671), 147.

140. Eliot to Boyle, 22 April 1684, in Birch, *The Life of the Honourable Robert Boyle* (1744), 442.

> man ... to manage the worship among them: him they call their teacher, and he beginneth with prayer, &c. When prayer is ended, they call forth such as are to answer the catechism. ... When catechism is ended, a chapter is read, sometimes in the old testament, and sometimes in the new; and sundry of the young men are trained up, and called forth to this service. ... When the chapter is read, a psalm is sung, which service sundry are able to manage well. That finished, the preacher first prayeth, then preacheth, and then prayeth again. If it be the day for the Lord's supper to be celebrated, the church address themselves unto it, and the minister doth exactly perform it, according to the scriptures. When that service is done, they sing a psalm, according to the pattern of Christ; then he blesseth the church, and so finisheth the morning service.[141]

Eliot continued to explain the afternoon worship service:

> In the afternoon they meet again, and perform all the parts of worship, as they did in the morning; which done, if there be any infant to be baptized, they perform that service according to the scriptures; which done, the deacon calleth for contributions; which done, if there be any act of public discipline ... then the offender is called forth (being with care and diligence prepared) and is exhorted to give glory to God, and confesses his sin; which, being penitent, they gladly accept him, forgive him, and receive him. If it be not a satisfactory confession, they shew him his defect, they admonish and exhort him to a more full confession; and of he is left to some other time. This finished, he blesseth the church, and so dismisseth the assembly.[142]

These descriptions are good evidences of the Praying Indians' Sunday worship service and Sabbath-keeping as one of the essential public practices of piety.

Conclusion

Puritan pastoral teaching was one of the primary tasks in Eliot's pastoral ministry. For Eliot, the teaching of the Word of God was the most important

---

141. Eliot to Boyle, 22 April 1684, in Birch, *The Life of the Honourable Robert Boyle* (1744), 443–44. Daniel Gookin and Cotton Mather also provided their descriptions of Praying Indians' worship service. See *HCINE*, 183; *LJE*, 82.

142. Eliot to Boyle, 22 April 1684, in Birch, *The Life of the Honourable Robert Boyle* (1744), 444.

ministerial task in his ministry. Preaching was the essential means of pastoral teaching of the Word of God. Despite the scarcity of Eliot's remaining sermon texts, through the Indians' sermons one can conjecture Eliot's understanding and practice of the puritan style of preaching. Alongside preaching, catechizing was also a significant means of pastoral teaching. For catechizing, public and private teaching and visitation were practiced by Eliot. Also, Eliot's teaching methodology in terms of a teaching tool was divided into text- and oral-based education. For Eliot, his strong involvement with translation and publication works, including the Bible, catechism, puritan literature, and *The Bay Psalm Book* (1640), shows what he thought about the necessity of written text, and how he wanted to use the texts for his ministry. Besides using the written texts, orality was still a powerful means of teaching for Eliot. Preaching and oral catechizing based on the questions and answers can be considered strong examples of oral pastoral education in Eliot's Indian ministry.

Eliot, following puritan tradition, regarded the puritan pastor not only as a teacher of the Word of God, but also as a pastoral counsellor and spiritual director. The training of Indian pastoral leaders was also a significant ministerial task for Eliot, which reflected the puritan tradition. Eliot's pastoral education of Indian ministerial leaders was not only because of the lack of ministers for Indian ministry, but also because he thought their work would have a better pastoral effect.

The practice of piety, along with puritan pastoral teaching and care, was one of the key tasks that Eliot practiced in Indian ministry. For Praying Indians, the practice of piety was not only a duty of Christians, but also a sign of Christian identity. Repentance, Bible reading and mediation, prayer, public fasting and thanksgiving, psalm-singing, and Sabbath-keeping as the representative practices of piety of Praying Indians, were regularly and seriously practiced under Eliot's pastoral direction.

Consequently, for Eliot, puritan pastoral teaching and care and practice of piety were the primary ministerial duties and tasks in his New England Indian ministry. At the same time, for Eliot, the puritan ministry was a significant means to turn the Indians into "sincere converts" who were ready to form a church. In the next chapter, we will investigate how the first Indian church members, who were approved as "sincere converts" by puritans, experienced conversion, and explore evidence for their understanding of Christianity.

6

Conversion Narratives and Indian Expression of Christianity

THE AIM OF THIS chapter is to explore the Praying Indians' understanding of Christianity as taught by John Eliot's Indian pastoral ministry. This will be done through an examination of the conversion narratives of Indians which were recorded by Eliot and published in *Tears of Repentance* (1653) and *Further Account* (1660), with the English settlers' narratives recorded by Thomas Shepard as a foil. Although the narratives of both Indians and English settlers survive only in the record of New England ministers, modern scholars have found them a valuable resource for exploring individuals' grasp of puritan teaching.[1]

As chapter 3 outlined, for puritans, conversion as a total ontological change was a primary pastoral duty and task, not only for individual religious change, but also for ecclesiastical and even national reformation.[2] D. Bruce Hindmarsh rightly stated: "the Puritan understanding of conversion stressed the transformation of the individual by grace, a transformation that took place through the agency of a gospel ministry and which only thus

---

1. See Selement and Woolley, *Thomas Shepard's Confessions*; Caldwell, *The Puritan Conversion Narrative*; Cohen, "Conversion among Puritans and Amerindians"; McGiffert, *God's Plot*.

2. See pp. 72–73, 83–87 above.

contributed to establishing a more pure church and godly commonwealth."[3] In fact, puritan understanding of conversion in terms of the individual, ecclesiastical, and national transformation is more conspicuous in the English context, as Hindmarsh stated, "Thus conversion functioned within English Puritanism as part of an ideal to transform the church and nation, and complete the Reformation."[4] Tom Webster's reflection on the formation of the puritan practice of piety supports this idea. Webster argued that English puritanism and puritan piety were formed through puritans' struggle with external opposition, as personal piety is generally formed through the dialectical relationship between internal and external tension and interaction.[5] In contrast, Mark A. Peterson argued that New England puritan piety was formed in the absence of severe external opposition to puritans that the English puritans experienced. However, despite the absence of external threats to puritans in New England, the multi-faceted influence of conversion was not changed in New England. It was still a powerful theological agenda for New England puritans, because certain practices of piety, which identified puritans, were "a central motivating force" for their migration to New England, as Peterson himself indicated. Further, the ultimate purpose of the puritan migrants was the realization of the reformation through puritan ministry and piety.[6] Thus, regardless of whether they were in Old or New England, for puritans, conversion was a quintessential factor in theology and ministry and "comprised the centerpiece of Puritan spirituality."[7] Furthermore, their conversion narratives included not only the confessions of what they believed and how they experienced the redeeming grace of God, but also significant declaratory statements of faith to be judged as sincere Christians. Like New England puritans, Praying Indians paid significant attention to polished style and fluent literal expression as well as rich content in their conversion narratives, to ensure approval of their sincere conversion. Also, the narratives were important for narrators themselves, as well as for other quasi- or full church members to follow and read as an instruction.[8] Therefore, considering the ecclesiastical significance of conversion narratives, for Praying Indians, the narratives were not just a means of testing for church membership, but also an essential source of

3. Hindmarsh, *The Evangelical Conversion Narrative*, 34.

4. Hindmarsh, *The Evangelical Conversion Narrative*, 53.

5. Webster, "The Piety of Practice and the Practice of Piety," 111–46. See also Brauer, "Conversion," 234–35.

6. Peterson, "The Practice of Piety in Puritan New England," 75–110. See also Brauer, "Conversion," 236; Hardman Moore, "New England's Reformation," 143–58.

7. Cohen, "Conversion among Puritans and Amerindians," 237.

8. Gordis, "The Conversion Narrative in Early America," 373, 383.

understanding Christianity and their identity as Christian converts, and a way to teach their neighbors.[9]

This chapter focuses on Indian narratives and will also pay attention to New England puritan narratives. Through the comparative analysis of puritan and Indian narratives, this chapter will reveal the similarities and differences between the narratives of puritans and Praying Indians. The Praying Indians' expressions and the contents of their narratives were strongly based on puritan theology as taught by Eliot. However, the Praying Indians' understanding of Christianity was also expressed in distinctive ways. This reflects the contextual difference between the ethnic groups, as well as the Praying Indians' unique understanding of puritanism in their own context. The strong theological continuity between the confessions of puritans and of Indians does not necessarily argue for enforced conversion to puritan Christianity, nor does the apparent absence of the Indians' own voice (since their confessions are mediated by English authors) ultimately reveal the conversion of Indians to be a sham.[10] In fact, Eliot emphasized the sincerity of the Indian confessions and clearly stated that he did his best to translate and show the exact contents of what they confessed. Eliot said when he recorded Indian confessions in 1652: "I have been true & faithful unto their souls, and in writing and reading their Confessions, I have not knowingly, or willingly made them better, than the Lord helped themselves to make them."[11] In 1659, he also said:

> These Confessions I wrote in English from their mouths with the best of my endeavours, both for diligence and also faithfulness; and so soon as they had done, I read them unto the Elders and Brethren and Sisters there present, and that the substance hereof was delivered by them, and faithfully translated and delivered by me (to the best of my understanding) I do here before the Lord testifie.[12]

In addition, Eliot added the following comment after each Indian's confession to show the validation of the confessions: "when he had finished, and I had read before the assembly this confession of his, we called upon the

---

9. Kathleen Lynch, in her book, has argued that personal spiritual experience as an "authorizing principle" is a "crux" of personal and social identity. Lynch, *Protestant Autobiography in the Seventeenth-Century Anglophone World*.

10. Jennings, *Invasion of America*, 228–53, has argued for forced conversion. Salisbury, "Red Puritans," suggested that the conversions were a sham.

11. *Tears of Repentance* (1653), 283.

12. *Further Account* (1660), 374.

witnesses to co-attest."[13] In this sense, as Cohen argued, even though Eliot prepared the narratives for publication, to win support from an English audience, "there is no compelling basis to discount the confessions."[14] The strong continuity and similarity between the narratives of puritans and Indians suggests how puritan pastoral ministry guided the Praying Indians, and how they described what they learned and experienced. Thus, Indian conversion narratives should perhaps be seen as a mirror which reveals not only the Praying Indians' image, but also puritanism itself.

In fact, the conversion narratives of puritans and Indians have not received much theological analysis by scholars. Although the conversion phenomenon of New England Indians has been treated as an interesting research topic, there has been virtually no investigation of Praying Indians' conversion narratives from a theological perspective.[15] For puritan conversion narratives, several scholars' works have been crucial resources. Two editions—Michael McGiffert' *God's Plot*, and the work of George Selement and Bruce C. Woolley, *Thomas Shepard's Confessions*— are significant. These two works not only contain the transcribed original texts of New England puritan narratives (as well as Shepard's autobiography and journal in the former), but also offer helpful introductions to puritan conversion theology.[16] Patricia Caldwell's *The Puritan Conversion Narrative* is also an important work of research for understanding puritans' thoughts on conversion through a comparison between conversion narratives of Old and New England puritans. In the book, Caldwell analyzes the difference between both Englanders' conversion narratives, mainly focusing on structures, forms of expression, styles, and the relationship between the contents and contexts,

---

13. *Further Account* (1660), 385.

14. Cohen, "Conversion among Puritans and Amerindians," 236. James Axtell as a revisionist of Jennings's theory demonstrating the one-sided victimization of the Indians and insincerity of puritans' Indian mission argued for the sincerity and quality of Indian conversions because of the qualification of puritan ministers for Indian evangelization, their pastoral teachings with various educational techniques, and the application of high standard for baptism and church admission to the Indians. Axtell, "Were Indian Conversions *Bona Fide*?," in *After Columbus*, 100–21.

15. Most studies have been undertaken by literary scholars. For information on these resources, see pp. 12–13 above. For an understanding of the New England Indians' conversion phenomenon in relation to puritan mission, see Simmons, "Conversion from Indian to Puritan," 197–218; Youngs, "The Indian Saints of New England," 241–56; Lonkhuyzen, "A Reappraisal of the Praying Indians," 396–428; McNally, "The Practice of Native American Christianity," 834–59; Fisher, "Native Americans, Conversion, and Christian Practice in Colonial New England," 101–24.

16. McGiffert, *God's Plot*; Selement and Woolley, *Thomas Shepard's Confessions*.

mainly from a social and cultural perspective, without providing a thorough theological analysis.[17]

There has been almost no comparative research on puritans' and Indians' conversion narratives, except for an article by Charles L. Cohen. Cohen provides a theological, social, and cultural analysis of Indian conversion narratives in relation to puritanism.[18] However, this research mainly focuses on Indian narratives, and relies on secondary sources to investigate puritans' understanding of conversion, rather than a direct comparison between the puritans' and Indians' narratives. Also, the article lacks a more thorough theological investigation of Indian conversion narratives in relation to Old and New England puritan theology in the writings of Eliot's contemporaries.

This chapter will look at Indian narratives, in comparison to the English settlers' narratives, to cast a light on Eliot's use of conversion theology in Indian ministry. The investigation will be based on the Indian narratives which were recorded by Eliot in 1652 and 1659, and published in *Tears of Repentance* (1653), and *Further Account* (1660), respectively, and puritan narratives recorded by Thomas Shepard in the 1630s–1640s. Also, Praying Indians' sermons delivered on 15 November 1658, a day of fasting and prayer at Natick, published in *Further Accompt* (1659), are significant resources.[19]

One can ask whether there was any change in Eliot's conversion theology after the Half-Way Covenant in 1662 in New England. Jerald C. Brauer describes a circumstantial shift in the function of conversion. Brauer argues for the different functions of conversion in Old and New England. According to him, before 1660, if conversion functioned "as a means of gathering support to transform a church and a nation" in the English context, conversion in the New England context "was the bedrock on which the church was built and on which the state rested." In this sense, conversion was a cornerstone for puritan society because of the strong relationship between conversion and church membership, which could secure one's social and ecclesiastical status in New England society. Brauer, furthermore, argues

---

17. Caldwell, *The Puritan Conversion Narrative*. For the resources for puritan understanding of conversion, see Nuttall, *The Holy Spirit in Puritan Faith and Experience*; Nuttall, *Visible Saints*; Morgan, *Visible Saints*; Norman, *The Heart Prepared*; Watkins, *The Puritan Experience*; Brauer, "Conversion," 227–43; Cohen, *God's Caress*. For further resources to gain an understanding of conversion in various disciplines, see Morrison, *Understanding Conversion*; Rambo, *Understanding Religious Conversion*; Mills and Grafton, *Conversion in Late Antiquity and the Early Middle Ages*; Mills and Grafton, *Conversion*.

18. Cohen, "Conversion among Puritans and Amerindians," 233–56.

19. *Tears of Repentance* (1653) represents "the first conversion narratives of any kind from New England that were printed for a reading audience across the Atlantic." Lynch, *Protestant Autobiography in the Seventeenth-Century Anglophone World*, 155.

that after the Half-Way Covenant in 1662 in New England, the term "conversion" sometimes implies "a statement of dissent from the majority culture."[20] However, it is probably true that Eliot's understanding of conversion in relation to his Indian ministry was not changed, even after 1662. His Indian ministry was not necessarily affected by the ecclesiastical declension and difficulty of New England churches in the mid- and late seventeenth century.[21] Also, as we confirmed in chapter 4, Eliot in fact still had strong sympathy with conversion-related church policy, although he officially supported the Half-Way Covenant. Alongside this, his conversion theology in *Indian Dialogues*, published in 1671, can be important evidence that his opinion on conversion was not different from what it had been at the beginning of the circumstantial change.[22] This chapter is based on the conviction of Eliot's unchanged theology on conversion, and his constant application of the ideology to his Indian ministry from the beginning to the end. In this sense, the comparative analysis of conversion narratives of puritans and Indians written before 1660 can still be an important source to reflect the meaning and function of conversion theology in Eliot's Indian ministry, even after 1662.

Through a comparative analysis of puritans' and Praying Indians' conversion narratives in this chapter, it will be suggested that puritan conversion theology was commonly shared by puritans and Praying Indians. Also, this chapter will examine Indians' understanding and knowledge of Christianity, based on Reformed theology mediated by the teachings of Eliot, as well as on their own experience. In addition, the analysis will confirm the relationship between puritan conversion theology and Eliot's ideological motive for Indian ministry (discussed in chapter 3).

Puritans on Conversion in Conversion Narratives

In this chapter, New England puritan conversion narratives signify Thomas Shepard's *Confessions*, a collection of fifty-one male and female church members of the First Church of Cambridge, Massachusetts, led by Thomas Shepard as the pastor who recorded the confessions in his private notebook between 1637 and 1645.[23] The conversion narratives in the *Confessions* show

20. Brauer, "Conversion," 234–38.
21. Bremer, *The Puritan Experiment*, 154–67; Noll, *A History of Christianity in the United States and Canada*, 48.
22. Eliot, *Indian Dialogues* (1671), 108, 116–17, 118–19, 159–60.
23. Part of the transcribed text of Thomas Shepard's *Confessions* is contained in McGiffert, *God's Plot* and the complete text can be found in Selement and Woolley, *Thomas*

Calvinist puritan conversion theology and soteriology, no doubt influenced by Shepard as the pastoral leader of the narrators.[24]

The *Confessions* strongly argued for the relationship between conversion and inner change, including a sense of sins, contrition, humiliation, anxiety, doubts, fear, and assurance. As argued in chapter 3, when people are in the process toward salvation, they initially experience, in the preparatory stages, a certain type of inner experience in the "pattern of regeneration" or "morphology of conversion."[25] Puritans' inner experience of conversion was ultimately in pursuit of salvation, and one of their most serious concerns was whether they were actually saved or not. Puritans' strong concern about assurance of salvation involved an inner search or self-examination accompanied by inner, spiritual, and psychological experience. This was the most common empirical phenomenon of conversion narrators in the *Confessions*.[26] For the puritan narrators, conversion was experiential rather than only a matter of intellectual acceptance. For example, Ann Errington's confession illustrates puritans' serious concern about inwardness and inner search. She confessed that when she heard Lamentations 3—let us search and turn to the Lord (Lam 3:40)[27]—it struck her heart as an arrow. And she said, "And it came as a light into me and the more the text was opened more I saw my heart. And hearing that something was lost when God came for searching."[28] Edward Hall expressed his serious thirst for a deep inner search in his narrative. "But his heart was not deep enough and hence he was put to more search whether ever he was humbled."[29]

Shepard's Confessions with Shepard's autobiography and journal. My research will be based on the text in Selement and Woolley's edition.

24. Cohen and Hindmarsh argued for the strong ideological influence of local pastor on the narrators. Cohen, *God's Caress*, 213n47; Hindmarsh, *The Evangelical Conversion Narrative*, 48. Gordis expressed the influence of the local pastor on conversion narratives as "clerical mediation." Gordis, "The Conversion Narrative in Early America," 377–78.

25. Shepard, *The Sound Believer* (1645), 115–37; Pettit, *The Heart Prepared*, 7; Morgan, *Visible Saints*, 66. While Morgan stated the "stereotype" of morphology in the New England puritan conversion experience, Caldwell argued that New England Puritan conversion narratives show less systematized and structured "morphology of conversion" than Old England narratives. Caldwell, *The Puritan Conversion Narrative*, 163–86; Morgan, *Visible Saints*, 68–69.

26. TSC. See also Cohen, *God's Caress*; Cohen, "Conversion among Puritans and Amerindians," 237–38; McGiffert, *God's Plot*, 9–19.

27. Selement and Woolley cited the Scriptures' chapters and verses in the footnotes in their edition, but I will indicate the Bible chapters and verses in the text hereafter. See Selement and Woolley, *Thomas Shepard's Confessions*.

28. *TSC*, 184.

29. *TSC*, 34.

Puritans understood that their serious concerns about inwardness and their pursuit of inner search were driven by God. Edward Collins confessed, "And so stayed my heart and in searching my heart, seeing sin die and growing in grace and I thought God would carry on His own work."[30] For Richard Eccles, God touched his heart: "And Lord broke my heart in the consideration of my own vileness and so I saw a necessity of Christ John 1:16."[31] For Martha Collins, the "Lord struck my heart and I thought it was for my sin and so let the Lord do with me what He will."[32] These examples lead us to consider the puritans' serious inner search not only as a process of conversion experience, but also as an important practice of piety, as argued by Lewis Bayly in his *The Practice of Piety* (2nd ed., 1612).[33]

This serious inwardness was related to their strong recognition of sinfulness and corruption in themselves. Many narrators confessed that they did not fully recognize their spiritual condition as being of a sinful nature before conversion. As Mary Griswald confessed: "But I had no fear wrought of sin but had some sad thoughts of that condition."[34] However, during the conversion experience, puritans' self-recognition of their sinfulness continually occurred in themselves. Shepard described George Willow's experience: "And now he saw the deadness of his heart under ordinances and the more he did strive against corruption, the more he was overcome by corruption."[35]

Puritans' recognition of their sinfulness was strongly related to the recognition of their total inability to "get out of it."[36] Elizabeth Olbon "knew Him not and so sin was heavy and she saw no possibility how to get out of it."[37] Shepard reported, "But she felt so much evil in her own heart she thought it impossible so poor a creature should be saved or received to mercy and so fell down in discouragements."[38]

Conversion narrators clearly understood the destiny of the "wicked" and "saints." As William Ames[39] mentioned, based on Reformed theological

30. *TSC*, 83–84.

31. *TSC*, 116.

32. *TSC*, 131.

33. Bayly, *The Practice of Piety* (2nd ed., 1612), 143–47, 185–88, 267, 278–79, 292–96, 306, 308, 329, 364.

34. *TSC*, 187.

35. *TSC*, 43.

36. Calvin, *Inst.*, II.i.5–8; II.iii.1; III.iii.9; III.xi.

37. *TSC*, 39.

38. *TSC*, 40.

39. William Ames here is a son of William Ames, the well-known puritan minister and professor who migrated from England to work in Holland. *TSC*, 209. Hereafter William Ames in this section is the same person.

understanding: "The first time I took notice of anything the Lord helped me to was the consideration of misery of wicked and happy estate of saints."[40] John Furnell expressed his understanding of the result of sinfulness through preaching: "And there being in that town three ministers the Lord brought to one Mr. Archer[41] who, when he came first, preached out of Ephesians showing every man's estate by nature to be dead in trespasses and sins [Eph 2:1]."[42] For puritans, the result of sins could cause God's wrath and deserved God's punishment. Conversion narrators clearly understood that they as sinners were in God's wrath: as Robert Daniel confessed, "But yet the Lord made me see my case to be miserable and so carried many years under a spirit of bondage and fear of God's wrath [Rom 8:15]."[43] The narrators in the *Confessions* explicitly mentioned hell as a terrifying punishment of sins, as seen in the puritan tradition. Shepard described George Willows's feeling: "And coming to hear a minister preach against that sin, he was terrified by it and so lay under the anger of God and sense of it and so saw nothing but hell due to him."[44] John Furnell also said, "And I considered if Hartford, I was one, and so considered I must to hell if I die in that condition. And he showing how Christ at first would."[45]

This serious recognition of sinfulness and the terrifying result of it through self-examination was related to puritans' emphasis on the urgency of conversion or being "born again." Ultimately, this concern was related to their desire for salvation. Mary Griswald confessed, "And hearing my mother speaking—I must be born again [John 3:3; 1 Pet 1:23]—I was sad but was cheered. But thinking without means, I thought God had ever left me and so I desired to learn things and I saw I had nothing but opposition against the Lord."[46]

For puritans, the subject of conversion and salvation was God. They believed that their conversion and salvation was absolutely dependent on God alone. Shepard reported that George Willows confessed his inability for conversion: "Yet he had no power to lay hold upon me, unless the Lord did draw His love to himself. Since this the Lord hath revealed Himself and

---

40. *TSC*, 210.

41. "John Archer (*d.* 1639) preached at All Saint's, Hertford, Hertfordshire, from 1631 until his death." *TSC*, 204n1.

42. *TSC*, 204.

43. *TSC*, 60. See *TSC*, 50.

44. *TSC*, 43.

45. *TSC*, 204. The fragmentary character of the prose here is fairly typical of the recorded confessions.

46. *TSC*, 187–88.

drawn Himself to him by His ordinances."[47] For Edward Hall, God first called and visited human beings: "[T]he son of man came to seek that which was lost. And he did not know but the Lord might seek him."[48] For Goodman Shepard, in this sense, even the change of heart is God's work because God is the subject of salvation: "The Lord could give a heart and a humble heart."[49] Because of this belief, for the New England puritans in the church at Cambridge, "Let Him do what He would" or "let Him do what He will" were frequent expressions declaring their faith in God as the only subject in their conversion.[50]

Puritans who believed in total dependence on God for salvation had a Christ-centered understanding of salvation.[51] Shepard reported a strong christological understanding of soteriology in Edward Hall's confession of the conversion experience: "[H]e saw more of his misery. . . . Hereby the Lord let him see he was Christless and built upon false foundations. . . . Now when the Lord did humble him, . . . he saw the want of Christ and that without Him he must perish."[52] Christ, for puritans, was the only means of salvation: William Ames said, "Christ saved them that were sinful and felt themselves full of sin and that Christ came to save them that had nothing of their own [Matt 9:12–13; 18:11]."[53] Puritans also mentioned free grace in Christ. For George Willows, "The Lord revealed Christ unto me by revealing the fullness of the riches of grace and help in Christ [Eph 2:7; Col 1:27; 2:2–3]."[54] Nicholas Wyeth also showed his belief of the free grace in Christ in his answer in the conversion narrative:

> Question. Do you remember nothing how God hath tendered Christ to you? Answer. In Ephesians 2 I hear when far off then made near [Eph 2:13] and Lord let me see no way to be save but by His own free grace. Question. What effects did it work? Answer. I saw it was His free grace to encourage me to go on. The Lord let me see I had nothing in myself.[55]

---

47. *TSC*, 43.
48. *TSC*, 34.
49. *TSC*, 174.
50. *TSC*, 52, 68.
51. Shepard, *The Sincere Convert* (1640), 46, 101. See Baxter, *The Reformed Pastor* (1656), 188; Baxter, *A Call to the Unconverted* (1658), 6, 15, 16, 21, 24.
52. *TSC*, 34.
53. *TSC*, 211–12.
54. *TSC*, 43.
55. *TSC*, 195.

This confession reminds us of the covenant of grace which means salvation was not based on good works, but totally on God's grace for his chosen people. Also, the covenant assured puritans of the constant sustaining of salvation for God's chosen people, as Miller argued. According to him, puritans "enjoyed clear sailing to the heaven of assurance. The covenant of grace defines the conditions by which Heaven is obtained, and he who fulfils the conditions has an incontestable title to glorification, exactly as he who pays the advertised price owns his freehold."[56]

Despite their strong belief in God and grace as the subject and foundation of salvation, the conversion narrators who were seriously concerned about salvation implicitly argued for their uses of will and determination for conversion. Narrators conceived that seeking and pursuing God for their salvation would be absolutely necessary. Elizabeth Olbon confessed the necessity of using will and determination based on Scripture. Shepard witnessed, "And then she heard—whoever is athirst come and buy without money [Isa 55:1]. Now she saw she had no money, yet hearing they that come to Christ might have comfort, then she felt fain she would have somewhat of Christ and something of her own."[57] Elizabeth who understood the Bible teaching, "blessed are those that hunger and thirst after Christ [Matt 5:6]" saw "she longed after Christ to save and sanctify."[58] This means that she realized her will and desire toward Christ. George Willows also expressed his will and determination toward Christ for conversion. Shepard said, "If He comes to seek the lost, why then not me? And so he was carried to long after Christ Jesus and heard those are blessed that did hunger and thirst [Matt. 5:6]."[59] Puritans also knew that they went against Christ with their will and also that they should pursue and follow Christ with their will and determination. Ann Errington confessed her own opposition to Christ, but after that she resolved to use means for her: "I saw I had rejected the Lord Jesus and I was very sorrowful and I was very sad. And going home I resolved I would use means for help and was very much cast down."[60] William Ames who "resolved and renewed resolution to seek after God" confessed that "I saw my will was the

---

56. Miller, *Errand into the Wilderness*, 71. See also Rohr, "Covenant and Assurance in Early English Puritanism," 195–203; Rohr, *The Covenant of Grace in Puritan Thought*; McGiffert, *God's Plot*, 12–16; Cohen, *God's Caress*, 47–74.

57. *TSC*, 40.

58. *TSC*, 41.

59. *TSC*, 43.

60. *TSC*, 185. See *TSC*, 191.

greatest hindrance."[61] These mentions tell us puritans' emphasis is on the use of will and determination to follow Christ.[62]

For conversion narrators, the will and determination to seek Christ should be from God, as Ann Errington confessed: "There I thought I had rejected Christ and the Lord gave me a heart as I thought to close with Christ as best good and to stoop to His will.... And I thought Lord gave me a willing heart, etc."[63]

Conversion narrators' understanding of the importance of will and determination toward conversion emphasized the significant role of means of grace.[64] Many narrators confessed that they could be changed by the means of grace. Their understanding of the importance of the means of grace reflected puritan understanding of preparationism.[65] Martha Collins's expression gives us a hint about the idea: "And hearing Mr. Shaw[66] that I should look after the Lord for Himself, I looked after that. And coming into the country I had no good Sabbaths nor blessing under that ministry. But hearing of soul's preparation for Christ, I was stirred up to seek."[67] Martha Collins implied the significance of means of grace through Shepard's question to her: "And coming to Mr. S[hepard] I was asked if I had not neglected means."[68] Katherine confessed that through the means of grace she could realize her spiritual situation: "First I went on in ignorance and had no means of light. So I went to an aunt who did, and where I was made by her to seek the means, praying with us before we went to the word. And she speaking of misery out of Christ, and so I saw many sins and so saw more."[69]

---

61. *TSC*, 211.

62. Shepard, *The Sincere Convert* (1640), 54–55. See Baxter, *A Call to the Unconverted* (1658), 12, 21–22, 29–30, 31, 35, 37, 49.

63. *TSC*, 185. Shepard, *The Sincere Convert* (1640), 51; Baxter, *A Call to the Unconverted* (1658), 6, 49.

64. Bayly, *The Practice of Piety* (2nd ed., 1612), 108–10. Shepard, *The Sincere Convert* (1640), 99, 106, 107. See Baxter, *The Reformed Pastor* (1656), 252–53; Baxter, *A Call to the Unconverted* (1658), 49.

65. Pettit, *The Heart Prepared*.

66. "John Shaw (1608–1672), a graduate of Christ's College, Cambridge and author of several religious tracts, in the 1630s held lectureships at Bramptom, Derbyshire (1630–1633), Chumleigh, Devonshire (1633–1636)—a post subsidized by London merchants with Puritan sympathies—and All hallows-on-the-Pavement, Yorkshire." *TSC*, 131n2.

67. *TSC*, 131.

68. *TSC*, 132.

69. *TSC*, 99.

All conversion narrators explicitly confessed that hearing of the Bible, especially through preaching, was an essential means of grace.[70] Katherine confessed the influence of preaching: "And afterward I heard Mr. Rogers[71] speaking—the just shall live by faith [Hab 2:4; Rom 1:17; Gal 3:11; Heb 10:38]. And so I had abundance of comfort from the word and I blessed the Lord for that condition."[72] For the conversion narrators, preaching had a significant impact on their heart. Richard Eccles confessed that through preaching, "Lord opened my heart showing me a way by confessing my sins."[73] Robert Holmes said that his "hardened heart was finally melted and could have joy by the Word."[74]

Puritan narrators' clear understanding of the importance of biblical teaching shows strong puritan Biblicism. Along with narrators' emphasis on preaching of the Bible, their direct citation of Scripture passages and application of them to their own situation are good examples of puritan Biblicism. For example, Shepard witnessed Edward Hall's case: "the first means of his good was Mr. Glover's[75] ministry he saw his misery from Jeremiah 7. . . . And afterward John 5:40 was opened. . . . And here he saw how freely Christ was offered and hereby the Lord did stay and comfort his spirit and so was stirred up with more vehemency to seek Christ."[76] George Willows's case was also described by Shepard: "And then thought, oh if I could but mourn under sin then I should be happy. But he could not, but hearing Isaiah 40 ult.—he gives strength to them that have no strength [Isa 40:29]—and this gave him peace and support and father heard Isaiah 30:6–7—then strength is to sit still in his ordinances."[77] Furthermore, many conversion narrators tried to identify the Bible passage with their own situation.[78] Martha Collins said, "And hearing on that text—gate is shut [Ezek 44:1–2]—and thinking

---

70. Calvin, *Inst.*, IV.i.5; Bernard, *The Faithfull Shepheard* (1607), 1–2; Baxter, *The Reformed Pastor* (1656), 103–4.

71. "John Rogers (1572?–1636), a Cambridge graduate and the author of The Doctrine of Faith (London, 1627) . . . served as the vicar of Dedham in Essex from 1603 until his death, although suspended for Nonconformity between 1629 and 1631." *TSC*, 65n1.

72. *TSC*, 100.

73. *TSC*, 116.

74. *TSC*, 143. See *TSC*, 193.

75. "Jose Glover (*d.* 1638) was the rector at Sutton in Surrey from 1628 until 1636, when he resigned with the intention of moving to New England." *TSC*, 33n1.

76. *TSC*, 33–34.

77. *TSC*, 43.

78. Caldwell, *The Puritan Conversion Narratives*, 141.

that surely now gate is shut for me."[79] Ann Errington confessed, "And on Sabbath day on sacrament day Hezekiah was humbled [2 Chr 32:26] and I thought I was not humbled."[80]

This strong Biblicism probably signifies Shepard's Calvinist theological understanding of the Bible and revelation, showing strong antagonism toward Antinomianism, which had been raised by Anne Hutchinson. According to Caldwell, Shepard "was one of the most vehement critics of Anne Hutchinson," and did not accept imaginative and rhetorical linguistic expression of people's spiritual experiences. That is to say, Shepard stressed the distinction between the revelation of God and the human's own voice, although he in fact paradoxically acknowledged the saint's recognition of "glorious impressions" which he or she could express in language. However, he was seriously concerned about human rhetorical invention in expressing inner religious experiences, and strictly emphasized self-examination to his church members.[81] In this sense, for puritan narrators, biblical expression was probably encouraged. So, through Elizabeth Olbon's confession, one can realize that the narrators thought that even inner feeling from God should be expressed through the words of the Bible: "Yet by this Scripture out of Isaiah and Matthew He let her feel His love."[82]

Shepard's emphasis on biblical teaching implies the narrators' intellectual acceptance and understanding of biblical knowledge. Although puritans strongly argued that human beings cannot understand God by human reason, they acknowledged the importance of biblical and doctrinal teaching for the knowledge of God (as argued in chapter 3). The pastoral teaching of the Bible premises the proper use of reason to know God. McGiffert indicated that Shepard stressed "the didactic and disciplinary uses of reason as a means."[83] Edward Collins expressed his appreciation of the knowledge that he could have through biblical and doctrinal teaching: "I looked after further means and helps and so attended on the means in the city.... And so hearing by letters that there was a lecture in Colne, hence I visited my friends and so hearing doctrine of man's misery, the Lord discovered myself more and more than before which I desired to see and hear."[84] Thus, the conversion narrators' mention of a change of heart due to biblical teaching, which often appeared in the *Confessions*, was probably because of the

79. *TSC*, 132.
80. *TSC*, 185.
81. Caldwell, *The Puritan Conversion Narratives*, 144–47.
82. *TSC*, 41.
83. McGiffert, *God's Plot*, 28.
84. *TSC*, 82–83.

influence of Shepard, who opposed Antinomianism, arguing that through reason "the spirit may let in his light and clear up the truth."[85]

Conversion narrators in the *Confessions* also mentioned various types of means of grace.[86] Katherine expressed the diversity of means of grace through "public and private" means: "And hence I sought the Lord in public and private and I looked upon Manasseh [2 Kgs 21:1–18; 2 Chr 33:1–20] and upon the scarlet sins of Isaiah made was white as snow [Isa 1:18]."[87] Edward Collins talked about "a private meeting of private conference" in particular: "And by a private meeting of private conference I heard diverse questions propounded and answered. . . . And the grace I saw in Christians did ashame me before the Lord. . . . Hence I endeavoured to get into private Christian meetings at London."[88] For Collins, the understanding of covenant was significant to him: "And there I took notice of covenant that it was free and saw promises made to such dispositions to lost to meek and hungry and thirsty [Matt 5:5–6] and to such as were confessors and forsakers of sin and hence I thought Jesus Christ was mine."[89] For Richard Eccles, the puritan ministry itself was a means of grace: "And I was settled under a powerful ministry and I was in a perplexed condition, my friends being taken away, which conscience said was for some sins I committed secretly. And under this ministry I had more and more light to see into my lost estate every day."[90] Robert Holmes experienced his change of heart even through sacrament: "And my heart was melted all sermon time and being sacrament time I went home and cried to Him."[91] For the narrators, puritan devotional literature was also a significant means of grace. Richard Eccles stated that he received strong influence from three popular writers: Lewis Bayly, William Perkins, and John Hart.[92] Eccles confessed:

> And in Practice of Piety I read torments of hell which affected my heart with my estate by Adam's fall. And by Mr. Perkins's Exposition of Creed I saw my condition bad. . . . And so getting some light I forsook ill company and reformed diverse things

---

85. Thomas Shepard, *The Parable of the Ten Virgins Opened and Applied* (1660), *The Works of Thomas Shepard*, II:283, cited in McGiffert, *God's Plot*, 28.

86. For the puritan understanding of pastoral teaching and the practice of piety as a means of grace, see pp. 91–92, 101–3, 105, 108–9 above.

87. *TSC*, 99.

88. *TSC*, 83.

89. *TSC*, 83.

90. *TSC*, 115–16.

91. *TSC*, 143.

92. According to Selement and Woolley, the author of *The Burning Bush* that Eccles mentioned was perhaps John Hart. *TSC*, 115n4.

and got light by reading The Burning Bush I saw there was some change wrought in my life which did stay me and so I rested.[93]

The conversion narrators who experienced heart-breaking recognition of sin and inner change through means of grace, and confirmed that their conversion came through the grace of God, confessed that they were still in unexpected and painful inner conflicts, including inner instability, fear, and doubt in their hearts. For the narrators, their common experience was the inner instability and unsettledness from the repetition of appearance and disappearance of inner doubt. Shepard described Joanna Sill's experience:

> Not long after having a day of fast the Lord helped her to seek Him. And the day after when at her calling she had much joy and consolation from Luke 1— blessed is he that believeth [Luke 1:45]. But she could not believe in deed and she knew not where she was. Then she questioned whether it was true joy . . . joy was gone, and then there were questions what her grounds were.[94]

William Ames expressed a complicated mind mixed with doubt, fear, temptations, and inner corruptions that he could search:

> And I have no faith yet desires after faith are beginning of it and hereupon my soul being encouraged to seek after Him. And the Lord brought me to this place by unexpected means and here the Lord kept me full of doubts and fears, not only with temptations but inward corruptions, which though I felt yet I did labor and pray against.[95]

As mentioned above, this inner instability can be understood as a result of puritans' self-examination or inner search. Also, through the inner search and meditation for their spiritual condition, they felt discouraged and humiliated as well. Joanna Sill experienced that:

> And so God hid Himself and [she] fell into a sinking condition. . . . But Hosea 14:4 supported her in the fatherless find mercy [Hos 14:3] and so she saw her nature how vile it. . . . Then there saw her nature and so she was discouraged. . . . And so seeing more and more of their vileness but hearing in a day of humiliation that if she sought the Lord with whole heart find.[96]

---

93. *TSC*, 115.
94. *TSC*, 52. See *TSC*, 40, 67, 100, 116, 131, 143.
95. *TSC*, 212.
96. *TSC*, 51–52.

Mary Angier had the same experience: "And when God changed her estate, she went to a place of more ignorance and so rested more quietly . . . speaking with one which did encourage her which was odious to her she continued under means and grew worse and worse."[97]

Caldwell has stressed the narrators' continuous inner instability and conflict with their migration experience. According to her, the unexpected difficult experiences and unpredictability of the wilderness of New England caused inner conflict and instability of mind, although they were still seeking God and a purer Christian faith as their strong motive for crossing the Atlantic. Caldwell suggests that the narrators expressed their worse inner condition and conflict after their migration.[98] In fact, a narrator like Nicholas Wyeth confessed that he could enjoy more freedom in New England: "Hence I came to New England being persecuted and courted for going from the place where we lived and hence I used means to come hither where we might enjoy more freedom. And I had much joy in going about this work."[99] However, many narrators commonly confessed their worse situation after migration. Elizabeth Olbon confessed that her heart became "more dead and dull" after migration.[100] George Willows also confessed his spiritual condition since he came to New England: "Since I came hither that hath been my grief that I walked no more closely with God in the place where I came."[101]

Along with the difficulties that the narrators had to face in the wilderness in New England, it is probably true that uncertainty of salvation was more likely to be the ultimate reason for their continuous inner conflict. In fact, the narrators expressed their hope for salvation and believed that they were in the process of moving towards it. Shepard reported Mary Angier's case: "And hearing the Lord called to any, she thought she was one of those any and seeing nothing would satisfy her but the Lord, and nothing in heaven or earth she desired nothing like Him. She thought the Lord called her to Himself."[102] Nicholas Wyeth implies his assurance cautiously through his answer to several questions:

> Question. Did the Lord ever give you any assurance of His love in Christ? Answer. The Lord let me see if not born again I could not enter into Kingdom of God [John 3:3]. Question. What ground of assurance? Answer. Because love began. Question.

---

97. *TSC*, 65–67.
98. Caldwell, *The Puritan Conversion Narratives*, 119–34.
99. *TSC*, 194.
100. *TSC*, 41.
101. *TSC*, 43.
102. *TSC*, 69. See *TSC*, 84, 116, 173.

> How know that? Answer. Because of that good I see in them and would get from them and I think myself unfit to come into their society.[103]

However, most narrators in the *Confessions* ended their narratives with the expression of less assurance and weak confidence in salvation. Nicholas Wyeth, whose confession of some evidence of assurance had been cited above, showed his ongoing uncertainty of salvation: "Question. Have you no fears? Answer. Yes, of death in regard of unprofitableness, unsensibleness of my condition and want of assurance."[104] Robert Daniel confessed his lack of assurance of salvation: "Yet when my soul was at lowest the Lord held forth some testimony of love, but yet I did depend upon Him without assurance."[105] Mary Angier's case was not so different: "And hearing how know whether united to Christ and mentioning a Scripture, was asked whether she had assurance. She said no but some hope."[106] In this sense, although the conversion narrators fully recognized the covenant of grace, and that for them, the covenant could help them to measure the assurance of salvation, it, in fact, did not guarantee their salvation.[107]

The conversion narrators' feeling of uncertainty and lack of assurance was derived from their understanding of Reformed soteriology. That is to say, their Reformed theological understanding of predestination can be a crucial reason for the uncertainty of salvation. William Ames's confession is a good example. He said that Satan tempted him and led him to think that he might not be elected and might seek God in vain:

> Presently the Lord was pleased to let Satan come forth upon me with manifest temptations and all at once as: that I was not elected and hence in vain for me to look after any salvation and that it was impossible I should attain to any work of law and Gospel hence in vain to set about it. That I did apprehend all the power of darkness did resist me and that I should never have any relief. That I was young and if I would seek after God it would be time enough hereafter. And I was almost quite discouraged from seeking after God and mercy but I could not be quieted and the Lord removed that temptation. I was not elected

---

103. *TSC*, 195–96.
104. *TSC*, 196.
105. *TSC*, 61.
106. *TSC*, 69.
107. McGiffert, *God's Plot*, 16.

because that was a secret to be left with God and to attend upon Him in His own way.[108]

This quotation shows how puritans' theological understanding affected their various inner experiences in conversion. In fact, for Shepard, the experience of anxiety in the conversion experience was normal and mandatory. Also, for Shepard, the more inner anxiety and conflict, the more assurance people could have. He said in his *Journal* on 7 December 1642:

> On lecture morning this came into my thoughts, that the greatest part of a Christian's grace lies in mourning for the want of it. ... And hence I saw that he who hath his grace lying and appearing chiefly in feeling of it is a Pharisee and proud ... that a poor Christian lamenting his wants is the most sincere; that the Lord when he shows mercy to any of his, it is in withholding much spiritual life and letting them feel much corruption.[109]

So, for Shepard, anxiety and assurance in conversion narrators' hearts "tend to fuse: to be anxious is to be assured; to be assured is to be, or become, anxious."[110] In that sense, Shepard understood that the experience of continuous inner conflict and anxiety in seeking God with assurance is a sign that the person is on the right track toward conversion. Therefore, conversion narrators considered their uncomfortable and instable mind to be a matter of course. Also, it might be possible that they tried to express their inner conflict and instability or unsettledness as much as they could in order for it to be recognized that they were on the right track of conversion.[111] This might be the reason why, for example, Robert Daniel said this: "How came you to assurance? Answer. By feeling a qualification as mourning not only for wrath but because of my sins to sin against such a God."[112]

Praying Indians on Conversion in Conversion Narratives

Praying Indians' conversion narratives, recorded by Eliot and published in *Tears of Repentance* (1653) and *A Further Account* (1660), are essential resources for explaining Indian understandings of conversion and soteriology. Along with the narratives, the sermons which were delivered by

108. *TSC*, 210–11.
109. Shepard, *The Journal*, in McGiffert, *God's Plot*, 123. See also McGiffert, *God's Plot*, 19–20.
110. McGiffert, *God's Plot*, 19–26.
111. Morgan, *Visible Saints*, 69–72.
112. *TSC*, 61.

Praying Indians on 15 November 1658, a day of fasting and prayer at Natick, are also worth reading, because the sermons were a kind of confessional exhortation.[113]

Like puritans, for Praying Indians, conversion was an ontological change.[114] This change was related to the change of identity. The term, "Praying Indians," signifies their ontologically changed identity after or in the process of conversion. Basically, for Indians, the expression, "Praying Indians" or "praying to God" meant that they believed in God as Christian converts. For them, as Eliot said, praying is not just "Ordinance and Duty of Prayer only, but of all Religion" reflecting on their confession of faith, because for Indians, "praying to God" meant their spiritual or religious identity as Christians.[115] For Piumbukhou, a Praying Indian, "praying to God" meant religion itself: "I am glad that you are so desirous to speak with me about our religion, and praying to God."[116] A statement by Totherswamp, a Praying Indian, conveys the general meaning of "praying to God":

> Before I prayed unto God, the English, when I came unto their houses, often said unto me, Pray to God; but I having many friends who loved me . . . they cared not for praying to God, and therefore I did not . . . soon after . . . I thought, that now I will pray unto God, and yet I was ashamed to pray. . . . Then you came unto us, and taught us, and said unto us, Pray unto God; and after that, my heart grew strong, and I was no more ashamed to pray, but I did take up praying to God.[117]

Here, one can understand that when a puritan minister encouraged him to "pray to God," this meant becoming Christian through believing in God, and that the Indian also understood the expression in this way.

For Praying Indians, "praying to God" was not about earthly values, but about the more fundamental "spiritual and heavenly" values. Piumbukhou, a Praying Indian, said:

> [T]he benefits of praying are spiritual and heavenly, it teaches us to know God, and the evil of sin; it teacheth us to repent of sin,

---

113. *Further Accompt* (1659), 333–39.

114. Shepard, *The Sincere Convert* (1640), 52; Baxter, *A Call to the Unconverted* (1658), 17, 55–56. See Calvin, *Inst.*, III.iii.5.

115. For Eliot's explanation of the meaning of "praying," see *Light Appearing* (1651), 202; *Tears of Repentance* (1653), 261. For the Indian use of the term, "praying," see the Indian confessions: *Tears of Repentance* (1653), 270–95; *Further Account* (1660), 361–95.

116. Eliot, *Indian Dialogues* (1671), 64.

117. *Tears of Repentance* (1653), 269.

and seek for pardon, and it teacheth us to forsake sin forever....
And yet I further tell you, that religion doth teach the right way
to be rich and prosperous in this world.... For religion teacheth
us to be diligent in labor six days, and on the seventh day to rest,
and keep it an holy Sabbath; and God hath promised that the
diligent hand shall make rich [Prov 10:4].[118]

Praying Indians' recognition of an ontological change after or in the conversion experience was obtained through their inner experience of conversion. Like puritans, Praying Indians seriously experienced inner change in their conversion. One can read many comments about the noticeable inward changes after conversion in the Indians' conversion experience stories. The inner changes include sense of sins, contrition, humiliation, anxiety, doubts, fear, and assurance. Thomas Mayhew reported that one of the Indians who received the gospel complained "against head knowledge and lip prayers, without heart holinesse" and said "I desire my heart may taste the word of God, repent of my sinnes, and leane upon the Redemption of the Lord Jesus Christ."[119] This story, as Mayhew told it, shows that Praying Indians understood that conversion should be followed by inner change. So, the strong inwardness in the Indian conversion experience matches a key point in the puritan understanding of conversion. Like puritans, Praying Indians' inner experience was a process of self-examination directed towards conversion and salvation. Thus, like the puritans, conversion for Praying Indians was experiential rather than only a matter of intellectual acceptance.[120] In order to consider inwardness and self-examination as a characteristic of the Indians' conversion experience which reflects puritan teaching, we need to focus on the Indians' reference to sin in their hearts. The author of *Day-Breaking* (1647) observed the early meetings with the Indians in 1646:

> That it is very likely if ever the Lord convert any of these Natives, that they will mourn for sin exceedingly, and consequently love Christ dearely, for if by a little measure of light such heart-breakings have appeared, what may wee thinke will bee, when more is let in they are some of them very wicked, some very ingenious, these latter are very apt and quick of understanding and naturally sad and melancholy ... and therefore there is the

---

118. Eliot, *Indian Dialogues* (1671), 65–66.

119. *Light Appearing* (1651), 183.

120. Shepard, *The Sound Believer* (1645), 115–237; Baxter, *A Call to the Unconverted* (1658), 20. See also pp. 72–74 above.

greater hope of great heart-breakings, if ever God brings them effectually home, for which we should affectionately pray.[121]

The Indian converts commonly pursued self-examination for sin in their hearts, which reminds us of inwardness and self-examination in the puritan tradition. Praying Indians' continuous references to "heart" and their heartbreaking recognition of sinfulness and contrition clearly show their inwardness in the conversion experience. John Speene, a Praying Indian, mentioned in his sermon that the "heart" is the first place where one must search for sin, and outward behaviour such as "words" and "works" and "doings" are the next.[122] Ponampam said, "I was ashamed of my sins, and my heart melted."[123] Monotunkquanit confessed, "Now my heart was broken, and I was a great sinner."[124] Waban also confessed, "I saw my mourning for sin was not good. . . . Lord break my heart, that I may pray to God aright . . . no man could work faith in me, but the Word which I heard doth it."[125] For Praying Indians, the compunction of sin, expressed as "my heart broken"[126] because of their recognition of their sins, was a serious inner experience. Totherswamp's confession implies his understanding of self-examination:

> But after I came to learn what sin was, by the Commandments of God, and then I saw all my sins, lust, gaming, &c. . . . You taught, That Christ knoweth all our heart, and seeth what is in them, if humility, or anger, or evil thoughts, Christ seeth all that is in the heart; then my heart feared greatly, because God was angry for all my sins; yea, now my heart is full of evil thoughts, and my heart runs away from God, therefore my heart feareth and mourneth. Every day I see sin in my heart.[127]

Piumbuhhou also said, "because my heart checketh mee for sin. . . . And the Word of God now sheweth me that there is a God; therefore my heart sayes, I desire to pray to God."[128] Praying Indians' experience of self-examination highlights the Indians' understanding of the process of having the Christian faith: Wutasakompauin confessed: "I learned in a Catechism, that Christ

---

121. *Day-Breaking* (1647), 95.

122. *Further Accompt* (1659), 337. John Speene appears as John Speen in different resources.

123. *Tears of Repentance* (1653), 280.

124. *Further Account* (1660), 372.

125. *Further Account* (1660), 375.

126. *Further Account* (1660), 372.

127. *Tears of Repentance* (1653), 269.

128. *Further Account* (1660), 371. Piumbuhhou may be Piumbukhou in *Indian Dialogues* (1671).

sendeth his Spirit into my heart, to break it, to make it repent, to convert me, to cause me to believe: my heart said, therefore I desire to pray to God, and to believe for pardon, and adoption, and peace with God."[129] This understanding reminds us of "morphology of conversion" in puritan conversion theology, although Indians showed a less detailed description of their experience than puritans.

Indian converts who had a clear recognition of their innate corruption strongly believed human total depravity through the Scriptures taught by puritan ministers.[130] Totherswamp showed his understanding of total depravity and original sin derived from Adam: "One man brought sin into the Word, I am full of that sin, and I break Gods Word every day. I see I deserve not pardon, for the first mans sinning; I can do no good . . . nothing but evil thoughts, and words, and works. I have lost all likeness to God, and goodness . . . and I deserve death and damnations."[131] Anthony clearly understood original sin: "I confess that in my Mothers Womb I was conceived in sin, and that I was born in iniquity."[132] Ponampiam also stated, "my heart was full of originall sin, and my heart was often full of anger."[133] For Nishohkou, original sin was "the roots of sin" in his heart.[134] In addition, Indian narrators showed their understanding of the dichotomy of sin into original sin and actual sin.[135] Praying Indians who understood original sin were seriously concerned about their actual sins in their lives. Anthony confessed, "but still I sinned, and especially the sin of Lust, & I made light of any sin."[136] Praying Indians' serious concern about their actual sins came from their understanding of the

129. *Further Account* (1660), 393.

130. Bayly, *The Practice Piety* (2nd ed., 1612), 4, 28, 53, 95, 102, 122, 397; Baxter, *The Reformed Pastor* (1656), 94, 196, 245–46; Baxter, *A Call to the Unconverted* (1658), 2, 3, 6, 12–13, 15–17, 38, 44, 54–55. See also Calvin, *Inst.*, I.xv.1–8; II.i.1–11. According to Cohen, unlike puritans, Praying Indians' narratives "pay less attention to the soul's innate corruption" and do not show serious desperate feeling in humiliation due to their sinfulness. Cohen, "Conversion among Puritans and Amerindians," 252. However, the expression of sinfulness and their humiliation is one of the main issues in their narratives. The observation of the different points between puritans and Indians' narratives is probably because puritan narratives more focused on humiliation and self-examination searching Christ in their deep recognition of sinfulness as a sign of being in proper process towards conversion. Rather, Indian narratives focused on not only their repentance and humiliation, but also their confidence and assurance in the Indians.

131. *Tears of Repentance* (1653), 269–70. See *Tears of Repentance* (1653), 278; *Further Account* (1660), 361.

132. *Further Account* (1660), 382.

133. *Further Account* (1660), 386.

134. *Further Account* (1660), 362.

135. Cohen, "Conversion among Puritans and Amerindians," 246–47.

136. *Further Account* (1660), 365.

Ten Commandments. Anthony continually said: "I heard, and understood the Commands of God, Thou shalt not murder, commit adultery, steal, bear false witness, covet; and that made me afraid to commit sin afore man, lest I should be punished or put to death, but I feared not God."[137]

For the Praying Indians, their pagan religious life was one of their worst actual sins. They frequently repented concerning their pagan religious life in their confessions. Anthony confessed, "my father and mother prayed to many gods, and I heard them when they did so; and I did so too . . . and in my childhood . . . I did delight in it, as dancing and Pawwaug."[138] This confession reveals one of the characteristics of Indian confession which is different from that of puritans. The Praying Indians' confession about their former religious life as a serious sin reflects the contextual difference in terms of religion between the native Indians and the puritans: puritan conversion happened within Christian cultures, but Indian conversion happened within a culture where Indians believed, "there be many Gods."[139]

The Praying Indians had a clear recognition of the results of their sinfulness. The results were God's punishment of misery, death, and hell. Nishohkou confessed: "therefore I see I deserve hell torments: and then I cryed, Oh Christ pardon all these my sins. Then afterward my heart desired strongly to pray unto God, but I saw I deserved misery and punishment, and I was weak."[140] Anthony also stated, "I saw that I had offended against God, and sinn'd against him, and that I had the root of sin in me, and that I had deserved all miseries, and death, and hell."[141] Speen understood that the result of his sins was "eternal damnation."[142]

For Praying Indians, the result of conversion was "eternal life." Nataôus confessed, "I beleeve that when believers d[ie], Gods Angels carry them to Heaven."[143] Ponampam also said, "I saw Christ came to give eternal life. . . . I believe only in Christ for eternal life; and what Christ will do with my soul, so let it be; and my soul desireth that I may receive the Seals to make strong my heart."[144]

Praying Indians' clear recognition of the difference between their ontological condition before and after their conversion made them very eager

137. *Further Account* (1660), 365. See *Further Account* (1660), 368.
138. *Further Account* (1660), 364.
139. *Further Account* (1660), 365.
140. *Further Account* (1660), 363.
141. *Further Account* (1660), 366.
142. *Further Account* (1660), 369.
143. *Tears of Repentance* (1653), 273.
144. *Further Account* (1660), 371.

to convert; for example, the more miserable their situation, the more urgent and necessary conversion became. In other words, Praying Indians' clear understanding of sinfulness, through self-examination and God's punishment as the result of their sinfulness, led them to recognize the urgency of conversion and salvation. The Indians' strong desire to pray to God, which meant conversion for them, was related to their concern about how they could be converted.[145]

Like the puritans, the Praying Indians definitely acknowledged God's sovereignty in salvation.[146] Praying Indians understood that being converted or "praying" to God is total dependence on God. Ponampam confessed:

> I should for ever perish in Hell, because God hath cast me off. ... [W]hat shall I do if I be damned! Then I heard that word, If ye repent and believe, God pardons all sins; then I thought, Oh that I had this, I desired to repent and believe, and I begged of God, Oh give me Repentance and Faith, freely do it for me; and I saw God was merciful to do it.[147]

For Anthony, God is the subject of the knowledge of Christ: "Yea Lord, no man has taught mee Christ, onely God hath taught my heart to know Christ."[148] Praying Indians' christological understanding of conversion and salvation is evident in their narratives. The death speech of Wamporas, a Praying Indian, indicated his strong desire to be converted through Christ. Eliot wrote, "his last words which he spake in this world were these; Johova Aninnumah Jesus Christ, (that is), Oh, Lord, give mee Jesus Christ; and when hee could speak no more, he continued to lift up his hands to Heaven, according as his strength lasted, unto his last breath; so that they say of him he dyed praying."[149] Ponampiam said, "Then I fully saw that Christ only is our Redeemer, and Saviour, and I desire to believe in Christ; and my heart said, that nothing that I can do can save me, only Christ: therefore I beg for Christ, and a part in him."[150] Like puritans, they understood the grace of Christ. Nataôus said, "I do now want Graces, and these Christ only teacheth us, and only Christ hath wrought our redemption, and he procureth our

---

145. Shepard, *The Sincere Convert* (1640), 58; Baxter, *A Call to the Unconverted* (1658), 21. See Baxter, *A Call to the Unconverted* (1658), 11–13.

146. Shepard, *The Sincere Convert* (1640), 46, 101; Baxter, *The Reformed Pastor* (1656), 188; Baxter, *A Call to the Unconverted* (1658), 6, 15, 16, 21, 24.

147. *Tears of Repentance* (1653), 281–82.

148. *Further Account* (1660), 367.

149. *Strength out of Weaknesse* (1652), 222.

150. *Further Account* (1660), 386.

pardon for all our sins."[151] Ponampam confessed that "I heard Gods free mercy in his word, call all to pray, from the rising of the Sun to the going down thereof."[152] Praying Indians showed their clear understanding of the covenant of grace as the "new covenant." Monequassun said, "Christ hath provided the new Covenant to save Beleevers in Christ, therefore I desire to give my soul to Christ, for pardon of all my sins: the first Covenant is broke by sins, and we deserve Hell; but Christ keepeth for us the new Covenant, and therefore I betrust my soul with Christ."[153] Praying Indians' understanding of the covenant of grace is also well described in *Indian Dialogues* (1671). Waban said:

> God hath made a new covenant of grace which he hath opened in the gospel, and Jesus Christ hath published it to all the world. And the sum of it is this, that whosoever shall penitently turn from sin towards God, and believe in Jesus Christ, he shall have a pardon for all his sins, and be partaker of eternal life, through the grace and mercy of God in Jesus Christ.[154]

Praying Indians also expressed their trinitarian understanding of soteriology. For Piumbuhhou, the entire converting process, including repentance, is led by God in the Trinity: "I learned in a Catechism, that Christ sendeth his Spirit into my heart, to break it, to make it repent, to convert me, to cause me to believe: my heart said, therefore I desire to pray to God, and to believe for pardon, and adoption, and peace with God."[155]

It is perhaps true that Praying Indians understood Reformed soteriology in terms of God's absolute sovereignty in salvation, so only God's elect can be saved. Waban said in *Indian Dialogues* (1671): "Christ hath undertaken to conquer the world of all God's elect (for it is only the elect of God whom Christ hath undertaken for) and the Father and the Son have sent forth God the Holy Ghost to effect this work."[156]

Like puritans, Praying Indians who understood God's absolute sovereignty on salvation also believed that God calls the unconverted.[157] The references of Piumbukhou, a Praying Indian, in *Indian Dialogues* (1671),

---

151. *Tears of Repentance* (1653), 273.

152. *Tears of Repentance* (1653), 280.

153. *Tears of Repentance* (1653), 278–79.

154. Eliot, *Indian Dialogues* (1671), 102.

155. *Further Account* (1660), 393. Praying Indians' understanding of Trinity is evident. See Eliot, *Indian Dialogues* (1671), 93, 101, 115–16.

156. Eliot, *Indian Dialogues* (1671), 102–3.

157. Shepard, *The Sincere Convert* (1640), 43; Baxter, *A Call to the Unconverted* (1658), 3, 8, 12, 13, 14, 29–30, 32.

imply this understanding. Piumbukhou said: "We shall endeavour to convince and persuade all your friends to turn unto God also. . . . Let us therefore get your friends and neighbors together, and labor to persuade them all first to hear the word of God preached among you."[158] The reason is that, for Praying Indians, God seeks and calls the unconverted rather than abandons and ignores them. Piumbukhou said: "But God is wiser than our fathers, and he hath opened to us this way of wisdom and life, and calleth us to enter, and walk therein. Therefore be wise, and submit your selves to the call of Christ."[159] Waban, in his short sermon in *Indian Dialogues* (1671), argued for this: "And now Jesus Christ calleth us to come to him. Some of us have submitted unto Christ, and he hath mercifully accepted us, and so he will accept you, if you will come in unto him."[160]

Like puritans, Praying Indians seemed to consider the use of will and determination important in their thoughts on conversion. The Praying Indians seemed to understand that repentance for conversion was not only the work of God, but also something that needs human determination as the response to God's calling. Also, they believed that they had to repent in order to be forgiven and delivered by God to walk with Christ, and to pray to God as the sign of salvation. This idea can be found in their references to their desire and will to repent. At every confession, the Praying Indians indicated their strong desire, which highlighted their determination to repent and their dedication to the Christian faith. John Speen confessed, "I desire to be washed from all my filthy sins . . . therefore I desire to repent, and Confess before God, and before the Church: and I desire not only to confess, but to have repentance, and faith, that I may have grace, mercy, and pardon: and such repentance as workes obedience."[161] Monotunkquanit also said:

> When I heard of the great works of Christ, I said, Oh what shall I do, that I may get Christ? & I said in my heart, Oh the holy Spirit help me, for I am ashamed of my sins; melted is my heart, and I desire pardon of all my sins; now I desire to forsake all my sins . . . by the blood of Jesus Christ, and this I do by believing in Jesus Christ.[162]

One of the most common aspects of the Indians' confession was that in the early stages of their conversion, they did not want to believe the gospel and

---

158. Eliot, *Indian Dialogues* (1671), 82.
159. Eliot, *Indian Dialogues* (1671), 87.
160. Eliot, *Indian Dialogues* (1671), 119.
161. *Further Account* (1660), 369, 389.
162. *Further Account* (1660), 372. See *Further Account* (1660), 334; *Strength out of Weaknesse* (1652), 236.

to follow what the gospel said. They confessed that they said, "I will not pray so long as I live" and "my heart did a little desire to pray to God." However, later on, they changed their minds and expressed a strong desire to believe, and finally decided to repent: "I desire to believe in Christ and I will pray to God as long as I live."[163] The important thing is that they believed that if they wanted to be forgiven and converted, they must do something. For them, repentance was imperative and was something they could do. They expressed "desire" as something they could do. This theological idea is found in a puritan's answer to an Indian's question which was asked when they had a meeting in 1646. When an old Indian asked, "whether it was not too late for such an old man as hee, who was neare death to repent or seeke after God," the puritan answered by describing God as a father who "call after his childe to returne and repent promising him favour." Therefore, the puritan argued, "if at last that sonne fall downe upon his knees and weepe and desire his father to love him, his father is so mercifull that hee will readily forgive him and love him; so wee said it was much more with God who is a more mercifull father to those whom hee hath made."[164]

In addition to their determination to repent, the Praying Indians showed their understanding of the means of grace for conversion.[165] Like puritans, Praying Indians heavily relied on biblical passages to describe their conversion experience. Like puritans' narratives, Indians' narratives contain many direct quotations from the Scriptures. Although Indian conversion narratives in both *Tears of Repentance* (1653) and *Further Account* (1660) commonly included biblical quotations to describe Indians' religious experiences, the latter have more quotations with a clear indication of the titles, chapters and verses of the Scriptures, and show a more biblically-structured form of confession through their strong dependence on the biblical passage, while the former did not have many biblical quotations. Most biblical passages in the narratives in *Tears of Repentance* (1653) were cited without any indication of titles and chapters except for two Scriptures—Matthew without an indication of the chapter and Psalms with chapter and verse.[166] Although this may reflect the way the confessions were prepared for publication, it is perhaps because the Indian Bible had not yet been translated at that time, 1652.[167] So, one can surmise that Praying Indians heavily relied

163. *Further Account* (1660), 355–96; in particular, 378, 380, 382, 388.
164. *Day-Breaking* (1647), 89.
165. Bayly, *The Practice of Piety* (2nd ed., 1612), 108–10; Shepard, *The Sincere Convert* (1640), 99, 106; Baxter, *The Reformed Pastor* (1656), 252–53; Baxter, *A Call to the Unconverted* (1658), 32–33.
166. *Tears of Repentance* (1653), 275, 287.
167. Cohen, "Conversion among Puritans and Amerindians," 245, 250. In the

on the minister's oral teaching of the Bible without actual access to the text, at least in 1652. Monequassun expressed in his conversion narrative in 1652 his strong desire for reading the Bible and for learning to read it for himself: "I desired to learn to read Gods Word, and hearing that if we ask wisdom of God, he will give it, then I did much pray to God, that he would teach me to reade."[168] This signifies that for Praying Indians, the Scriptures were the most important means of grace which encouraged them to repent, and made them determined to believe in and follow Christ. Nishohkou explained his repentance experience after hearing the Scriptures:

> Again, I heard . . . Mat. 5. Whoever breaks the least of Gods Commandements, and teach men so to do, shall be least in the Kingdom of heaven. Then I was trouble, because I had been an active sinner, in lust, and other sins, and I was worse than a beast in my sins. Then I cryed to God, Oh Christ pardon all my sins. Thus I cryed and desired pardon, but I was weak in believing.[169]

According to Anthony, the Scriptures made him want to believe in Christ: "Again I heard, Mat. 3. The axe is laid to the root of the tree, every tree that bringeth not forth good fruit is hewen down, and cast into the fire: then I feared my own case, because my fruit were sin, and I deserved to be cut down; then I desired to believe in Christ."[170]

Furthermore, for the Praying Indians, catechizing was a significant means of grace. Waban, a Praying Indian, said:

> Again, I learn in the Catechize, Q. What hath Christ done for us? A. He dyed for us, hee was buried, he rose again for us, and by his resurrection hee raiseth our souls unto grace, and also at the last day: And my heart said, Oh let it be so in me! . . . Again it is said in Catechism, Why is Christ a Prophet? A. To teach me

---

conversion narratives in *Further Account* (1660), Genesis in Old Testament and Matthew in New Testament were mainly quoted and only Nishohkou and Ponampiam's narratives contained other Scriptures as well such as Psalm, Isaiah, Luke, John, and James in the first and second narrative of Nishohkou and 1 Chronicles, Malachi, and John in Ponampiam's narrative. *Tears of Repentance* (1653), 362, 379, 385, 386. This reflects the translation process of the Indian Bible by Eliot. Eliot published *The First Book of Moses called Genesis* and *The Gospel of Matthew* in the Indian language in 1655 and *The Psalter* in 1658. Also, the publication of *The New Testament of Our Lord and Saviour Jesus Christ* and *The Holy Bible* was 1661 and 1663 respectively.

168. *Tears of Repentance* (1653), 277.
169. *Further Account* (1660), 363.
170. *Further Account* (1660), 367.

the way to heaven: therefore my heart desireth that Christ may ever lead me by his Word.[171]

The Praying Indians understood that the means of grace were a "fort" which helped them to keep their faith, protecting and safeguarding their salvation. Nishohkou confessed, "Then I desired my heart might be made strong by Church-covenant, Baptism, and the Lords Supper, which might be as a Fort to keep me from enemies, as a Fort keepeth us from our outward enemies."[172] Here one can find the puritans' understanding of the means of grace as a kind of preparation for believers to lead them into conversion and salvation.[173] In addition, for the Praying Indians, the means of grace gave them confirmation of their faith. Nishohkou said:

> Again, Mat. 16. Christ saith, Thou art Peter a Rock, and on this Rock I will build my church, and the gates of Hell shall not prevail against it: Therefore my heart said, I desire this; because Christ dwells in the Church, and in the midst of them where two or three are met together in my name. Oh! I do therefore desire Church Ordinances, that I might be with Christ, and that I might have the Seals.[174]

Praying Indians who understood that they could be saved through the grace of God with serious recognition of sinfulness and the painful result of it, still expressed continuous serious inner conflict as a common phenomenon in the puritan conversion experience.[175] Piumbuhhou confessed, "my heart rejoiced to hear of the mercy of God; yet I doubted, and my heart was hard again."[176] Piumbuhhou also confessed "then my afflicted poore heart came in, and the Minister came to me and said, pray to God, because God afflicteth and tryeth you; my heart said, when the Minister spake to me, let it be as you say, that God may shew me that mercy."[177] Nishohkou also said, "but if I truly believe then he will pardon, but true faith I cannot work; Oh Jesus Christ help me, and give it me."[178] In his later confession, Nishohkou said, "Then I hear this promise; If you repent and believe, you shall have

171. *Further Account* (1660), 376. See *Tears of Repentance* (1653), 276, 280, 281, 285, 290, 291, 293.

172. *Further Account* (1660), 363.

173. Cohen, "Conversion among Puritans and Amerindians," 249. See also Pettit, *The Heart Prepared*.

174. *Further Account* (1660), 363.

175. See pp. 78–80, 205–8 above.

176. *Further Account* (1660), 371.

177. *Further Account* (1660), 392.

178. *Tears of Repentance* (1653), 289.

pardon and be saved: and therefore sometime I believe, and sometimes I doubt again."[179] Indians considered their inner instability to be a weakness of their faith: "Then I cryed to God, Oh Christ pardon all my great sins, Oh Christ have mercy on mee, Oh God remember mee, to pardon all my sins. Thus I cryed and desired pardon, but I was weak in believing. But then, about two years after, I was greatly troubled about my weakness."[180] Anthony also confessed, "therefore now I prayed, Oh Christ Jesus pardon mee, but my heart is weak and doubting, and I cannot believe."[181] In fact, according to Cohen, the native Indians' conversion narratives "lack any sense of assurance," especially in their narratives of 1659 recorded in *Further Account* (1660).[182]

However, Praying Indians' inner conflict did not seriously imply their lack of assurance and confidence in conversion. This is a clear difference between Indian narratives and puritan narratives, which emphasized uncertainty more and assurance of faith less. Praying Indians highlighted the sincerity of their conversion experience and Christian faith. This can be found in their confessions, as it explains their process of repentance. Most of them experienced a kind of process towards real repentance and conversion. In the early stages they experienced doubt and did not believe in themselves, even though they received the gospel and "prayed to God," but after that they could earnestly desire repentance. Nishohkou confessed, "After wee pray'd to God about three years, my heart was not right, but I desired to run wilde, as also sundry others did."[183] John Speen also confessed that "at first when I prayed, my prayer was vain, and only I prayed with my mouth."[184] Throughout the process they said they had matured considerably as they repented sincerely and confessed their faith earnestly. John Speen later confessed that he "earnestly entreated God to pardon and deliver."[185] Anthony, a Praying Indian, desired, "Let God do with mee what hee will: but I beg mercy in Christ, onely I desire to pray to God as long as I live."[186] This confession of true repentance and conversion is one of the most important common aspects of the Praying Indians' confession. Also, this aspect is one of the most noticeable differences between the conversion narratives of

179. *Further Account* (1660), 362.
180. *Further Account* (1660), 363.
181. *Further Account* (1660), 367.
182. Cohen, "Conversion among Puritans and Amerindians," 252.
183. *Further Account* (1660), 361.
184. *Further Account* (1660), 368.
185. *Further Account* (1660), 369.
186. *Further Account* (1660), 368.

Praying Indians and those of New England puritans, as appeared between the conversion narratives of Old and New England puritans. Praying Indians clearly understood their original destiny because of their sins. Also, they fully acknowledged that their conversion was not complete and they were still experiencing inner troubles and conflicts, including mixed feelings of assurance and doubt, so sometimes they thought they were hypocrites. Nishohkou confessed: "I sometimes think Christ doth not delight in me because I do much play the hypocrite, but if I truly beleeve then he will pardon, but true faith I cannot work; Oh Jesus Christ help me, and give it me."[187] However, Praying Indians' expression of hope for the pardon and mercy of Christ implicitly argued for their assurance and confidence in conversion and salvation. Totherswamp confessed his strong belief in pardon and redemption through the mercy of Christ:

> The first man brought sin first, and I do every day ad[d] to that sin, more sins; but Christ hath done for us all righteousness, and died for us because of our sins, and Christ teacheth us, that if we cast away our sins, and trust in Christ, then God will pardon all our sins; this I beleeve Christ hath done . . . therefore I do hope for pardon. . . . Again, When I heard, and understood Redemption by Christ, then I beleeved Jesus Christ to take away my sins. . . .[T]he greatest mercy of all is Christ, to give us pardon and life.[188]

The closing statements of many Indian narratives are worth attention. Many ended with an expression of hope in the promises of God for redemption, and a strong commitment to follow Christ as converts. This also implies their assurance in conversion. For example, Nataôus ended his narrative with his strong belief and dependence on Christ as the saviour: "I want faith to beleeve the Word of God, and to open my Eyes, and to help me to cast away all sins; and Christ hath deserved for me eternall life: I have deserved nothing my self; Christ hath deserved all, and giveth me faith to beleeve it."[189] Robin Speen also ended his narrative as follows: "God in Heaven is very merciful, and therefore hath called me to pray unto God. God hath promised to pardon al[l] their sins, who pray unto God, and beleeve in the Promise of Christ, and Christ can give me to beleeve in him."[190] Piumbuhhou at the end of his narrative confessed:

---

187. *Tears of Repentance* (1653), 289.
188. *Tears of Repentance* (1653), 270.
189. *Tears of Repentance* (1653), 273.
190. *Tears of Repentance* (1653), 287.

> Then hearing of the mercy of Christ, my heart said, I am like a dead man, and therefore I desire to be with Christ as long as I live: my heart did not know how to Convert, and turn to God, therefore my heart did gladly pray to God for it; my heart did desire to pray, because I heard, Christ is our redeemer, and doth deliver our soules. . . . I desire that Christ may be my deliverer: therefore I betrust my soul with Christ as long as I live.[191]

The expression "as long as I live," which often appeared in the narratives, signifies Praying Indians' will to follow Christ. Ponampam confessed his will to follow Christ and his belief in God's promise of redemption: "I thought I wil[l] give my self to God and to Christ, and do what he will for ever; and because of this promise of pardon to al[l] that repent and beleeve, my heart desireth to pray to God as long as I live."[192] Nishohkou also said, "Again, I heard Mat. 9. The Son of Man hath power to pardon sin on earth, and therefore me O Lord; then my heart did desire Christ, and to pray as long as I live."[193] These references explicitly declared not only what they actually believed, but also their strong hope and expectation from this belief. Also, it is probably true that Indian confessions show more assurance and confidence in conversion than some of the English settlers did in their narratives.[194]

Consequently, through the Praying Indians' confession of the Christian faith with assurance and confidence, we can discover that Eliot's ministerial purpose had finally been achieved. Also, the narratives reveal Eliot's primary and lasting motive for Indian ministry. That is to say, Eliot's fundamental and lasting motive to push ahead with preaching the gospel to the Indians was his strong concern for conversion and unquenchable aspiration for conversion-oriented ministry.

Conclusion

Through a comparison of the conversion narratives of puritans and Praying Indians, one can discover a common understanding of puritan conversion theology and soteriology which appears in the writings of both puritans and Indians. It is true that native Indians' understanding of puritan thoughts on conversion and salvation was due to the strong influence of Eliot as their

191. *Further Account* (1660), 393.
192. *Tears of Repentance* (1653), 280–81.
193. *Further Account* (1660), 380.
194. Caldwell, *The Puritan Conversion Narratives*, 87, points out that the narratives from Thomas Shepard's congregation at Cambridge, Massachusetts, were more open-ended and tentative.

pastoral leader. In this sense, a comparative analysis of the conversion narratives of English settlers and converted Indians clearly reveals the strong continuity between puritans and Indians on puritan theology.

However, the Praying Indians gave voice to their unique expression in their own contexts. Praying Indians' consideration of their former pagan religious customs as serious sins reflects the contextual difference in terms of religion between the Indians and the puritans. Also, Praying Indians' strong expression of their confidence and assurance in conversion, which was not found easily in puritan confessions, signifies a clear difference between the two narratives.

The strong theological continuity of Praying Indians' confessions with those of puritans is not necessary a sign of the unilateral enforcement of Christianity by puritans. It could just as well suggest the success of Eliot's puritan pastoral ministry to Praying Indians.[195] In consideration of the significance of conversion as a core part of Christianity in the puritans' ecclesiastical understanding, and conversion narratives as statements of the Christian faith, the Indian conversion narratives clearly reveal how the Indians in fact understood Christianity itself.

A comparative analysis of the conversion narratives of English settlers and converted Indians strongly suggests that the fundamental and lasting motive for Eliot's preaching of the gospel to New England Indians was rooted in puritan conversion theology and a conversion-oriented puritan pastoral ministry. In the Indians' conversion narratives, John Eliot, who had preached the gospel to the Indians, could finally see the fruits of his ministry through the Indians' faithful and sincere confessions of Christian faith.

---

195. Cohen, "Conversion among Puritans and Amerindians," 236.

7

Conclusion

THE AIM OF THIS book has been to investigate John Eliot's puritan ministry to the New England Indians. Eliot's passionate and devoted pastoral ministry to the Indians has been mainly interpreted as "mission" in modern Protestant missiological perspectives. This research initially questions whether we can apply the term "mission" to Eliot, and whether it is always right to understand his seventeenth- century pastoral activities with the Indians in the modern perspective and ideological paradigm of "mission." Along with this initial question, the historiographical analysis of dominant scholarly perspectives in Eliot research—including the modern Protestant "mission" perspective—led us to realize the significance of the understanding of puritan theology and ministry in the seventeenth-century transatlantic world, which is the crucial basis for this book. In other words, through the relocation of Eliot in his own historical contexts, this book ultimately seeks to understand Eliot's pastoral activities with the Indians, which have previously been understood simply as "mission," and have not been properly analyzed theologically, particularly in relation to Eliot's contemporary puritan tradition, focusing on Eliot's theological and ministerial background and how he practiced and applied these ideas and traditions to New England Indians.

In addition to the perspectival shift, this book in chapter 2 offers a new reflection on the mutual relationship among the Great Migration, puritan millenarianism, and Indian conversion, in particular their relation to the motives for Eliot's Indian ministry. Through a fresh interpretation of the purpose of the puritans' Great Migration, based not only on new scholarship, but also on resources in the Eliot Tracts describing the early period of puritan migration, we realize that the missiological understanding of Indian "mission" as the motive for the Great Migration based on Perry Miller's "errand into the wilderness" thesis needs to be corrected. Puritans' main reason for migration to New England was further reformation and pure Christianity that they could not realize under Laudian policy in England. Also, this chapter refutes previous research arguing that puritans migrated to New England under the strong influence of millenarianism in the seventeenth-century transatlantic world in order to establish a model society in the imminently-coming millennium in New England as a "New Jerusalem." However, despite the influence of millenarianism on puritans in the seventeenth century, millenarianism was not the main impetus for them to migrate to New England, and their purpose in migration was not to make a model society in the coming millennium, but rather to pursue further reformation and purity within Christianity. This fact is surely supported by the fact that Eliot's millenarianism was formed not only by his contemporaries, but also in response to radically shifted circumstances during the Interregnum (1649–60) and after the Restoration (1660), which was when Eliot experienced his ideological revision. In this sense, for Eliot, millenarianism was not the initial motive for his migration nor for his Indian ministry, although it is evident that Eliot's thoughts on the millennium and his strong expectation of it became significant stimuli for his Indian ministry. This can be well understood when we consider his thought on the origin of the New England Indians as the descendants of "Gentile Hebrews," and the possibility of their mass conversion in relation to the millennium. However, after 1660, because of rapid circumstantial change, Eliot's millenarian vision could not be a strong and continuous motive for his Indian ministry, just as it was before, despite his continuous vision of the Kingdom of Christ and Indian conversion until his death. These new reflections on the motives for Eliot's Indian ministry require us to have an alternative answer about the more fundamental and lasting stimuli for Eliot's Indian ministry. This book proposes puritan conversion theology and soteriology. Although Indian conversion was not Eliot's primary reason for migration in 1631, the primary reasons for his strong involvement with Indian ministry from 1646 on were puritan fundamental concern for the conversion of the unconverted, and puritan conversion theology and soteriology. These were the strong motives for continuous Indian ministry and made Eliot's vision of Indian evangelization stronger.

In addition, the research for the motives for Indian ministry based on a new historical interpretation strongly proves the necessity and justification for a historical and circumstantial lens for reinterpretation, and a better understanding of Eliot as a seventeenth-century figure.

Chapter 3 investigated seventeenth-century puritan pastoral ministry as the background for Eliot's Indian ministry. For puritans, conversion was the most important pastoral duty and task. Puritans' thoughts on conversion as fundamental ontological change of not only the internal, but also the external, reflects puritans' strong introspective piety and their practical application of this piety in their everyday life. Puritans who regarded conversion as an important measure of salvation focused on how human beings can be saved. Despite their strong emphasis on God's initiative and sovereignty based on Reformed theology, puritans seemed to argue that God's calling for conversion implicitly urged human determination and response. Also, puritans allowed the use of free will and the means of grace toward the calling of God for salvation.

For puritans, the primary means of ministry was pastoral teaching, focusing on the Word of God through various methodologies, including personal or private instruction, and visitations based on text-based and oral education, due to their belief in the preaching of the Word as the crucial means of conversion. Also, puritans developed counselling and spiritual direction as significant components of pastoral teaching and pastorship. In addition, pastoral teaching for pastors was also an important task of puritan ministry.

For puritans, the practice of piety was a visible sign of conversion as well as a means of conversion, and a lifelong duty, ultimately another significant ministerial task. Puritans pursued a conversionist and Bible-centered practice of piety. Through "heart religion" pursuing inner spiritual experience, and communion with God through meditation, prayer, fasting and singing psalms, puritans revealed their strong introspective pietistic tendency. Also, puritans understood piety not only as a duty, but also as a sign of being "visible saints." In addition, puritans understood that the ultimate pursuit of puritan ministry was the reformation of church and society. Puritans believed that reformation could be actualized through conversion-oriented pastoral ministry based on pastoral teaching and care and the practice of piety.

Lastly, this chapter suggested puritan conversion theology and pastoral theology were the initial and most lasting motives for Eliot's Indian ministry. Although for Eliot, Indian conversion was not his primary motive for migration to New England, one of the primary reasons that he finally became involved with Indian ministry was puritan fundamental ministerial concern for "soul-saving worke" and conversion theology as they appear in the Eliot Tracts. Also, the rhetoric in the Eliot Tracts urging reformation provides a crucial hint of the relationship between reformation and Indian conversion. As puritans conceived that true conversion is a sign and process of reformation, for Eliot, Indian conversion was a visible and effective means not only for fundraising, but also a strong stimulus for further reformation in England. At the same time, for New England, Indian conversion was an impetus for evoking interest and support for Indian ministry, as well as an efficient means for the process and actualisation of the values of reformation in New England as well. Along with chapter 2, this chapter highlighted the importance of historical and theological perspectives for understanding Eliot as a seventeenth-century puritan figure and a theological basis on which we can define Eliot's pastoral work with the Indians, which has been normally understood as "mission."

Based on the puritan background, chapters 4–6 focus on Eliot's practice of puritan ministry to New England Indians. Chapter 4 examined Praying Towns and Indian churches. The fourteen Praying Towns established by Eliot based on the Bible and millenarian vision were the ideal Indian Christian settlements in his vision. Eliot's vision of ideal Christian community could be completed through the establishment of an Indian church. Eliot applied his theological understanding of the church in the Indian pastoral context. Eliot's application of strict church membership based on the "New England Way" reflects not only his conversion theology and congregationalist ecclesiology, but also his clear distinction between Praying Towns and Indian churches. For Eliot, Praying Towns were Indian Christian settlements for civility and religion, and Indian churches were reformed visible churches composed of "sincere converts." The distinction between Praying Towns and Indian churches, and between normal Praying Indians and official Indian church members in Eliot's ministry, can probably be compared to English puritan ministerial contexts, in which puritan ministers urged parishioners to be "sincere converts," and pursued a purely reformed church, particularly through focusing on preaching of the Word and well-regulated church membership policy. Although Praying Towns were Indian Christian settlements of covenant, worship, Christian teaching and piety, as well as theocracy under Eliot's pastoral direction, the reason that Eliot eagerly tried to establish Indian churches in the towns was his strong aspiration for the establishment of reformed church in the Praying Towns. In addition, congregational polity practiced in the Indian churches is another good example of Eliot's practical application of his own ecclesiology. The Indian churches' teaching and ruling elder system, and the autonomy in place in individual Indian churches, show not only Eliot's congregationalist ecclesiology, but also the contextual and strategic application of his own ideology. Consequently, for Eliot, Praying Towns as the biblical and covenanted

Indian Christian settlements, and Indian churches as purely reformed and congregational churches directed by puritan ministry, were not only his pastoral fields, but also the actualization of his values of the Kingdom of Christ which would be realized in the future in his expectation.

In chapter 5, we examined Eliot's actual practices of Indian ministry in the special communities. Chapter 5 argued the extent to which Eliot practiced and applied puritan theology and ministerial ideas and traditions to the Indians as his new parishioners. Through this chapter, we can realize that the theological and ministerial ideas and practices in seventeenth-century puritan tradition were applied almost exactly to Praying Indians by Eliot. In this sense, we can understand the strong continuity between puritans and Indians, and that Indian ministry for Eliot was a very puritan ministry. Also, this chapter gave a significant insight for Eliot research that Eliot's pastoral activities, which have normally been interpreted as "mission" in previous research, can and should be re-analyzed via a seventeenth-century puritan theological and historical angle.

In chapter 6, we finally came to Praying Indians' own voices regarding Christianity as taught by and mediated through Eliot. While we focused earlier on puritan understanding of Indian ministry, this chapter focused on what the Indians understood and experienced, how they felt about what they learned, and how they responded via their own means of expression in their own context. For this aim, this chapter investigated Indian conversion narratives in comparison to New England puritan narratives. Considering the significance of conversion and conversion narratives as the core of Christian faith, and the declaratory statement of puritan faith and understanding of Christianity, it is probably true that the narratives revealed the Indians' understanding of Christianity itself despite their focus on conversion experience. In the comparative analysis of the conversion narratives, we could conclude that puritans and Indians shared the same theology of conversion and salvation. This significantly reveals the strong puritan influence on the Indians. However, this does not mean the total absence of Indian voice, nor unilateral transplantation of puritanism to the Indians, but rather implies that the result of Eliot's puritan ministry for Praying Indians and their Christianization was realized based on puritanism. This chapter confirms that puritan conversion theology and soteriology are important in terms of the motive for Eliot's Indian ministry, as argued in chapter 3.

Some scholars concluded that Eliot's "mission" had failed.[1] This judgment might be from their Indian-centered ethnohistorical assessment of

---

1. Morrison, "'That Art of Coyning Christians,'" 77–92; Jennings, *The Invasion of America*, 251; Fisher, "Native Americans, Conversion, and Christian Practice in Colonial New England," 103. Jean Fittz Hankins and John Frederick Woolverton argued

English colonialism and quantitative assessment, based only on visible achievements. In fact, Eliot's Indian ministry was severely hampered by King Philip's War in 1675-76, which was the most serious conflict between puritans and Indians in seventeenth-century New England. It was a serious disaster that led Praying Towns and Indian churches into an unrecoverable situation, as it were. During the war, about 5,000 Indians, approximately 40 percent of the Indians in southern New England at that time, were killed. Many English colonists were also killed. The casualties exceeded 10 percent of the forces. More than a dozen towns were totally destroyed. For Eliot, the more serious difficulties were the severe distrust and hatred of the English toward Praying Indians, although most of the Praying Indians sympathized with the English, while one-fourth of the Indians generally did so.[2] After the war, Eliot faced rapid and unrecoverable ministerial decline. Eliot described his ministerial situation after the war:

> Praying to God was quenched, the younger generation being debauched by it, and the good old generation of the first beginers gathered home by death. So the Satan imp[ro]ved the op[por]tunity to defile, debase, & bring into contempt the whole work of praying to God, a great apostacy defiled us. And yet through grace some stood & doe stand, and the work is on foot to this day, praised be the Lord . . . po[o]re soules . . . left theire goods, books, bibles, only some few caryed their bibles, the rest were spoyled & lost.[3]

However, Eliot's Indian ministry was not ended after the war, and the work of breaking through the severe visible and invisible difficulties continued. William Kellaway argues that the Indian-language publications funded by the New England Company after the war outnumbered the publications before 1675.[4] These included John Eliot's publication of revised editions of his works, including *Harmony of the Gospels* (1678), *A*

Protestant missions to New England Indians in eighteenth century were also failed. Hankins, "Bringing the Good News," 6; Woolverton, *Colonial Anglicanism in North America*, 103. See Fisher, "Native Americans, Conversion, and Christian Practice in Colonial New England," 103n7.

2. Eliot to Robert Boyle, Governor of the Company, 17 December 1675, in *CGT-NEC*, 53–55; *HCINE*, 196; *HADSINE*, 429–525; "Roxbury Church Record" in *A Report of the Record Commissioners*, 195–96; Kellaway, *The News England Company*, 116–20; Vaughan, *New England Frontier*, 315–22; *ID*, 52–54; Morrison, *A Praying People*, 151–83; Lepore, *The Name of War*; Wyss, *Writing Indians*, 52–80; Breen, *Transgressing the Bounds*, 145–96; *ET*, 22; Hermes, "King Philip's War," 439–40.

3. "Roxbury Church Record" in *A Report of the Record Commissioners*, 195–96.

4. Kellaway, *The New England Company*, 147.

Christian Covenanting Confession (1680), *The Psalter* (1682), *The Holy Bible* (1685), *The Practice of Piety* (1685), *A Call to the Unconverted* (1688), and *The Sincere Convert* (1689). Eliot's passion for Indian ministry continued unchanged, and contributed to the noticeable survival of Christian Indians in the last quarter of the seventeenth century. Sixteen Praying Indians of Natick sent a letter to Eliot on 19 March 1683/4. Their sincere thanks to and admiration for Eliot as their pastoral leader reveals Eliot's unchanged ministerial passion for them:

> God hath made you to us and our nation a spiritual father, we are inexpressibly ingaged to you for your faithful constant Indefatigable labours, care and love, to and for us, and you have always manifested the same to us as wel[l] in our adversity as prosperity, for about forty years making know to us the Glad tidings of Salvation of Jesus Christ; for which we desire to give your our Hearty thanks, and whereas you are now grown aged, soe that we are deprived of seeing your face and hearing your voice . . . soe frequently as formerly, wee presume to make this our Addresse to you.[5]

Through Eliot's devotion—as evidenced by the report of Grindal Rawson and Samuel Danforth, who were sent to Indian communities around Massachusetts in 1698 to count the number of Indian churches and active participants—"there were thirty congregations in Massachusetts, with thirty-seven Indian ministers or schoolmasters and seven or eight English ministers overseeing them."[6] This report most likely signifies that Eliot's Indian ministry was not ended after the war, and that it overcame the difficulties and continued even to the end of his life. We cannot say that Eliot's Indian ministry was failed and unsuccessful, because pastoral ministry as "soul-saving work" can never be judged by visible quantitative measures. Eliot's Indian ministry was not failed, but merely buried in the stream of history.

Samuel Sewall, who had a strong friendship with Eliot and called him "brother," introduced Eliot's vision of Ezek 37 in his diary of 1 June 1690: "June 1. Mr. Taylor, Mr. Pierpont and Mr. Walter dine with me; Mr. Walter tells me of a small Paraphrase of Mr. Eliot's upon Ezekiel 37., written about half a year before his death."[7] It seems that Eliot still had in mind the vision

---

5. *CGTNEC*, 74.

6. "Account of an Indian Visitation, A.D. 1698," in *MHSC* 10 (1809), 129–34, quoted from Fisher, "Native Americans, Conversion, and Christian Practice in Colonial New England," 104n8.

7. Sewall, *The Diary of Samuel Sewall*, 252, 279. Graham, "Sewall, Samuel."

of Ezek 37, which was the first text on which he preached to the Indians in 1646, when he began the unprecedented project of Indian ministry. Thomas Shepard reported: "It is somewhat observable . . . that the first Text out of which Mr. Eliot preached to the Indians was about the dry bones, Ezek. 37. where it's [sic] said, Vers. 9, 10. that by prophesying to the wind, the wind came and the dry bones lived."[8] What did the vision of the dry bones' revival mean for Eliot? Eliot associated the vision of Ezek 37 with a vision of preaching for Indian conversion. This was the vision of John Eliot, "the Apostle to the Indians," and as this book has shown, his vision of preaching for conversion was rooted in and shaped by the ethos of seventeenth-century puritanism.

---

8. *Clear Sun-Shine* (1648), 135.

Bibliography

Primary Sources

Ames, William. *Conscience with the Power and Cases Thereof.* Leiden, 1639.
———. *Medulla theologica* (*The Marrow of Theology*) (1623). Translated from the 3rd Latin edition (1629). Edited by John D. Eusden. 2nd ed. Grand Rapids: Baker, 1997.
Baillie, Robert. *A Dissuasive from the Errours of the Time.* London, 1645.
Baxter, Richard. *A Call to the Unconverted.* London, 1658. Reprint, edited by Jay P. Green. Lafayette, IN: Sovereign Grace, 2000.
———. *The Reformed Pastor.* London, 1656. Reprint, edited by William Brown. Edinburgh: Banner of Truth Trust, 1974.
———. *Reliquiae Baxterianae: Or, Mr. Richard Baxter's Narrative of the Most Memorable Passages of His Life and Times.* Edited by Matthew Sylvester. London, 1696. Reprint, abridged by J. M. Lloyd Thomas, edited by N. H. Keeble. *The Autobiography of Richard Baxter.* London: Dent, 1931. Totowa, NJ: Rowman & Littlefield, 1974.
———. *The Saints' Everlasting Rest.* London, 1650. Reprint, Ross-shire, Scotland: Christian Focus, 2005.
Bayly, Lewis. *The Practice of Piety.* 2nd ed. London, 1612.
Bernard, Richard. *The Faithfull Shepheard.* London, 1607.
Birch, Thomas. *The Life of the Honourable Robert Boyle.* London, 1744.
———. *The Works of Robert Boyle.* 6 vols. London, 1772.
Broughton, Hugh. *A Require of Agreement.* London, 1611.
Calvin, John. *The Bondage and Liberation of the Will: A Defense of the Orthodox Doctrine of Human Choice against Pighius.* Edited by A. N. S. Lane. Translated by G. I. Davies. Grand Rapids: Baker, 1996.
———. *Commentaries: Genesis.* Translated by John King. Grand Rapids: Eerdmans, 1963.
———. *Institutes of the Christian Religion.* Translated by Ford Lewis Battles. Edited by John T. McNeill. Library of Christian Classics 20–21. Philadelphia: Westminster, 1960.
Clark, Michael P., ed. *The Eliot Tracts: With Letters from John Eliot to Thomas Thorowgood and Richard Baxter.* Westport, CT: Praeger, 2003.
Clark, Thomas. *Historical Account of John Eliot.* MHSC 1st series 8 (1802) 5–35.
Clarke, Samuel. *The Lives of Thirty-Two English Divines.* London: William Birch, 1677.
Cotton, John. *A Brief Exposition of the Whole Book of Canticles.* London, 1642; 1648.

———. *Churches Resurrection*. London, 1642.

———. *The Correspondence of John Cotton*. Edited by Sargent Bush Jr. Chapel Hill: University of North Carolina Press, 2001.

———. *An Exposition upon the Thirteenth Chapter of the Revelation*. London, 1655.

———. *Gods Promise to His Plantation*. London, 1630.

———. *The Keyes of the Kingdom of Heaven*. London, 1644; Reprinted in *John Cotton on the Churches of New England*, edited by Larzer Ziff. Cambridge: Belknap, 1968.

———. *The Way of the Churches of Christ in New-England*. London, 1645.

———. *The Way of Congregational Churches Cleared*. London, 1648; Reprinted in *John Cotton on the Churches of New England*, edited by Larzer Ziff. Cambridge: Belknap, 1968.

———. *The Way of Life*. London, 1642.

Eames, Wilberforce. "Discovery of a Lost Cambridge Imprint of John Eliot's Genesis, 1655." *Colonial Society of Massachusetts* 34 (1937) 11–15.

Edwards, Jonathan. *Letters and Personal Writings*. In vol. 16 of *The Works of Jonathan Edwards*, edited by George S. Claghorn. New Haven: Yale University Press, 1998.

———. *Religious Affection* (1746). In vol. 2 of *The Works of Jonathan Edwards*, edited by John E. Smith. New Haven: Yale University Press, 1959.

Eliot, John. "An Account of Indian Churches in New-England" (1673). First published in *MHSC* 1.10 (1809) 124–29.

———, ed. *A Brief Narrative of the Progress of the Gospel amongst the Indians in New England, in the Year 1670*. London, 1671. *Old South Leaflets* 1:21. Boston: Old South Meeting House, n.d.

———. *A Call to the Unconverted* (1658). Translated by Richard Baxter. Cambridge, 1664, 1688.

———. *The Christian Commonwealth*. London, 1659.

———. *A Christian Covenanting Confession*. Cambridge, 1680.

———. *The Communion of Churches*. Cambridge, 1665.

———. *Dying Speeches & Counsels of Such Indians as Dyed in the Lord*. Cambridge, 1685.

———. *The First Book of Moses Called Genesis*. Cambridge, 1655.

———, ed. *A Further Accompt of the Progresse of the Gospel amongst the Indians in New-England and of the Means Used Effectually to Advance the Same*. London, 1659. Sabin's Reprint, Quarto Series 6. New York, 1865.

———, ed. *A Further Account of the Progress of the Gospel amongst the Indians in New England: Being a Relation of the Confessions Made by Several Indians (in the Presence of the Elders and Members of Several Churches) in Order to Their Admission into Church-Fellowship*. London, 1660.

———. *The Gospel of Matthew*. Cambridge, 1655.

———. *Harmony of the Gospels*. Boston, 1678.

———. *The Holy Bible: Containing the Old Testament and the New. Translated into the Indian Language, and Ordered to be Printed by the Commissioners of the United Colonies in New England, at the Charge, and with the Consent of the Corporation in England for the Propagation of the Gospel amongst the Indians in New England*. Cambridge, 1663, 1685.

———. *Indian Dialogues for Their Instruction in That Great Service of Christ, in Calling Home Their Country-Men to the Knowledge of God, and of Themselves, and of Iesus Christ*. Cambridge, 1671. Reprinted in *John Eliot's Indian Dialogues:*

A Study in Cultural Interaction, edited by Henry W. Bowden and James P. Ronda. Westport, CT: Greenwood, 1980.

———. *The Indian Grammar Begun: Or, An Essay to Bring the Indian Language into Rules.* Cambridge, 1666.

———. *The Indian Primer.* Cambridge, 1669.

———. *John Eliot and The Indians, 1652–1657: Being Letters Addresses to Rev. Jonathan Hanmer of Barnstaple, England.* Edited by Wilberforce Eames. New York: Adams and Grace, 1915.

———, ed. *A Late and Further Manifestation of the Progress of the Gospel amongst the Indians in New-England . . . Being a Narrative of the Examinations of the Indians, about Their Knowledge in Religion, by the Elders of the Churches.* London, 1655. MHSC 3.4 (1834) 261–87.

———. "The Learned Conjectures of Reverend John Eliot Touching the Americans" (1653). In Thomas Thorowgood, *Jews in America, or Probabilities That Those Indians Are Judaical.* London: Thomas Slater, 1660; Reprinted in *The Eliot Tracts: With Letters from John Eliot to Thomas Thorowgood and Richard Baxter*, edited by Michael P. Clark, 409–27. Westport, CT: Praeger, 2003.

———. *The Logick Primer.* Cambridge, 1672.

———. *The New Testament of Our Lord and Saviour Jesus Christ.* Cambridge, 1661, 1685.

———. *Our Indians' ABC.* Cambridge, 1671.

———. *The Practice of Piety.* Translated by Lewis Bayly. 2nd ed., 1612. Cambridge, 1665, 1685.

———. "Primer and Catechism." Cambridge, 1654, 1662, 1669, 1686, or 1687. 3rd ed., the only one extant in its entirety, was published as *The Indian Primer* (1669). The title page and several other portions of the 4th ed. are not extant.

———. *The Psalter.* Cambridge, 1658 or 1659, 1663 or 1664, 1682.

———. *The Sincere Convert* (1640). Translated by Thomas Shepard. Cambridge, 1689.

Eliot, John, and Thomas Mayhew Jr., eds. *Tears of Repentance: Or, A Further Narrative of the Progress of the Gospel amongst the Indians in New-England: Setting forth, Not Only Their Present State and Condition, but Sundry Confessions of Sin by Diverse of the Said Indian.* London, 1653. MHSC 3.4 (1834) 197–260.

Eliot, John, et al., eds. *The Whole Book Psalmes Faithfully Translated into English Metre.* Cambridge: Stephen Day, 1640. Reprint, *The Bay Psalm Book: A Facsimile of the First Edition of 1640*, edited by Zoltan Haraszti. Chicago: University of Chicago Press, 1956.

Emerson, Wilimena H., et al. *Genealogy of the Descendants of John Eliot, "Apostle to the Indians," 1598–1905.* New Haven: Tuttle, Morehouse & Taylor, 1905.

Francis, Convers. *Life of John Eliot, the Apostle to the Indians.* Boston: Hilliard, Gray, 1836.

Ford, John W., ed. *Some Correspondence between the Governors and Treasurers of the New England Company in London and the Commissioners of the United Colonies in America the Missionaries of the Company and Others between the Years 1657 and 1712 to Which Are Added the Journals of the Rev. Experience Mayhew in 1713 and 1714.* London: Spottiswoode, 1896.

Fulke, William. *A Brief and Plaine Declaration.* London, 1584.

Gookin, Daniel. *Historical Account of the Doings and Sufferings of the Christian Indians in New England in the Years 1675–1677.* Transactions and Collections of American

Antiquarian Society 2. Cambridge: Printed for the Society at the University Press, 1836.

———. *The Historical Collections of the Indians in New England* (1674). MHSC 1st series 1 (1792) 141–226.

Greenham, Richard. *The Works of the Reverend and Faithful Servant of Jesus Christ, M. Richard Greenham*. Edited by Henry Holland. London, 1599. Reprint, *Practical Divinity: The Works and Life of Richard Greenham*, edited by Kenneth L. Parker and Eric J. Carlson. Brookfield, VT: Ashgate, 1998.

Hall, David D., ed. *The Antinomian Controversy, 1636–1638: A Documentary History*. Middletown, CT: Wesleyan University Press, 1968.

Israel, Menasseh Ben. *The Hope of Israel: The English Translation by Moses Wall* (1652). Translated by Richenda George. Edited by Henry Mechoulan and Gerard Nahon. Oxford: Oxford University Press, 1987.

Jackson, John. *A Sober Word to a Serious People*. London, 1651.

Lechford, Thomas. *Plaine Dealing: Or, Newes from New-England*. London, 1642. Edited by J. Hammond Trumbull. Boston, 1867. Reprint, New York: Garrett, 1970.

Mather, Cotton. *The Triumphs of the Reformed Religion in America. The Life of the Renowned John Eliot; a Person Justly Famous in the Church of God*. Boston, 1691; Reprint, Cotton Mather, *Magnalia Christi Americana*. London. 1702. Edited by T. Robbins. 2 vols. Hartford: Silas Andrus & Son, 1853. Edited by Kenneth Murdock. Cambridge: Harvard University Press, 1977.

Perkins, William. *The Arte of Prophecying*. Translated from the Latin ed. (1592). London, 1607.

———. *A Discourse of Conscience*. London, 1596.

———. *A Golden Chain, or, Description of Theology*. London, 1591.

———. *Of the Calling of the Ministerie*. London, 1605.

———. *The Workes of That Famous and Worthy Minister of Christ, in the University of Cambridge*. 3 vols. London, 1608–31.

Powicke, F. J., ed. *Some Unpublished Correspondence of the Rev. Richard Baxter and the Rev. John Eliot, "The Apostle to the American Indians," 1656–1682*. Manchester: Manchester University Press, 1931.

Pulsifer, David. C., ed. *Records of the Colony of New Plymouth in New England, vol. 1: 1643–1651*. Boston: William White, 1859.

A Report of the Record Commissioners, Containing the Roxbury Land and Church Records. Boston: Rockwell and Churchhill, 1881.

Rogers, John. *Ohel or Beth-shemesh: A Tabernacle for the Sun*. London, 1653.

Roxbury Land and Church Records: Sixth Report of the Boston Record Commissioners. Boston: Rockwell and Churchill, 1884.

Sewall, Samuel. *The Diary of Samuel Sewall, 1674–1729*. Edited by M. Halsey Thomas. New York: Farrar, Straus and Giroux, 1973.

[Shepard, Thomas?], ed. *The Clear Sun-Shine of the Gospel Breaking forth upon the Indians in New-England*. London, 1648. MHSC 3.4 (1834) 25–67. Sabin's Reprint, Quarto Series 10. New York, 1865.

[———], ed. *The Day-Breaking, If Not the Sun-Rising of the Gospell with the Indians in New-England*. London, 1647. MHSC 3.4 (1834) 1–23. Sabin's Reprint, Quarto Series 9. New York, 1865.

———. *The Sincere Convert*. London, 1640. Reprint, *The Works of Thomas Shepard*, vol. 1., edited by John A. Albro. Boston: Doctrinal Tract and Book Society, 1853. Ligonier, PA: Soli Deo Gloria, 1991.

———. *The Sound Believer*. London, 1645. Reprint, *The Works of Thomas Shepard*, vol. 1., edited by John A. Albro. Boston: Doctrinal Tract and Book Society, 1853. Ligonier, PA: Soli Deo Gloria, 1991.

———. *Thomas Shepard's Autobiography, Journal, and Confessions*. Reprinted in *God's Plot: Puritan Spirituality in Thomas Shepard's Cambridge*, edited by Michael McGiffert. Amherst, MA: University of Massachusetts Press, 1972; 1994.

———. *Thomas Shepard's Confessions*. Edited by George Selement and Bruce C. Woolley. Publications of The Colonial Society of Massachusetts Collections 58. Boston: Colonial Society of Massachusetts, 1981.

Shurtleff, Nathaniel B., ed. *Records of the Governor and Company of the Massachusetts Bay in New England (1626–1686)*. Boston, 1853–54. Reprint, New York: AMS, 1968.

Shurtleff, Nathaniel B., and David C. Pulsifer, eds. *Records of the Colony of New Plymouth (1855–1861)*. New York: AMS, 1968.

Society for Propagation of the Gospel in New-England. *The New England Company of 1649 and John Eliot. The Ledger for the Years 1650–1660 and the Record Book of Meetings between 1656 and 1686 of the Corporation for the Propagation of the Gospel in New England*. New York: B. Franklin, 1967.

Thorowgood, Thomas. *Jewes in America; or, Probabilities That the Americans Are of That Race*. London, 1650.

Walker, Williston, ed. *The Creeds and Platforms of Congregationalism*. New York: Scribner's Sons, 1893.

[Weld, Thomas, Hugh Peter, and Henry Dunster], eds. *New Englands First Fruits; in Respect, First of the Conversion of Some, Conviction of Divers, Preparation of Sundry of the Indians*. London, 1643. Sabin's Reprint, Quarto Series 7. New York, 1865.

Whitfield, Henry, ed. *The Light Appearing More and More towards the Perfect Day or a Farther Discovery of the Present State of the Indians in New England*. London, 1651. MHSC 3.4 (1834) 101–47. Sabin's Reprint, Quarto Series 3. New York, 1865.

———, ed. *Strength out of Weaknesse, Or a Glorious Manifestation of the Further Progresse of the Gospel among the Indians in New England*. London, 1652. MHSC 3.4 (1834) 149–96. Sabin's Reprint, Quarto Series 5. New York, 1865.

Williams, Roger. *The Complete Writings of Roger Williams*. Edited by J. Hammond Trumbull. 7 vols. New York: Russell and Russell, 1963.

———. *A Key into the Language of America*. London, 1643.

Winters, William. "The Eliot Family." *The New England Historical and Genealogical Society* 39 (1885) 365–71.

———. "Notices of the Pilgrim Fathers, John Eliot and His Friends." *Transactions of the Royal Society* 10 (1882) 267–311.

Winslow, Edward, ed. *The Glorious Progress of the Gospel amongst the Indians of New England*. London, 1649. MHSC 3.4 (1834) 69–98.

Winthrop, John. *The Journal of John Winthrop*. Edited by Richard S. Dunn et al. Cambridge: Harvard University Press, 1996.

———. *The Winthrop Papers, 1498–1654*. Edited by Allyn B. Forbes et al. 6 vols. Boston: Massachusetts Historical Society, 1929–.

Secondary Sources

Adams, Nehemiah. *The Life of John Eliot; with an Account of the Early Missionary Efforts among the Indians of New England*. Boston: Massachusetts Sabbath School Society, 1847.
Albro, John A. *The Life of Thomas Shepard*. Boston, 1847.
American National Biography. 24 vols. Oxford: Oxford University Press, 1999. https://www.anb.org.
Amory, Hugh. *Bibliography and the Book Trades: Studies in the Print Culture of Early New England*. Edited by David D. Hall. Philadelphia: University of Pennsylvania Press, 2005.
———. "'Gods Altar Needs Not Our Pollishings': Revisiting the Bay Psalm Book." In Hugh Amory, *Bibliography and the Book Trades: Studies in the Print Culture of Early New England*, edited by David D. Hall, 34–57. Philadelphia: University of Pennsylvania Press, 2005.
———. "Printing and Bookselling in New England, 1638–1713." In Hugh Amory, *Bibliography and the Book Trades: Studies in the Print Culture of Early New England*, edited by David D. Hall, 105–45. Philadelphia: University of Pennsylvania Press, 2005.
Amory, Hugh, and David D. Hall, eds. *A History of the Book in America, vol. 1: The Colonial Book in the Atlantic World*. Cambridge: Cambridge University Press, 2000.
Anderson, Gerald H. *Biographical Dictionary of Christian Missions*. New York: Macmillan, 1998.
Anderson, Robert C., ed. *The Great Migration Begins: Immigrants to New England 1620–1633*. 3 vols. Boston: New England Historic Genealogical Society, 1995. http://www.greatmigration.org.
———. "A Note on the Changing Pace of the Great Migration." *New England Quarterly* 59 (1986) 406–7.
Atherton, Ian. "Reynolds, Edward (1599–1676)." In *ODNB* (Online).
Avis, Paul D. L. *The Church in the Theology of the Reformers*. Atlanta: John Knox, 1981.
Axtell, James. *After Columbus: Essays in the Ethnohistory of Colonial North America*. Oxford: Oxford University Press, 1988.
———. *America Perceived: A View from Abroad in the 17th Century*. West Haven, CT: Pendulum, 1974.
———. *Beyond 1492: Encounters in Colonial North America*. Oxford: Oxford University Press, 1992.
———. "The Ethnohistory of Early America: A Review Essay." *William and Mary Quarterly* 3rd series 35 (1978) 110–44.
———. *The European and the Indian: Essays in the Ethnohistory of Colonial North America*. Oxford: Oxford University Press, 1981.
———, ed. *The Indian Peoples of Eastern America: A Documentary History of the Sexes*. Oxford: Oxford University Press, 1981.
———. *The Invasion Within: The Contest of Cultures in Colonial North America*. Oxford: Oxford University Press, 1985.
———. *White Indians of Colonial America*. Fairfield, WA: Ye Galleon, 1979.
Bainton, Roland H. *Christendom: A Short History of Christianity and Its Impact on Western Civilization*. New York: Harper & Row, 1966.

Balmer, Randall, ed. *Encyclopedia of Evangelicalism*. Waco, TX: Baylor University Press, 2004.

Baritz, Loren. *City on a Hill: A History of Ideas and Myths in America*. New York: Wiley & Sons, 1964.

Battenhouse, Roy W. "The Doctrine of Man in Calvin and in Renaissance Platonism." In *Articles on Calvin and Calvinism, vol. 4: Influences upon Calvin and Discussion of the 1559 Institutes*, edited by Richard C. Gamble, 155–79. New York: Garland, 1992.

Battles, Ford Lewis. *The Piety of John Calvin*. Grand Rapids: Baker, 1978.

―――. "True Piety according to Calvin." In *Interpreting John Calvin*, edited by R. Benedetto, 289–306. Grand Rapids: Baker, 1996.

Bauckham, Richard. "Fulke, William (1536/7–1589)." In *ODNB* (Online).

Beeke, Joel R. *Puritan Reformed Spirituality: A Practical Theological Study from Our Reformed and Puritan Heritage*. Webster, NY: Evangelical, 2004.

Benedict, Philip. *Christ's Churches Purely Reformed: A Social History of Calvinism*. New Haven: Yale University Press, 2002.

Bercovitch, Sacvan. *The American Jeremiad*. Madison: University of Wisconsin Press, 1978.

―――, ed. *The American Puritan Imagination: Essays in Revaluation*. Cambridge: Cambridge University Press, 1974.

―――. *The Puritan Origins of the American Self*. New Haven: Yale University Press, 1975.

Bilodeau, Christopher. "'They Honor Our Lord among Themselves in Their Own Way': Colonial Christianity and the Illinois Indians." *American Indian Quarterly* 25 (2001) 352–77.

Biglow, William. *History of the Town of Natick*. Boston, 1830.

Black, J. William. *Reformation Pastors: Richard Baxter and the Ideal of the Reformed Pastor*. Milton Keynes, UK: Paternoster, 2004.

Bosch, David J. "Mission and Evangelism: Clarifying the Concepts." *Zeitschrift für Missionswissenschaft und Religionswissenschaft* 68 (1984) 161–91.

―――. *Transforming Mission: Paradigm Shifts in Theology of Mission*. American Society of Missiology Series 16. Maryknoll, NY: Orbis, 1991.

―――. *Witness to the World: The Christian Mission in Theological Perspective*. London: Marshall, Morgan & Scott, 1980.

Bouwsma, William. "The Spirituality of John Calvin." In *Christian Spirituality: High Middle Ages and Reformation*, edited by Jill Raitt, 318–33. New York: Crossroad, 1987.

Bowden, Henry W. *American Indians and Christian Missions: Studies in Cultural Conflict*. Chicago: University of Chicago Press, 1982.

Bowden, John, ed. *Christianity: The Complete Guide*. London: Continuum, 2005.

Bozeman, Theodore Dwight. "Biblical Primitivism: An Approach to New England Puritanism." In *The American Quest for the Primitive Church*, edited by Richard T. Hughes, 19–32. Chicago: University of Illinois Press, 1988.

―――. "Thomas Brightman (1562–1607)." In *ODNB* (Online).

―――. *To Live Ancient Lives: The Primitivist Dimension in Puritanism*. Chapel Hill: University of North Carolina Press, 1988.

Brachlow, Stephen. *The Communion of Saints: Radical Puritan and Separatist Ecclesiology, 1570–1625*. Oxford: Oxford University Press, 1988.

Brautigam, Dwight. "Prelates and Politics: Uses of 'Puritan,' 1625-40." In *Puritanism and Its Discontents*, edited by Laura Lunger Knoppers, 49-66. Newark, NJ: University of Delaware Press, 2003.

Breen, T. H. *The Character of a Good Ruler: A Study of Puritan Political Ideas in New England, 1630-1730*. New Haven: Yale University Press, 1970.

Brauer, Jerald C. "Conversion: From Puritanism To Revivalism." *The Journal of Religion* 58.3 (1978) 227-24.

———. "Types of Puritan Piety." *Church History* 56.1 (1987) 39-58.

Breen, Louis A. *Transgressing the Bounds: Subversive Enterprises among the Puritan Eliot in Massachusetts, 1630-1692*. Oxford: Oxford University Press, 2001.

Bremer, Francis J. *Congregational Communion: Clerical Friendship in the Anglo-American Puritan Community, 1610-1692*. Boston: Northeastern University Press, 1994.

———. "Cotton, John (1585-1652)." In *ODNB* (Online).

———. "Endecott, John (d. 1665)." In *ODNB* (Online).

———. *John Winthrop: America's Forgotten Founding Father*. Oxford: Oxford University Press, 2003.

———. *The Puritan Experiment: New England Society from Bradford to Edwards*. New York: St. Martin's, 1976. Revised ed. Hanover, NH: University Press of New England, 1995.

———, ed. *Puritanism: Transatlantic Perspectives on a Seventeenth-Century Anglo-American Faith*. Boston: Massachusetts Historical Society, 1993.

———. "Whitfield [Whitfeld], Henry (1590/91-1657)." In *ODNB* (Online).

———. "Williams, Roger (c.1606-1683)." In *ODNB* (Online).

———. "Wilson, John (c.1591-1667)." In *ANB* (Online).

———. "Winthrop, John (1588-1649)." In *ODNB* (Online).

Bremer, Francis J., and Lynn A. Botelho, eds. *The World of John Winthrop: Essays on England and New England, 1588-1649*. Boston: Massachusetts Historical Society, 2005.

Bremer, Francis J., and T. Webster, eds. *Puritans and Puritanism in Europe and America: A Comprehensive Encyclopedia*. 2 vols. Santa Barbara, CA: ABE-Clio, 2006.

Brenner, Elise. "To Pray or Be Prey; That is the Question: Strategies for Cultural Autonomy of Massachusetts Praying Town Indians." *Ethnohistory* 27 (1980) 135-52.

Bross, Kristina Kae. *Dry Bones and Indian Sermons: Praying Indians in Colonial America*. Ithaca, NY: Cornell University Press, 2004.

———. "Dying Saints, Vanishing Savages: 'Dying Indian Speeches' in Colonial New England Literature." *Early American Literature* 36 (2001) 325-52.

———. *Early Native Literacies in New England*. Amherst: University of Massachusetts Press, 2008.

———. "'That Epithet of Praying': The Praying Indian Figure in Early England Literature." PhD diss., University of Chicago, 1997.

Brown, Anne S., and David D. Hall. "Family Strategies and Religious Practice: Baptism and the Lord's Supper in Early New England." In *Lived Religion in America: Towards a History of Practice*, edited by David D. Hall, 41-68. Princeton: Princeton University Press, 1997.

Browne, John. *The Congregational Church at Wrentham in Suffolk: Its History and Biographies*. London: Jarrold & Sons, 1854.

———. *A History of Congregationalism, and Memorials of the Churches in Norfolk and Suffolk*. London: Jarrold & Sons, 1877.

Butin, Philip. *Reformed Ecclesiology: Trinitarian Grace according to Calvin.* Princeton: Princeton Theological Seminary, 1994.
Byington, Ezra Hoyt. "John Eliot, the Puritan Missionary to the Indians." *Papers of the American Society of Church History* 8 (1896) 109–45.
Caldwell, Patricia. *The Puritan Conversion Narrative: The Beginnings of American Expression.* Cambridge: Cambridge University Press, 1983.
Calloway, Colin G. *New Worlds for All.* Baltimore: Johns Hopkins University Press, 1997.
Cambers, Andrew. *Godly Reading: Print, Manuscript and Puritanism in England, 1580–1720.* Cambridge: Cambridge University Press, 2011.
———. "Reading, the Godly, and Self-Writing in England, circa 1580–1720." *Journal of British Studies* 46 (2007) 796–825.
Cambers, Andrew, and Michelle Wolfe. "Reading, Family Religion, and Evangelical Identity in Late Stuart England." *Historical Journal* 47 (2004) 875–96.
Cameron, Euan. *The European Reformation.* Oxford: Clarendon, 1991.
Carlson, Eric Josef. "The Boring of the Ear: Shaping the Pastoral Vision of Preaching in England, 1540–1640." In *Preachers and People in the Reformations and Early Modern Period*, edited by Larissa Taylor, 249–96. Leiden: Brill, 2001.
———. "Greenham, Richard (early 1540s–1594)." In *ODNB* (Online).
Carpenter, John B. "The New England Puritans: The Grandparents of Modern Protestant Missions." *Missiology* 30.4 (2002) 519–32.
Castillo, Susan P., and Ivy Schweitzer, eds. *A Companion to the Literatures of Colonial America.* Oxford: Blackwell, 2005.
Caverly, Robert Boodey. *Lessons of Law and Life from John Eliot, the Apostle to the Indian Nations of New England.* Boston: Sargent and Sons, 1880.
Cesarini, Joseph Patrick. "Reading New England's Mission: Indians Conversion and the Ends of Puritan Rhetoric in the Seventeenth Century." PhD diss., Rutgers, The State University of New Jersey, 2003.
Chamberlain, David. *Eliot of Massachusetts.* London, 1928.
Chan, Simon. *Spiritual Theology: A Systematic Study of the Christian Life.* Downers Grove, IL: InterVarsity, 1998.
Chi, Joseph Jung UK. "'Forget not the wombe that bare you, and the brest that gave you sucke': John Cotton's Sermons on Canticles and Revelation and His Apocalyptic Vision for England." PhD diss., University of Edinburgh, 2008.
Clark, Thomas. "Historical Account of John Eliot." *Massachusetts Historical Society Collections* 1st series 8 (1802) 5–35.
Coffey, John, and Paul C. H. Lim, eds. *The Cambridge Companion to Puritanism.* Cambridge: Cambridge University Press, 2008.
Cogley, Richard W. "Idealism vs. Materialism in the Study of Puritan Missions to the Indians." *Method & Theory in the Study of Religion* 3.2 (1991) 165–82.
———. "John Eliot and the Origins of the American Indians." *Early American Literature* 21 (1986–87) 210–25.
———. "John Eliot and the Millennium." *Religion and American Culture* 1.2 (1991) 227–50.
———. "John Eliot in Recent Scholarship." *American Indian Culture and Research Journal* 14.2 (1990) 72–92.
———. *John Eliot's Mission to the Indians before King Philip's War.* Cambridge: Harvard University Press, 1999.

———. "John Eliot's Puritan Ministry." *Fides et Historia* 31.2 (1999) 1–18.
———. "The Millenarianism of John Eliot, 'Apostle to the Indians.'" PhD diss., Princeton University, 1983.
———. "Pagans and Christians on the New England Frontier: A Study of John Eliot's Indian Dialogues (1671)." *Mission Studies* 16.1 (1999) 95–109.
———. "Seventeenth-Century English Millenarianism." *Religion* 17.4 (1987) 379–96.
Cohen, Charles L. "Conversion among Puritans and Amerindians: A Theological and Cultural Perspective." In *Puritanism: Transatlantic Perspectives on a Seventeenth-Century Anglo-American Faith*, edited by Francis J. Bremer, 233–56. Boston: Massachusetts Historical Society, 1993.
———. *God's Caress: The Psychology of Puritan Religious Experience*. New York: Oxford University Press, 1986.
Collinson, Patrick. "Antipuritanism." In *The Cambridge Companion to Puritanism*, edited by John Coffey and Paul C. H. Lim, 19–33. Cambridge: Cambridge University Press, 2008.
———. *The Birthpangs of Protestant England: Religious and Cultural Change in the Sixteenth and Seventeenth Centuries*. Basingstoke: Macmillan, 1988.
———. "The Cohabitation of the Faithful with the Unfaithful." In *From Persecution to Toleration: The Glorious Revolution and Religion in England*, edited by Ole Peter Grell et al., 51–76. Oxford: Oxford University Press, 1991.
———. "A Comment: Concerning the Name Puritan." *Journal of Ecclesiastical History* 31 (1980) 483–88.
———. "England and International Calvinism 1558–1640." In *International Calvinism 1541–1715*, edited by Menna Prestwich, 197–223. Oxford: Oxford University Press, 1985.
———. *The Elizabethan Puritan Movement*. London: Jonathan Cape, 1967. 2nd ed. London: Methuen, 1982.
———. "Elizabethan and Jacobean Puritanism as Forms of Popular Religious Culture." In *The Culture of English Puritanism, 1560–1700*, edited by Christopher Durston et al., 32–57. Basingstoke: Macmillan, 1996.
———. *English Puritanism*. London: Historical Association, 1983.
———. *Godly People: Essays on English Protestantism and Puritanism*. London: Hambledon, 1983.
———. *The Puritan Character: Polemics and Polarities in Early Seventeenth-Century English Culture*. Los Angeles: Clark Library, 1989. Reprinted in Patrick Collinson, *From Cranmer to Sancroft*. London: Hambledon, 2006.
———. *The Religion of Protestants: The Church in English Society, 1559–1625*. Oxford: Oxford University Press, 1982.
———. "Shepherds, Sheepdogs, and Hirelings: The Pastoral Ministry in Post-Reformation England." In *The Ministry: Clerical and Lay*, edited by W. J. Sheils et al., 185–220. Oxford: Blackwell, 1989.
Como, David R. *Blown by the Spirit: Puritanism and the Emergence of an Antinomian Underground in Pre-Civil-War England*. Stanford: Stanford University Press, 2004.
Conforti, Joseph A. *Imagining New England: Explorations of Regional Identity from the Pilgrims to the Mid-Twentieth Century*. Chapel Hill: University of North Carolina Press, 2001.
Cooper, James F., Jr. *Tenacious of Their Liberties: The Congregationalists in Colonial Massachusetts*. New York: Oxford University Press, 1999.

Cornish, Louis C. "John Eliot." *Proceedings of the Unitarian Historical Society* 7.1 (1940) 1–20.
Cressy, David. *Bonfires and Bells: National Memory and the Protestant Calendar in Elizabethan and Stuart England.* London: Weidenfeld & Nicolson, 1989.
———. *Coming Over: Migration and Communication between England and New England in the Seventeenth Century.* Cambridge: Cambridge University Press, 1987.
Cressy, David, and Lori Anne Ferrell, eds. *Religion and Society in Early Modern England: A Sourcebook.* 2nd ed. London: Routledge, 2005.
Cross, F. L., ed. *The Oxford Dictionary of the Christian Church.* Rev. ed. Oxford: Oxford University Press, 2005.
Dailey, Barbara Ritter. "Lechford, Thomas (d. in or after 1642)." In *ODNB* (Online).
Davies, Horton. *Worship and Theology in England.* 5 vols. Princeton: Princeton University Press, 1961–75.
———. *The Worship of the American Puritans, 1629–1730.* Morgan, PA: Soli Deo Gloria, 1999.
Dawson, Jane E. A. "The Apocalyptic Thinking of the Marian Exiles." In *Prophecy and Eschatology Studies in Church History,* edited by Michael Wilks, 75–91. Studies in Church History: Subsidia 10. Oxford: Blackwell, 1994.
———. *Campbell Letters, 1559–83.* Scottish History Society, 5th series 10. Edinburgh: Lothian, 1997.
———. *John Knox.* New Haven: Yale University Press, 2015.
———. *The Politics of Religion in the Age of Mary, Queen of Scots: The Earl of Argyll and the Struggle for Britain and Ireland.* Studies in Early Modern British History. Cambridge: Cambridge University Press, 2002.
———. *Scotland Re-formed: 1488–1587.* The New Edinburgh History of Scotland 6. Edinburgh: Edinburgh University Press, 2007. Reprint, 2010, 2011, 2012.
Delbanco, Andrew. "The Puritan Errand Re-Viewed." *Journal of American Studies* 18 (1984) 343–60.
———. *The Puritan Ordeal.* Cambridge: Harvard University Press, 1989.
Dexter, Henry Martin. *The Congregationalism of the Last Three Hundred Years, As Seen in Its Literature.* New York, 1880.
A Dictionary of World History. Oxford University Press, 2000. http://www.oxfordreference.com/views/GLOBAL.html.
Dickens, A. G. *The English Reformation.* 2nd ed. London: B. T. Batsford, 1965.
Ditmore, Michael G. "Preparation and Confession: Reconsidering Edmund S. Morgan's Visible Saints." *New England Quarterly* 62 (1994) 298–319.
Dixhoorn, Chad B. Van. "Reforming the Reformation: Theological Debate at the Westminster Assembly, 1643–1652." PhD diss., University of Cambridge, 2005.
Donagan, Barbara. "Puritan Ministers and Laymen: Professional Claims and Social Constraints in 17th Century England." *The Huntington Library Quarterly* 47.2 (1984) 81–111.
Douglas, J. D. *The New International Dictionary of the Christian Church.* Grand Rapids: Zondervan, 1974; revised ed., 1978.
Drake, Francis. *The Town of Roxbury.* Roxbury, MA: Published by the Author, 1878.
Duffy, Eamon. "The Godly and the Multitude in Stuart England." *The Seventeenth Century* 1 (1986) 31–55.

———. "The Long Reformation: Catholicism, Protestantism and the Multitude." In *England's Long Reformation, 1500–1800*, edited by Nicholas Tyacke, 33–70. London: UCL, 1998.

———. *The Stripping of the Altars: Traditional Religion in England, 1400–1580*. New Haven: Yale University Press, 1992.

Dunkle, Robert J., and Ann S. Lainhart. *The Town Records of Roxbury, Massachusetts, 1647 to 1730: Being Volume One of the Original*. Boston: New England Historic Genealogical Society, 1997.

Dupré, Louis, and Don E. Sailers, eds. *Christian Spirituality: Post Reformation and Modern*. New York: Crossroad, 1989.

Durston, Christopher, and Jacqueline Eales, eds. *The Culture of English Puritanism, 1560–1700*. Basingstoke: Palgrave Macmillan, 1996.

Durston, Christopher, and Judith Maltby, eds. *Religion in Revolutionary England*. Manchester: Manchester University Press, 2006.

Eales, Jacqueline. *Puritans and Roundheads: The Harleys of Brampton Bryan and the Outbreak of the English Civil War*. Cambridge: Cambridge University Press, 1990.

Elliott, Emory. *Power and the Pulpit in Puritan New England*. Princeton: Princeton University Press, 1975.

Ellis, Charles M. *The History of Roxbury*. Boston: Samuel G. Drake, 1847.

Fairbanks, Jonathan L., and Robert F. Trent, eds. *New England Begins: The Seventeenth Century*. 3 vols. Boston: Museum of Fine Arts, 1982.

Fausz, J. Frederick. "Eliot, John [*called* the Apostle to the Indians] (1604–90)." In *ODNB* (Online).

Fenton, William N. *American Indian and White Relations to 1830: Needs and Opportunities for Study*. Chapel Hill: University of North Carolina Press, 1957.

Fiering, Norman S. *Moral Philosophy at Seventeenth-Century Harvard*. Chapel Hill: University of North Carolina Press, 1981.

Fincham, Kenneth, ed. *The Early Stuart Church, 1603–1642*. Basingstoke: Macmillan, 1993.

Fincham, Kenneth, and Peter Lake, eds. *Religious Politics in Post-Reformation England*. Woodbridge, Suffolk: Boydell & Brewer, 2006.

Firth, Katherine. *The Apocalyptic Tradition in Reformation Britain, 1530–1645*. Oxford: Oxford University Press, 1979.

Fisher, Linford D. "Native Americans, Conversion, and Christian Practice in Colonial New England, 1640–1730." *Harvard Theological Review* 102.1 (2009) 101–24.

Fletcher, A., and P. Roberts, eds. *Religion, Culture and Society in Early Modern Britain*. Cambridge: Cambridge University Press, 1994.

Ford, James Thomas. "Preaching in the Reformed Tradition." In *Preachers and People in the Reformations and Early Modern Period*, edited by Larissa Taylor, 65–88. Leiden: Brill, 2001.

Foster, Stephen. "English Puritanism and the Progress of New England Institutions, 1630–1660." In *Saints & Revolutionaries*, edited by David D. Hall et al., 3–37. New York: Norton, 1984.

———. *The Long Argument: English Puritanism and the Shaping of New England Culture, 1570–1700*. Chapel Hill: University of North Carolina Press, 1991.

———. *Notes from the Caroline Underground: Alexander Leighton, the Puritan Triumvirate and the Laudian Reaction to Nonconformity*. Hamden, CT: Archon, 1978.

———. *Their Solitary Way: The Puritan Social Ethic in the First Century of Settlement in New England.* New Haven: Yale University Press, 1970.
Fox, Adam. *Oral and Literate Culture in England 1500–1700.* Oxford: Oxford University Press, 2000.
———. "Religious Satire in English towns, 1570–1640." In *The Reformation in English Towns, 1500–1640,* edited by Patrick Collinson et al., 221–40. Basingstoke: Macmillan, 1998.
Freeman, Thomas S. "John Foxe (1516/17–1587)." In *ODNB* (Online).
Gauci, Perry. "Ashurst, Henry (1616?–1680)." In *ODNB* (Online).
Giles, Paul. "The Culture of Colonial America: Theology and Aesthetics." In *A Companion to the Literatures of Colonial America,* edited by Susan Castillo et al., 78–93. Oxford: Blackwell, 2005.
Gilpin, W. Clark. *The Millenarian Piety of Roger Williams.* Chicago: University of Chicago Press, 1979.
George, C. H. "Puritanism as History and Historiography." *Past and Present* 41 (1968) 77–104.
Glover, Robert Hall. *The Progress of World-Wide Missions.* New York: Harper & Brothers, 1924, 1939. Revised and enlarged by J. Herbert Kane, 1960.
Godbeer, Richard. *The Devil's Dominion: Magic and Religion in Early New England.* New York: Cambridge University Press, 1992.
Goddard, Ives, and Kathleen J. Bragdon. *Native Writings in Massachusett.* Philadelphia: American Philosophical Society, 1988.
Gordis, Lisa M. "The Conversion Narrative in Early America." In *A Companion to the Literatures of Colonial America,* edited by Susan Castillo et al., 369–86. Oxford: Blackwell, 2005.
———. *Opening Scripture: Bible Reading and Interpretive Authority in Puritan New England.* Chicago: University of Chicago Press, 2003.
Graham, Judith S. "Sewall, Samuel (1652–1730)." In *ODNB* (Online).
Gray, Edward G. *New World Babel: Languages & Nations in Early America.* Princeton: Princeton University Press, 1999.
Gray, Kathryn Napier. "Speech, Text and Performance in John Eliot's Writing." PhD diss., University of Glasgow, 2003.
Greaves, Richard L. "Bernard, Richard (*bap.* 1568, *d.* 1642)." In *ODNB* (Online).
———. "The Puritan Non-Conformist Tradition in England, 1560–1700: Historiographical Reflections." *Albion* 17 (1985) 449–86.
Green, Ian. *The Christian's ABC: Catechisms and Catechising in England, c.1530–1740.* Oxford: Clarendon, 1996.
———. *Print and Protestantism in Early Modern England.* Oxford: Oxford University Press, 2000.
Green, Jack P. *The Intellectual Construction of America: Exceptionalism and Identity from 1492 to 1800.* Chapel Hill: University of North Carolina Press, 1993.
Gribben, Crawford. "After Left Behind: The Paradox of Evangelical Pessimism." In *Expecting the End: Millennialism in Social and Historical Context,* edited by Kenneth G. C. Newport et al., 113–30. Waco, TX: Baylor University Press, 2006.
———. "Baptist and Millennialism in Early Modern England." In *Exploring Baptist Origins,* edited by Anthony R. Cross et al., 101–22. Oxford: Regent's Park College, 2010.
———. "Before Left Behind." *Books & Culture* (July/August 2003) 11.

---. "The Church of Scotland and the English Apocalyptic Imagination, 1630 to 1650." *Scottish Historical Review* 88.1 (2009) 34–56.

---. "The Eschatology of the Puritan Confessions." *Scottish Bulletin of Evangelical Theology* 20.1 (2002) 51–78.

---. "Evangelical Eschatology and 'the Puritan Hope.'" In *The Emergence of Evangelicalism: Exploring Historical Continuities*, edited by Michael Haykin et al., 375–93. Leicester: Apollos, 2008.

---. *Evangelical Millennialism in the Trans-Atlantic World, 1500–2000*. Basingstoke: Palgrave Macmillan, 2011.

---. "The Future of Millennial Expectation." In *Expecting the End: Millennialism in Social and Historical Context*, edited by Kenneth G. C. Newport et al., 237–40. Waco, TX: Baylor University Press.

---. *God's Irishmen: Theological Debates in Cromwellian Ireland*. Oxford: Oxford University Press, 2007.

---. "Introduction: Antichrist in Ireland — Protestant Millennialism and Irish Studies." In *Protestant Millennialism, Evangelicalism and Irish Society, 1790–2005*, edited by Crawford Gribben et al., 1–30. Basingstoke: Palgrave Macmillan, 2006.

---. *An Introduction to John Owen*. Carol Stream, IL: Crossway, 2020.

---. "John Gill and Puritan Eschatology." *Evangelical Quarterly* 73.4 (2001) 311–26.

---. *John Owen and English Puritanism: Experiences of Defeat*. Oxford: Oxford University Press, 2016.

---. "Protestant Millennialism, Political Violence and the Ulster Conflict." *Irish Studies Review* 15.1 (2007) 51–63.

---. *The Puritan Millennium: Literature and Theology, 1550–1682*. Dublin: Four Courts, 2000. 2nd ed. Milton Keynes: Paternoster, 2008.

---. "Rapture Fictions and the Changing Evangelical Condition." *Literature and Theology* 18.1 (2004) 77–94.

---. *Rapture Fiction and the Evangelical Crisis*. Webster, NY: Evangelical, 2006.

---. *The Rise and Fall of Christian Ireland*. Oxford: Oxford University Press, 2021.

---. *Survival and Resistance in Evangelical America: Christian Reconstruction in the Pacific Northwest*. Oxford: Oxford University Press, 2021.

---. "'The worst sect that a Christian man can meet': Opposition to the Plymouth Brethren in Ireland and Scotland, 1859–1900." *Scottish Studies Review* 3.2 (2002) 34–53.

---. *Writing the Rapture: Prophecy Fiction in Evangelical America*. Oxford: Oxford University Press, 2009.

Gribben, Crawford, and Elizabethanne Boran, eds. *Enforcing Reformation in Ireland and Scotland, 1550–1700*. Aldershot: Ashgate, 2006.

Gribben, Crawford, and Timothy C. F. Stunt. "Introduction." In *Prisoners of Hope? Aspects of Evangelical Millennialism in Britain and Ireland, 1800–1880*, edited by Crawford Gribben et al., 1–17. Studies in Evangelical History and Thought. Milton Keynes: Paternoster, 2004.

Gribben, Crawford, and Mark S. Sweetnam, eds. *Left Behind and the Evangelical Imagination*. Sheffield: Sheffield Phoenix, 2011.

Gribben, Crawford, and David G. Mullan, eds. *Literature and the Scottish Reformation*. Aldershot: Ashgate, 2009.

Gura, Philip. *A Glimpse of Sion's Glory: Puritan Radicalism in New England, 1620–1660*. Middletown, CT: Wesleyan University Press, 1984.

Ha, Polly, and Patrick Collinson, eds. *The Reception of Continental Reformation in Britain*. Oxford: Oxford University Press for the British Academy, 2010.

Hageman, Howard G. "Reformed Spirituality." In *Protestant Spiritual Traditions*, edited by Frank C. Senn. Eugene, OR: Wipf & Stock, 2000.

Haigh, Christopher, ed. *The English Reformation Revised*. Cambridge: Cambridge University Press, 1987. Reprint, 1992.

Hale, Richard Walden. *Tercentenary History of the Roxbury Latin School, 1645-1945*. Cambridge, MA: Riverside, 1946.

Hall, Basil, "Puritanism: The Problem of Definition." In vol. 2 of *Studies in Church History*, edited by G. J. Cuming, 283-96. London: Nelson, 1965.

Hall, David D. *Cultures of Print: Essays in the History of the Book*. Amherst: University of Massachusetts Press, 1996.

———. *The Faithful Shepherd: A History of the New England Ministry in the Seventeenth Century*. New York: Norton Library, 1974. 2nd ed. Cambridge: Harvard University Press, 2006.

———, ed. *Lived Religion in America: Toward a History of Practice*. Princeton: Princeton University Press, 1997.

———. "On Common Ground: The Coherence of American Puritan Studies." *William and Mary Quarterly* 3rd series 44 (1987) 193-221.

———. *The Puritans: A Transatlantic History*. Princeton: Princeton University Press, 2019.

———, ed. *Puritans in the New World: A Critical Anthology*. Princeton: Princeton University Press, 2004.

———. "Toward a History of Popular Religion in Early New England." *William and Mary Quarterly* 3rd series 49 (1984) 49-55.

———. *World of Wonders, Days of Judgment: Popular Religious Belief in Early New England*. Cambridge: Harvard University Press, 1989.

Hall, David D., and Alexandra Walsham. "'Justification by Print Alone?': Protestantism, Literacy, and Communications in the Anglo-American World of John Winthrop." In *The World of John Winthrop: Essays on England and New England, 1588-1649*, edited by Francis J. Bremer et al., 334-85. Boston: Massachusetts Historical Society, 2005.

Hall, David D., et al., eds. *Saints and Revolutionaries: Essays on Early American History*. New York: Norton, 1984.

Hall, Michael G. "Mather, Cotton (1663-1728)." In *ODNB* (Online).

———. "Mather, Richard (1596-1669)." In *ODNB* (Online).

Haller, William. *Liberty and Reformation in the Puritan Revolution*. New York: Columbia University Press, 1955.

———. *The Rise of Puritanism*. New York: Columbia University Press, 1938; Philadelphia: University of Pennsylvania Press, 1972.

Hambrick-Stowe, Charles E., ed. "III. Puritan Spirituality in America." In *Christian Spirituality: Post Reformation and Modern*, edited by Louis Dupre et al., 338-53. New York: SCM, 1990.

———. *Early New England Meditative Poetry: Anne Bradstreet and Edward Taylor*. Sources of American Spirituality. New York: Paulist, 1988.

———. *The Practice of Piety: Puritan Devotional Disciplines in Seventeenth-Century New England*. Chapel Hill: University of North Carolina Press, 1982.

Hammond, J. A. *Sinful Self, Saintly Self: The Puritan Experience of Poetry*. Athens: University of Georgia Press, 1993.

Hankins, Jean Fittz. "Bringing the Good News: Protestant Missionaries to the Indians of New England and New York." PhD diss., University of Connecticut, 1993.

Hardman Moore, Susan. "Arguing for Peace: Giles Firmin on New England and Godly Unity." In *Unity and Diversity in the Church*, edited by R. N. Swanson, 251–61. Studies in Church History 32. Oxford: Blackwell, 1996.

———. "Calvinism and the Arts." *Theology in Scotland* 16 (2009) 75–92.

———, ed. *The Diary of Thomas Larkham, 1647–1669*. Church of England Record Society 17. Woodbridge, Suffolk: Boydell & Brewer, 2011.

———. "New England's Reformation: 'Wee shall be as a Citty Upon a Hill, the eies of all people are upon us.'" In *Religious Politics in Post-Reformation England*, edited by Kenneth Fincham et al., 143–58. Woodbridge, Suffolk: Boydell & Brewer, 2006.

———. *Pilgrims: New World Settlers & The Call of Home*. New Haven: Yale University Press, 2007.

———. "Popery, Purity and Providence: Deciphering the New England Experiment." In *Religion, Culture and Society in Early Modern Britain*, edited by Anthony Fletcher et al., 257–89. Cambridge: Cambridge University Press, 1994.

———. "'Pure Folkes' and the Parish: Thomas Larkham in Cockermouth and Tavistock." In *Life and Thought in the Northern Church c.1100–1700*, edited by Diana Wood, 489–509. Woodbridge, Suffolk: Boydell, 1999.

———. "Sexing the Soul: Gender and the Rhetoric of Puritan Piety." In *Gender and Christian Religion*, edited by R. N. Swanson, 175–86. Studies in Church History 34. Oxford: Blackwell, 1998.

———. "Wie der Calvinismus nach Amerika kam: Die Geschichte der Susanna Bell." In *Calvin heute: Impulse der reformierten Theologie für die Zukunft der Kirche*, edited by Ulrich Möller et al., 59–68. Neukirchener, 2009.

Harling, Frederick F. "A Biography of John Eliot, 1604–1690." PhD diss., Boston University, 1965.

Hawkes, R. M. "The Logic of Assurance in English Puritan Theology." *Westminster Theological Journal* 52 (1990) 247–61.

Hawkins, Anne Hunsaker. *Archetypes of Conversion: The Autobiographies of Augustine, Bunyan, and Merton*. Lewisburg, PA: Bucknell University Press, 1985.

Hazlett, W. Ian P. *The Reformation in Britain and Ireland: An Introduction*. London: T. & T. Clark International, 2003.

Heal, Felicity. *Reformation in Britain and Ireland*. Oxford: Oxford University Press, 2003.

Hedges, Andrew H. "Strangers, Foreigners, and Fellow Citizens: Case Studies of English Missions to the Indians in Colonial New England and the Middle Colonies, 1642–1755." PhD diss., University of Illinois at Urbana-Champaign, 1996.

Heimert, Alan. "Puritanism, the Wilderness, and the Frontier." *New England Quarterly* 26 (September 1953) 361–82.

Heimert, Alan, and A. Delbanco, eds. *The Puritans in America: A Narrative Anthology*. Cambridge: Harvard University Press, 1985.

Hermes, Katherine. "King Philip's War." In *PPEA* 439–40.

Hill, Christopher. *The English Bible and the Seventeenth Century Revolution*. London: Allen Lane, 1993.

———. *Puritanism and Revolution*. London: Secker and Warburg, 1958.

———. *Society and Puritanism in Pre-Revolutionary England*. London: Secker and Warburg, 1964.
———. *The World Turned Upside Down: Radical Ideas during the English Revolution*. London: Temple Smith, 1972.
Hindmarsh, D. Bruce. *The Evangelical Conversion Narrative: Spiritual Autobiography in Early Modern England*. Oxford: Oxford University Press, 2005.
Hinson, E. Glenn. "Puritan Spirituality." In *Protestant Spiritual Traditions*, edited by Frank C. Senn. Eugene, OR: Wipf & Stock, 2000.
Hoffer, Peter Charles. *Sensory Worlds in Early America*. Baltimore: Johns Hopkins University Press, 2003.
Hoopes, James. *Consciousness in New England: From Puritanism and Ideas to Psychoanalysis and Semiotic*. Baltimore: Johns Hopkins University Press, 1989.
Holifield, E. Brooks. *The Covenant Sealed: The Development of Puritan Sacramental Theology in Old and New England, 1570–1720*. New Haven: Yale University Press, 1974.
———. *Theology in America*. New Haven: Yale University Press, 2003.
Holstun, James. *A Rational Millennium: Puritan Utopias of Seventeenth-Century England and America*. New York: Oxford University Press, 1987.
Howard, Joseph Kinsey. *Strange Empire: A Narrative of the Northwest*. New York: Morrow, 1952.
Huddleston, Lee E. *Origins of the American Indians: European Concepts, 1492–1729*. Austin: University of Texas Press, 1967.
Hughes, Ann. *Gangraena and the Struggle for the English Revolution*. Oxford: Oxford University Press, 2004.
Hughes, Richard, ed. *The American Quest for the Primitive Church*. Chicago: University of Illinois Press, 1988.
Hunt, Arnold. *The Art of Hearing: English Preachers and Their Audiences, 1590–1640*. Cambridge: Cambridge University Press, 2010.
Huntley, Frank Livingstone. *Bishop Joseph Hall and Protestant Meditation in Seventeenth-Century England: A Study with the Texts of The Art of Divine Meditation (1606) and Occasional Meditations (1633)*. Binghamton: Center for Medieval and Early Renaissance Studies, 1981.
Ingram, Martin. "Reformation of Manners in Early Modern England." In *The Experience of Authority in Early Modern England*, edited by Paul Griffiths et al., 47–88. London: Macmillan, 1996.
Jalalzai, Zubeda. "Puritan Imperialisms: The Limits of Identity and the Indians Missions of Massachusetts Bay." PhD diss., State University of New York at Buffalo, 2000.
Jedin, Hubert, and John Dolan, eds. *Handbook of Church History*. 10 vols. London: Burns & Oates, 1965–81.
Jennings, Francis. *The Ambiguous Iroquois Empire: The Covenant Chain Confederation of Indian Tribes with English Colonies form Its Beginnings to the Lancaster Treaty of 1744*. New York: Norton, 1984.
———. *The Founders of America: How the Indians Discovered the Land, Pioneered It, and Created Great Classical Civilizations; How They Were Plunged into a Dark Age by Invasion and Conquest; and How They Are Reviving*. New York: Norton, 1993.
———. "Goals and Functions of Puritan Missions to the Indians." *Ethnohistory* 18 (1971) 197–212.

———. *Invasion of America: Indians, Colonialism, and the Cant of Conquest*. Chapel Hill: The University of North Carolina Press, 1975.
Jinkins, Michael. "Perkins, William (1558–1602)." In *ODNB* (Online).
———. "Shepard, Thomas (1605–1649)." In *ODNB* (Online).
Jong, James A De. *As the Waters Cover the Seas: Millennial Expectations in the Rise of Anglo-American Missions, 1640–1810*. Kampen, Netherlands: Kok, 1970.
Jones, G. Lloyd. "Broughton, Hugh (1549–1612)." In *ODNB* (Online).
Jones, J. Gwynfor, and Vivienne Larminie. "Bayly, Lewis (c.1575–1631)." In *ODNB* (Online).
Jones, Serene. *Calvin and the Rhetoric of Piety*. Louisville: Westminster John Knox, 1995.
Jongeneel, J. A. B. "The Protestant Missionary Movement up to 1789." In *Missiology: An Ecumenical Introduction: Texts and Contexts of Global Christianity*, edited by F. J. Verstraelen et al., 222–28. Grand Rapids: Eerdmans, 1995.
Jue, Jeffrey K. "Puritan Millenarianism in Old and New England." In *The Cambridge Companion to Puritanism*, edited by John Coffey and Paul C. H. Lim, 259–76. Cambridge: Cambridge University Press, 2008.
Kane, J. Herbert. *A Concise Dictionary of the Christian World Mission*. Grand Rapids: Baker, 1978.
Kapic, Kelly M., and Randall C. Gleason, eds. *The Devoted Life: An Invitation to the Puritan Classics*. Downers Grove, IL: InterVarsity, 2004.
Katz, David S. *The Jews in the History of England, 1485–1850*. Oxford: Clarendon, 1994.
———. "Menasseh ben Israel (1604–1657)." In *ODNB* (Online).
———. *Philo-Semitism and the Readmission of the Jews to England, 1603–1655*. Oxford: Clarendon, 1982.
Kaufman, U. Milo. *The Pilgrim's Progress and Traditions in Puritan Meditation*. New Haven: Yale University Press, 1966.
Keeble, N. H. "Baxter, Richard (1615–1691)." In *ODNB* (Online).
———. "Puritanism and Literature." In *The Cambridge Companion to Puritanism*, edited by John Coffey and Paul C. H. Lim, 309–24. Cambridge: Cambridge University Press, 2008.
———. *Richard Baxter: Puritan Man of Letters*. Oxford: Clarendon, 1982.
Keeble, N. H., and Geoffrey F. Nuttall, eds. *Calendar of the Correspondence of Richard Baxter*. 2 vols. Oxford: Clarendon, 1991.
Kellaway, William. *The New England Company, 1649–1776: Missionary Society to the American Indians*. London: Longmans, 1961.
Kendall, R. T. *Calvin and English Calvinism to 1649*. Oxford: Oxford University Press, 1979.
Kerr, Anne, and Edmund Wright, eds. *A Dictionary of World History*. Oxford: Oxford University Press, 2000.
Khun, Thomas Samuel. *The Structure of Scientific Revolution*. Chicago: University of Chicago Press, 1962.
Kibbey, Ann. *The Interpretation of Material Shapes in Puritanism: A Study of Rhetoric, Prejudice, and Violence*. Cambridge: Cambridge University Press, 1986.
King, John N. "John Bale (1495–1563)." In *ODNB* (Online).
Kirk, J. Andrew. *What Is Mission?: Theological Explorations*. London: Darton, Longman and Todd, 1999.

Knappen, M. M. *Tudor Puritanism*. Chicago: University of Chicago Press, 1939; Gloucester, MA: Peter Smith, 1963.
Knight, Janice. *Orthodoxies in Massachusetts: Re-reading American Puritanism*. Cambridge: Harvard University Press, 1994.
Knoppers, Laura Lunger, ed. *Puritanism and Its Discontents*. Newark, NJ: University of Delaware Press, 2003.
Kupperman, Karen Ordahl. "Climate and Mastery of the Wilderness in Seventeenth-Century New England." In *Seventeenth-Century New England*, edited by David D. Hall et al., 3–38. Publications of The Colonial Society of Massachusetts 63. Boston: Colonial Society of Massachusetts, 1984.
———. "Errand to the Indies: Puritan Colonisation from Providence Island through the Western Design." *William and Mary Quarterly* 3rd series 45 (1988) 70–99.
———. *Indians and English: Facing Off in Early America*. Ithaca, NY: Cornell University Press, 2000.
———. *Providence Island, 1630–1641: The Other Puritan Colony*. Cambridge: Cambridge University Press, 1993.
———. "The Puzzle of the American Climate in the Early Colonial Period." *American Historical Review* 87 (1982) 1262–89.
———. *Settling with the Indians: The Meeting of English and Indian Cultures in America, 1580–1640*. Totowa, NJ: Rowman and Littlefield, 1980.
Kwiat, Joseph J., ed. *History of American Missions to the Heathen, to the Present Time*. Worchester: Spooner & Howland, 1840.
Lake, Peter. "Anti-Popery: The Structure of a Prejudice." In *Conflict in Early Stuart England: Studies in Religion and Politics 1603–1642*, edited by Richard Cust et al., 72–106. London: Longman, 1989.
———. *The Boxmaker's Revenge: 'Orthodoxy,' 'Heterodoxy,' and the Politics of the Parish in Early Stuart London*. Manchester: Manchester University Press, 2001.
———. "Calvinism and the English Church 1570–1635." *Past and Present* 114 (1987) 32–76.
———. "Defining Puritanism—Again?" In *Puritanism: Transatlantic Perspectives on a Seventeenth-Century Anglo-American Faith*, edited by Francis J. Bremer, 3–29. Boston: Massachusetts Historical Society, 1993.
———. "The Historiography of Puritanism." In *The Cambridge Companion to Puritanism*, edited by John Coffey and Paul C. H. Lim, 346–71. Cambridge: Cambridge University Press, 2008.
———. *Moderate Puritans and the Elizabethan Church*. Cambridge: Cambridge University Press, 1982.
Lake, Peter, with Michael Questier. *The Antichrist's Lewd Hat: Protestants, Papists and Players in Post-Reformation England*. New Haven: Yale University Press, 2002.
Lake, Peter, and Michael Questier, eds. *Conformity and Orthodoxy in the English Church, c.1560–1660*. Woodbridge: Ashgate, 2000.
Lamont, William. *Godly Rule: Politics and Religion, 1603–60*. London: Macmillan, 1969.
———. *Marginal Prynne, 1600–1669*. London: Routledge and Kegan Paul, 1963.
———. *Puritanism and Historical Controversy*. London: UCL, 1996.
———. *Richard Baxter and the Millennium: Protestant Imperialism and the English Revolution*. London: Croom Helm, 1979.
Lang, Amy Schrager. *Prophetic Woman: Anne Hutchinson and the Problem of Dissent in the Literature of New England*. Berkeley: University of California Press, 1987.

Latourette, Kenneth Scott. *A History of Christianity*. Vol. 1. Peabody, MA: Prince, 1953, 1975; revised ed., 1999.

———. *A History of the Expansion of Christianity*. 7 vols. New York: Harper & Row, 1937–45.

Lee, Sou-Young. "Calvin's Understanding of Pietas." In *Calvinus Sincerioris Religionis Vindex*, edited by Wilhelm H. Neuser et al., 225–39. Kriksville, MO: Sixteenth Century Studies, 1997.

Lepore, Jill. *The Name of War: King Philip's War and the Origins of American Identity*. New York: Vintage, 1998.

Leverenz, David. *The Language of Puritan Feeling: An Exploration in Literature, Psychology, and Social History*. New Brunswick, NJ: Rutgers University Press, 1980.

Levy, B. M. *Preaching in the First Half Century of New England History*. Hartford, CT: The American Society of Church History, 1945.

Lim, Paul C. H. *In Pursuit of Purity, Unity, and Liberty: Richard Baxter's Puritan Ecclesiology in Its Seventeenth-Century Context*. Leiden: Brill, 2004.

Lockridge, Kenneth. *A New England Town: The First Hundred Years*. New York: Norton, 1970.

Lonkhuyzen, Harold W. Van. "A Reappraisal of the Praying Indians: Acculturation, Conversion, and Identity at Natick, Massachusetts, 1646–1730." *The New England Quarterly* 63.3 (1990) 396–428.

Lovelace, Richard. *The American Pietism of Cotton Mather: Origins of American Evangelicalism*. Grand Rapids: Christian University Press, 1979.

Lowance, Mason I., Jr. *The Language of Canaan: Metaphor and Symbol in New England from the Puritans to the Transcendentalists*. Cambridge: Harvard University Press, 1980.

Luder, Laura. "Pequot War (1636–1637)." In *PPEA* 477.

Lynch, Kathleen. *Protestant Autobiography in the Seventeenth-Century Anglophone World*. Oxford: Oxford University Press, 2012.

MacCulloch, Diarmaid. *The Later Reformation in England*. Basingstoke: Palgrave, 1990; 2nd ed., 2001.

———. *The Reformation: A History*. New York: Viking, 2003.

Maclear, James F. "'The Heart of New England Rent': The Mystical Element in Early Puritan History." *Mississippi Valley Historical Review* 42 (1956) 621–52.

———. "New England and the Fifth Monarchy: The Quest for the Millennium in Early American Puritanism." *William and Mary Quarterly* 3rd series 32 (1975) 223–60.

MacDonald, Alan. R. *The Jacobean Kirk, 1567–1625*. Aldershot: Ashgate, 1998.

Maffly-Kipp, Laurie, et al., eds. *Practicing Protestants: Histories of Christian Life in America, 1630–1965*. Baltimore: Johns Hopkins University Press, 2006.

Mandell, Daniel R. "Mayhew, Thomas (*bap.* 1593, *d.* 1682)." In *ODNB* (Online).

Mayers, Ruth E. "Vane, Sir Henry, the Younger (1613–1662)." In *ODNB* (Online).

McGee, J. Sears. *The Godly Man in Stuart England: Anglicans, Puritans, and the Two Tables, 1620–1670*. New Haven: Yale University Press, 1976.

McGiffert, Michael. "From Moses to Adam: The Making of the Covenant of Works." *Sixteenth Century Journal* 19 (1988) 131–55.

———. *God's Plot: Puritan Spirituality in Thomas Shepard's Cambridge*. Amherst: University of Massachusetts Press, 1972; 1994.

———. "Grace and Works: The Rise and Division of Covenant Divinity in Elizabethan Puritanism." *Harvard Theological Review* 75 (1982) 463–502.

———. "The Perkinsonian Moment of Federal Theology." *Calvin Theological Journal* 29 (1994) 117–48.

McIntyre, Sheila, and Len Travers, eds. *The Correspondence of John Cotton Junior*. Boston: The Colonial Society of Massachusetts, 2009.

McKee, Elsie Anne, ed. and trans. *John Calvin: Writings on Pastoral Piety*. New York: Paulist, 2001.

McLoughlin, William G. *New England Dissent, 1630–1833: The Baptists and the Separation of Church and State*. 2 vols. Cambridge: Harvard University Press, 1971.

———. *Soul Liberty: The Baptists' Struggle in New England, 1630–1833*. Hanover, NH: Brown University Press, 1991.

McNally, Michael D. "The Practice of Native American Christianity." *Church History* 69 (2000) 834–59.

Miller, Perry. *Errand into the Wilderness*. Cambridge: Harvard University Press, 1956, 1984.

———. *The New England Mind: From Colony to Province*. Cambridge: Harvard University Press, 1953.

———. *The New England Mind: The Seventeenth Century*. Cambridge: Harvard University Press, 1939; rev. ed., 1954; 3rd ed., 1982.

Miller, Perry, and T. H. Johnson, eds. *The Puritans: A Sourcebook of their Writings* (2 vols.). New York: Harper, 1963.

Mills, Kenneth, eds. *Conversion: Old Worlds and New*. Rochester: University of Rochester Press, 2003.

Mills, Kenneth, and Anthony Grafton, eds. *Conversion in Late Antiquity and the Early Middle Ages: Seeing and Believing*. Rochester: University of Rochester Press, 2003.

Milne, Graeme J. "New England Agents and the English Atlantic, 1641–1666." PhD diss., University of Edinburgh, 1993.

Milton, Anthony. *Catholic and Reformed: The Roman and Protestant Churches in English Protestant Thought, 1600–1640*. Cambridge: Cambridge University Press, 1995.

———. "Laud, William (1573–1645)." In *ODNB* (Online).

Moody, Michael E. "Ainsworth, Henry (1571–1622)." In *ODNB* (Online).

Moore, Cynthia Marie. "'Rent and Ragged Relation(s)': Puritans, Indians, and the Management of Congregations in New England, 1647–1776." PhD diss., State University of New York at Stony Brook, 1999.

Moore, Martin. *Memoirs of the Life and Character of Rev. John Eliot, Apostle of the N.A. Indians*. Boston: T. Bedlington, 1822.

Moreau, A. Scott, ed. *Evangelical Dictionary of World Missions*. Grand Rapids: Baker, 2000.

Morgan, Edmund S. *Visible Saints: The History of a Puritan Idea*. Ithaca, NY: Cornell University Press, 1963.

Morgan, John. *Godly Learning: Puritan Attitudes toward Reason, Learning, and Education, 1560–1640*. Cambridge: Cambridge University Press, 1986.

Morison, Samuel Eliot. *The Founding of Harvard College*. Cambridge: Harvard University Press, 1935; 2nd ed., 1968.

———. *Harvard College in the Seventeenth Century*. 2 vols. Cambridge: Harvard University Press, 1936.

———. "John Eliot." *Builders of the Bay Colony*. Boston, 1930.

Morrill, John. "The Church in England, 1642-9." In *Reactions to the English Civil War, 1642-1649*, edited by John Morrill, 89-114. Basingstoke: Macmillan, 1986.
———. "The Impact of Puritanism." In *The Impact of the English Civil War*, edited by John Morrill, 50-66. London: Collins & Brown, 1991.
———. "A Liberation Theology? Aspects of Puritanism in the English Revolution." In *Puritanism and Its Discontents*, edited by Laura Lunger Knoppers, 27-48. Newark, NJ: University of Delaware Press, 2003.
———. "The Making of Oliver Cromwell." In *Oliver Cromwell and the English Revolution*, edited by John Morrill, 19-48. London: Longman, 1990.
———. *The Nature of the English Revolution*. Harlow: Longman, 1993.
Morrison, Dane. *A Praying People: Massachusett Acculturation and the Failure of the Puritan Mission, 1600-1690*. New York: Lang, 1995.
———. "The Puritan Revolution." In *The Cambridge Companion to Puritanism*, edited by John Coffey and Paul C. H. Lim, 67-88. Cambridge: Cambridge University Press, 2008.
Morrison, Karl F. *Understanding Conversion*. Charlottesville: University of Virginia Press, 1992.
Morrison, Kenneth M. "'That Art of Coyning Christians': John Eliot and the Praying Indians of Massachusetts." *Ethnohistory* 21 (1974) 77-92.
Muller, Richard A. *After Calvin: Studies in the Development of a Theological Tradition*. Oxford: Oxford University Press, 2003.
———. "A Golden Chaine: Predestinarian System or Schematized *Ordo Salutis*?" *Sixteenth Century Journal* 9 (1978) 69-81.
———. *Post-Reformation Dogmatics: The Rise and Development of Reformed Orthodoxy, ca.1520 to ca.1725*. 4 vols. Grand Rapids: Baker, 2003.
Murdock, Graeme. *Beyond Calvin: The Intellectual, Political and Cultural World of Europe's Reformed Churches, 1540-1620*. Basingstoke: Palgrave Macmillan, 2004.
Murrin, John M. "Magistrates, Sinners, and a Precarious Liberty: Trial by Jury in Seventeenth-Century New England." In *Saints and Revolutionaries: Essays on Early American History*, edited by David D. Hall et al., 152-206. New York: Norton, 1984.
Naeher, Robert James. "Dialogue in the Wilderness: John Eliot and the Indian Exploration of Puritanism as a Source of Meaning, Comfort, and Ethnic Survival." *New England Quarterly* 62 (1989) 346-68.
Neill, Stephen. *A History of Christian Missions*. London: Penguin, 1964; rev. ed., 1986, 1990.
Neuser, Wilhelm H., and Brian G. Armstrong, eds. *Calvinus Sincerioris Religionis Vindex*. Kriksville, MO: Sixteenth Century Studies, 1997.
Nock, A. D. *Conversion: The Old and the New in Religion from Alexander the Great to Augustine of Hippo*. Boston: University Press of America, 1988.
Noll, Mark A. *America's God: From Jonathan Edwards to Abraham Lincoln*. Oxford: Oxford University Press, 2002.
———. *A History of Christianity in the United States and Canada*. London: SPCK, 1992.
Normandie, James De. *Address on the Apostle Eliot*. N.p. 1907.
———. *An Historical Sketch of the First Church in Roxbury*. N.p., 1896.
———. "John Eliot, the Apostle to the Indians." *Harvard Theological Review* (July 1912) 249-370.

Nuttall, Geoffrey F. *The Holy Spirit in Puritan Faith and Experience*. Oxford: Oxford University Press, 1946.
———. *The Puritan Spirit*. London: Epworth, 1967.
———. *Richard Baxter*. London: Nelson & Sons, 1965.
———. *Visible Saints: The Congregational Way 1640-1660*. Oxford: Blackwell, 1957.
O'Brien, Jean M. *Dispossession by Degrees: Indian Land and Identity in Natick, Massachusetts, 1650-1790*. Cambridge: Cambridge University Press, 1997.
Oh, Deok Kyo. 'The Churches Resurrection': *John Cotton's Eschatological Understanding of the Ecclesiastical Reformation*. Suwon, Korea: Hapdong Theological Seminary Press, 2001.
Oxford Dictionary of National Biography. 61 vols. Oxford: Oxford University Press, 2004. https://www.oxforddnb.com.
Packer, James I. *The Redemption and Restoration of Man in the Thought of Richard Baxter: A Study in Puritan Theology*. Vancouver: Regent College Publishing, 2003.
Parker, Kenneth. *The English Sabbath: A Study of the Doctrine and Discipline from the Reformation to the Civil War*. Cambridge: Cambridge University Press, 1988.
Parker, Kenneth, and Eric J. Carlson, eds. *'Practical Divinity': The Works and Life of Revd Richard Greenham*. Brookfield: Ashgate, 1998.
Parker, T. H. L. *Calvin's Preaching*. Edinburgh: T. & T. Clark, 1992.
Payne, Rodger M. *The Self and the Sacred: Conversion and Autobiography in Early American Protestantism*. Knoxville: University of Tennessee Press, 1998.
Pestana, Carla Gardina. *The English Atlantic in an Age of Revolution, 1640-1661*. Cambridge: Harvard University Press, 2004.
———. *Quakers and Baptists in Colonial Massachusetts*. Cambridge: Cambridge University Press, 1991.
Peterson, Mark A. "The Practice of Piety in Puritan New England: Contexts and Consequences." In *The World of John Winthrop: Essays on England and New England 1588-1649*, edited by Francis J. Bremer et al., 75–110. Boston: Massachusetts Historical Society, 2005.
———. *The Price of Redemption: The Spiritual Economy of Puritan New England*. Stanford: Stanford University Press, 1997.
Pettit, Norman. *The Heart Prepared: Grace and Conversion in Puritan Spiritual Life*. New Haven: Yale University Press, 1966.
Pilling, James Constantine. *Bibliography of the Algonquian Languages*. Washington: Government Printing Office, 1891.
Polack, W. G. *John Eliot: The Apostle to the Indians*. St. Louis, MO: Concordia, 1924.
Poole, Robert. *Time's Alteration: Calendar Reform in Early Modern England*. London: UCL, 1998.
Pope, R. G. *The Half-Way Covenant: Church Membership in Puritan New England*. Princeton: Princeton University Press, 1969.
Porter, Harry, ed. *Puritanism in Tudor England*. London: Macmillan, 1970.
Porterfield, Amanda. *Female Piety in Puritan New England: The Emergence of Religious Humanism*. New York: Oxford University Press, 1992.
Powell, Sumner Chilton. *Puritan Village: The Formation of a New England Town*. Middletown, CT: Wesleyan University Press, 1963.
Primus, John H. *Richard Greenham: Portrait of An Elizabethan Pastor*. Macon, GA: Mercer University Press, 1998.

Raitt, Jill, ed. *Christian Spirituality: High Middle Ages and Reformation*. New York: Crossroad, 1987.
Rambo, Lewis. *Understanding Religious Conversion*. New Haven: Yale University Press, 1993.
Reay, Barry, and J. F. McGregor. *Radical Religion in the English Revolution*. Oxford: Oxford University Press, 1984.
Reis, Elizabeth. *Damned Women: Sinners and Witches in Puritan New England*. Ithaca, NY: Cornell University Press, 1997.
Reynolds, Matthew. *Godly Reformers and Their Opponents in Early Modern England: Religion in Norwich c.1560–1643*. Woodbridge, Suffolk: Boydell, 2005.
Rice, Howard L. *Reformed Spirituality: An Introduction for Believers*. Louisville: Westminster John Knox, 1991.
Richard, Lucien Joseph. *The Spirituality of John Calvin*. Atlanta: John Knox, 1974.
Richardson, Alan, and John Bowden, eds. *A New Dictionary of Christian Theology*. London: SCM, 1983.
Richardson, Caroline Frances. *English Preachers and Preaching, 1640–1670*. New York: Macmillan, 1928.
Rivett, Sarah. "Evidence of Grace: The Science of the Soul in Colonial New England." PhD diss., University of Chicago, 2005.
Robinson, Charles Henry. *History of Christian Missions*. Edinburgh: T. & T. Clark, 1915.
Rohr, John Von. "Covenant and Assurance in Early English Puritanism." *Church History* 34.2 (1965) 195–203.
———. *The Covenant of Grace in Puritan Thought*. Atlanta: Scholars, 1986.
Ronda, James P. "Generation of Faith." *William and Mary Quarterly* 38 (1981) 369–94.
———. "'We Are Well as We Are': An Indian Critique of Seventeenth-Century Christian Missions." *William and Mary Quarterly* 3rd series 34 (1977) 66–82.
Rooy, Sydney H. *The Theology of Missions in the Puritan Tradition; A Study of Representative Puritans: Richard Sibbes, Richard Baxter, John Eliot, Cotton Mather, and Jonathan Edwards*. Grand Rapids: Eerdmans, 1965; 2nd ed., Laurel, MS: Audubon, 2006.
Rutman, Darrett Bruce. *American Puritanism: Faith and Practice*. Philadelphia: J. P. Lippincott, 1970.
———. "New England as Idea and Society Revisited." *William and Mary Quarterly* 3rd series 41 (1984) 56–61.
———. *Winthrop's Boston. A Portrait of Puritan Town, 1630–1649*. New York: Norton, 1972.
Salisbury, Neal. "Conquest of the 'Savage': Puritans, Puritan Missionaries, and Indians 1620–1680." PhD diss., University of California, Los Angeles, 1972.
———. *Manitou and Providence: Indians, Europeans, and the Making of New England, 1500–1643*. New York: Oxford University Press, 1982.
———. "Prospero in New England: The Puritan Missionary as Colonist." In *Papers of the Sixth Algonquian Conference, 1974*, edited by William Cowan, 253–73. Ottawa: National Museum of Man, 1975.
———. "Red Puritans: The 'Praying Indians' of Massachusetts Bay and John Eliot." *William and Mary Quarterly* 3rd series 31 (1974) 27–54.
———. "Squanto: Last of the Patuxets." In *Struggle and Survival in Colonial America*, edited by David G. Sweet et al., 228–46. Berkeley: University of California Press, 1981.

Sehr, Timothy J. *Colony and Commonwealth: Massachusetts Bay, 1649–1660.* New York: Garland, 1989.

———. "John Eliot, Millennialist and Missionary." *The Historian* 46 (1983–84) 187–203.

Selement, George. *Keepers of the Vineyard: The Puritan Ministry and Collective Culture in Colonial New England.* Lanham, MD: University Press of America, 1984.

———. "The Meeting of Elite and Popular Minds at Cambridge, New England, 1638–1645." *William and Mary Quarterly* 3rd series 41 (1984) 32–47.

Senn, Frank C., ed. *Protestant Spiritual Traditions.* Eugene, OR: Wipf & Stock, 2000.

Scherer, J. A. *Gospel, Church, and Kingdom: Comparative Studies in World Mission Theology.* Minneapolis: Augsburg, 1987.

Shea, Daniel B. *Spiritual Autobiography in Early America.* Princeton: Princeton University Press, 1968.

Sheils, W. J., and Diana Wood, eds. *The Ministry: Clerical and Lay.* Oxford: Blackwell, 1989.

Shipps, Kenneth W. "The Puritan Migration to New England: A New Source on Motivation." *NEHGR* 135 (1991) 83–97.

Scholz, R. F. "Clerical Consociation in Massachusetts Bay: Reassessing the New England Way and Its Origins." *William and Mary Quarterly* 3rd series 19 (1972) 391–414.

Seaver, Paul. *Wallington's World: A Puritan Artisan in Seventeenth-Century London.* London: Methuen, 1985.

Silverman, David J. *Faith and Boundaries: Colonists, Christianity, and Community among the Wampanoag Indians of Martha's Vineyard, 1600–1871.* New York: Cambridge University Press, 2005.

———. "Indians, Missionaries, and Religious Translation: Creating Wampanoag Christianity in Seventeenth-Century Martha's Vineyard." *William and Mary Quarterly* 62 (2005) 141–74.

Simmons, William S. "Conversion from Indian to Puritan." *The New England Quarterly* 52.2 (1979) 197–218.

Solberg, Winton U. *Redeem the Time: The Puritan Sabbath in Early America.* Cambridge: Harvard University Press, 1977.

Sommerville, C. John. *Popular Religion in Restoration England.* Gainesville: University of Florida Press, 1977.

Spindler, M. R. "The Biblical Grounding and Orientation of Mission." In *Missiology: An Ecumenical Introduction: Texts and Contexts of Global Christianity*, edited by F. J. Verstraelen et al., 123–43. Grand Rapids: Eerdmans, 1995.

Sprunger, Keith L. "Ames, William (1576–1633)." In *ODNB* (Online).

———. *The Learned Doctor William Ames: Dutch Backgrounds of English and American Puritanism.* Chicago: University of Illinois Press, 1972.

Spufford, Margaret. "Puritanism and Social Control?" In *Order and Disorder in Early Modern England*, edited by Anthony Fletcher et al., 41–57. Cambridge: Cambridge University Press, 1985.

Spurr, John. *English Puritanism, 1603–1689.* London: Macmillan, 1998.

———. "Later Stuart Puritanism." In *The Cambridge Companion to Puritanism*, edited by John Coffey and Paul C. H. Lim, 89–105. Cambridge: Cambridge University Press, 2008.

Stanley, Brian. *The Bible and the Flag: Protestant Missions and British Imperialism in the Nineteenth and Twentieth Centuries.* Leicester: Apollos, 1990.

———. "Carey, William (1761–1834)." In *ODNB* (Online).
Stannard, David E. *The Puritan Way of Death: A Study in Religion, Culture, and Social Change*. New York: Oxford University Press, 1977.
Stevens, Laura M. *The Poor Indians: British Missionaries, Native Americans, and Colonial Sensibility*. Philadelphia: University of Pennsylvania Press, 2004.
Stoeffler, F. Ernest. *The Rise of Evangelical Pietism*. Leiden: Brill, 1965.
Stoever, William K. B. *'A Faire and Easie Way to Heaven': Covenant Theology and Antinomianism in Early Massachusetts*. Middletown, CT: Wesleyan University Press, 1978.
Stout, Harry S. "The Morphology of Remigration: New England University Men and Their Return to England, 1640–1660." *Journal of American Studies* 10 (1976) 151–72.
———. *The New England Soul: Preaching and Religious Culture in Colonial New England*. Oxford: Oxford University Press, 1986.
Swanson, R. N., ed. *Unity and Diversity in the Church*. Studies in Church History 32. Oxford: Blackwell, 1996.
Szasz, Margaret Connell. *Indian Education in the American Colonies, 1607–1783*. Albuquerque: University of New Mexico Press, 1988.
Taylor, Larissa, ed. *Preachers and People in the Reformations and Early Modern Period*. Leiden: Brill, 2001.
"The Charter of Massachusetts Bay: 1629." http://avalon.law.yale.edu/17th_century/mass03.asp.
Thompson, Roger. "Gookin, Daniel (*bap.* 1612, *d.* 1687)." In *ODNB* (Online).
Thwing, Walter Eliot. *History of the First Church in Roxbury, Massachusetts, 1630–1904*. Boston: Butterfield, 1908.
———. *Vital Records of Roxbury, Massachusetts to the End of the Year 1849*. Salem, MA: Essex Institute, 1926.
Tipson, Baird. "The Development of a Puritan Understanding of Conversion." PhD diss., Yale University, 1972.
———. "Invisible Saints: The 'Judgment of Charity' in the Early New England Churches." *Church History* 44 (1975) 460–71.
———. "The Routinized Piety of Thomas Shepard's Diary." *Early American Literature* 13 (1978) 64–80.
Todd, Margo. *The Culture of Protestantism in Early Modern Scotland*. New Haven: Yale University Press, 2002.
———. "Puritan Self-Fashioning." In *Puritanism: Transatlantic Perspectives on a Seventeenth-Century Anglo-American Faith*, edited by Francis J. Bremer, 57–87. Boston: Massachusetts Historical Society, 1993.
Tooker, William Wallace. *John Eliot's First Indian Teacher and Interpreter, Cockenoe-De-Long Island: And the Story of his Career from the Early Records*. New York: F. P. Harper, 1896.
Toon, Peter, ed. *Puritans, the Millennium and the Future of Israel: Puritan Eschatology 1600–1660*. Cambridge: James Clarke, 1970.
Travers, Len. "Winslow, Edward (1595–1655)." In *ODNB* (Online).
Treat, James, ed. *Native and Christian*. New York: Routledge, 1995.
Trumbull, J. Hammond. "The Indian Tongue and Its Literature as Fashioned by Eliot and Others." In vol. 1 of *Memorial History of Boston*, edited by Justin Winsor, 465–80. Boston: J. R. Osgood, 1885.

Tyacke, Nicholas. *Anti-Calvinists: The Rise of English Arminianism, c.1590–1640*. Oxford: Clarendon, 1987.
———. *Aspects of English Protestantism, c.1530–1700*. Manchester: Manchester University Press, 2001.
———, ed. *England's Long Reformation 1500–1800*. London: UCL, 1998.
———. *The Fortunes of English Puritanism 1603–1640*. London: Dr. Williams's Trust, 1990.
Underdown, David. *Fire from Heaven: Life in an English Town in the Seventeenth Century*. London: Fontana, 1993.
Valeri, Mark R. *Heavenly Merchandize: How Religion Shaped Commerce in Puritan America*. Princeton: Princeton University Press, 2010.
Vaughan, Alden T. *New England Frontier: Puritans and Indians 1620–1675*. 3rd ed. Norman: University of Oklahoma Press, 1995.
———, ed. *The Puritan Tradition in America, 1620–1730*. Rev. ed. Hanover, NH: University Press of New England, 1997.
Wakefield, Gordon Stevens. *Puritan Devotion: Its Place in the Development of Christian Piety*. London: Epworth, 1957.
Wallace, Dewey D., Jr. *Puritans and Predestination: Grace in English Protestant Theology*. Chapel Hill: University of North Carolina Press, 1982.
Walls, Andrew F. *The Cross-Cultural Process in Christian History: Studies in the Transmission and Appropriation of Faith*. Maryknoll, NY: Orbis, 2002.
———. *The Missionary Movement in Christian History: Studies in the Transmission of Faith*. Maryknoll, NY: Orbis, 1996.
Walsham, Alexandra. *Charitable Hatred: Tolerance and Intolerance in England, 1500–1700*. Manchester: Manchester University Press, 2006.
———. "The Godly and Popular Culture." In *The Cambridge Companion to Puritanism*, edited by John Coffey and Paul C. H. Lim, 279–82. Cambridge: Cambridge University Press, 2008.
———. *Providence in Early Modern England*. Oxford: Oxford University Press, 1999.
Wardlaw, Thompson R., and Arthur N. Johnson. *British Foreign Mission, 1837–1897*. London: Blackie & Son, 1899.
Warneck, Gustav. *Outline of a History of Protestant Missions from the Reformation to the Present Time: With an Appendix concerning Roman Catholic Missions*. Edinburgh: Oliphant, Anderson & Ferrier, 1906.
Warren, Max. *The Missionary Movement from Britain in Modern History*. London: SCM, 1965.
Washburn, Wilcom E. *The Indian in America*. New York: Harper & Row, 1975.
Waterhouse, Richard. "Reluctant Emigrants: The English Background of the First Generation of the New England Puritan Clergy." *Historical Magazine of the Protestant Episcopal Church* 44.4 (1975) 473–88.
Watkins, Owen. *The Puritan Experience: Studies in Spiritual Autobiography*. London: Routledge and Kegan Paul, 1972.
Watts, Michael R. *The Dissenters: From the Reformation to the French Revolution*. Vol. 1. Oxford: Clarendon, 1978.
Webster, Charles, ed. *The Intellectual Revolution of the Seventeenth Century*. London: Routledge and Kegan Paul, 1974.
Webster, Tom. *Godly Clergy in Early Stuart England: The Caroline Puritan Movement, c.1620–1643*. Cambridge: Cambridge University Press, 1997.

———. "The Piety of Practice and the Practice of Piety." In *The World of John Winthrop: Essays on England and New England 1588–1649*, edited by Francis J. Bremer et al., 111–46. Boston: Massachusetts Historical Society, 2005.

———. "Writing to Redundancy: Approaches to Spiritual Journals and Early Modern Spirituality." *Historical Journal* 39 (1996) 33–56.

Weir, David A. *Church Covenanting in Seventeenth-Century New England*. Ann Arbor, MI: University Microfilms, 1992.

———. *Early New England: A Covenanted Society*. Grand Rapids: Eerdmans, 2005.

Weis, Frederick Lewis. *The Colonial Clergy and the Colonial Churches of New England*, Baltimore: Genealogical, 1977.

Wendel, Francois. *Calvin: The Origins and Development of His Religious Thought*. Translated by Philip Mairet. New York: Harper & Row, 1963.

Werge, Thomas. *Thomas Shepard*. Boston: Twayne, 1987.

White, Helen C. *English Devotional Literature [Prose], 1600–1640*. Madison: University of Wisconsin Press, 1931.

Wilbur, C. Keith. *The New England Indians: An Illustrated Source Book of Authentic Details of Everyday Indian Life*. Old Saybrook, CT: Globe Pequot, 1996.

Winship, George Parker. *The Cambridge Press 1638–1692: A Rexamination of the Evidence concerning the Bay Psalm Book and the Eliot Indian Bible as well as Other Contemporary Books and People*. Philadelphia: University of Pennsylvania Press, 1945.

———, ed. *The New England Company of 1649 and John Eliot*. Boston: Printed for the Prince Society at the Plimpton Press, 1920.

Winship, Michael P. "Hutchinson, Anne (bap. 1591, d. 1643)." In *ODNB* (Online).

———. *Making Heretics: Militant Protestantism and Free Grace in Massachusetts, 1636–1641*. Princeton: Princeton University Press, 2002.

———. *Seers of God: Puritan Providentialism in the Restoration and Early Enlightenment*. Baltimore: Johns Hopkins University Press, 1996.

———. "Were There Any Puritans in New England?" *New England Quarterly* 74 (2001) 118–38.

———. "Wheelwright, John (1592?–1679)." In *ODNB* (Online).

Winslow, Ola Elizabeth. *John Eliot: "Apostle to the Indians."* Boston: Houghton Mifflin, 1968.

Wood, Diana, ed. *Life and Thought in the Northern Church, c.1100–1700*. Woodbridge, Suffolk: Boydell, 1999.

Wood, Timothy. *Agents of Wrath, Sowers of Discord: Authority and Dissent in Puritan Massachusetts, 1630–1655*. New York: Routledge, 2006.

Woodhouse, A. S. P. *Puritanism and Liberty*. 3rd ed. London: J. M. Dent, 1992.

Woolrych, Austin. *Britain in Revolution, 1625–1660*. Oxford: Oxford University Press, 2002.

Woolverton, John Frederick. *Colonial Anglicanism in North America*. Detroit: Wayne State University Press, 1984.

Wright, Stephen. *The Early English Baptists, 1603–1649*. Woodbridge, Suffolk: Boydell, 2006.

Wrightson, Keith. *English Society 1580–1680*. London: Hutchinson, 1982. Reprint, London: Routledge, 1993.

———. "The Puritan Reformation of Manners, with Special Reference to the Counties of Lancashire and Essex, 1640–1660." PhD diss., University of Cambridge, 1973.

Wrightson, Keith, and David Levine. *Poverty and Piety in an English Village: Terling, 1525–1700*. 2nd ed. Oxford: Oxford University Press, 1995.
Wyss, Hilary E. *Writing Indians: Literacy, Christianity, and Native Community in Early America*. Amherst: University of Massachusetts Press, 2000.
Yates, Timothy. *Christian Mission in the Twentieth Century*. Cambridge: Cambridge University Press, 1994.
Young, John T. "Dury, John (1596–1680)." In *ODNB* (Online).
Youngs, J. William T. "The Indian Saints of New England." *Early American Literature* 16.3 (1981/1982) 241–56.
Zakai, Avihu. *Exile and Kingdom: History and Apocalypse in the Puritan Migration to America*. Cambridge: Cambridge University Press, 1992.
Ziff, Larzer. *The Career of John Cotton: Puritanism and the American Experience*. Princeton: Princeton University Press, 1962.

Index

Algonquian, 4n6, 13, 23, 65, 167, 169
Ames, William (a son of William Ames, the well-known puritan), 197n39
Anderson, Gerald H., 20
Angier, Mary, 206, 207
Anthony (a praying Indian), 212, 213, 214, 218, 220
Antinomian controversy, 79
Antinomianism, 80, 203, 204
Arbella, 36
Archer, John, 198n41
Autonomy, 145, 146, 154, 155
Axtell, James, 9, 10

Bainton, Roland, 19
Baxter, Richard, 4n7; training of pastors, 100n208; understanding of preaching and catechizing, 92n151
Bay Psalm Book (1640), 108, 185, 189
Bayly, Lewis, 65n1; *The Practice of Piety* (2nd edn., 1612), 65n2
Bernard, Richard, 91n140, 92, 93
Biblical civil covenant, 136, 137
Biblicism, 86, 93, 95 101, 102, 103, 118, 160, 166, 202
Black, J. William, 67
Bornkamm, H., 19
Bosch, David J., 15, 16, 17, 20, 21, 31
Bowden, Henry Warner, 9

Boyle, Robert (the Governor of New England Company), 25, 140, 154, 186
Bozeman, Theodore Dwight, 10, 33, 34, 36, 41, 45, 68, 69, 124
Brauer, Jerald C., 194
Brenner, Elise, 9
Brightman, Thomas, 42
Bross, Kristina Kae, 12
Broughton, Hugh, 52, 53
Bucer, Martin, 99

Caldwell, Patricia, 193
Calvin, John, 21, 72, 74, 75, 78, 89, 90, 92, 99, 102, 109
Cambers, Andrew, 67, 95
Cambridge Platform (1648), 142n78
Carey, William, 21
Carpenter, John B., 31
Cesarini, Joseph Patrick, 12
Chambon, J., 19
Charter of Massachusetts Bay (1629), 36
church membership, 110, 144, 145, 147, 148, 149, 153, 184, 191, 194, 227
church polity, 125, 141, 145, 146, 154, 155
city upon a hill, 19, 20, 30, 31, 32, 33, 34, 115
civil polity, 24, 66, 125, 133, 134, 136, 145

civilization, 112, 127, 128, 132
civilizedness, 128
Cogley, Richard W., 10, 11, 13, 32, 36, 51, 53, 54, 62, 111, 124
Collins, Edward, 197, 203, 204
Collins, Martha, 197, 201, 202
Collinson, Patrick, 66
compunction of sin, 80, 211
congregationalism, 142, 146
conversion, puritan understanding of, 72–83
conviction of sin, 80
Cotton, John, 23n75
covenant, 124, 133, 136, 137, 138, 139; of grace, 200

Danforth, Samuel, 230
Daniel, Robert, 198, 207, 208
De Jong, James A., 9
Durie [Dury], John, 115n298

Ebeling, G., 19
Eccles, Richard, 197, 202, 204
Eliot Tracts, 26n78
Eliot, John, Algonquian Indian language, 167–71; the apostle of the Indians, 3; biography, 3–5; ecclesiology, 141–46; history and process of Eliot's publications, 168n51; Indian origin, 50–62; John Eliot's first preaching to the Indians, 3; millenarianism, 43–50; Roxbury, 3; theological background, 65–66; translations, 167–69; translation of the Bible, 167; vision of Ezek 37, 230
Endecott, John, 40n46, 126
Errington, Ann, 196, 200, 201, 203
ethnohistory, 8n20
evangelism, meaning of, 16

Fifth Monarchists or Fifth Monarchy Men, 44
Fisher, Lindford D., 179
Floyd [Lloyd], Richard (a treasurer of the New England Company), 193

Fox, Adam, 95
Fulke, William, 91n137
Furnell, John, 198
further reformation, 20, 33, 35, 42, 48, 63, 95, 101, 115, 142

General Court of Massachusetts, 126
Glover, Jose, 202n75
Glover, Robert Hall, 21
Gookin, Daniel, 6n11
Gordis, Lisa M., 93
Gray, Kathryn Napier, 12
Great Migration, revised interpretation, 31–40
Green, Ian, 163, 165
Greenham, Richard, 67n10
Griswald, Mary, 197, 198
Gura, Philip F., 33

Half-Way Covenant, 194, 195
Hall, David D., 66, 172
Hall, Edward, 196, 199, 202
Hambrick-Stowe, Charles E., 95, 101
Hanmer, Jonathan, 149
Hardman Moore, Susan, 34, 35
Harling, Frederick F., 6
Hart, John, 204
Hassanemest, 139
Hawkes, R. M., 69
Hedges, Andrew H., 10
Hindmarsh, D. Bruce, 190, 191
Hinson, E. Glenn, 68, 69
Holmes, Robert, 202, 204
Holstun, James, 10
Hunt, Arnold, 67
Hutchinson, Anne, 79, 203

Indian church, establishment of, 139–41
Indian civil covenant, 136, 138
Indian Dialogues (1671), 26

Jalalzai, Zubeda, 12
Jennings, Francis, 7
Jongenell, J. A. B., 31

Kane, Herbert, 21
Kellaway, William, 229

King Philip's War (1675–76), 229
Kirk, J. Andrew, 20
Kwait, Joseph J., 31

Latourette, Kenneth Scott, 19
Laud, William, 39
Laudian policy, 5, 20, 30, 33, 114
Lechford, Thomas, 148
Leveri[t]ch, William, 116n300
Lim, Paul C. H., 67
Loewenich, W. von, 19
Lonkhuyzen, Harold W. Van, 9
lost ten tribes of Israelites, 53

Maclear, James F., 9
Martha's Vineyard, 139, 154
Mashpege, 139
Mather, Cotton, 6n12
Mather, Richard, 38n40
Mayflower, 31, 34, 38
Mayhew, Thomas, 38n37
McGiffert, Michael, 69, 193
means of grace, understanding in Reformed tradition, 77n61
Menasseh ben Israel, 53, 54
Miller, Perry, thesis of "errand into the wildernes," 5, 19, 20, 30
mission, traditional understanding, 14–18
mission, historical and theological interpretations, 18–22
Monequassun (a praying Indian), 215, 218
Monotunkquanit (a praying Indian), 158, 211, 216
Moore, Cynthia Marie, 12
morphology of conversion, 78
Morrison, Kenneth M., 9

Naeher, Robert James, 9
Nantucket, 139
Nataôus (a praying Indian), 213, 214, 221
Natick (the first Praying Town), 25, 123
New England Company, 126n13
Nishohkou (a praying Indian), 161, 186, 212; Nishohkou's sermon, 161

Nonantum, 125
Noonanetum, 173

Olbon, Elizabeth, 197, 200, 203, 206
ordo salutis, 78

pawwawes, 128, 181
pawwaws, 180, 181
Penitent (a praying Indian from *Indian Dialogues* (1671)), 174, 175
Perkins, William, 73, 78, 91, 93, 204
Peterson, Mark A., 191
piety, 69n18
Piumbubbon (a praying Indian), 161, 162
Piumbuhhou (a praying Indian), 211, 215, 219, 221
Piumbukhou (a praying Indian), 159, 176, 179, 180, 182, 183, 187, 209, 215, 216
Ponampam (a praying Indian), 211, 213, 214, 215, 222
Ponampiam (a praying Indian), 212, 214
Poquanum (a praying Indian), 164
praying Indians, Bible reading and meditation, 181–82; Biblicism, 133, 160; catechizing, 162–65; conversion, as an ontological change, 209; Indian communities around Massachusetts in 1698, 230; inwardness, 210; lack of assurance in conversion narratives, 220; meaning of the term, 4n6; pastoral counselling, 173–75; pastoral education for Indian pastoral leaders, 175–78; pastoral visitation, 165–66; pawwaws (Indian traditional religious custom), 180; prayer, 182–84; psalm-singing, 185–86; public fasting and thanksgiving, 184–85; repentance, 179–80; Sabbath-keeping, 186; self-examination, 210–14; sermons, 161–62; sermons (as a confessional exhortation), 209

praying Indians (*continued*) sincere thanks to and admiration for Eliot, 230; trinitarian understanding of soteriology, 215; understanding of God's absolute sovereignty on salvation, 215; understanding of Reformed soteriology, 215; understanding of the means of grace, 217–19

praying towns, after Natick, 127n18

Primus, John H., 67

puritan, catechizing, 67, 70, 86, 94, 97; conversion, understanding of, 72; conversion-oriented ministry, 118, 145; counselling, 97; fasting, 107; heart religion, 107, 108, 118; holy communion, 105, 110; inwardness, 69, 70, 74; Lord's Supper, 110; meditation, 106, 118; parish-centered ministry, 99; pastoral care, 97; pastoral teaching, 87; pastoral training and education, 99; piety, other expressions of, 104n238; prayer, 106; preaching, 88; preaching, Bible-centered and plain, 93; public profession of conversion, 110; repentance, 102, 104, 107; Sabbath-keeping, 109; sacraments, 109; Scripture reading, 95, 105, 106; self-examination, 105, 196, 203, 210; psalm-singing, 108; teachings, orality, 95; teachings, literacy, 95; theology, experimental nature of, 73; visible saints, 70, 103, 104, 110, 118, 143, 194; visitation, 94

puritanism, definition of, 68

Rawson, Grindal, 230

reformation, in England, 48, 114, 115, 116, 118, 119

reformation of manners, 85

Reformed theology, 89, 91

Reformed tradition, 86, 95, 97, 101, 103

Restoration of Charles II (1660), 48

Reynolds, Edward, 40, 168

Rice, Howard L., 68

Robinson, Charles Henry, 31

Rogers, John, 202n71

Ronda, James P., 9

Rooy, Sydney H., 6, 124

Sachem of Pautuket, 131

Salisbury, Neal, 9

Schmidt, K. D., 19

Selement, George, 193

Sewall, Samuel, 230

Shaw, John, 201n66

Shepard, Thomas, 65n1; confessions, 195–96; opposed Antinomianism, 204

Sibbes, Richard, 5

Sill, Joanna, 205

Society for the Propagation of the Gospel in New England, 126n13

Speen, John (a praying Indian, pastoral leader in Natick), 174

Speen, Robin (a praying Indian), 221

Spindler, M. R., 15

Stoeffler, F. Ernest, 68

Symonds, Samuel, 39

Thorowgood, Thomas, 52, 53

Totherswamp (a praying Indian), 173, 209, 211, 212, 221

uncivilizedness, 58, 127, 128, 130

Vaughan, Alden T., 6, 7, 124

Waban (a praying Indian), 113, 161, 164, 165, 180, 184, 211, 215, 216, 218

Walsham, Alexandra, 172

Wamporas (a praying Indian), 140, 141, 214

Warneck, Gustav, 21

Washburn, Wilcome E., 9

Webster, Tom, 66, 191

Weir, David A., 136

Whitfield, Henry, 161n14

wigwams, 165n38
William (a praying Indian), 160
Williams, Roger, 170n60
Willows, George, 197, 198, 199, 200, 202, 206
Wilson, John, 123n2
Winslow, Edward, 128, 166, 172
Winslow, Ola Elizabeth, 6, 124
Winthrop, John, 32n7; "A Modell of Christian Charity," 31
Woolley, Bruce C., 193
Wutasakompauin (a praying Indian), 164, 211
Wyeth, Nicholas, 199, 206, 207

www.ingramcontent.com/pod-product-compliance
Lightning Source LLC
Chambersburg PA
CBHW070241230426
43664CB00014B/2379